Penguin Books
Worlds Apart

Gavin Young spent most of his youth in Cornwall and South Wales. He studied modern history at Oxford University and spent two years with a shipping company in Basra, Iraq, before setting out to live in wilder places – first, with the Marsh Arabs in southern Iraq between the Tigris and Euphrates rivers, then with the people of the plains and mountains of south-western Arabia. From Tunis he joined the *Observer* as a foreign correspondent in 1960 and subsequently covered fifteen wars and revolutions throughout the world. He has also been the *Observer* correspondent in Paris and in New York.

Gavin Young's first book, *Return to the Marshes* (1977), describes his adventures in Iraq with the Marsh Arabs, who inhabit the ancient land of Sumer and Babylonia, and was the basis of a BBC film in 1979. His second book, *Iraq: Land of Two Rivers*, an account of a journey through the historic landscape of Mesopotamia, was published in 1980. Gavin Young then travelled round the world by whatever waterborne transport he could find at the time. The story of that extraordinary voyage was told in his next two bestselling books, *Slow Boats to China* (1981, Penguin 1983) and *Slow Boats Home* (1985, Penguin 1986).

Worlds Apart

Travels in War and Peace

Gavin Young

Illustrations by Salim

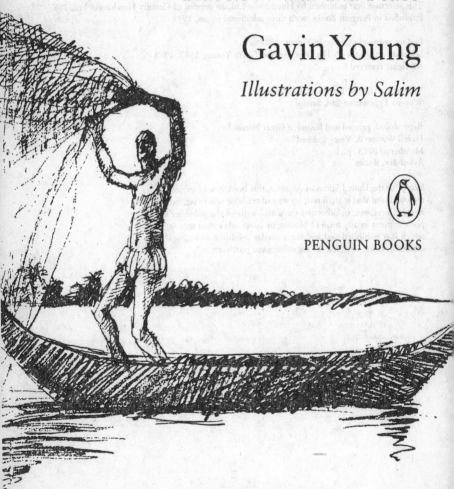

PENGUIN BOOKS

PENGUIN BOOKS

Published by the Penguin Group
27 Wrights Lane, London W8 5TZ, England
Viking Penguin Inc., 40 West 23rd Street, New York, New York 10010, USA
Penguin Books Australia Ltd, Ringwood, Victoria, Australia
Penguin Books Canada Ltd, 2801 John Street, Markham, Ontario, Canada L3R 1B4
Penguin Books (NZ) Ltd, 182–190 Wairau Road, Auckland 10, New Zealand

Penguin Books Ltd, Registered Offices: Harmondsworth, Middlesex, England

This selection first published by Hutchinson Ltd, an imprint of Century Hutchinson Ltd, 1987
Published in Penguin Books, with three additional pieces, 1988

Typeset in 11/13pt Linotron 202 Sabon by
Wyvern Typesetting Ltd, Bristol

Reproduced, printed and bound in Great Britain by
Hazell Watson & Viney Limited
Member of BPCC plc,
Aylesbury, Bucks

To
David Astor
Michael Davie
and
the late Ian Fleming
and
the late Ian Fleming

without whom . . .

ACKNOWLEDGEMENTS

Most of these pieces have appeared in the *Observer* or its Colour Magazine. *Casualties of Peace* was also published in the *New York Review of Books*, and *Italy under Siege* in the *Australian Bulletin*. I am most grateful for permission to republish them here.

My profoundest thanks are due to my friend Dennis Enright for his cheerful and invaluable help in the unenviable task of selection; and as usual to my sea anchor Gritta Weil, who helped to get things together. Thanks also to Mike Cottingham for his excellent maps.

Finally, Roddy Bloomfield of Hutchinson is the sort of editor one prays for.

Contents

Contents

Preface

'What is written is written,' pious characters in *A Thousand and One Nights* used to say. I admit that I, too, have become more than a half-believer in Kismet, as those old Arabs used to call destiny or fate. After all, I can see now what the writing said.

Some children dream of growing up to be writers, as others dream of becoming engine drivers. I have met people who, when practically at the toddler stage, saw themselves as trench-coated foreign correspondents eyewitnessing the assassinations of presidents, or, safari-suited and pale ochre with jaundice, rattling out a front-page scoop in a jungle lean-to. I was not one of them. Far from it. I fell into journalism as a drunken man falls into a pond.

I really wanted to explore all sorts of untamed mountain ranges, jungles and deserts – not to write about them at all. (How to earn the money to do this was a secondary, if not a tertiary, consideration.) Outrageous fortune may have shunted me to journalism and books despite myself, but with me travel was never a matter of chance; I ran away to it deliberately, as boys once ran away to sea. By 1950, at the age of twenty-two, with the dramas and excursions of military service in Palestine, good health and a fair general education behind me, I felt there must be more to do in this world than join the ranks of sombrely suited people sitting behind desks. Sitting at desks was a good way to make money. But money, in my view, wasn't everything – a point upon which my parents and I signally failed to see eye to eye.

What was needed, I realized, was a job – any job – to get me off the old home ground. It was very fortunate, then, that Ralli Brothers, a well-known firm of traders with worldwide connections, agreed to take me on as a clerk at £5 a week, and luckier still that they soon posted me to a branch office they were opening in Basra, the port of Iraq. There, in the palm-shaded tranquillity of Sindbad's ramshackle but still picturesque city, the Lawrence of Arabia bug got its teeth into me, and refused to let go. I found an Arabic teacher and began to look around for a camel to carry me across the widest Arabian desert; only the widest would do. It was then that Kismet first noticeably intruded – in the unusually austere person of Wilfred Thesiger, the last of the great Arabian explorers, famous for having crossed the great sands of Arabia's Empty Quarter twice to only two other white men's once. He told me to forget the camel and think about the Marsh Arabs, the practically unknown descendants of the ancient Sumerians, who lived less than a hundred miles north of my Basra office.

From that moment I was away and travelling. Soon I left Ralli's and took, like a duck, to the Marshes. I loved the Marsh Arabs, and stayed with them for two years. Still, there were other things to be seen; I had to move on. Advised by Thesiger, I left the Marshes for the wilds of south-western Arabia and two years cheek-by-jowl with the Bedu, helping them to control their locust swarms. I was a great reader, and in the southern Hejaz my tent was cluttered with the books I ordered from Heywood Hill's bookshop in London, which came to me on camelback months later. Already I had had about four years of rare excitement, and I suppose now and again I may have dreamed of emulating Thesiger – this was before he wrote *Arabian Sands* – by sending occasional stiffly authoritative articles to the *Royal Central Asian Magazine* on, say, Bedu migration routes of the Asir, or stone well construction in the Wadi Dawasir. But to me serious journalism, leave alone book writing, were things far above my head – wonderful things that other people were born to do, like waltzing on ice.

The Anglo-French Suez fiasco swiftly made any odd wanderer like me *persona non grata* in the Middle East. Obliged to leave Arabia, I decided to take all I had – my Arab experience and rough-and-ready Arabic – to North Africa, the other half of the Arab world. I was able to land a part-time job with Radio Morocco's English service in Rabat that allowed me days off in which to explore the country. And a good thing, too, because it was here in Tangier that Kismet once again put an oar into my affairs.

One evening in Dean's Bar, a famous meeting place for expatriates on the way to the Socco Grande, I ran for the first time into Ian Fleming, a tall, handsome man with a cigarette holder in one hand and a pint tumbler of vodka and tonic in the other. Ensconced in the Minza Hotel round the corner, he was engaged by day in dictating two books to an English secretary whom he described as 'a good girl with a drunken nose'. One of the books was the second, or possibly the third, James Bond adventure and became *Diamonds Are Forever*; the other was a documentary about diamond smuggling in Africa. We got on very well. He questioned me closely about the Marsh Arabs – Ian seemed to think I must have been almost incredibly intrepid, or simply mad, to have lived with them. He took to referring to me as 'my Zulu' – I suppose Zulus and Marsh Arabs were indistinguishably outlandish to him – and as we walked together along the wide sickle-shaped bay of Tangier, talking of this and that, he collected seashells in a battered briefcase. And, of course, I wondered out loud what I could possibly do to avoid returning to England to beg for conventional work in a nine-to-five office.

Ian, I should explain here, was not yet world-famous as the millionaire creator of James Bond. He was, however, Foreign Manager of the *Sunday Times*. 'Look here,' he said, on my last evening at Dean's, 'there's only one job in the world that pays people to be independent, to travel anywhere on this globe, and to hobnob with heaven-knows-who from a president to a prostitute. That job is journalism.'

'Not a job for me,' I said, weak as dishwater. 'I can't write. Even if I could, my name appearing in print . . . my God . . . too terrifying. . . .'

'Well,' Ian said across his levelled cigarette holder, 'you know where to find me.'

A vital seed had been ineradicably sown.

Soon my situation changed as, life tells one, situations invariably do. In the course of my meagre duties at Radio Morocco I met Algerian intellectuals, and having watched Colonel Nasser riding the unstoppable tidal wave of Arab nationalism in the Middle East – a phenomenon that caught the Western world on quite the wrong foot – I understood their point of view. At the same time, my job at Radio Morocco was leading inexorably to penury. I had also learned two facts of immediate importance to my future life. First: the headquarters of the Algerian government-in-exile – the men who at that moment were running a most bloody rebellion against the French – was in Tunis. Second: not a single British newspaper kept a correspondent in Tunis; up to then their editors had covered the war from Paris.

With the spectre of lifelong servitude to banking gibbering at my heels, to pack my bags and fly from Rabat to Tunis seemed like the work of seconds. Despair made me uncharacteristically bold. From the Tunisia Palace Hotel I wrote a letter to England that said in essence, 'Here I am. Unemployed. Youngish, fit and in Tunis. Sitting on top of a front-page story. Immediate access to every top Algerian.' This was not strictly true, but I knew that were I to walk up the right street I might be lucky enough to elbow at least one top Algerian off the pavement. I went on: 'Would you – by any remote chance – like me – ever – to send you some news? I've lived in the Middle East and know something about Arab nationalism.' I believe I added, 'I think your paper is wonderful.' That really was about all. I avoided any mention of the Marsh Arabs or Bedu – romantic nonsense, all that, irrelevant to the realities of the grim subject in hand. And I said nothing about money. I would have *paid* to have a job in Tunis.

This letter I duly sealed with a dry tongue and stamped with a shaking hand. And then I addressed it – but not to my inspiration and friend, Ian Fleming, at the *Sunday Times*. In my newly discovered sympathy for the Algerian side in the war, I knew that the *Observer*, unlike Ian's bosses, had taken the minority view that Arab nationalism was here to stay. Accordingly, it had courageously opposed the Suez adventure, lost half its readership in doing so, and was still trying to rise above that setback. So I sent my letter to David Astor, the Editor of the *Observer*. Ever prone to magnify fate, like George in E.M. Forster's *A Room with a View*, I see now that destiny's web was almost spun.

It was lucky for me that the Algerian conflict was at its climax, otherwise I doubt if Mr Astor would have bothered to reply. But a reply came. Would I please come to London to discuss my proposal? *Would* I? I would and did. At the *Observer*'s Dickensian offices in Tudor Street Robert Stephens, the paper's Diplomatic Correspondent, grilled me very sweetly about recent events on the Arab scene, and evidently my replies were not unacceptably idiotic, because shortly afterwards the Editor himself received me. A floppy-haired, shy-voiced man, popping multicoloured sweets into his mouth from a tin on his desk, David Astor told me I would be taken on as a 'stringer' – that is, as a locally based correspondent paid a small retaining fee and so much extra for every word printed. Astounding . . . I had suddenly embarked on a new career. Luckily for me, considering my total lack of self-confidence as a writer and with the *Observer* actually demanding copy, I was spared both the usual soul-rending struggle to get my first efforts even so much as looked at by an editor, and the rejection slips that so often put the swift kibosh on an aspiring writer's hopes.

Only the other day I read in P.G. Wodehouse's autobiography that in his early years the master of all those apparently effortless magazine serials had spent night after night writing in his bed-sitting room in

London, and got out of it nothing more than a collection of rejection slips with which he reckoned he could have papered the walls of a good-sized banqueting hall. While he was prepared to grant that some of them were rather pretty – the ones *Tit-Bits* used to send him had a picture of Newnes' offices in an attractive shade of green – he admitted that 'What I feel about rejection slips is that their glamour soon wears off,' adding, 'When you've seen one, I often say, you've seen them all.'

Wodehouse makes a joke of it. But what a lucky escape fate had handed me. Indeed, having been accepted into the deep end of journalism before I had even learned to dog-paddle, I was too ignorant of the business to grasp just how lucky I was, or else too preoccupied with a terrible conflict of emotions. You might think that, on the memorable afternoon when David Astor popped a violet-coloured sweet into his mouth and between crunches informed me that hence-forth I could consider myself the Tunis stringer for the *Observer*, I gambolled down his staircase like a starving puppy unexpectedly presented with a juicy bone. Not at all. Believe it or not, I even considered letting the whole thing drop.

The reason was simple: panic. The sheer mind-freezing panic accompanying the knowledge that, as certain as death and sooner rather than later, a cable signed by a remorseless editor in London would slip under the door of my Tunisian hotel room, requesting – urgently and at length – elucidation of some devastating development in the Algerian War that I had heard nothing about. 'Why?' London would imperiously demand to know; and 'Search me' would be my feeble, involuntary response. The dreadful certainty of that cable struck me like a sandbag to the back of the neck. It stopped me dead on the corner of Tudor and Bouverie Streets, besieged by terror, while passers-by audibly wondered if I thought I was a bloody lamp-post. I imagined that I was actually holding that deadly cable in my hand. I would have preferred a tarantula.

Where on earth, I asked myself, would I scavenge enough informa-tion to compose an answer authoritative enough to publish? Another thing: *Observer* correspondents, the cats' whiskers of Fleet Street, were famous for their lucid, lively prose. How was I going to write like them at the drop of a hat? And still another: if, by some miracle, I did scrabble out a not too visibly undernourished answer, who would tell me how to wire the wretched thing to London in the accepted form? As clear as sunshine, I was going to be found wanting. 'Young is not up to it,' the Tudor Street people would mutter. I would fluff the opportunity of a lifetime. I would find myself back more or less where I had started with Ralli Brothers eight years before.

Luckily, absolute fear driveth out dithering. There was only one thing for it. Cornered by fate, I must follow the advice that a popular if over-hearty form master at school had handed out to the flagging pupils he called his 'byes'. 'Now, then,' I could hear him saying, 'buckle to, byes, buckle to.' I would buckle to. I had already realized that journalism – perhaps above all professions – is something no one can fudge. Nobody on earth can write your stuff for you. You stand or fall by your own (signed) effort. An exhilarating thought, but an alarming one too. Thank heavens, then, that before I left for Tunis kind people took pity on me.

Fred Tomlinson, an *Observer* veteran who doubled as Air Correspondent and Deputy News Editor, swiftly recognized in me the stumbling personification of Evelyn Waugh's William Boot of *The Beast*. He tactfully advised me not to send my dispatches by air mail to 'Mr David Astor, *The Observer*, Tudor Street, London EC4', or to end them, 'All best wishes, yours sincerely, Gavin Young. PS: It's really very fine here for the time of year.' Not only that. This was in the days before telex and the ubiquitous long-distance telephone, and pages of copy had first to be reduced to cablese – a sort of poor man's pidjin – then cut into strips and pasted messily onto cable forms. You pushed these sticky scraps through a grille to a bad-tempered post office official who counted the words – often between leisurely intervals of picking his nose – then counted them again because he had forgotten the number he'd first thought of. Fred explained this strange language – how such phrases as 'for me', 'from Algiers' and 'to Paris' shortened into 'prome', 'exalgiers' and 'pariswards' respectively. 'Phew. Good proyou,' he quipped with a fatherly wink when at last I appeared to have hoisted this in. And then – good old Fred – he made me feel almost one of the boys by suggesting a pint at the Rose and Crown ('Auntie's', to *Observer* people) around the corner.

A professional tip of a different kind came from one of the paper's finest writers, the late John Gale, an immensely warm and manically humorous man of about my own age. During the Suez affair he had sent dispatches of near-genius from Nasser's Cairo while French and British bombs were falling on the city's suburbs, and we had met and got on famously when he passed through Rabat on his way to see the French side of the Algerian carnage. Now, as I blurted out my self-doubt, he told me, 'For God's sake don't worry. Look, mate – the Jews of Tunisia make a fantastic liqueur called *boukha*, some sort of fig brandy. Bloody strong stuff. Before you sit down to write a word, take a hefty slug of it, I would. It'll relax you no end.'

Good advice for some; unfortunately, I couldn't follow it. Not that in the normal way I am in the least averse to booze – on the contrary. My trouble is that owing to some metabolic quirk I invariably find that the combination of alcohol and a blank sheet of typing paper, far from composing my mind, increases its natural confusion to an untameable degree. So I confined my *boukha* tippling to drinking John's health on Saturday nights when my week's copy was safely on the wire to London. The real bonus I gleaned from John, apart from some much-needed moral comfort, came from reading and rereading his *Observer* articles, which with their cool, urgent simplicity and precise use of idiosyncratic quotes (his 'ear' was miraculous) had made him a phenomenon in the world of reporters.

Patrick O'Donovan was another *Observer* star whose work I read and reread. Admired and loved, he was a tall, stately galleon of a man, a former Irish Guards officer and an authentic wit, uproarious at play and at work. He was also an inspired writer who could write a word picture of a military rout in central Mongolia, a Christmas Eve in Bethlehem with bomb accompaniment, or a relatively uneventful Miss World contest ('Miss South Korea was in unfortunate puce,' I remember) with such deft, resonant and unexpected imagery that you felt you were standing at his elbow. In early middle age, to nobody's surprise, Patrick developed a fine W.C. Fields nose and the phrase 'a legend in his lunchtime' could easily have applied to him, although it was actually coined for an *Observer* Sports Editor later on.

An even more valuable bonus came my way in the person of my first News Editor, Michael Davie. Michael was (and, happily, still is) a feature writer of dazzling skill who had emerged, as have many of the English-speaking world's finest journalists, from the ranks of sports reporters. As News Editor, he possessed an unmatchable ability to instil confidence into a neurotic correspondent shivering at the end of a telegraphic cable hundreds of miles long. And a golden gift it was – for, as I have already mentioned, this was long before the day when you could snatch up a telephone in Baghdad, Peking and probably Timbuktu to beg your newspaper for a shoulder to weep on or a pat on the back. Sometimes it was a toss-up whether your news stories reached London at all. From Guinea once – the nightmare comes back to me as I write – my fifteen hundred words of urgent copy (incidentally containing one of my very few scoops) only got through to London thanks to the friendly perseverance of a bare-chested African in a ramshackle hut who sweated through most of a steamy afternoon, painfully dotting and dashing it out to distant Tudor Street on a rusty morse key that might once have been the property of Henry Morton Stanley. At such times one aged a decade in a couple of hours.

Michael's messages, so soothing and encouraging, were often able to reduce that decade to a mere twelvemonth. His notes and prompt cables of congratulations – he signed them 'Love, Michael' – acted on me like handfuls of pep pills. More than that, I soon discovered that we shared delight and admiration for magazine writers such as Ring Lardner, A.J. Liebling, James Thurber and S.J. Perelman – most of our reporter-heroes were stalwarts of the *New Yorker* of that time.

By their example Gale, O'Donovan and Michael Davie showed me that the *Observer* was the Rolls-Royce of British weekly journalism – something I never really doubted. Thanks to them, I began to see how things could, and should, be done. I even began, little by little, to acquire that minimal degree of self-confidence without which it is impossible to do any good work at all.

I haven't kept a copy of the piece I sent to the *Observer* from Tunis in answer to Michael's first cabled request – the cable in fear of which I had stood quaking on the corner of Tudor and Bouverie Streets. I only remember that it concerned the death in action near the Tunisian border of Amirouche, a notorious Algerian guerrilla commander. As inexperienced people usually do, I grossly overfiled and my twelve hundred words were cut down in London to about five hundred. I didn't mind. What mattered was that there, over the top of them, in print for the first time ever, were the words, 'from Gavin Young, Tunis'. As soon as the *Observer* arrived I scuttled off with it, like a squirrel with a nut, to a café on the main boulevard, ordered a Ricard, and read and reread those measly five hundred words as proudly as if I were Flaubert gawking at the first printed pages of *Madame Bovary*. After a while, I glanced furtively round at the other tables. Surely I was the object of everybody's interest today – exposed since this morning to every spy in town as the *Observer*'s man in Tunisia. The café was full of life and people who looked as though they might read newspapers, including English ones. I was staggered to see that no one was paying me the faintest attention.

*

Time went by. Pieces (getting larger) went on appearing in the *Observer* under my name. Presently the Algerian war was overtaken by a larger crisis – the Congo blew up and filled the world's front pages for the best part of the next two years. Shooting started when the United Nations moved troops in to deal with the Congo's eccentric Prime Minister, Patrice Lumumba, and Michael Davie cabled me to go there and take over from the great O'Donovan. I was soon buckling to very hard indeed, and six months later David Astor promoted me onto the staff of the *Observer*. Was he wise? I couldn't help wondering.

An early piece of mine in this book (it appeared in three parts in the *Observer*) is an account of an unusual assignment that remains one of my favourite adventures. How it fell into my lap may be worth a brief word; it strikes me now as marvellously John Buchan-esque. I received in Leopoldville a letter from David Astor which said, in effect, 'How do you feel about a trip to Nagaland? The war there looks very much like an *Observer* story. Come back to London and let's talk about it.' I was thrown into confusion. Nagaland? Where on earth was that? I sat down to work it out calmly. I couldn't believe that the Editor would want to send me very far from the turbulent Congo: surely, I was an *Observer* 'Africa man'. Obviously then, Nagaland was in Africa. Wherever it was, nothing on earth would have induced me to confess to anyone that I had never heard of it. I cabled back, 'Agree Nagaland well worth a visit.'

I found there was no need to panic. Back in London no one at the *Observer* had heard of Nagaland before that week. Small wonder, since it is one of the world's remotest areas – a tangle of jungle-covered mountains in north-eastern India where the borders of India, Burma and China converge. The Nagas, a tribal people, had formerly been head-hunters, but thanks to the efforts of energetic missionaries they were now hymn-singing Baptists. Stocky and high-cheekboned like Gurkhas, they cultivated rice and lived in thatched houses that clung to precipitous hillsides in a region not far removed from Shangri-la. Having remained almost insanely loyal to the British through the worst days of the Japanese advance into India, they had hoped to be allowed to continue as part of the British Commonwealth when India became independent in 1947. Outraged when these hopes were dashed, many Nagas had taken up arms against the Indian Army. Their leader, a Mr Phizo, had recently arrived in London by devious routes and once there had talked a great deal about resistance ... bombing ... burning villages ... in fact a relatively large-scale war.

All of which Mr Nehru, the Indian Prime Minister, had dismissed as rubbish.

'Do you think what Phizo says is true?' I asked.

'That's what we want you to find out,' was David Astor's reply. 'Actually, I don't suppose you'll manage to get there, but I think you ought to try.'

I felt I was well and truly in the erratic wake of Buchan's Sandy Arbuthnot when my first step towards Nagaland and the East took me due north to the Scottish island of Mull. There, of all places, in a converted croft, dwelt a Mrs Betts, the greatest living expert on the Nagas; she had parachuted down to them in the war and been received as a sort of white goddess. From Mull the trail led to an office in the Vauxhall Bridge Road in London where Mr Phizo, overjoyed to hear that I was off to Nagaland, advised me to fly to Rangoon (since India would be closed to me) and take a sampan to the higher reaches of the Chindwin River, where it approached the Indian and Chinese frontiers. From there I should be able to skip quite easily across a small ocean of razor-backed mountains into India and the Naga Hills region where the war was.

I had a number of questions. Where was I to find the place to board a sampan? How would I know when to get off it? Upper Burma was a closed military region; wasn't I likely to be arrested in the first five minutes? And the Burmese were notoriously tough on foreign intruders.

Imperturbably, over green tea, Mr Phizo replied that he would instruct his people in Nagaland (how, I wondered: by telepathy?) to send a secret emissary down the Chindwin to meet me in Rangoon. I should wait for him – he might be delayed by the monsoon rains – on successive Mondays and Thursdays in Rangoon Zoo. The Zoo? Between the giraffe house and the monkey cage, Mr Phizo unsmilingly added.

Ten days later I pushed through the turnstiles at Rangoon Zoo, reached the monkey cage, and saw – no one. It was only on my fifth visit that, to my intense relief, a short, muscular man with high cheekbones and wearing a Burmese sarong bobbed out smiling from behind the giraffes. My first Naga. It was Prem – fearless, impassive, resourceful Prem. He got me up to Nagaland and back again in two months, and became a friend (he was killed in a skirmish a few years later). My progress up the Chindwin consisted of ten days on a sampan crowded with Burmese policemen and soldiers, under whose inquisitive scrutiny I was obliged to impersonate a missionary. In mid-Burma I was exposed as a fraud by a real missionary, a Methodist named Edwards from Woking. But that's another story.

Fate – and David Astor – then sent me to New York. I stepped off the *Queen Elizabeth* in a blizzard and spent the next two years exploring that city as minutely and enthusiastically as I had explored the Marshlands of Sumer and Babylon. It's contrast that keeps the life-force flowing.

It was in New York that I realized the *Observer* was a newspaper of international and not merely national renown. I would tentatively introduce myself as its representative and watch doors fly open. The paper itself was unfailingly obtainable at the out-of-town news-stand under the old 'flatiron' building in Times Square as well as at Gordon's bookstore a door or two east of the St Regis Hotel on 55th Street, and these two destinations provided me with a regular Monday amble from where I lived on Second Avenue between 52nd and 53rd Streets, in a fourth-floor walk-up apartment with a hole in the ceiling.

It's still there, that unpretentious little walk-up. I usually give it a wave when I'm in the city. By some miracle that stretch of Second Avenue has hardly changed, although I miss Ferraro's, the grocer's that occupied the north-east corner of 53rd Street, and this year I saw that the friendly Chinese restaurant on my ground floor had changed its name from the Gold Coin to something Irish.

From 1963 to 1987 is twenty-four years, but as usual I stood staring at No. 994 Second Avenue with the feeling that I'd left it the year before last. Was it really in 1962 that I almost severed a fingertip in the springs of my Castro Convertible sofa-bed as I struggled to fold the damned thing away one blurry morning? Had the hole in the ceiling (it was between fireplace and window) been patched up yet? If not, it was about time.

New York City in the 'Kennedy Spring' was much more than just another adventure. Living and working there added a great city, a continent, a horizontal and vertical world to my experience. It had been an enormous step from the Arabian outback to the *Observer*. New York was another giant step. Writers from Norman Mailer to P.G. Wodehouse, editors, artists, cartoonists, youth gangs, jazz men, boxers, the Harlem dance halls, Broadway directors and actors populated a New York that was exactly, thrillingly, what I had expected it to be. No wonder that whenever I go back there I throw a tender glance at No. 994.

This collection includes a few slight pieces from New York, and a few more about Beverly Hills and Hollywood. The impressions of Fidel Castro's Cuba just before the missile crisis were the product of a visit I made from New York during which I ended up, very early one morning, in a Havana nightclub with Castro himself. I found him genial, but he had a habit of emphasizing a point by poking a forefinger like a chisel into my short ribs. When I clambered aboard the plane to Miami that same morning I could feel the bruises. But there is nothing here of the American political scene. I had no contact with goings-on in Washington where, in any case, the *Observer* had a correspondent, nor did I want anything to do with it. Seats of power bore me, and Washington life has always seemed to me to be about as interesting as a Bank Holiday weekend in Guildford. The throb of hot-blooded American life was, and still is, to be felt in New York and points west. A number of the pieces included here concern places farther-flung than New York, or people whom I got to know in the course of repeated encounters. Continuity is an important element in foreign reporting.

The Shah of Iran takes up a good deal of room. I think he remains an interesting phenomenon. I knew him fairly well from 1963 onwards and found him in some ways a touching, even likeable, figure before his crazy obsession with pre-Islamic grandeur took hold and doomed him to end like Ozymandias.

Zulfikar Ali Bhutto, that brilliant cad, hanged like Kipling's Danny Deever and in almost the same spot, was interesting too – and his political soul goes marching strongly on. Unlike the Shah, he was too bright for anyone's good. Many of his countrymen could never forgive him for being so much, and so obviously, cleverer than they were, and at the same time so openly scornful of them. So they strung him up, as General Zia al-Haq, himself a Bhutto protégé, inadvertently gave me the tip that they would. 'If the Supreme Court says, "Hang the bastard," I'll hang him,' were Zia's exact words to me. Later, a flustered major telephoned my hotel from Zia's office begging me to change 'bastard' to 'blighter'. I did so. But the word 'bastard' had made the hanging a certainty.

Ian Smith is vastly different, but he too once lived in unreality, a failing he shared with such disparate men as the Shah, Bhutto and Egypt's Anwar Sadat (Sadat's book – I have included my review of it –

demonstrated that). The piece here describes what I considered to be the dream world Ian Smith constructed round his fellow Rhodesians when he was Prime Minister. I was not too sorry when he declared me *persona non grata* on the strength of it.

Of all the articles resurrected here, those that gave me most satisfaction to write – though it was a tortured kind of satisfaction – are those about the effect of war on a typical Vietnamese family. Madame Dinh's family was neither rich nor well connected. She and her relations had no axe to grind in that miserable affair. Like most Vietnamese in the city of Hué, they prayed to be left alone – by both sides. What naïvety! I was lucky to meet Tam and Chinh and the rest of them soon after I arrived in Vietnam in early 1965. The Vietnamese are possibly the warmest-hearted people in the world, and I was soon accepted as one of the family. And so I was privileged to watch, at close quarters, as year after year the accidents of a miserable war whittled away the family – a son here, a brother or a cousin there. No written words of mine can speak adequately for that tormented family – whose torments are even now not at an end. Seven years of 're-education' and hard labour did not strike the Communists as enough punishment for these unimportant people, so they destituted them as well. The concept of forgiveness is a casualty of the peace in Vietnam today.

Nevertheless, there is still a slender hope for Madame Dinh's family. Her son, daughter-in-law and grandchildren are on a list – it is a long one – of Vietnamese who have been sponsored by foreigners and so may receive official permission from Hanoi to exile themselves from their own country. Perhaps in four or five years I may be reunited with them in London or Los Angeles: who knows? As for Madame Dinh herself, I wouldn't be surprised if she decided to stay, whatever happens. What would she do in Pasadena or Dallas, far from the spirits of her parents, her husband, uncles and aunts, a son, various nephews and nieces, all of whom lie in the Buddhist cemetery in Hué? As for my friend Vien, who also appears in this book, I'm sorry to say I have had no word of him from that day to this.

There is something in this book of the Marsh Arabs. A first love is never forgotten. I wrote a book, called *Return to the Marshes*, about my life with them but I had not managed to pursue their further doings in print until the Iran–Iraq War gave me an opportunity – a grim one, but still an opportunity. It was shattering to find a people as old as old Sumer, people I loved, suddenly plunged – reed houses, canoes, water buffaloes and all – into a world of ground-to-ground missiles, heavy artillery and helicopter gunships. They had endured, indeed even thrived on, seven thousand years of tribal skirmishing, but this was very different. Going back, I found many old friends who, I think, were delighted to be revisited *in extremis*, enduring the kind of terrors and bereavements that Madame Dinh had endured for so long in her corner of this wicked world.

In so far as writing can be 'fun', I am sure it is not surprising that the pieces comprising the People and Places section of this book were the ones I most enjoyed researching and getting down. People and places, after all, were what I had set out to find when I fled the shipping office in the bazaar of Basra for the waterlogged bosom of the Marshes.

The piece about Wilfred Thesiger, however, has nothing to do with our beloved Marsh Arabs or that time. It was the result of a most enjoyable visit I paid to him in wildest Kenya up near Lake Rudolf, where he 'went native' some years ago among the Samburu. I think I've caught the authentic Thesigerian tone of voice – it *should* be familiar enough to me after thirty-five years – but he has since pointed out to me, in gently reproving tones, that Lawi is a Catholic and not, as I had it, a Protestant. Nor, he says, is it a buffalo that can turn on a sixpence; it is a charging rhino. As your life, dear reader, may one day depend upon it, I thought I should make that clear.

Investigating Brighton was a sort of working holiday, rather as it was, I suppose, in pre-war days for the private detectives who hung about the lobby of the Metropole Hotel jotting down evidence, between the occasional Scotch-and-splash, of the comings and goings of erring husbands and their 'little friends' (hired from an agency for the occasion) to be used in impending divorce cases. The stony narrowness of Brighton beach took me aback, but the ghosts in the streets more than made up for it. Not so much the shades of Prinny, Mrs Fitzherbert and Mrs Hester Thrale as those of Patrick Hamilton, author of *Hangover Square*, of Graham Greene's vicious boy Pinkie, and music hall's Max Miller, the 'Cheeky Chappie'. And there was compensation in the living, too – in the large and most unspectral lady I found waiting in the heat for the miniature railway to Black Rock, who, kicking off her shoes, gasped to her husband, 'I'm fooked!' Pinkie's girlfriend, Ida, compared Brighton rock to life itself: 'Bite it all the way down, you'll still read Brighton. That's human nature.' So it is, Ida.

Graham Greene himself is in this book – not at all dour or seedy, but delightfully relaxed over a pink gin, longing to burst into song in the staid coffee room of the Travellers' Club. And the courageous, romantic Colonel David Stirling, whom I met in another club, is here too, though I imagine he has long since given up his plans to run Britain's power stations, sewers and the like.

I have slipped in a mildly amusing (I hope) defence of foreign correspondents, particularly those whose special task is to cover wars, revolutions and natural disasters. I wrote it in the heat of indignation stoked by a decade or two of ignorant and supercilious criticism of people who were my colleagues for so many years. The usual sneer was that 'those journalist johnnies write everything from the hotel bar, doncha know.' Well, there are conmen in every part of life, but I have been lucky to work with people who must have been the most meticulous and courageous professionals in any business. So I wrote this rebuttal of senseless criticism after a bizarre couple of weeks spent sculling about in canoes and paddleboats among the drowned islands of the Bay of Bengal immediately after one of the most savage cyclones in living memory. It might have been a regatta if it hadn't been for the stench of bodies.

Since the Vietnam and Cambodian wars such thoughtless criticism has died down, if not out: you can hardly accuse the media of sloth and cowardice when it's clear that the battle pictures on your TV screen were filmed by human beings, and not by a computer floating in space. As a matter of fact, about seventy-five correspondents and photographers were listed as killed or missing in Vietnam and Cambodia. That figure, it seems to me, speaks for itself.

People – young people, usually – sometimes ask me how to set about a life of travel. I am sadly compelled to answer that, as far as the journalistic variety is concerned, it is hard to be very encouraging. Every British national newspaper used to have its stable of foreign correspondents. But these are penny-pinching days. As never before, newspaper owners are cutting back on just about everything in order to protect their millions, and usually the first thing they cut back on is

Abroad. 'It's the air fares,' they groan. 'It's the hotels. We're going broke.' It would be heartless not to feel sorry for them.

Among other things they use to justify turning a cold shoulder on the wider world are opinion polls claiming that readers are only attracted by football, TV gossip, fashion, chat shows and party political twaddle. Perhaps the polls know best, but can this really be so? Has the cosy but uninspiring symbol of the parish pump really replaced Long John Silver's parrot, Blind Pew's tapping stick and the good old Jolly Roger in the hearts of the young? I can't believe that the red-blooded Stevensonian wanderlust has quite evaporated. To anyone who feels it in the blood, a word of advice. Remember, if there's one certainty in all this it is that youth is worth more than bags of gold. What worse fate could befall one than to end up in old age moaning, 'If only I had tried to do that . . . if only . . .'?

In the centenary portrait of John Buchan included here I quote from his autobiography, *Memory Hold the Door*. 'I regard the shrinking of opportunity as one of the gravest facts of our age. The world must remain an oyster for youth to open. If not, youth will cease to be young and that would be the end of everything.'

As I started by saying, I believe in Kismet: what is written is written. Fate turned me up an oyster or two. Here are a few samples of what came out of them.

Gavin Young
Dar Sinclair, Tangier
1987

Confessions of a Long-distance Wanderer

Why do so many of us in the West go on travelling? Why do hordes of Britons seem to welcome the least opportunity to be jostled about in airports, to endure inexplicable delays corralled in departure lounges redolent of *1984*? Or risk entrapment by a gaudy brochure into a shaky Spanish hotel two blocks from a polluted beach? Is it worth the anguish and expense? After all, television nightly lays the world on our hearthrugs like a faithful dog bringing in his master's slippers. Travel books are published and read as never before. And if to buy them demands what S.J. Perelman used to call 'a hefty chunk of coin', they are certainly far cheaper than the cheapest air tickets.

I suppose one major spur to travel is simply the change, the escape from boredom that Graham Greene talks about. Evidently a great many people (including me) still believe that getting away from the hundredth episode of *Dallas* and the party political broadcasts is worth a journey that could end in sandflies and diarrhoea. More seriously, many of us, too, feel what Greene described as 'the desire to see a little bit further before the surrender to old age and the blank certitude of death'.

The *nakhoda* (captain) of a semi-derelict Baluchi launch in which I crossed the Arabian Sea in 1979 asked me why I travelled with him – why didn't I fly like other people? I wanted to give him Greene's reason, or a burst of Kipling's 'For to admire an' for to see this world so wide'. But my Arabic wasn't nearly good enough, and so I said, 'To meet you,' which in its way came to the same thing. Merely meeting foreigners makes a wonderful change. Among perfect strangers our own strangeness is a better disguise than any the Caliph Harun al Rashid found to prowl in through the streets of moonlit Baghdad. Abroad, our upbringing, class, education, even our financial condition, go for nothing. We start again with a clean slate. The anonymity of travel is one of its greatest attractions.

There's little point in making pompous distinctions between long journeys and short ones. Max Beerbohm, in *Ichabod*, an essay fondly dedicated to the labels on his much-travelled hatbox, talks of the 'delicious glamour' of long journeys. But short ones, too, excited him; a single frontier crossed at dead of night, a strange tongue and strange uniforms meant for him an expansion and enrichment of his soul. So it is with most of us who travel, however far or near we go. And a short journey can provide the joy of train or boat travel which long distances usually rule out.

Technological progress has affected long-distance travel in unexpected ways. For example, the old explorers would be astonished to find that it is now relatively easy to travel to Lhasa on foot, yak or bus, traversing the Himalayas from Kulu, where Kipling's Kim and his friend the Lama crossed a snowy pass in cold moonlight, up to their knees 'like Bactrian camels – the snow-bred sort that come into the Kashmir Serai'. Now, where Kim, beaten down by the silences and the appalling sweep of the cloud-shadows after rain, burst out, 'Surely the Gods live here,' tourist guides pilot holidaying Western businessmen and their wives. On the other hand, I am told that the jetliners hopping across the principal islands in the Pacific have made many smaller islands virtually inaccessible by eliminating the passenger ships that only a decade ago linked them all up.

Why travel? I am such a travel addict that I even like Frank Sinatra's swinging version of Kipling's 'Road to Mandalay' ('. . . out of China 'croo-oo-ooss the bay'). Not something my old English teacher would have approved of. In connection with whom, I wonder how much people think these days of travel as an essential element in a well-rounded education? Does it really broaden the mind? That it did was taken for granted in the days of the eighteenth-century Grand Tour.

But if you go to Venice or Florence can you see anything to learn from? A friend of mine pooh-poohed the Grand Tour idea, declaring that decent views of the Great Sights of Europe are obliterated by surging groups. Well, obviously it's best to avoid the Louvre on a Sunday and the Forum in Rome during the school holidays; at other times they can rise above the drawback of a few score tourists. In Ephesus recently I was temporarily enmeshed in converging groups of Americans and Swedes outside the ruined front door of what my Turkish guide assured me had been the biggest brothel in the Ancient World ('was made to protect the girls of the East from the lusty seamens,' he said). Despite the crowds I was able to get a very satisfactory squint at that antique cathouse. I believe places become really intolerable when they are adopted by hordes of tourists or colonized by tourist organizations implanting their wretched resorts. Examples of this: Bali; Pattaya in Thailand; the Maldive Island resorts, where everything – even the fish in an ocean full of fish – is expensively imported.

Of course, group travel has made it very difficult for the single traveller. I have too often been faced with suspicious immigration officers muttering, 'Where's your group, then, eh?' On the other hand, it has made it extraordinarily easy for almost any Dad, Mum and Kid to become his or her own Intrepid Victorian. In the nineteenth century, enterprising British officers returning to England on leave from India often trekked across ancient trade routes through Afghanistan, Persia and wild Kurdistan to Beirut, sketching as they went. There are folios in the Victoria and Albert print room of beautiful sketches by – as it were – Major Carstairs of the Bengal Fusiliers or Captain Bagshawe of the Guides; watercolours of the mosque at Meshed or the Rowanduz Gorge. Nowadays, certain tour operators cater for just that sort of thing. You can join small groups of amateur hunters of, say, a rare Kashmiri lotus or a semi-extinct crested chitchat in High Armenia. Eminent Oxford professors lead you by the hand through Petra or Troy. How much better than second-hand views on the telly. You can feel the wind and sun. You don't have to be young or fit; only keen.

To my mind, it is pointless to complain that the world has been quite turned over like an overworked ploughed field – that there's nothing new left under the sun. Or to sneer that trains, ships, buses and cars have made all travel a clangorous purgatory. Beerbohm asks, reasonably, 'To see what one has not seen before, is not that almost as good as to see what no one has ever seen?' Of course it is. And, of course, as he says, the noise of great ports and great railway stations is as dear to the traveller as the bugle note to the warhorse. The shouts of 'All visitors ashore!', '*En voiture!*' and '*Partenza!*' were as sweet to him as the first twittering of the birds in the hedgerows. So they are to us.

The din of airports is not dear at all. Air travel is to be undergone, not thought about. But sea travel, delectable, rare as caviare, is something to savour. I even believe ocean airs carry a special spiritual balm. Seafarers seem more tolerant than other men. Perhaps it's due to a lifetime of suspension between sea and heaven. Earthbound religious, political, racial tensions miraculously dissolve on the pure briny. Recently, in a Gulf tanker manned by Iranians, I found bearded

Muslim fundamentalist seamen with photographs of Ayatollah Khomeini pinned over their bunks apparently quite unconcerned by the nude pin-ups torn from *Playboy* by their colleagues. 'How's that for tolerance?' the British captain asked me proudly. In Tehran, the pin-ups would have led to instant jailings and floggings, perhaps the severing of hands.

Two sorts of travel lack the sublime element: the first is the travel of the very rich who move about at a level of slickness that has nothing to do with anything else on earth. And second, I'm afraid some business-men, however many Club Class miles they notch up, will never see anything through those boardroom eyes but other box wallahs bearing contracts. En route to Ostend as much as to Samarkand, trafficking alone cannot fan the fiery heart of a true pilgrim-traveller on the Golden Road. The sublime and contracts cannot co-exist.

Admittedly, some formidable voices have spoken out sharply against travel. J.B. Priestley, for example, determined to give up attending conferences abroad; he just couldn't stand the 'abroadness' of it all. The foreign delegates, he grumbled, were altogether *too foreign* – 'To begin with, they always pretend not to understand a word of English.' G.K. Chesterton pointed out that a deeper and sharper question than 'What can they know of England who only England knows?' is 'What can they know of England who know only the world?' 'The more dead and dusty a thing is,' he wrote, 'the more it travels about. Dust is like this and the thistledown and the High Commissioner in South Africa. The rolling, echoing stone is dead, but the moss, although silent, is alive.' Fertile things, he added, are heavier, like the fruit trees in the pregnant mud of the Nile.

Strong words; but personally I don't believe one of them. I cannot agree with Chesterton that the man in the cabbage field who has seen nothing at all is none the less thinking of the things that unite men – hunger, babies and the beauty of women, and the promise and menace of the sky – and thus 'sees' everything worth seeing. I, too, like to stand in cabbage fields now and again, thinking of babies and things. But to my mind it is just not enough: that's how you become a stick-in-the-mud. And while you are there among the cabbages, even while the television men are gathering together their travellers' cheques and the apparatus to film whatever part of the globe they are going to show you next, what is the world doing? Not standing still, you can bet your bottom dollar on that. There is no substitute for getting out and catching the world on the wing. Never mind discomfort; it shifts the adrenalin about. There are worse things in life than lice in the seams of your shirt or even bedbugs in your jeans. Stagnation, for example.

Approach travel in a lively spirit. Remember that when your plane lifts up through the clouds, you'll find, as you found before, that your heart, like that of William Boot in *Scoop*, will 'rise with it and glory lark-like, in the high places'. 'Away! Our camels sniff the evening and are glad.' It would be nice to see you over a gin pahit or a stengah on the Shanghai Bund. Or even, at a pinch, in a sleeping bag at Heathrow's Terminal One. *En voiture! Partenza!*

1982

Foreign Parts

Outpost in the Congo

A curious incident marred the independence celebrations in Leopoldville that in 1960 ended Belgian rule in the Congo (now Zaire). An African dashed out of the crowd lining the capital's widest boulevard to see King Baudouin ride past, mounted the running-board of the royal car, yanked the king's ceremonial sword from its scabbard and brandished it in triumph before his delighted countrymen. It was an omen. Nothing went right after that. Soon, the Congolese Army mutinied against its Belgian officers – the signal for a panic-stricken exodus of most of the considerable Belgian population. They forsook houses, cars, servants, pets, and left the new state looking something like the Marie Celeste. I heard it said that meals were left half-eaten, half-smoked cigarettes burning in ashtrays, baths still running. Certainly bewildered pet dogs roamed the streets of Leopoldville for weeks afterwards.

Meanwhile law and order crumbled away. The machinery of administration, deprived of its Belgian experts (they had kept things pretty much in their own hands), ceased to function. Civil war broke out in parts of the country. In despair, the new Congolese Prime Minister, Patrice Lumumba, a clever but eccentric former beer salesman, invited the United Nations Secretary General, Dag Hammarskjold, to send an international force to restore order, and soon a motley collection of Ethiopians, Swedes, Indonesians, Ghanaians, Sudanese and Irish in UN blue berets fanned out through this vast and largely jungle-covered country. In the next year or two, a number of them were killed in action, and several were eaten by tribesmen and crocodiles. The soldiers were followed by civilian experts on everything from finance to telecommunications and health.

I reached Leopoldville shortly after independence in a Soviet Ilyushin turbo-prop aeroplane carrying Lumumba back home from a visit to Moscow. By then he was more or less mentally overcome by power and the international attention he had achieved through disaster. I remained a year in the Congo – a doom-laden place if ever I *saw one – more and more convinced that, if we stayed too long – UN experts, soldiers, journalists, everyone – we would be sucked down into this fatal morass that Joseph Conrad called the Heart of Darkness.*

COQUILHATVILLE, CONGO, 24 OCTOBER 1960

There is an inescapable seediness about the Ancion Hotel at Coquilhatville that the potted tropical plants and bright red and green steel chairs on the terrace do little to dispel. Friendly Congolese waiters, as regularly as their counterparts in wartime London, announce that everything on the menu except pork and potatoes is 'off'. The only telephone is padlocked. Below the terrace the flat, blue-grey Congo slides past to the sea 750 miles away, flecked with the tufts and giant tangles of the invidious water hyacinth which, lower down, become a menace to the smaller river craft. Once a week the steamer from Leopoldville pulls up to the jetty near the hotel, her attendant barges clustering round her like pilot fish round a shark. Four hundred and fifty miles, two days up and two days down. There are no roads or rails between Coquilhatville and the capital.

Equateur Province is for the most part thickly blanketed by dense rain forest. Lying astride the Equator, it has an unenviably hot and humid climate. Towns and villages are widely scattered, communications are non-existent except by river, through a maze of jungle-bound waterways, crocodile-haunted. Rather less than two million Congolese are divided into numerous tribal associations all more or less at violent loggerheads. And tribal rivalries have now extended into urban politics.

Coquilhatville has a depressed look about it that has probably nothing to do with independence. It is a shapeless town of small, curiously ugly villas and shops that straggle inland from the river. It is the capital of the Province, its administrative centre and its port. Palm oil, rubber, rice, cotton and coffee are shipped down the river from the plantations far up in the interior. Founded by Henry Morton Stanley, who arrived there with the Belgian Lieutenant Coquilhat, in 1883, it has grown while the surrounding countryside has remained as Stanley found it.

Simply because the Ancion is the only hotel it is something of a social centre. Visitors and Congolese officials eat there, Belgian businessmen and plantation managers in shirts and shorts come to drink whisky and soda in the sticky noon heat and stare resentfully at

9

United Nations officials who lunch there. Before independence there were about 1500 Belgians in the city, now only 140 remain. Few if any have a good word to say for the UN mission that arrived three weeks ago. 'What good do those——[the epithet was Rabelaisian] think they are doing here?' they say. 'They don't understand the first thing about the Congo. The best thing they can do is help us to come back.'

Such criticism of the UN officials is unjust. It is not their fault that the post-independence panic stampeded nearly all the Belgian officials out of the Province – including all but two doctors. The health services have only been kept alive, precariously, by the arrival of experts from the World Health Organization. The scattered village dispensaries are unstaffed, the danger of epidemics is grave. The incidence of leprosy is very high. At the leprosarium near Coquilhatville five Sisters of Notre Dame du Sacré Coeur continue to look after 775 leprosy patients. They are directed for the moment by a gentle, sensitive Negro, Dr Phil Edwards, who captained the Canadian Olympic team at Berlin in 1936. Now he is an expert on tropical diseases.

The new Congolese Provincial Ministers are well-intentioned but harassed by political insecurity. The young Provincial President received me in a spacious residence formerly occupied by the Belgian Provincial Governor. He stood under the chandeliers, twitching his fingers together like a nervous undergraduate. A framed photograph of himself with jaw jutting in heroic pose stood on a massive radio-gram, hardly recognizable. He was polite and talked of his desire to cooperate with the UN mission. At one stage he left me to go and argue with a band of Congolese private soldiers in the garden. They showed him no respect. Shouting and waving their arms, they eventually moved off; but one had the feeling they would be back. 'If only the Army could be disbanded . . . ,' the President said dimly. He glanced continually out of the window to see if the soldiers had returned. I didn't blame him. The Congolese Army is as much a menace in Coquilhatville as it is anywhere else in the Congo today. Undisciplined and rapacious, it threatens to paralyse at any moment all normal life in the town.

The real hope for the maintenance of law and order lies in the UN military force; 1100 neat, bright Indonesian 'Rangers'. Already the diminutive Indonesians are playing football with the Congolese, who find judo too rough. And however critical the remaining Belgians may be of the UN, all are thankful for the presence of the UN troops.

The Belgians believe that the only hope for the Congo lies in their own return, but the UN mission has something more to do than simply reorganize and administer. The Congolese must be trained to take over positions of responsibility in what is now their own country. The Belgians who insult UN officials in the Ancion Hotel apparently don't see it that way. They hardly seem to realize that the restrictive and debasing paternalism of earlier years is as dead as the explorers who founded Coquilhatville eighty-seven years ago. It is no longer a question of looking after the Congolese, but of teaching and assisting the Congolese to look after themselves.

Clinging to Freedom on the Hilltops

I lost over a stone scrambling across those Naga Hills, but it was a thrilling adventure. Back in London, David Astor rewarded me with a bonus of £250, a tidy sum in those distant days when bonuses were still relatively commonplace. And at a small Observer *party at the Waldorf Hotel, he described my trip as one of the two or three most memorable adventures in the history of the newspaper. Kind words. That history has yet to be written. How I found my way to the Naga War is described in the preface to this book.*

NAGALAND, 30 APRIL 1961

I said goodbye to the General at the top of a pass 8000 feet above the sea, 7500 feet above the Indian plain. He was Kaito Sukhai, Commander-in-Chief of the Naga Nationalist Army, now fighting for the sixth year running a war of independence against India. The General and his staff had come to see me off. 'Don't forget Nagaland,' they said, and 'Tell Uncle we are praying for him.'

Behind us the jungle rose like a cliff. Below us the sharp hill ridges of Nagaland stretched away into the haze like waves on a petrified ocean. There was no sign anywhere of an Indian patrol; only the watchful figures of the General's Home Guard, stocky and alert in jungle green, tommy guns and rifles at the ready. Yet somewhere in the woods beneath us were 30,000 soldiers (the figure is Indian and official) sent by the Indian Army to suppress the Nagas' rebellion. The General's Home Guards (a mere 2000 according to Indian sources) have kept them at bay since 1955.

The 'Uncle' for whom they are praying is fifty-seven-year-old A.Z. Phizo, President of the Naga National Council, the political organization of which the Naga Home Guard is the military arm. Mr Phizo has been in London for nearly a year. He is the first Naga of any political consequence to escape from his remote country in north-east India to state the case for Naga independence, freely and at length, to a wide international audience. For years he has been stating it to the Indian Government in vain. Now, from an office in the Vauxhall Bridge Road, he is in constant clandestine contact with his nationalist supporters at home.

For too long, the Naga rebels feel, they have been fighting a war that is righteous but unknown. Phizo has sought to change all that. His object in coming to England has been to break the screen of silence which, he says, the Indian Government has erected round events in Nagaland and to try to mobilize international support for an appeal to the United Nations. He chose London, he says, because his people are Christians and traditionally democratic. They wish to avoid for as long as possible what may prove to be an ultimate necessity – an appeal for help from Communist China. Nagaland does not border China, but it very nearly does so. Although they recognize the risk of such an appeal, the Nagas say, 'If the West will not help us, we must seek aid elsewhere, no matter what its source.'

Last year Phizo publicly accused the Indians of committing a series of atrocities against Naga civilians. He produced lists of villages burnt by the Indian Army, and the names of individual victims killed, tortured, raped and maimed by Indian troops. These allegations were forcefully denied by the Indian Government, although Indian press reports admitted that guilt was established in twenty-two cases of alleged atrocities. Indian counter-allegations blamed the Naga nationalists for atrocities against their own people, and Phizo himself for the murder of one of his former supporters. Last year a warrant was issued for his arrest.

According to Indian Government statements, a compromise settlement acceptable to the great majority of the Naga people could be reached. The rebels, the statements said, were a handful of violent extremists representing no more than 25 per cent of the population. It was difficult to arrive at any objective estimate of the truth. No foreign newspaper correspondents had been allowed to visit Nagaland for several years.

From time to time reports emanating from the region went some way to confirm Phizo's atrocity stories. Very little was known of the character of the Naga Home Guard – the Nationalist Army of so-called 'underground hostiles', whose numbers were said by the Indians to be dwindling but who evidently continued to be briskly active: who ambushed convoys, attacked and besieged Indian Army posts, and shot down an Indian Air Force aeroplane. (The Governor of Assam's personal pilot is still a prisoner.)

The Nagas are a people of Mongolian origin, most of whom inhabit the mountainous Naga Hills and Tuensang areas that fringe the Indo-Burmese border. About 350,000 Nagas, divided into more than fifteen tribes, are scattered throughout this beautiful but savage tangle of jungle-covered hill country 100 miles wide by 400 long. There are many thousands more in the neighbouring State of Manipur, which they share with an alien tribe – the Kukis – and in north-west Burma. The total Naga population has been estimated at 600,000. Naga tribes are culturally and linguistically closely related and form a homogeneous bloc. For the last two or three generations at least they have been conscious of a common Nagahood.

Nagas are stocky, muscular, cheerful people. Most of them are Christians – Baptists converted by American missionaries who were expelled from the area by the Indian Government soon after independence in 1947. For centuries they led an uncomplicated, isolated life cultivating the sides of their mountains in a jungle backwater unruffled by outside influences. But they are formidable warriors and formerly, because of their bizarre fashion of trophy gathering, earned themselves a reputation as head-hunters. In fact head-hunting began to die out as the British gradually pacified the area at the end of the nineteenth century.

The British administered the Nagas on a very light rein. They were ensured peace and a greater measure of security; their village organizations (essentially democratic) were left to function intact. In both world wars Nagas volunteered for service with the British forces. Nagas served on the Western Front in World War I. When in 1944 the Japanese troops were in full control of the Naga Hills area the Nagas remained inflexibly loyal. Virtually the only exception was A.Z. Phizo himself, who now admits that he was won over by a Japanese promise to recognize Nagaland's independence.

The imminence of Indian independence in 1946 sparked off intense Naga political agitation for a separate homeland. The agitation was led by the Naga National Council, which had been formed some years

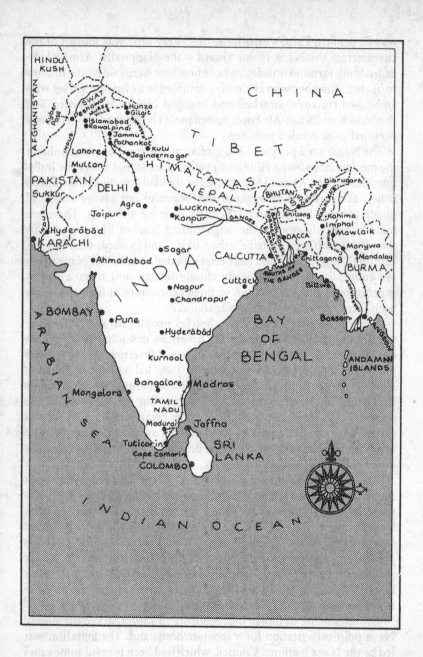

earlier to further the social and cultural advancement of the Nagas. The NNC consisted of the Naga tribal leaders, including Mr Phizo. Nagas had never been dominated by the plainsmen nor, they said, had they ever been part of India. They had nothing in common with India culturally, racially or linguistically. They were Mongols related rather to the races living in the east: the Burmese, for example, or the Thais. They are probably most closely related to the Dyaks of Borneo and to Philippine hill tribes.

In 1947 an agreement was reached between the Naga National Council and the Indian Government of Assam that went a fair way to granting the Naga claims. The ninth clause of the agreement said:

The Governor of Assam, as the agent of the Government of the Indian Union, will have a special responsibility for a period of ten years to ensure the due observance of the agreement; at the end of this period the Naga National Council will be asked whether they require the above agreement to be extended for a further period, or a new agreement regarding the future of the Naga people arrived at.

Although the agreement contained no explicit guarantee of self-determination, to the Naga National Council any later agreement, as proposed, would be certain to lead towards independence. But it was soon clear to them that the Indian Government had no intention of sanctioning Naga secession from the Union, either then or later. The Indian case was (and is) that the Indian Union legally includes all the territories formerly embraced by British India. Nagaland was one such territory.

The degree of underdevelopment and the primitive state of the Nagas themselves have also been used as arguments against Naga independence. But Nagas point to the independent status of the mountain kingdoms of Sikkim and Bhutan and ask if these are not precedents. They complain that many Indians regard them as semi-naked savages. The Indian Air Force officers still held prisoner by the Home Guard told me when I visited them recently, 'Before our capture we believed the Nagas were head-hunters and cannibals. This is the impression we had formed from hearsay in India. We expected to be eaten.'

In December last year a group of foreign journalists were permitted to visit western Nagaland. They heard the views both of members of the Naga People's Convention (the moderate political group favouring Statehood within the Indian Union) and a number of 'overground' nationalists. According to the special correspondent of *The Times*, the nationalists bombarded the journalists with written statements, allegations about atrocities and the like, conveyed to them, for the most part, clandestinely.

The press party was rarely out of the amiably curious observation of officials and in retrospect seems to have spent a disproportionate time bumping along by motor vehicle and watching tribal dances. Correspondents were not permitted to visit the places where they might have been able to ascertain for themselves which of two contradictory reports was nearer the truth.

Estimates of popular support for the 'moderates' (who are branded as 'traitors' by the nationalists) vary considerably. The Indian External Affairs Ministry is said to put it at 75 per cent of the population. The moderates themselves claim 40 per cent, with 12 per cent supporting Phizo and 48 per cent 'don't knows'. Phizo ridicules both these estimates and insists he has an overwhelming majority. The moderate Naga group (the NPC) is now cooperating with the Indian Government under an agreement signed last July by which Nagaland will become an autonomous State within the Indian Union. The new State – the sixteenth in the Union – will comprise the former Naga Hills and Tuensang areas. Mr Phizo and the rebel Federal Government point out that thousands of Nagas are excluded from the area of the new State, and that any agreement with the Indian Government is meaningless which is not the result of negotiations with the NNC leaders. Until such negotiations come about, they say, the war will continue.

Many details of the situation in Nagaland remained obscure. How well organized and armed were the Naga rebel troops, for example? Did they enjoy the support of the Naga civilians? How was their morale? There had been newspaper reports alleging Naga contacts with the Chinese and Burmese Communist groups and the infiltration of Communist arms to the Home Guard. Was this true?

Any assessment of the situation seemed to require answers to these and other questions. They could be answered only on the spot. At the end of an eighteen-day march through the tangled switchback jungles of the Naga Hills country, I felt I could answer some of them.

7 MAY 1961

The typewritten letter was dated February 1961, and headed 'Urra Camp, Nagaland'. 'I am very glad to hear that you are coming to meet us,' it said. 'For your escort I am sending one section of our Home Guard. They will do all the needful. We are all anxious to meet you. Yours faithfully, Isak Swu, Secretary for Foreign Affairs, Government of Nagaland.'

Beside me in the kitchen of the house stood the smiling young Naga Home Guard lieutenant who had delivered the letter, and behind him his sergeant, stiffly at attention. Smoke eddied upwards from a pinewood fire in the middle of the bamboo-thatched room, filling it with an aromatic haze filtering the harsh light of the pressure lamps. On the fire a monstrous cauldron of tea had been put to boil; giant haunches of buffalo meat and sides of pork hung from hooks in the ceiling; and twenty Nagas, wearing red and black embroidered tribal blankets over shirts and trousers, stared at us with bright, expectant eyes.

A few minutes before midnight I and four Naga guides had reached this cluster of houses on the threshold of Nagaland proper – our rendezvous with the Naga Nationalist Army – about 8000 feet above the Indian plains. It had taken us five days, walking ten or twelve hours a day, to negotiate the precipitous, threadbare hill ranges. The lieutenant and the letter had arrived half an hour before us: news of our progress had reached Naga headquarters in good time. This was the first example (but by no means the last) of the efficiency of the Naga rebel intelligence grapevine. Proof also of the efficacy of the nationalists' secret lines of communication with President Phizo in London.

Lieutenant P. Vikura was the first Naga soldier I saw. He was short but strongly built, with the muscular legs and high-cheekboned, humorous face that is typically Naga. His jungle green uniform was that of a lieutenant in the Indian Army and he wore a bush hat turned up at one side. As well as the Sten gun slung on his shoulder, he carried a Webley pistol and two hand grenades in his belt. Vikura, his features apart, could have been a smart young officer in any army in the world. His face was impassive as he told me his story. His father had been bayoneted to death by Assamese riflemen of the Indian Army in 1956, and his mother jailed. Vikura, eighteen at the time, was at school in central Nagaland. He and two hundred other students ran off into the jungle when the Indians began to organize Naga students into labour squads. He has been with the Home Guard ever since.

Outside in the trees Vikura's section stood guard or rested, oiling and cleaning their weapons. Like Vikura, they wore jungle green and had bound their tribal blankets round their chests and shoulders. 'The Indians send a good number of Gurkha and Assamese troops against us. In the jungle it is sometimes difficult to tell our men from theirs in the heat of battle,' explained Vikura. Several Nagas wore Gurkha *kukris* – curved single-edged daggers – captured from the Indian regiments. Each man carried a rifle, with a full magazine and a bandolier of twenty rounds of .303 ammunition: the NCOs carried Sten or tommy guns. All were in full battle order. When we approached they were called up to attention by their sergeant (he had served several years in the Indian Army). They crowded cheerfully round offering cigarettes. Later, as I waited with the guides before we moved off on the last stage of our march to headquarters, I saw them kneeling in three ranks under the trees, heads bowed and hatless, as the sergeant said prayers.

I was to learn later that among the Home Guard Christianity is a strong and living faith – a Cromwellian ingredient in the Naga struggle. In camp or in the jungle, morning and evening – unless circumstances of war absolutely forbid it – the men are paraded for prayers. Before an attack or a hazardous march Naga officers and men kneel to ask God's protection. In the camp mess rooms, no one dips his hand into his bowl before the most senior man present has said grace. Before he wraps himself in his blanket to sleep, a Naga soldier kneels to pray in silence. Christianity in Nagaland seems to be flourishing, the number of converts growing. The Nagas have their own Baptist pastors; they are usually among the better educated of the villagers and many of them speak English. Others are more or less permanently on the move, visiting a wide circuit of villages which have no resident pastor, distributing Bibles – in the Naga dialects – and dispensing religious instruction. These 'travelling pastors' say they have incurred the suspicion of the Indian Army in Nagaland – the Army of Occupation, they call it. They claim that many of them have been arrested, and some killed, by Indian troops.

From discussions with senior Naga officers and officials, it was evident that the conviction of their 'apartness' from the Indians is based at least partly on their religion. But not to the extent ascribed to it by some Indians, who have thrown the blame for the Naga tragedy onto alleged para-political activities by the American missions – for which, incidentally, there seems to be no evidence at all – and past British imperialist policies which, they say, have deliberately denied Nagas mind-broadening political access to the plainsmen. But the

Nagas' spirit of independence – and their readiness to fight for it – is far older than their recently acquired Christianity.

Yet Christianity is one of the factors which has led most Nagas to feel closer affinities with the Christian West rather than with what some of them describe as 'the dark empty faiths' of their immediate neighbours – a feeling shared by other Christian peoples in Asia, notably the Karens and the Shans in Burma. The Nagas may secretly despise Hindus as unenlightened, but they have no wish to convert them, still less destroy them as infidels. The Naga War is not a jehad. But their Christianity is undoubtedly one reason why, for the moment, the Nagas are seeking sympathy from the West rather than elsewhere and why Mr Phizo is in London rather than Peking.

Urra ('Our Land' in Naga) is a large semi-permanent camp, the headquarters base of one of four military zones. It houses about 250 Naga soldiers, civilians, scouts and refugees. Neat, stoutly built bamboo structures face onto the parade ground; the thick upper foliage of sixty-foot trees screens it from the air; sturdy log stockades and a system of slit trenches protect it from ground attack. The red, green and white flag of Free Nagaland, with its three blue stars for the northern, central and southern provinces, flies from a flagstaff behind a saluting base. General Sukhai and some of his staff had arrived there a few days before from central headquarters. The head of the rebel Federal Government was attending a Cabinet meeting near Kohima, but his brother J.K. Sukhai, the Minister of Justice, were in the reception committee.

The camp is well equipped. The officers' mess is a long, spacious building with neat tables and benches of bamboo under decorated signs which say 'Praise God from whom all blessings flow, Praise Him all creatures here below.' Outside it is a badminton court and behind it the cookhouse, barrack rooms, butcher's shop and the offices of the headquarters staff equipped with typewriters, filing cabinets and mounds of documents – orders of the day to be dispatched to other units, battle reports, news bulletins. All documents are in English, neatly typed, and bear the round blue official stamp of the Federal Government of Nagaland. In an information room two clerks collect and file the most recent cuttings from the Indian press, and summaries are made and distributed of all news broadcasts from the BBC, the Voice of America, All-India Radio, Moscow, Peking and Pakistan. Naga officers are well versed in current affairs.

Isak Swu is typical of Naga civilian officials. He is the younger brother of the present leader of the Federal Government which opposes the Indian 'puppets' in Kohima. As the holder of a degree in politics and economics from Gauhati University in Assam, twenty-nine-year-old Swu would have preferred to have continued his studies at a Baptist seminary in the United States.

'But I could no longer tolerate seeing the Nagas treated like beasts by Indian officials and Army officers,' he told me. 'I tried my best to explain the position of my people in an attempt to minimize their maltreatment, but my efforts were in vain. After the burning of six villages, including my own, in the Sema area round Chishi, I found I had no reasonable alternative but to come away and work in the national movement.'

Swu is an intelligent, gentle man and speaks good English. He said that Naga students were disgusted at what he alleged was the betrayal of the nationalist cause by the Naga People's Convention leaders, when they recently agreed to Indian proposals for a Naga State inside the Indian Union. Swu claimed that hundreds of Naga students in Kohima and elsewhere had boycotted the celebrations in February which inaugurated the new State. 'They, and we, know,' said Swu, 'that many of the Naga collaborators are men who have been working in the Indian Administration. That much has been admitted in the Indian press. Others are no-goods who would do anything for money. The Indians give them money and food – buy them in fact. They have no standing in the villages where most of the population lives. Many of them dare not set foot outside Indian-protected Kohima. What, I ask you, can they represent? But their case is better known to the outside world because the Indian Government provides them with means of communication which are denied to us.'

Naga officials and officers were unanimous in their condemnation of the new agreement. They admit that the Indians have now gone further to meet Naga claims than ever before ('but only because *we* drove them to it'). But, they say, the grant of Statehood is an Indian trick to encourage the Nagas to forget their real objective, which is complete independence. 'We want to be rid of these Indians once and for all, after all the crimes they have committed in our land. They say we are poor and backward and that they will bring us prosperity. We say, rather poverty and rags and freedom to choose our friends and allies than all the schools and hospitals in the world with Indian overlords.' Thirty-seven-year-old Mr Kuhoto Sukhai told me: 'The Indians aren't the only people who can develop our country. Why shouldn't we invite technicians we choose and trust? You see, we simply can't afford to trust the Indians any more.'

But the Naga Home Guards I saw seemed surprisingly free from poverty and rags. All were correctly uniformed, well fed and well armed. Morale and discipline were obviously high. Privates and orderlies stamped and saluted as smartly as in most British Army camps. Their two meals a day – according to Naga tradition – were substantial. There was an increasing shortage of rice – normally the staple food – as a result, I was told, of Indian scorched-earth tactics. Later I saw several village rice stores that had been reduced to charred rubble in Indian attempts, the villagers said, to cow them into neutrality. But a mixture of pulses, chillis, yams, salt, maize and a variety of jungle leaves well cooked together in a massive earthenware pot makes an excellent vegetarian stew. Monkey meat (not unlike lamb) and wild fowl can be added to taste. Despite Indian attempts at intimidation, the villages continue to supply most of the Home Guard's requirements. And the four Indian prisoners held by the Home Guard since August told me they were accustomed to the food now and found it nourishing.

Similarly the Naga National Council and the Home Guard seem to have few financial worries. Expenses are met by donations and voluntary subscriptions. Main expenditure is on clothing, arms, ammunition, medicine and stationery. Home Guards are not paid, but fed and clothed. They are all volunteers. A significant item in the budget covers payments to Indian civil servants and soldiers, including officers. When I asked Naga officials if Indians did indeed accept bribes, they laughed as if the question were hardly worth answering. 'Some Indians who realize the true state of affairs sympathize with us. In some cases officers secretly tip us off before an attack, and they have helped us in other ways. But they wouldn't dare express their views openly.'

The Indians have sometimes said that the Home Guard is obliged to terrorize the civilians into supporting the NNC and that a majority are politically indifferent. Ridiculing these claims, Nagas point out that the Home Guards could hardly have fought so long and so successfully without the support of the civilian population. 'If we had been terrorizing them,' the nationalists say, 'is it likely that they would have remained neutral? Still less would they have cooperated as they are doing.' I was shortly to see evidence of this cooperation.

Nagas are a people who feel bedevilled by their picturesque past. Today many Nagas are educated and bilingual – English is their second language – and they accuse the Indians of trying to project an image of them as a primitive, colourful tourist attraction. Another charge is that the Indian Administration has done its best to create a false picture of civil war in Nagaland. Although there are upwards of sixteen Naga tribes, domestic conflict has usually been confined to incidents between village and village rather than between tribe and tribe, and the prevailing Christianity is a detribalizing and unifying factor. Every Home Guard recruit, if he is not already a Christian, is soon converted.

According to Naga leaders Indians have attempted to sow discord among the Naga population by inducing avaricious Naga 'no-goods' to search and burn villages on their behalf. I heard many stories of the activities of the 'Flying Scouts' – bands of Naga youths, organized into strong-arm groups to terrorize suspected NNC supporters in town and village. In theory, the NNC says, these boys are employed as village guards to protect the Naga civilians from marauding Home Guards. They are paid by the Indian Government. One twenty-four-year-old Sema Naga soldier told me how he had joined the 'Flying Scouts' under duress. In October 1959, he said, he and fifty-eight others were ordered to search a village where, it was suspected, the Naga 'underground' had hidden a duplicating machine. He witnessed the prolonged torture of five villagers, one of whom was finally obliged to reveal the duplicator. Earlier, with a detachment of the Assam Rifles, he had seen a Naga girl raped several times and male villagers beaten, on the orders of an Indian officer, at a village called Lunchang. My informant presently escaped to the Home Guard, taking six Indian rifles with him.

The jungle is a perfect cloak for the Home Guard. Regular tracks are few and the Nagas tend to shun them. Often their soldiers move from village to village and camp to camp, cutting paths as they go with their long curved machetes – the indispensable *daos*. They move in single file, their flanks covered by 'Road Protection' groups – civilian or military – which police the neighbouring spurs. In the jungle, units communicate by shouting or imitating selected bird and animal calls. They have no fear of moving by day, and smoke and sing and chatter happily on the march. A newcomer to the Naga Hills finds even a short walk a gruelling experience but the strong-legged Nagas stride blithely up the steepest incline, talking and laughing.

I saw Naga scouts emerging from the undergrowth, like fleas from a rug, to bring reports of Indian movements and other information from Imphal, Kohima and other battle areas. Some carried shotguns, others simply pistols or *daos*. One such messenger arrived with bundles of dispatches and letters after a week's walk. He reported to the local area commander (a general) that Indian artillery had been in action near Kohima in an effort to destroy Home Guard hideouts. The general was anxious to know if there had been any Naga casualties. 'No,' was the answer, 'we were expecting the bombardment.'

The Nagas seem to have plenty of arms at the moment, nearly all captured from the Indian Army and in good condition. The remainder are Japanese rifles – relics of the last war. Ammunition is plentiful enough to permit shooting competitions; I was even invited to take on the nimble Commander-in-Chief with a Bren gun. Visiting the wreck of the Indian Air Force DC-3 shot down by the Home Guards last August, I took tea with Naga officers sitting on a bullet-scarred wing, as soldiers tossed grenades into a nearby river to catch fish for the evening meal. But the time is coming, Naga officers say, when they will need heavier weapons – light anti-aircraft guns and heavy mortars. They hope the Chinese will provide them if other sources prove fruitless.

A by-product of the war is the refugee problem; they had fled from their villages to escape 'regroupment' by the Indians and forced labour. Some have been given shelter in Naga Home Guard camps; others have gone deep into the jungle. They live now in crude bamboo shelters, clearing enough of the undergrowth to plant essential crops – Job's tears, pulses and other edible seeds. Many of the children have the swollen bellies and matchstick legs that are the product of malnutrition; others the puffy bodies caused by deficiency of Vitamin B. The Home Guards give them what food they can spare. Their medical officer – briskly businesslike in khaki drill suit and sun helmet – was active distributing medicine and injecting refugees with vitamins. Far from showing fear, these refugees evidently welcomed the arrival of Home Guard patrols.

In the larger villages, the population provided liberal hospitality with every appearance of good will. There was no evidence of coercion or intimidation by the Home Guards; on the contrary they were greeted with cheerful shouts of recognition. Villagers and Home

23

Guards mounted guard together when we decided to stay the night in Naga houses, and neighbouring villagers were asked to keep an eye open for Indian patrols.

The Indian Army has constructed a network of military posts on prominent spurs about two to three miles apart. The Nagas invited me to inspect them through binoculars. Indian Air Force aircraft, including jets, regularly patrol the area. I saw relics of Indian air attacks – fragments of bombs and 20 mm cannon shells – and heard the sound of heavy firing farther north, probably from mortars. The arrival of Indian troops is a risk the villagers are apparently willing and able to take. On one occasion a group of forty Nagas came secretly from their Indian-occupied village to spend the night dancing and carousing with the Home Guard. They slipped home before dawn, and the Indians were unaware that they had been away.

When Naga Home Guards leave, the population accompany them to the village confines. They call 'Safe journey' as volunteers follow the soldiers into the jungle carrying baskets of rice provided by the village, and sides of pork and massive gourds of *zu* – potent rice wine that tastes like smoky cider.

The tenor of Naga civilian complaints of Indian injustice was unvarying. Villagers jostled their way forward to describe personal sufferings in vivid detail. The stories of burnt rice stores and houses seemed endless. Individuals told how they had been beaten and tied up for hours without water; how they had been bound and hung head downwards from trees to be flogged; how sons, brothers and fathers had been bayoneted to death. Refugee women described how Indian troops had arrived in their village on 6 September last year, searching for Home Guards and the four captive Indian airmen. 'We were all rounded up and the men separated from the women. Our men were forced to run the gauntlet of Indian troops armed with stout sticks. Then they were kicked like footballs as they lay helpless on the ground. Three men died then – one of them a travelling pastor. Later we women were told to run into the jungle and scatter. Afterwards we heard from survivors that most of the men had been shot "trying to escape". We were about 120 men and women before the Indian patrol arrived. There were thirty survivors, only three of them men. All our crops were burnt. How can we dare go back?'

These woman and their children are being cared for now by the Home Guard. Other villagers complain that they are forced to work for the Indian Army as menials without pay, facing a beating if they refuse. Nagas ask: 'Are we animals to be treated like this? Isn't there some international law to protect us from this treatment?' They say that whole villages have been moved to other areas of Nagaland and regrouped in 'concentration camps'.

In the base camp at Urra, as I prepared to leave Nagaland, General Zuheto Swu, the tough, good-natured area commander, was drawing up battle plans with the Commander-in-Chief; on the parade ground a sergeant-major – barking English words of command – was drilling a squad of young Home Guard recruits; some officers were playing badminton; from a barrack room wireless set came the sound of American dance music; a queue was forming at the barber's shop. Clerks prepared envelopes for lists of recent incidents and alleged Indian atrocities to be sent to the United Nations Secretary-General with copies for Queen Elizabeth and President Kennedy.

Naga Ministers and officials said to me: 'Nagas served the British in both wars. The British know what we were like and our character hasn't changed. Why can't they speak up for us?' Isak Swu handed me a statement which he said quoted a speech made by the Indian Prime Minister, Mr Nehru, in 1952: 'We want no people in the territory of India against their will and with the help of the Armed Forces. We want no forced marriage or forced unions. This great Republic of India is a free, voluntary and friendly and affectionate Union of the States of India.' Swu went on: 'Mr Nehru has an international reputation as a great liberal and humanitarian. When he speaks the world listens and believes. But here is the harsh reality which is the other side of the picture. Perhaps Mr Nehru is not aware of what is going on here. But surely as Prime Minister he should be? We ask for recognition by the Indian Government for what we are – the true representatives of the Naga people. The Indians may parade their puppets around Delhi and Kohima, but the war will only end with negotiations with us.'

Nagas have no supporting bloc of racially related nations; no neighbouring state in which to establish a 'Free Government'. The Naga nationalists talk now of complete independence, and believe that with outside help a separate Nagaland – with strong Commonwealth ties – could be economically viable. It may be that if mutual problems of 'face' could be overcome, and political negotiations initiated by the Indian Government, the Naga leaders would moderate their demands. A final, total break with India and the danger of a Naga call for outside intervention in a strategically important area might thus be avoided. The alternative seems to be the perpetuation of a costly struggle which is no less tragic for being remote.

Twenty-six years later, the conflict continues, albeit on a diminished scale.

Cuba Revisited

Before the missile crisis of October 1962 Communist Cuba was an enigma. No one was certain what course Fidel Castro would take. I went down from New York to take a look.

HAVANA, 17 JUNE 1962

Fidel Castro's Cuba is the only Communist state outside Eurasia. But it is Communism with a difference. Cuba is neither a satellite, like East Germany, nor an uncommitted country, like Yugoslavia. Castro himself is a self-educated Marxist who has never visited either Moscow or Peking. So, to both East and West, Cuba is of intense interest. To the East it is a proof that a country may choose Communism without the help of Russian or Chinese armies. To the West it is evidence that Communism today may take many different forms.

'Cubans sometimes give you the impression they invented Marxism –Leninism,' a Communist diplomat told me ruefully in Havana. Cubans enjoy being the 'odd men out' in Latin America. They know that if the phrase 'evolution or revolution' has become an urgent cliché throughout the continent, they are responsible. They know that President Kennedy's multi-billion-dollar Alliance of Progress aid project for Latin American democracies is, in reality, the child of Fidel Castro's success. 'And a very bad child it is,' Castro told me recently, adding contemptuously: 'It's a failure.'

This premature judgement is wholeheartedly endorsed by every Fidelista. To them only Communism can save Latin America, and Communist revolution there is inevitable. In Cuba itself, Communism begins at the airport. Behind the Cuban Airlines Ilyushins and visiting Czech airliners, papier mâché peace doves hover over printed quotations from Lenin, Mao and Fidel. The gleaming skyscraper walls of

Havana are plastered with hammers and sickles. Among signs saying Kit Kat Club, Sloppy Joe's Bar and Floor Show Twice Nitely, neon lights shout: 'We shall Win'.

There are well-designed signs for every occasion. Cartoon workers, homerically muscled, exhort comrades to exceed production norms, comrade waiters (*compañeros gastronomicos*) are advised to brush their teeth before serving customers, to shave and keep their thumbs out of the soup. Absenteeism is condemned as a 'dark and subtle enemy'. It has become a revolutionary duty to 'study a little each day' and to go and cut sugar cane at seasonal intervals.

To keep the revolution on its toes, danger of invasion is constantly invoked. To me, Castro himself would go no further than to say such a thing is 'possible'; nevertheless anti-aircraft guns point skywards over Havana's Malecón seaside promenade. They are manned round the clock. Behind them, somewhere in the island, there are perhaps 50 or 60 MiG fighters, an estimated 150 Soviet tanks, assault and field guns, and 70,000 men of the Regular Army. Uniformed militiamen guard most office and hotel doorways, nonchalantly holding rifles or small Czech sub-machine guns. There are a number of militiawomen, too, businesslike but carefully made up and manicured. They wear tight-fitting olive-green trousers that zip provocatively up the back. There are signs now that the militia is to be pared down and the revolution-ary army purified by purges. The militia – about a quarter of a million strong – has proved a setback to work norms and administrative efficiency. It is not unusual for a Ministry official to glance at his watch during an end-of-morning conversation and hurry out of his office explaining: 'Sorry, I should be on guard duty all this afternoon. Come back tomorrow.'

Somehow Havana has little of the outward 'under siege' grimness one would expect of a European city in a similar revolutionary situation. The city's fabulous night clubs are still open and offer two glittering shows nightly to full houses of Cubans and foreign visitors. In equal proportions the smarter bars still do a brisk trade, although beer is rare and the Scotch mélanged. You can drink Russian champagne at £3 a bottle, vinegary Egyptian or Albanian red wine, and reasonable rum at reasonable prices.

In some respects Havana has the end-of-term atmosphere of a vast scout camp. Thousands of young Cubans have poured into the city since the regime began a deliberate nationwide mobilization of youth, in efforts to build up revolutionary cadres as quickly as possible.

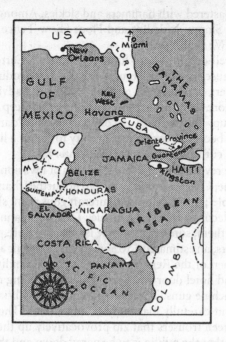

Upwards of 60,000 'scholarship holders', mostly in their teens, have been installed in the luxury villas that once belonged to Havana's *haute bourgeoisie*. Despite a serious shortage of teachers and supervisors, the Government is trying to provide them with a basic general education, technical training and a solid grounding in Marxism–Leninism. They are 'the inheritors', and are treated as such. They are well housed and fed and are clothed in neat grey uniforms. They are happy with the revolution, with their new-found importance and freedom. Representatives of the new generation growing up, they may hardly remember what life in a non-Communist country is like. With teachers from Soviet bloc countries, who speak little Spanish, they study Russian, Czech or German. Eventually hard-working students will be given scholarships to technical colleges and universities in Eastern Europe. A large English-speaking group told me they would like to go to Britain, 'but we haven't got enough money'. When I asked how many of them were still Catholic and churchgoers they explained: 'People don't go to church in a Socialist state.' An official abruptly chimed in: 'There's nothing to stop anyone going who wants to.'

The island is the scene of a vast indoctrination effort that spares no one. On the edge of the remaining slums of Havana children of three and four years old, rescued from the most brutal squalor but now well fed and clothed, are being cared for in one of thirty bright new infant centres constructed by the Government. It is a well-run, essential project that no one had thought necessary under Batista. Each morning the toddlers are formed up to follow their teacher in singing the 'Internationale' and to shout *Viva Cuba Socialista* and *Cuba si, Yanqui no.*

Last year, 'the year of education', an impressive number of young student volunteers took to the hills to teach the alphabet to thousands of illiterate peasants. They took with them handy teaching manuals that combined education and political instruction. 'A', they taught, stands for 'agrarian reform', one of the pillars of the revolution; 'A' also stands for 'Associated Press, counter-revolutionary mouthpiece of the imperialist United States'. As a result of these student efforts the Cuban Government now claims that illiteracy has been eliminated. A side product of the 'alphabetization' effort is a sad, sweet song called 'The Awakening', now one of Cuba's top pops. The singer recalls the bitter time when she was separated from her lover on the other side of the island, unable to communicate because of her illiteracy. Now, she sings, the Government has taught her to write and she is in touch with him again.

Unlike all too many Latin American politicians, Cuba's leaders have realized that extensive housing and slum clearance policies are not only humane but can be politically rewarding as well. In spite of Castro's recent dissatisfaction with the achievements of Cuban construction workers, the revolution has some impressive new housing to show. Cuba's slum dwellers have cause to be grateful. Hundreds of new schools have gone up in the interior. One particularly ambitious educational project is under way in Oriente Province. Named after one of Castro's principal guerrilla lieutenants, killed in an air accident in 1959, the Camilo Cienfuegos school is scheduled to board 20,000 illiterate children from the remote valleys of the Sierra Maestra mountain range. A few hundred children are already installed. Complete with classrooms, dormitories, library, cafeteria, sports ground and a small farm, it has been built by the Army. 'In other Latin American countries the Army is an expensive parasite,' says the grizzled Army captain who administers the school. 'Here the Army works for the people.' The whole project is expected to cost $80 million. The revolution is particularly proud that a number of Batista police barracks have been turned into schools – and neon signs advertise the fact.

But shortage of money and efforts to industrialize the country are now leading to a cutback in 'good works' schemes. 'Priorities now are production and industrialization,' Castro told me. 'Economic problems are going to hold up our school plan. And although we shall continue building new houses, their quality will have to suffer.' Up to now standards of building construction and design have been impressive.

There is a good deal of talk in the present Planning Year of a formidable industrial expansion. But details are obscure. Statistics, as the Minister of Industries, 'Ché' Guevara, has been moved to complain, are in a tangle or non-existent. Essentially all Cuba's industrialization plans depend on the Soviet bloc, to a much lesser extent on trade with non-Communist countries like Canada and Japan. Non-Western diplomats in Cuba believe China's inability to deliver goods in accordance with earlier glowing promises has been both an eye-opener and a disappointment to the Cubans. If published figures are to be believed, Cuban–Soviet trade in 1962 should reach a record equivalent of $750 million. Russia is already pledged to take the greater part of Cuba's sugar crop, and other 'bloc' countries and China to take virtually all the rest. In exchange the Russians are to provide such essentials as machinery, vehicles, pumps, machine tools, petrol, flour and fats. They will also supply twenty assorted factories – including a large steel plant and an oil refinery. 'The Russian people' have donated a complete 1400-bed hospital. The Czechs and Romanians are selling a cement factory apiece.

It is difficult to judge the present state of Cuban industrial production and expansion. It seems unwise to accept at face value the glowing figures published in the official press, when Cuban leaders themselves express periodic dissatisfaction. In the interior I saw in process of construction new Czech and East German plants for making household goods and one British sack factory. But none of them will be in production before 1963 or 1964.

Cuba is now desperately short of technicians: most of the best have left. Those who remain combine, according to foreign technicians, a desperate inexperience with a stubborn refusal to take advice. Soviet bloc technicians have learnt that it is wiser to proffer advice to a Cuban only when advice is asked for: it seldom is.

Senior officials at the Central Planning Board (Juceplan) in Havana blame a number of factors for the frustrating delays. First there is a crippling shortage of transport: the old American trucks are wearing out, as are the country's buses. There is a shortage of spare parts for everything American, from rolling mills to television sets. Although Soviet ships have delivered tons of electrical equipment and machine parts, planners complain that much of it is mouldering on the docks or in store. One Juceplan official told me: 'We've got warehouses full of bits all over Cuba, but so far there are no plants to put them in. For example, we've got 50,000 voltameters. What the hell can we do with them?'

But few Cubans fear that things are in real danger of grinding to a paralysing halt. There is the sense of adventure, the excitement of starting from scratch in a new world of their own creation, that enables the Cuban revolutionaries to rise above burgeoning problems. Cuba has become, both politically and economically, a country of day-to-day improvisation, a 'do-it-yourself' state. 'We'll manage, some-how' is the general feeling. It is sustained by a formidable confidence in the 'maximum leader', Fidel Castro.

24 JUNE 1962

I met Castro by chance outside a Havana night club at half-past two in the morning. I invited him in. Strong and paunchy-framed, with straggled beard, he sat in a steel-framed chair and propped his back against the wall of the bar. 'I don't drink,' he said, 'but I'll have a coffee and a quarter of an hour with you.' He talked animatedly for more than an hour and a half; five guards with machine pistols stood around watchfully.

Although Castro is Cuba's Prime Minister, he refuses to keep office hours. He is liable to pop up almost anywhere at any time, usually late at night. He works fourteen hours a day. After gruelling television appearances he likes to drop into the kitchen of the former Havana Hilton Hotel for a scratch meal. His unavailability is a source of complaint to subordinates with documents to be signed. He is a restless talker. He speaks fair, fluent English better than he understands it. His voice is soft and hoarse. He listens intently to questions, narrowing small, shrewd, watchful eyes in a fleshy face. Three-quarter view he looks like Peter Sellers taking off Ustinov taking off Castro.

He said he had no desire to meet President Kenedy even if invited. 'I've no interest.' He shifted irritably in his seat. He believes the Americans are still plotting against him; but he wouldn't go further than to say another invasion is 'possible'. Nevertheless he would be willing to discuss compensation to nationalized American firms if the United States buys Cuban sugar again. When he mentions the Americans he looks sad. 'I am a friend of the Americans. I don't hate the American people. I was very popular over there, you know. But they can't get the truth. Their radio and newspapers are controlled by big business. All give them a false story.'

He said he'd abandoned non-alignment because Cuba's circumstances were different from those of Yugoslavia or Egypt. 'As time went on I found I had more in common with the Socialist bloc.' On his way out to his car, he stopped to sign autographs for a group of Canadians.

More than three years after the fall of the American-backed dictator Batista, Fidel Castro is still the political weathercock of the Cuban revolution. His towering, turbulent personality dominates his collaborators. What Castro says, what Castro does, what happens to Castro are of immense importance to Cuba. Castro himself personifies and typifies the revolution to a remarkable degree. Like other Cubans he is reckless, mercurial, proud. He can be emotional and blatantly ruthless; absurdly histrionic and devastatingly frank. He is at his best on television, identifying himself unfailingly with the common man.

He has personally condemned the 'cult of personality', but his earthy informality has made him adored by the Fidelista in the street. He told me: 'I've been compared to Simón Bolívar. But this is the century of the masses – the need produces the leader. It wasn't Churchill who won the war but the soldiers and workers. Here it's not Fidel – or Juan or Pedro either – it's the people that matter.' But the cult is there nevertheless; in terms of political reality it is Fidel who matters more than any other Cuban leader. No one has any idea what would happen if he were somehow removed from the scene: but everyone agrees there would be chaos.

The 'Old Guard' Cuban Communist Party (PSP) collaborates with a cautious enthusiasm. Last March the party leadership meekly endorsed Castro's violent denunciation and exile of another old Communist stalwart, Aníbal Escalante. Escalante's crime was 'sectarianism' – he had used his position in the National Directorate of ORI (the Integrated Revolutionary Organizations, forerunner of the United Party of the Revolution) to infiltrate PSP members into key positions throughout the Administration. It is hard to believe that Escalante's close party colleagues were unaware of his activities. They had evidently decided that in the event of detection and denunciation Escalante would make a worthy scapegoat. Blas Roca, Secretary-General of the PSP, Escalante's collaborator and now editor of the Communist newspaper *Hoy* (*Today*) told me: 'Escalante was condemned unanimously. He used his position in a thrust for personal power.'

Members of Fidel's own 26th-of-July Movement are plainly relieved by Castro's attack on Escalante. It demonstrated their ascendancy over the Communist traditionalists. Escalante's tactics were causing serious administrative dislocation. Differences between the PSP and the 'New Communists' can hardly have had an ideological basis; they are both treading the same Marxist–Leninist path. But the PSP leaders, experienced organization men, may well have mistrusted the erratic character of the 26th-of-July leaders.

Castro's denunciation of Escalante is seen by a number of independent observers, as well as by some Fidelistas, as the outcome of a silent struggle for power. The weakness of the PSP was never to have been a party of the masses; in the days before its leaders hastily jumped on Castro's victory bandwagon the party drew its main following from a comparatively small section of industrial workers. Moscow's easy acceptance of Escalante's dismissal is evidence that the Russians rate Castro's political importance higher than that of any Communist faithful.

Today the leaders of Cuban power seem fairly evenly distributed. The Revolutionary Army is controlled by Raúl Castro, Fidel's younger brother, who has the white clenched face of a fanatic. He is considered political heir-apparent, but has none of 'Big Brother's' popular appeal. The ubiquitous security service, G2, is run by a staunch Fidelista Minister of the Interior. The key National Agrarian Reform Institute (INRA), main instrument for Cuba's economic socialization, is headed by the PSP Communist closest to Castro, Carlos Rafael Rodríguez. But the Argentine Ernesto 'Ché' Guevara, a Castro lieutenant, is Minister for Industries. In general 'Old Communists' run the propaganda machine.

Efforts are now being made to forge a new alliance between industrial workers and peasants (*campesinos*). Theoretically, the *campesinos* have benefited most from the revolution. Since the break-up of private landholdings under the agrarian reform plan they have found themselves working variously on state farms, cooperatives, or independently in a Government-controlled association of small farmers. Partly because of the inexperience of farm managers appointed from Havana, food production has suffered. At the same time Cuba's sugar production dropped this year to 4,800,000 tons, the lowest for many years, though this was partly due to drought earlier in the year. Blatant anomalies in food distribution are apparent. In Havana food is strictly rationed – three-quarters of a pound of meat a week per person, five eggs a month, one litre of milk a day for every five people. Every child under seven qualifies for one litre a day, and usually seems to get it. Because of inefficient distribution adults are obliged to queue for hours for basic necessities. Yet in the country I saw farmers selling turkeys, chickens and eggs at the roadside. There is a good deal of complaint about food shortages. Officials point out that, although many Cubans are eating less today, more people are eating regularly.

Although food shortages encourage resentment against the revolution, they do not seem likely to cause its overthrow. The main pillars of the regime, after all – the Army, Militia and youth organizations, get priority. So do hospitals, schools and other Government institutions. Nevertheless such privations are partly responsible for the continuing exodus of Cubans to Miami, Mexico and elsewhere. An estimated 6000 are leaving monthly, and by now the total number of exiles is probably between 250,000 and 500,000. They are not prevented from leaving, though they are not encouraged. Cuban officials refer to them contemptuously as *gusanos* (worms) 'waiting for the US Marines to land'. An official told me he was sick of hearing 'worms' in his department pining for 'the good old days'. 'They're simply childish, talking about the days when they could still get their Virginia hams. Let them leave.' But most of those who pine for Virginia hams have long since left for Miami, where they are presumably getting them. The exodus began in 1959 with Batista supporters and the *haute bourgeoisie*. Since then thousands of professional men and shopkeepers have left. Catholics have snatched their children away to avoid political indoctrination in state schools. Now some of the small people are going too.

While the drain in technical know-how poses serious problems for the regime, the continuing resentful presence of these people could be even more troublesome. There are probably thousands of counter-revolutionaries in Cuba. They include the rump of the middle class, professors, some students, taxi drivers, cabaret showgirls. Some of them crowd the bars and night clubs of Havana on a Saturday night.

After a few drinks they like to air their pathetic grievances to anyone who looks like a foreign journalist. They don't seem to worry that they'll be overheard by agents of Castro's secret service. Talkative *gusanos* are seldom arrested or even admonished. But the anti-regime men I met denied any ability to initiate a blow against the regime. That, they said, would have to come from outside. Their job was to wait for 'D-Day'.

An important question in Cuba today is: in the long term, will repression and Marxist–Leninist indoctrination prove sufficiently thorough to offset the unrest caused by a continuing economic depression? For all his personal charm Castro is a dictator who tolerates no opposition. Six hundred and seventy-five Cubans have died before firing squads, according to official statements – the real figure may be higher. The press, radio and television are captives of the Government. The single 'party' permeates every sphere of activity; almost every street has its 'Committee for the Defence of the Revolution'. Education is blatantly yoked to political orientation. The number of political prisoners is estimated to be between 10,000 and 20,000. And the elections promised by a younger, more romantic Castro have long been forgotten.

Cuba, officials say, is blazing a trail for Latin America. Banners proclaim Cuba 'the first Socialist state in America'. Fidelistas believe the whole Western hemisphere will ultimately take Cuba's path. Thus the Kennedy Administration, American big business and the press are under bitter and unrelenting attack. But the Cuban attitude to individual American visitors is one of friendly condescension and of pity. Cuban leaders lay the blame for economic shortcomings about equally on their own errors and the American trade embargo. Some of the more realistic – including 'Old Communists' – see the desirability of renewed trade relations with the US. But a political rapprochement is less attractive. 'America,' said Castro, 'is our only enemy.'

Birth of a Nation

A report on the New Palestinians – young, vigorous and well educated – who represent the intellectual and technical resources of this disrupted nationality.

JERUSALEM, 12 APRIL 1969

'What a delightful place,' said the Western diplomat's wife up from Tel Aviv, gazing round the lobby of my hotel in East (Arab) Jerusalem. 'When did the Israelis take it over?' I pointed out that it was not quite five years old and was owned and run to this day by Palestinian Arabs. She seemed confused. Could Arabs possess such skills? I hurried her off to the bazaars of the Old City. And there in the humpbacked streets of the Via Dolorosa, among the Holy Land souvenir shops with their owners smiling – 'Welcome, take a look' – the smell of fresh vegetables and old donkey droppings, she recovered her poise. 'Poor Arabs,' happily she patted a heavily laden mule, 'always two hundred years behind the times.'

It would be more to the point to say poor Palestinians – still fighting, among so much else, the lingering prejudice of the European romantic tradition that ordains it thus: Arabs, in the fastnesses of their suqs and tents, good; Arabs in urban villas, good for little. It is a prejudice not necessarily held by Israelis who lived side by side with Arabs in Palestine under the British Mandate before Israel came into being in 1948. But it is detectable in more recent arrivals in Israel who try to show their basic sympathy for Palestinians by speaking with patronizing warmth of the Arab odd-job man round the corner.

I have found young Israelis quite surprised to hear that thousands of Arab students dress and talk like them, and have interests and a way of life very similar to their own. This persisting ignorance nearly two years after the 1967 war – which gave Israelis an unprecedented chance to meet Palestinians in East Jerusalem or on the West Bank – seems to show that an invaluable opportunity for future understanding has been missed, seemingly through indifference. The opportunity was invaluable because the whole Arab–Israeli conflict, twenty years old and still going strong, is basically the problem of the Palestinians who have seen their land taken and continue to resent their banishment. A solution must eventually depend, if not on war, on some sort of agreement between the two peoples to coexist peacefully.

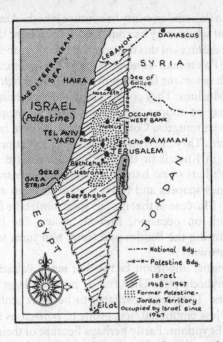

What kind of people are the Palestinians of 1969, and what are their attitudes to life and politics? There are upwards of two and a half million of them, over a million living in the two occupied areas of the West Bank and the Gaza Strip and in Israel itself, and the rest scattered throughout the Arab world and overseas. Most of them are the descendants of people who lived in Palestine since the Muslim conquest thirteen centuries ago, or even before that, until the creation of the State of Israel in 1948. So much they have in common. They have, however, become overmuch identified with three popular categories. The first is represented by the colourful, though pungent, throngs in the bazaars with which one can lump the peasant and his camel. The second is made up of the commando groups of dangerous, uniformed men based mainly in the caves of East Jordan. Finally, there are the sad, tattered refugees, humping their bundles and babies ever eastwards, hoarding twenty years of hate in one wretched tent after another.

Together, these three groups perhaps account for a third of the total Palestinian population. It is the remaining two-thirds — the New Palestinians — which should be considered more than it usually is when there is talk of a Palestinian entity or a future Jewish–Arab state. These people (some of whom may be commandos) represent the intellectual and technical resources of this disrupted nationality, and it is they who will determine Palestinian – and perhaps Arab – politics, and they are the people with whom the Israelis will have to live or fight. They can be Christians or Muslims. They could come from the families of lawyers, or pharmacists, or tourist guides, or farmers, or professors, or engineers or even refugees. Could they run a modern hotel? Some of them can and do. They also run big businesses and cope with modern city planning (in Kuwait or Beirut); have long since given up tarboushes for felt hats or no hats at all; are college deans, priests and bishops; edit newspapers and run TV stations; read anything from Shakespeare to Marcuse (if that is a fair spectrum); take *Le Monde*, the *Economist* and, on occasion, *Pravda*; design fine buildings and construct them; dig the Beatles and 'soul' and form successful pop groups of their own.

The undramatic, important fact is that many Palestinians are not very unlike anybody else. They feel at home in large European or American cities. They tend, perhaps, to be more stolid than other Arabs, a little less emotional, less prone to boisterous good humour than, say, the Egyptians. Partly perhaps because of their recent tragic history, they are a very serious people. And partly because of what they lack. They have no country. Out of all the rich lands of their ancestors, they retain control over not one inch. The West Bank is under occupation, and even before that Palestinians did not run it; it was firmly administered from Amman. Palestinians blame the fact that it has no industry to speak of on King Hussein, who, they say, gave economic preference to his East Bank before 1967.

But the West Bank is not poverty-stricken. It is intensely cultivated. Nor are its cities slums. Ramallah, Bethlehem, Tulkarm and other towns are graceful places. East Jerusalem is smaller than West, but more beautiful. The roads through the West Bank pass rows of well, if sometimes garishly, designed houses and villas; there are many private cars, perhaps too many for comfort; television aerials rise like reed beds. There is also some poverty, as elsewhere.

If things go peacefully, and there's an Israeli withdrawal behind the pre-1967 borders, it seems unlikely that Hussein will be able to deny self-government to the West Bank. There are two reasons for this: the soldering of Palestinian society through education, and the sudden new thrust of Palestinian self-awareness. The first has been the booster rocket to the second. A striking aspect of the West Bank is the number of schoolchildren. For years, 'school' has been an almost holy word for any young Palestinian. Now an even holier word is 'university'. Many have attained it. Driven eastwards, Palestinians had imperative reason for seeking education. Hundreds of families, deprived of their own land, had to depend on the ability of young Palestinians to find and hold jobs in foreign countries where the demand was for skilled rather than unskilled labour, and for academic qualifications. The Palestinian diaspora, in fact, forced the Palestinians into much the same single-minded attitude to education as that of overseas Chinese – or even of the Jews of the diaspora themselves. Through family sacrifice, Palestinians have fanned out into colleges and universities from California to Pakistan. Schools and colleges of the Arab world are stocked with Palestinian professors of law, physics, political science; others are teaching in America and Europe. In the professions, a high percentage of Arab lawyers and doctors and technicians of various kinds are Palestinian.

Education is the golden prize. I have seen graduation certificates from German and other European universities framed proudly on West Bank drawing room walls, like flags of victory. And teenage children, determined to finish their homework, dropping with sleep, their backs firmly turned away from the tempting distraction of *The Avengers* on television from Amman. Male students wear blazers or roll-top sweaters, the girls something slightly longer than a mini-skirt. According to your viewpoint, you could argue that their moral standards are high or that they are tiresomely square. Among Palestinian youth, beards and long hair are a joke; hippies and pot smokers are anathema. 'Pre-marital sex is rare,' an intelligent girl told me a little wistfully: 'Palestinian men still prefer to marry Palestinian virgins or foreigners.' After the 1967 war there was an initial curiosity about Israeli life. Now, disenchantment – together with bombs and politics – explains why Palestinians seldom stroll the short distance to West Jerusalem.

Another kind of educational process has taken hold since 1967 – and here, supremely important for the future of the area, is where the new feelings of national ambition, the Palestinian renaissance, fit into the picture. Almost two years of occupation and under-employment have driven Palestinians on the West Bank to a frenzy of political self-education and debate. In homes and restaurants, night and day, the past, the nightmare present and the impenetrable future are ceaselessly analysed. Textbooks on social, political, historical matters, right-wing or left-wing, are passed about. People are keeping scrapbooks of press cuttings and photographs of the occupation. True stories of Israeli arrests, beatings or the blowing up of houses mix with rumours of torture and death and Fedayeen exploits to feed the high fires of Palestinian nationalism. As the days pass, the 600,000 people on this always intimate and claustrophobic territory are brought closer together.

But at the same time, the occupation is deepening the generation gap. It is the younger people, including women and girls, who are the most daringly active thorns in the flesh of the Israeli occupation or at least the most bitterly passive. Elderly mayors, elderly parents cannot curb their acts or feelings, even if they want to. After 1948 and before 1967, West Bank politics was completely dominated by the older members of the few 'good' families who worked for the non-Palestinian regime in Amman. There were no indigenous organizations that the average Palestinian cared to join. The catastrophe of the war forced them into a new self-reliance. By now, the evolution of the Palestinian ethos is not only bound to change the political face of the West Bank after an Israeli withdrawal, but conceivably that of the East Bank as well. Withdrawal will mean the release of some 1500 or more Palestinians from Israeli jails – 'graduates' of that famous political college, an enemy prison. These men, plus the commandos still at large, are likely to be the spearhead of a nationalist, social revolution which many Palestinians would no doubt welcome. It might be men such as Dr Subhi Ghoshi, now under arrest in Jerusalem, who has a left-wing reputation and the attractive habit of treating his poorer patients for nothing, who would come to the top. Another contender would be the mayor of El Bureh, Abdul Jawad Saleh, who sits in his office in an open-necked shirt, khaki shorts and boots – a new look for the New Palestinian – who recently refused an Israeli invitation to resign and take a 'paid holiday' in Europe. There are others. Women might storm a particular Bastille of their own.

The driving nationalist role women are now playing in and outside the West Bank will launch them, over the last carpings of male traditionalists (a fast-fading breed among Palestinians), into the right to vote. Many Palestinian women are, of course, simple village people still living traditional lives – though they have always been more independent in their ways than the usual stereotype of Arab women wrapped up like black bundles and entirely subservient to their menfolk. But more typical of Palestinian middle-class women is Mrs el Musri, of Nablus. Her husband, who studied at Aberystwyth and Cardiff universities, runs a modern farm, discussing his herd of Friesians with his farmhand, wearing cloth cap, windcheater, gum boots and carrying pipe and stick like any farmer in England. She herself runs a comfortable houseful of children, is smartly dressed, like her husband speaks excellent English, and has four brothers. Two of them are doctors working in Düsseldorf, another is in Kuwait. The fourth is in an Israeli jail in Jenin. He is seventeen years old and was captured last year during a battle in the Jordan Valley. And there is nothing downtrodden about the smartly dressed young women running information centres in Beirut. Or among the Palestinian girl students in St Germain des Prés or Kensington. 'I imagine we'll get the vote automatically after all this is over,' a fifth-year student at the American University of Beirut said hopefully.

Yet social revolution on the West Bank obviously implies a prior Israeli pull-back. This is not bound to happen. For one thing, the Israelis show little willingness to do so. For another, the militant Palestinian organizations and their followers are hanging their hopes, at least openly, on much more. Simply to accept the West Bank in return for a peace settlement with Israel, they argue, is a sell-out. It would bury, perhaps irretrievably, the basic problem of Palestine: the recovery of lost lands and the resettlement in Israel of the refugees.

Not every young Palestinian would agree with the commandos. And here unanswerable questions pose themselves. For the Fedayeen are themselves among the younger generation. Many of them are educated men; their leaders are teachers, engineers and the like, not unemployables or drop-outs. They represent the strong arm of the diaspora Palestinians, give hope to their compatriots on the West Bank, are the steel in the new Palestinian political entity, are composed of the New Palestinians themselves. 'The Fedayeen are not ideal, as some Arabs think they are,' an economics student in Beirut told me, 'but they represent a new type of man and they need graduates.' As soon as he leaves college he is going off with them. Another student said: 'It's coming to be thought a crime for anyone to go off to America or somewhere when we have so much work to do here for Palestine.'

If, after months of humiliation, the chance of a peace settlement comes up and the Arab leaders are able to bargain for an Israeli withdrawal in some 'honourable' way, will people on the West Bank oppose it? Will even the Fedayeen split on that issue? I feel that many of the militants would agree to a peaceful life. Their fight is a genuine one and deeply felt, but it is largely against the occupation and for the restoration of East Jerusalem and refugee rights. Their political zeal might later be channelled into the politics of a Palestinian state and conflict with King Hussein, but that is another thing. Others might want to carry on. How many? Few ask. The thought, for most Palestinians, of an Israeli withdrawal with all these fine conditions seems remote. Only one or two things seem fairly certain.

One is that those few middle-aged West Bankers, lawyers and businessmen, who urge separating the West Bank from Jordan now to achieve an immediate special economic and defence relationship with Israel as a prelude to confederation, seem cut off from the mainstream of thought and feeling of their compatriots. A second is that if the occupation continues, another large-scale tragedy looms – perhaps through an Israeli decision to shift large numbers of Palestinians eastwards once again, this time across the Jordan; or perhaps a popular uprising with bloody consequences. It cannot be ruled out that at some time despair might lead to a settling of scores between Palestinians themselves. And if 'collaborators' and Arab informers begin to be purged by the Fedayeen, things on the West Bank will be a mess indeed. The irony of the tragedy is that, partly thanks to the shock of the 1967 war, Palestinians are better prepared today to inherit a state of their own in peace than ever before. Run a hotel? The Palestinians of 1969 could run a nation.

The Bangladesh War, 1971

With only four other British newspaper correspondents I was besieged in Dacca, then the capital of East Pakistan, during the two-week-long Indo–Pakistan War that ended in the city's capture by the Indian Army and the birth of a new Bengali nation called Bangladesh. I managed to be the only journalist present in the Governor's air-raid bunker when the Government of East Pakistan collapsed under the pressure of an Indian air bombardment, and later I attended the 'surrender lunch' with the victorious Indian and defeated Pakistan generals. What the Pakistani generals told me then was at that time not

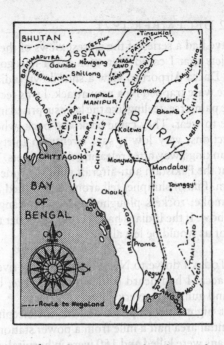

generally known, as far as I am aware. What they said was that the war could have ended a week earlier (and many lives been saved) had Pakistan's President Yahya Khan not cabled his hopelessly outnumbered and surrounded generals in Dacca with the misinformation that they only had to hang on and America and China would come to their aid.

My Bengali friend who on victory day predicted, 'There's going to be such disruption here. Coups and murders. Political assassination,' was tragically right. Even Sheikh Mujibur Rahman, the infant country's hero-President, who returned from a Pakistani jail to a jubilant welcome in Dacca, was soon gunned down by his own countrymen. Since then there have been other coups and killings. The poor Bangladeshis have had to face far too many disappointments since that day of 'Joi Bangla!' – 'Long live Bengal!'

I was extraordinarily lucky to have been so close to the centre of the tragedy and victory of Bangladesh. I was relieved when I was given that year's Journalist of the Year Award, sharing it with Peter Hazelhurst of The Times. So many of my contemporaries had already got it that I was beginning to develop a complex.

DACCA, 12 DECEMBER 1971

Tuesday: I have had a series of the closest views of the undersides of Indian MiG jets that I could ever wish for. I had gone with other journalists to Dacca Airport to view a shot down Indian plane. And while there we were trapped by a new attack. I was recumbent under an inadequate palm tree, feeling like the lady surprised in her bath with only a sponge to wear. They came back and back, wheeling in from different directions, very low – say, twenty to thirty feet directly overhead – banking away after releasing their rockets. The noise was shattering, but the Pakistani anti-aircraft guns – a wide variety – out-shattered them. Bits of shrapnel fell around. A United Nations plane went up in smoke; rockets ploughed through a hangar. It was an exhilarating show. If the Indians had had bombs under their wings, or napalm, few of us would be left alive.

Wednesday: Today I drove to Naryanganj, the big river port twelve miles from Dacca. I had heard of devastation there, but saw little. Barbed wire and guns were everywhere.

Bombing at night: Indian pilots had hit the sleeping heart of a pauper residential area half a mile from a power station. Four or five hundred civilians were killed and 150 were in hospital; the dead were buried in the mud as they slept.

Other things remind us that all is not black and white – some hamlets demolished by fire on the roadside, not by bombs, but by the Pakistan Army.

God knows what editors in London are making of the news they get about Dacca. Correspondents of daily newspapers and agencies here are still receiving much-delayed cables from London demanding to know why they have received no daily file on events and details of life, smells and sounds. Don't they know we can't get out? And that cables have massive delays? One newsman was asked why he could not fly out by Pakistan International Airlines if others were suspended. Does his editor really think that any airline at all has been coming here since last Friday?

Thursday: The worst of it till now is the horror of the Islamic orphanage, hit by Indian bombs at four o'clock this morning. Three hundred boys and girls were sleeping there. I saw the place soon after dawn. Bombs had ploughed everyone into a vast and hideous mud-cake, most of them dead. Some under the heap were breathing, no doubt, but how far down, how badly injured, no one could tell.

Bombing at night is a deadly thing, and unnecessary here. These bombs were aimed at the airport runway, but the Indians had been attacking it for five days by daylight. Only at midday today did a jet pilot finally put a bomb right on it. But up to then we had all agreed with an Australian correspondent here who muttered on the first day: 'The Indians couldn't hit a bull in the bum with a banjo.' That was when we saw the Indian jets careening out of the sky, shot down one by one, seven or nine of them, probably more. The big Sukhoi-7 Russian bombers are the most spectacular in their fall, slow and graceful, like a sad ballet. That seems a month ago.

After the bombing we emerge into the streets and I look at my fellow cover-takers. We make a grotesque miscellany. Dapper clerks in white shirts and trousers and black shoes and with glistening hair; impassive, lean rickshaw men careering in packs through the dogs and crows picking at offal in the roads; strange groups of tattered people, dark-skinned, wild eyes in bony faces, crouching under a huge banyan tree – the ultimate poor. What do they make of the sirens, the earth-shaking noise of bombs? The old man striding nowhere through the city, his dirty white locks flying, with a bundle and a long stick, like a mad prophet possessed by the belief that he would see his strangest prophecy come true if he can only get there, somewhere, in time.

Friday morning: The sirens drowned out the muezzin's early call to prayer. And now we hear the guns. The front can't be far away. The propeller-driven Indian aircraft drops huge bombs. The tall steel structure of the Intercontinental Hotel quivers like a sapling.

Again the mercy flights scheduled for the umpteenth time by the UN, and today by the RAF in Singapore, have been cancelled. The women and children are stranded. Who, we ask here with increasing indignation, is preventing these innocents from leaving – the Indian Government? The Pakistanis have no reason to do so.

One thing international opinion could do is to urge the Indians to stop night bombing, at which they are as inept as most other air forces. Another is to try to have Dacca declared an open city. I believe the Pakistanis would agree to this under certain conditions, designed solely to prevent massacres and a civilian uprising and shoot-out in these teeming streets, where two rickshaws abreast can cause a traffic block.

There has been a calmness in the city, despite the raids. Banks and shops go on as before. People shelter under doorways and walls when the Indian jets go over or the shrapnel from the Pakistani anti-aircraft guns falls. Slit trenches are everywhere: the hotel lawns have been cut into neatly and in straight lines, like a sliced cake. Is there to be a heroic last stand, a miniature *Götterdämmerung*, for East Pakistan? Impossible to say.

We listen to the BBC and learn that the Indian Army has amphibious armoured personnel carriers and can throw a bridge across the waterways hereabouts with fair speed. But the armies are probably about on the line of the real rivers, the Ganges on the west and its biggest tributary to the east. These are huge stretches of water, as big as lakes. It is not easy to throw an Army across them if they are defended. Besides, the ground is too wet and cut across with canals which are natural tank traps. All this could help the Pakistanis, provided they still have supplies, communications and ammunition. But do they?

Friday evening: A United Nations attempt to make Dacca an open city failed today. The Indians would not agree, I understand, fearing some tactical disadvantage for themselves. The UN (U Thant in person, at the behest of Paul-Marc Henri, the UN representative here) urged the plan on humanitarian grounds. Henri, a bustling figure of almost Falstaffian proportions who might easily have made an outstanding Gaullist Minister, has now decked out the UN compound with blue and white signs of neutrality. He is in daily conference with consular representatives, to arrange flights out for the women and children.

One objection after another arises and has to be eradicated – the Indians insist on relief planes flying into Dacca through Calcutta, to emphasize the existence of a 'Bangladesh' Government there. So we are now nearly a week without those flights. An Indian bomb fell not far from the UN complex this morning. But there, later, was Henri and his motley group, shooting off messages to New York surrounded by papers and files and half-empty whisky glasses.

Rumours abound, some spreading from radio sets which pick up snippets and stories from Delhi. One strong rumour two days ago was that the Pakistani commander, General Niazi, had skipped out of Dacca in a small propeller-driven plane at night. The story was heard on the news from Delhi. But the rumour was proved false today when Niazi appeared in the Dacca streets large as life (which is very large) in the middle jeep of three, surrounded by his escort. Niazi has never been faulted for his courage. He wears the ribbon of the Military Cross, won in World War II fighting the Japanese. Second to him, Major-General Farman Ali Khan has once or twice in the past week appeared to journalists, but he too, like all the small in-group of top administrators here, has been working relentlessly round the clock. And there was nothing much they cared to say. Their lot is not a happy one.

18 DECEMBER 1971

Now the shouts of '*Joi Bangla!*' deafen us. Our hands are sore with shaking the hands of jubilant Bengalis. The jail has been broken into and hooligans, too, are on the streets of Dacca. The shooting is sporadic. Law and order teeters; the water may give out.

Sikh officers, all turban and tangled hair, crowd into the reception lobby of the Intercontinental Hotel, where so recently big Punjabi majors shouted to the bar pianist to play 'Roll Out the Barrel'. Now the problems begin, and the Indian officers are clearly appalled by the prospect.

Piles of dead soldiers lie about the roads and ditches at the entrance to Dacca. With the advance guard of the Indian Army, the first Indian general into the city, Major-General Gandharu Nagra, said: 'Casualties are severe. Very messy.' I asked him if he had already met General Niazi, the Pakistani Army commander in the east. 'Oh, yes. He said he was very happy to see me. We knew each other at college.'

That first morning of the ceasefire, when victors and vanquished met at last at Army Headquarters in north Dacca, I saw the officers of both sides looking at one another bleakly but without rancour. There was no Indian jubilation, simply a drained sense of sad futility. Officers who had been comrades at the same staff colleges, who wear the same North Africa or Burma Stars on their chests, and use the same British slang ('What's the drill, sir?'), stood looking at one another wondering who to blame. The Indian troops – dusty in buses, jeeps or trucks – took the garlands and embraces, the cries of '*Joi Bangla*' from leaping, near-hysterical Bengalis, smiling but aloof. When the Indian Eastern Command chief of staff, General Jacob, arrived in Dacca at noon by helicopter, he looked desperately tired and cast down. I lunched with him, General Niazi and General Farman Ali.

It was an embarrassing meal. We stood up and picked at curried chicken legs and bananas. Indians and Pakistanis hardly spoke to one another. The surrender had not yet been signed. 'Niazi could have made a better defence if he had concentrated his forces in a tighter ring round Dacca,' Jacob said quietly to me. 'But he stuck to the frontiers, and we came between them and behind them and separated them up. We don't feel like crowing. You may know that I was not happy about this war in the beginning.' (The generals were doves, the Indian politicians hawks for this war.) Niazi told me: 'We surrendered because otherwise we'd have had to destroy the city between our two armies. We would have had to surrender in the end, so what was the point in continuing?' He gave a pale smile.

A similar meal that I had had with Niazi in the garrison town of Mymensingh the day the war started seemed a very long time ago. Then he had cracked jokes and talked of fighting to the last man. Now he still wore his pistol, but was a man whose occupation had gone. He is not at all a brilliant man, not a political thinker, but he is a dedicated soldier.

Now, two weeks later, the end has come. The humiliation of defeat is shocking to see. The sight of Farman Ali, grey-faced and desolate, wandering alone across the Dacca racecourse after the surrender, was not something one wanted to see again. Nor – despite his faults – do I ever again want to contemplate a man like General Niazi, large and portly, heeling and toeing it across the grass to the howls of the jubilant Bengalis. Or to see him stand reading the surrender terms, crowded by television cameramen and the probing microphones that cheapen the dignity and tragedy of great defeat. Or to see him sitting to sign the several copies of the humiliating document that ended his career. Still less would I care again to see the crowning insult, the unbuckling of his gun belt and its handing over to the turbaned Indian commander, General Aurora. At that point, I saw Niazi's face blurring with misery. One hoped more than anything that he would not cry. Niazi has been castigated by foreigners in Dacca as well as by Bengalis. But he is a simple man. He had no chance of ultimate victory once general war was on. I know he feels abandoned by his boss, Yahya Khan. 'The President said he did not expect general war,' Farman told me at that amazing surrender-day lunch.

Now that the siege of Dacca is over, and we are again able to be in contact with the outside world, those fourteen strange days of isolation are becoming hard to recall. But some of it will stay with me for a long time.

The Pakistani Sabre pilots came into the hotel in the early days, in flowery shirts and silk cravats, all cock-a-hoop, but after three days they admitted sadly into their whisky that they could not take off any more, since the runway was cut up by bombing. Soon the hotel was taken over by the Red Cross and became a neutral zone, so they could not come back. And shortly after that their mess at the airport was destroyed by a large bomb. Several of them were said to have been killed.

The hotel soon instituted a one-menu regime, which was hardly surprising since Indira Gandhi said the war would go on a long time, and Yahya Khan implied it would last for ever. There was no beer. The last shipment was hijacked by the Mukti Bahini, the Bangladeshi 'freedom fighters', near Chittagong.

Before the women and children were evacuated the hotel was like a railway station, full of civilian men, women and children, Red Cross and United Nations people – even a poodle. The only British doctor in Dacca, Dr Basset, who has been here twenty years, was handing out tranquillizers in handfuls. We felt more vulnerable when the RAF planes that evacuated the civilians had been and gone. No one was sure that the Pakistanis would not fight to the end and take the city down with them. The UN people thought we might be used by the Pakistani Army as hostages in the crunch. Most people thought Niazi capable of that, but they maligned him.

We were not pleased to find that several Red Cross men had left on the British planes, including the American responsible for the security of the hotel. Not one but two West German television teams had fled as well, leaving behind them, we found later, all their equipment, worth thousands of dollars. The remaining journalists organized themselves as security guards to prevent any Tom, Dick or Harry sneaking into the hotel. If it was not really neutral we might have had the Mukti Bahini guerrillas in, knocking off some of the West Pakistani civilians. We searched the rooms one by one, unearthing quantities of pistols and ammunition and several guns belonging to Pakistanis. The Pakistanis in the hotel huddled together on the sixth floor, for some reason, sometimes eight to a room.

Bernard Holt, the tough hero-manager of the hotel, was superb. No emergency seemed to get him down. All his staff were Bengali, and obviously many of them were Mukti Bahinis in disguise. As soon as the war ended, receptionists, doormen and room boys emerged as persons of some authority around town. A network had surfaced. Holt had to cope with hysterical civilians – not all of them women – frightened

West Pakistanis, tricky Bengalis. He even carried a large slab of plastic explosive out of the ladies' lavatory into the garden.

He had suggested clearing the top three floors in case the shells started coming in when the Indians reached the city. But the view was so good that we chose to remain up there. In the bombing the hotel shook like a blancmange.

Despair became palpable nine days after the war began, on 11 December. Mr Malik, the Governor, wanted to surrender then. So did his adviser, Major General Farman Ali Khan, an academic-looking soldier who talked more sense than other Pakistani bigwigs around Dacca. On 10 December Farman Ali sent a message to Yahya Khan in Islamabad proposing a 'ceasefire leading to a peaceful transfer of power to a Government here of elected representatives of East Pakistan'. The Pakistani troops would not have laid down their arms, but would have ceased fire and been repatriated to West Pakistan. The Indians, too, would have evacuated East Bengal under this scheme. No surrender, Farman stressed, but a 'peaceful transfer of power'.

Yahya vetoed it. Then for the first time – but not the last – he used the intervention story to put new fire into Niazi: the Chinese and Americans would intervene, he promised, to save Pakistan. Hearing this, Niazi threw up his hands, crowing, 'We are off the hook.'

Farman Ali never believed the intervention story. He told me as much on the day of surrender. But he confirmed that Niazi believed it. So did General Jacob, whose code breakers intercepted these gung-ho messages from Islamabad.

The Bengalis have been deeply confused. A Bengali friend tells me they have been torn between fear and dislike of the Indians and fear and dislike of West Pakistanis. 'There's going to be such disruption here,' he says. 'Coups and murders. Political assassination.' This man is staunchly Awami League (the party of Sheikh Mujibur Rahman) and leans to the left. He wants Sheikh Mujibur Rahman back, but fears he will be killed.

Retribution is in the air. I remember vividly the burning villages I saw just before the war outside Dacca, destroyed by the Razakars – the hated gendarmes locally recruited by the Army from the non-Bengali minority – because they thought Mukti Bahinis had been there. Every pot and pan had been systematically smashed with boot or rifle butt. The peasant bodies were still there to see and the stink of burnt flesh as strong as the stink of retribution in the air now. Is Yahya aware of what has gone on here? I remember, too, a scene up-country when a dead Razakar, shot higher up by the Muktis, floated through a riverside village. Peasant children pelted the body with stones, shouting: 'How many Bengalis did you kill? Go on, tell us.' Their parents looked on with grim smiles.

On Tuesday I went to see the ultradynamic Paul-Marc Henri of the United Nations. He had moved into a missionary college, fearing that he and his people would be used as hostages by the Pakistanis. A sustained air attack, very low and very noisy, came in. I heard later that during it the Soviet Consul, Mr Popov, lay on the floor with the US Consul in the American's office.

Smoke billowed from the nearby Governor's palace. I learned that John Kelly, a short, ex-Balliol New Zealander, who normally specializes in refugee relief for the UN, was inside the palace because Mr Malik was meeting his Cabinet to decide whether he would resign. Was Kelly dead, we wondered? No – soon he drove up shaken but alive. The Governor's house, he said, had been badly hit. But Malik was still undecided. His wife and daughter were there. 'As I dived out of the window into a slit trench,' said Kelly, 'I saw General Farman Ali loping past, white-faced, crying: "Why are the Indians doing this?" and not stopping for an answer.'

'Let's go and see if Malik's all right,' I suggested.

Kelly said, 'Well, if we make it quick. The Indians may be back.'

We arrived. The house smoked and was shattered. A calm colonel led us to an above-ground bunker in the garden. In it we meet Malik and his Ministers.

Malik clutched my hand as if he would never let it go. He was elderly and frightened. 'Should we give up now, do you think?' he quavered to Kelly. Kelly did not want to commit the UN to any of this, so he hedged.

In another room I found Malik's Austrian wife and her daughter looking distraught against the stark concrete of the bunker. An old carved four-poster bed added a surrealist touch. They had been crying.

'Should I send my family to the hotel now, or would tomorrow morning be all right?' Malik asked me. I opened my mouth to say 'Right away' – just as another raid started. The jets made a shattering row. The ground crashed and heaved outside. 'We are refugees now, too,' choked Mr Malik. There seemed nothing to say to that. Kelly looked at me, silently saying, 'What induced me to come back here?'

Then Malik produced a shaking pen and a sheet of office paper. The Ministers mumbled, heads together. Between one crash and the next

Kelly and I looked at the paper and saw that it was addressed to President Yahya Khan and that Malik had at last resigned. Then, the raid still seething round us, Malik, a devout Muslim, took off his shoes and socks, carefully washed his feet in a small washroom opening into the bunker, spread a white handkerchief over his head, and knelt down in a corner of the bunker and said his prayers. That was the end of Government House. That was the end of the last Government of East Pakistan.

Nervous and encumbered by wives and numerous children, the Ministers adjourned to the hotel. All, Malik included, are Bengalis, so their future is far from happy – they cannot cheerfully be flown out to West Pakistan like Farman Ali or Niazi or the troops. Their homes are here. Millions of Bengalis think of them as traitors.

Malik had another blow to endure. When that same afternoon Yahya agreed to Niazi's surrender, his cable to Niazi and Malik said: 'You should now take all necessary measures to stop the fighting and preserve the lives of all armed forces personnel, all those from West Pakistan and all loyal elements.' Malik evidently did not find himself sufficiently covered by the phrase 'all loyal elements'. He felt bitterly that the message was a sign of Yahya's cynicism towards East Pakistan and those Bengalis who had loyally served him and had to take the direct consequences. Malik huddled in the hotel, listening no doubt to the heavy firing outside as Razakars and Muktis shot it out and some Bengalis loudly suggested storming the hotel to get the 'puppets'.

I asked General Jacob later whether the raid on the Governor's house – a civilian target after all – had been intended specifically as psychological pressure on Malik to resign. Jacob did not like the word 'psychological' for some reason. But his answer meant 'yes'.

Then it was all over bar the shouting – and much shooting. Indian MiG 21s came over again and again during the last days. You could see the pilots' heads from my window. The jets hit civilians, and I have the strong impression from talking to General Jacob and other senior Indian officers this week that there was a failure of intelligence. A university dormitory block was strafed time and again. But the Pakistan troops were hardly there to speak of. They were in the university proper. Bengali families died from the rocket fire.

Under this ear-breaking bombardment I began to notice small things. A group of racehorses cantered down the road by the racecourse as the jets dived. But later they were grazing quite peacefully as I waited on the racecourse with half a dozen journalists for the Indian and Pakistani generals to arrive to sign the surrender while streams of unidentifiable machine gun bullets sizzled low over the grass. The scavenger birds over Dacca rode out the raids with hardly a quiver.

At ground level the Soviet Consul, Mr Popov, a lanky intellectual with a bow tie and domed forehead, raced about breathing brandy fumes, in high elation, inquiring how many Pakistani Government officials had taken refuge in the hotel, offering sanctuary to any other diplomats he met, and occasionally dropping off to play a game of chess with American journalists at the hotel. The Iranian Consul was detected in the act of making lots of West Pakistanis instant Iranian citizens, and so was asked to leave the hotel himself.

On the last day of the war, Wednesday, Farman Ali made a final effort to convince Yahya not to fight on. He had Niazi's support this time. Messages went back and forth to Islamabad. But the Indians forestalled all that with a straight ultimatum. Ceasefire, unconditional surrender. It was due to expire at 9.30 a.m. Thursday. And it is a sign of the chaos in Dacca and in men's minds here then that at 9.15 Farman and Niazi were actually incapable of telling the Indians that they accepted because their communications at GHQ were not working.

Luckily the ubiquitous John Kelly decided to contact Farman and discovered the danger. A flash on the UN radio saved the day – saved Dacca from a massive shelling and bombing, from destruction in fact. General Jacob said later, 'Oh, yes. If they had not replied in time, I would have let you all have it.'

To the end, Niazi refused to call it surrender. Even Farman Ali took the pointless trouble to tell journalists at midday on Wednesday that there was no question of a ceasefire. So East Pakistan went down in muddle and noise and blood.

And the second largest Muslim nation – East Bengal (Bangladesh) – was born in the crash of Indian guns and the joyous screams of Bengalis who have countless disappointments to face yet. The size of the problem was there to read on General Jacob's sensitive Jewish face – victorious but feeling nothing of victory. He could not smile. He might have been the defeated one. He will leave the elation and the shouting to the politicians and intellectuals in their villas in Delhi or Bombay.

When will the Indians leave East Bengal? How can they? Who will keep law and order? The UN? To the Mukti Bahini, Jacob said: 'If there's any bloody trouble, I'll slap a curfew on.' It will be needed, by the look of things. Indians have been killed since the ceasefire. There are pockets of frightened Razakars. The Mukti Bahini roam about crazily firing in the air, bearded, long-haired, wild-eyed.

Bangladesh is born. But bringing up this baby in surroundings of such disaster is going to tax the world.

Far from Those Hotel Bars

24 DECEMBER 1970

Several months of journalistic travel this year in some of the hotter spots of the world have reminded me, as seldom in the past, how Carruthers, the adaptable Buchan-esque spy, has been replaced by Carruthers, the trouble-shooting foreign correspondent. It is literally true that last November, at the height of the cyclone relief effort in the tangle of remote islands devastated by tidal waves at the top of the Bay of Bengal, one of the world's least-visited places, one could have met a dishevelled, turbaned figure, paddling a lone canoe up some uncharted creek and shouting cheerfully: 'I'm Witherspoon, *Daily Blast*. Which way to Dacca?'

These reflections are prompted by the fact that regularly, at Christmas or New Year, a foreign reporter is bedevilled by the smoothness of diplomats and, to a lesser extent, businessmen abroad, who claim they never believe anything they read in the press, 'because it is all written in a hotel bar'. No foreign correspondent has escaped that tiresome experience. It is one of the lesser but more irritating hazards of the profession.

The example of the Bengal cyclone comes to mind for two reasons: first, because of the problem confronting the press in getting to the disaster area, 150 miles from anywhere, and under their own unaided steam; second, because of a harangue I personally received from a very high personage in Pakistan. 'Disgraceful,' he fumed, 'that British–Pakistani relations should be placed in jeopardy by inaccurate British journalists, reporting on the failure of the Pakistani Government [in West Pakistan] to show immediate and effective concern for the plight of the cyclone victims in East Pakistan.' Disgraceful, too, he added, that the extent of the damage had been exaggerated by those same journalists who had spent their time in the comfortable bar of Dacca's Intercontinental Hotel. Anglo-Pakistani relations (not of the best) were, of course, that official's main concern. What rankled was the remarks about that comfortable bar. The press effort, in terms of physical effort and initiative, was something extraordinary and memorable in a hideously memorable episode. Despite the disaster, it was also funny in a cruel, Evelyn Waughish way.

The Bengal disaster area was about 10,000 square miles of flat green islands and treacherous sandbanks, slashed through with countless serpentine waterways. Maps are few and inaccurate. The local Bengalis, shocked and bereaved by disaster, were friendly but unhelpful. The place was scattered with stinking corpses, and the water was thought to be contaminated. There might have been a serious cholera epidemic. For a few days the markets of Dacca were cluttered with foreign journalists, haggling like old women at a sale, stocking up with supplies for the plunge into the interior.

London's Thames Television, a team of three, collared a massive Ganges hulk that must have been built a hundred years ago, during the Indian Mutiny or slightly before. With its three decks, massive wheel and paddles, it looked like a cross between the *African Queen* and a decaying wedding cake. The three young Englishmen stocked it up with two weeks' food – largely, it seems, pineapples, cocoa and whisky. I was at a Royal Marine relief base on a remote island when it staggered round a corner, and clanking and gurgling came to rest at a primitive jetty after an accident-ridden two-day trip from Dacca. We sat on its enormous poop that evening, something out of Conrad's *Outcast of the Islands*, while hordes of hungry Bengalis crowded round and were given supplies by Marines. Stan, the cameraman, was cook and potato peeler. Frank, the sound man, was a virtuoso on the Primus stove. The pilot and steersman, an elderly Bengali with a grey fringe beard, was introduced as 'Frisby' and, as translator, liaised with the local world. A boy-of-all-jobs nicknamed 'Ashtray' bustled about killing insects. Below decks a crew of fifteen Bengalis from Dacca cooked curry.

The BBC *Panorama* TV team, in a similarly grotesque craft, had landed on an island with the intention of staying there, self-supporting, for three weeks. A press photographer was dropped off on a sandbank by seaplane. A party of Marines, approaching an island for the first time, were stunned to find a tall, gaunt but white figure with a stubbled face striding nonchalantly towards them and crying, 'Hello.

Welcome. Any room aboard?' He had arrived there by canoe three days before and had been filming and sharing tea and hard-boiled eggs with the locals.

There were many other instances of journalistic enterprise. And so the news of the flood damage in East Bengal was not exaggerated. Yet, admittedly, sometimes news is almost bound to be. During the fighting in Jordan between royal troops and Palestinian guerrillas in September, journalists locked up in another Intercontinental Hotel by the shot and shell considerably exaggerated the damage to Amman. Words like 'Hiroshima' were too cavalierly thrown about, even though the battle was horrific enough. That, though, was undoubtedly largely due to the fact that journalists could not – though not through want of trying – get out and see for themselves.

In Cambodia this summer, things were far from a joke. It is far more dangerous even than Vietnam. There is no official transport for journalists, no helicopter cover or means of evacuation from a tight place in a countryside riddled with Communist troops who have shown that they will shoot on sight, or – worse – stop you, beat you, then kill you or take you away. If a journalist goes out of the capital, Phnom Penh, he is on his own in his car and he is only safe when he gets back. No other foreigner ventures out: no businessmen, certainly, and diplomats are not allowed to. More than twenty correspondents have been reported missing or killed since March this year. The most recent, Frank Frosch of United Press International, a quiet, amiable man with whom I discussed these risks in August, was in November beaten and shot to death twenty miles from Phnom Penh.

On one trip I took to visit the South Vietnamese troops in Cambodia – a drive of fifty miles – I was strolling with Ian Mackenzie of Reuter's through a riverside town, relatively remote from civilization, when we were approached by a haversacked figure in beard and jeans who asked the way to Phnom Penh. We pointed, and he plodded on. He was a British freelance photographer in from Vietnam, but he might have been hitch-hiking through Somerset or Maine.

No foreign correspondent who has covered more than one or two wars – *one* war would do if that one was Vietnam or Cambodia – should be accused of bragging if he says he has lost count of the times when he felt he carried the risk-taking too far. But mostly they talk about it only among themselves – when they get back to that bar. It is easy for foreign residents who live with families and wives in houses or flats to sneer at people who use hotel bars. But if you live in hotels, when you're not in the field where are you to drink? And in any case journalists are not too worried. As circulation figures comfortingly show, those who say they never believe what the papers say still go out and buy them.

The China No One Wants to Know

Suddenly Chiang Kai-shek's offshore islands found themselves cold-shouldered, kicked out of the United Nations, virtually disclaimed by Nixon, even denied a British Consulate.

TAIWAN, 14 MAY 1972

Fleeing from the victorious Communists in 1949, General Chiang Kai-shek arrived on Taiwan with a million or two mainland Chinese, and imposed a split-level personality on the island. That makes it difficult to do the Taiwanese justice.

It is necessary when saying that Taiwan, originally called Formosa, is a likeable place (which it is) to apologize for aspects of it that are clearly unlovable: Fortress Taiwan, the whiffs of totalitarianism from on high, the stubborn absurdities of an octogenarian élite. An intelligent Englishman once said to me in Hong Kong, 'Why worry about those gangsters?' It was a crudely inhuman slander. Taiwanese, Vietnamese, Cubans – of all the peoples I have met in twenty years of travel these, though not necessarily in that order, are the ones I have felt happiest with. Yet, walking into Taiwan's National Assembly one morning in March, I had a momentary feeling that Taiwan is simply too absurd to exist as a separate entity. Most Assemblymen, for example, came from the mainland with Chiang. They were elected in 1954 and haven't shifted since. In this legislature, middle-aged means young. We had to dodge enfeebled ancients with long white beards staggering in and out of the massive chamber of the College of Chinese Culture, some supported by the arms of their elderly wives. Under a great picture of Dr Sun Yat-sen, the founder of the Chinese Republic from whom Chiang took over in 1925 – an aeon ago – old gentlemen quavered into a microphone. The shaky Chinese gutturals fell across rows of heedless seats where other elderly members of non-

Communist China's National Assembly slumped, slept, read. People pottered down the aisles to the tea urns. One old man seemed to be repairing his false teeth. At the doors, smooth-cheeked young military policemen, immaculately turned out, their thoughts carefully immured behind impassive snub-nosed faces, continuously saluted with white-gloved hands as members wobbled in and out.

'Mao, after all, does not represent *all* China,' an old man was saying over the loudspeaker system. There was scattered applause. I came across a middle-aged Member, a jolly, square-built woman called Mrs Grace Hsu. She claims to represent Shanghai, and she lives in New York. Now President Nixon is embracing Mao Tse-tung in Peking. What did she think of that? 'Well, I think it's terrible, of course. Though I voted for Nixon.' Could she be a Chinese Assemblywoman in Taipei *and* vote in American elections? 'Oh, yes. It's good to have people like me living in America. We have so many overseas Chinese living there, someone must speak for them.'

Taking care not to jostle any of the brittle old boys, we walked down the college steps and back into the real world. In Taipei's streets, newspapers said: 'Gimo Rededicates Self to National Task'. 'Gimo' (pronounced 'Geemo') is short for Generalissimo Chiang Kai-shek, who had just been re-elected President, unopposed, at eighty-four. And what we had been witnessing in the superb setting of the golden dragon-wreathed Assembly was another victory of the Gimo's elderly old guard over younger reformers. The old boys had voted against wider representation in the highest Government bodies of Taiwanese – who outnumber the 'refugee' mainlanders, of whom Chiang is one, 12 million to 2 million, but whose say in Taiwan's future is minimal.

In the past, too, the indigenous Taiwanese have been the victims of political circumstance. A province of Imperial China from 1886, Taiwan was ceded to Japan in 1895. The island became a rice and sugar powerhouse for Japan and an extensive 'Japanicization' policy was introduced. Already economically useful to the Japanese, Taiwan became important as a military staging post during Japan's onslaught on South-East Asia. On Japan's defeat, the switch back was completed, and Taiwan was returned to the arms of a floundering China. Soon Mao Tse-tung's armies overcame Chiang Kai-shek's Nationalists and Chiang and his defeated followers took over Taiwan – where they have stayed.

It is the old guard's last stand. Neither they nor Chiang can last much longer. Yet their presence does a disservice. For their activities conceal a pathetic aspect of Taiwan, which deserves world sympathy. The Taiwanese, mainland or indigenous, may seem to be suffering under a tyranny of blimps, but they *know* that the alternative of the Maoist dictatorship would be worse. No one I met on Taiwan believes that Communism is even a minimal force on the island. On the other hand, everyone realizes the virtually universal desire for independence from Peking. A harmless and legitimate desire, the Taiwanese feel, which the West, Britain particularly, by removing all diplomatic recognition with ignominious haste in March, now seems to disparage.

Taipei is not old or beautiful. It is rather grim in a Japanese way. But it has something else: warmth and an amazing friendliness. You walk the pavements fielding smiles from all sides – not smarmy, give-us-a-cigarette-johnny smiles, but smiles that mean 'How nice you are in our city. I can speak a little English. Anything you particularly want to see?'

My companion, the photographer Ian Berry, was wandering around one Sunday when to his surprise he was invited by a young girl student to visit her flat. She simply wanted to chat with a real live Englishman and make him feel welcome. A student in a bus asked me to come and meet his mother and father next evening. I went to their small flat to find an enormous meal ready and Chinese wine. We sat cheerfully in a neat room with a tiny rock garden in it; the mother's prize for acting stood on the television set beside photographs of an elder son in Air Force cadet uniform. Big Chinese characters in gold on a wall said 'Good health' and 'Bless this house'.

The son in the Air Force is characteristic of Taiwan. It is Fortress Taiwan today. The Army is 600,000 strong and every young man serves two or three years, a state of affairs quietly accepted, like everything here, if not with joy. There is the continuing talk from the big brass of 'recovering the mainland' and 'suppressing the Communist rebellion', but that is far less of a Taiwanese priority than simply Being Prepared – for anything.

Strict discipline, in some ways similar to that on Mao's mainland though less severe, is understandable on Taiwan. The island hangs in the China Sea like a tiny pilot fish under the belly of a monstrous whale. Invasion may or may not come, but the Taiwanese have to be able to act as if it will. The mountains are honeycombed with tunnels and bunkers.

On Quemoy, along with Matsu an island outpost that sits on the very lip of the mainland – only about 3000 yards from Communist China – you get the impression that the entire military population lives underground. The military C119 (GIs called it the 'flying coffin') that carries you to Quemoy from Taiwan comes in at about 400 feet to avoid detection by the mainland radar, they say. Wherever you drive on this green little island, bunker mouths yawn at you in the undergrowth. Up above, the stocky, dark-skinned people of Quemoy plough rich-looking fields. Deep red farm buildings with beautifully arched roofs nestle under great crags bristling with radar antennae. Tons of cement protect huge guns. We peered out nervously at the low bulk of the mainland.

'No explosive shell has fallen on Quemoy for twelve years,' said the lieutenant. Amazing news. The last bombardment was terrifying: 175,000 shells in two days, the lieutenant told us. Father Bernard Druetto, a Franciscan, dramatically bearded, who runs a small mission on Quemoy, played us a tape he had made in his living room of that bombardment. It is an uninterrupted sound of explosions the like of which I haven't heard in ten years of wars. 'It didn't do the Communists any good,' Father Druetto said. 'No one left Quemoy. There were 32,000 civilians on the island then. Now there are 62,000.' Why no shellings since then? The question meets shrugs all round. The obvious answer, though, is an agreement between Peking and Taipei to save money.

Instead of high explosives, however, there is a childish war of propaganda shells and balloons. Nationalist troops fire over pop records, leaflets saying 'President Chiang is concerned about you', inflatable Donald Ducks (yes), photographs of Stalin's daughter Svetlana, and pictures of prosperity on Taiwan. The Communists fire back small radio sets, tinned foods and leaflets urging the Taiwanese to get rid of the American imperialists (something they no longer have to do since Nixon went to Peking).

We saw the most astonishing psychological warfare ploy of all from a tip of Nationalist rock near a Communist tip of rock. Across the narrow strait, over the fishing boats, a tremendous voice, metallic, echoing, like an angry god roaring in a cave, boomed out towards us harsh, throaty Chinese sounds. A pause, and from behind us came an answering voice, unearthly, titanic, but female this time. Later we were led into a granite hillside. Here we found the owners of 'our' voices – no giants but a small pale young man and a smiling girl, both in glasses, shouting slowly into a microphone at the Communists across the water. Were the Communists threatening to come and grab Quemoy? Not a bit of it. 'They never insult President Chiang,' a major told us. 'That last bit you heard was telling us that after twenty-two years Shanghai is now an important industrial base.' Godlike voices bellowing boredom. We felt sorry for the fishermen who have to listen to it day after day.

Even here, facing the enemy, the lovable side of non-official Taiwanese crept out to us. We watched a parade of airmen. Their general made a speech and they pledged allegiance to newly re-elected 'Gimo' Chiang. Orders were bawled about; heels stamped; all rigidly disciplined. As soon as the parade was stood at ease, however, I noticed men in the rear ranks peering round the men in front, grinning to us and quickly waving; not something you see on Horse Guards Parade.

We had asked to see the Chinese military academy at Kaosiung in the south of the island. We went by train, a sleek Japanese-made train with Pullman seats. In the academy, the pleasant general-commandant welcomed us with green tea and a briefing on the history of China's Sandhurst. The first commandant had been Chiang Kai-shek on the mainland at Whampoa in 1925. His picture was on a wall – a crisp young officer standing beside a seated Sun Yat-sen. 'The Whampoa spirit,' said a military voice as slides clicked across a screen, 'means responsibility and sacrifice.' Outside, vast buildings stood around green lawns. 'Look at your programme,' said the general in a kindly voice. It said: 'Tour of Academy. Visit: Library, Chemistry Lab., Workshop, Electrical Engineering Lab. . . .' All empty schoolrooms. No cadets. No military training.

Irritation overcame timidity; we said 'No'. In the trees, we glimpsed experts practising karate. We headed for them, trailing a comet tail of anxious officers. The officers need not have worried. These youngsters are full of the Whampoa Spirit all right. More than 60 per cent of them apparently are original Taiwanese.

The next most impressive thing in Kaosiung was something quite different: workers, mostly neatly dressed girls, pedalling home from the great export processing plant like a locust swarm on wheels. It's their low salaries ($40–50 a month plus lodging in a YMCA-run dormitory) that keep Taiwan's trade booming. But some girls I talked to were able to save half their salaries for Mother. Electrical products, electronics, scooters, lathes, wigs stream out of this duty-free area to Europe and America in a growing flood. On economic success

Taiwan, under new pressures now from the mainland, stands or falls. Is it wavering? Not according to someone I saw at the solid British office of Butterfield and Swire in Taipei. 'No sign of trade taking a dip,' he said. 'Anxiety here, yes, since some trading partners are recognizing Peking. But lots of confidence here underlying the gloom.'

Now that Japan and Communist China are looking coyly at one another, will Japanese businessmen obey Peking's insistence that if they want the mainland market they must pull out of Taiwan? That would be a desperate blow for Taiwan. But commercial people in Taipei think that the Japanese will find a convenient compromise. In fact, one British businessman is confidently putting his own money in to the hilt. Dennis Gregson, once of Llanelly, now living in Richmond, Surrey, has snapped up nearly a hundred contracts to sell Taiwanese goods in Britain. Why? 'Taiwan is bursting with energy and expertise,' he said, and that was obvious. What about quality? 'Second to none,' he said. 'And low salaries, low cost of living, so low prices. There's a boom like in Japan twenty years ago.'

Indeed, a drive into the country revealed the energy, industry and tradition of the Taiwanese. Every wrinkle in the ground was terraced. Paddy fields ran up to the factory gates. The landscape was amazingly cluttered. Dragons on temple roofs writhed among industrial chimneys and pylons. In the cities there is very little of the expected mixture of traditional Chinese and smatterings of American. The room boy in my hotel in Tainan told me, 'Your luggage coming okay. No sweat.' At the Taipei Golf Club, Taiwanese in co-respondent shoes tee off near a sign that says 'Snake bite is a rare accident. The best treatment is DON'T GET BIT!' But these were exceptions.

In general Taiwan is delightfully uncontaminated by foreign influences. Taipei may have a look of workaday grit about it, but it also has perhaps the finest museum in the Chinese world, with a hollow mountain full of art treasures brought from the mainland to draw on.

In a small round market, ordinary Chinese sat rosy with beer on Sunday afternoons at marble-topped tables, eating squid, oysters, mussels, dark grey crabs imprisoned in jackets of seaweed. There were eels in tanks, too, and crayfish for a song. Nearby was a street of nothing but small eating shops at one end; at the other, quackery: snake soup shops, places selling powdered gazelle horn, dried turtles or seahorses for strength. In one doorway, for no apparent reason, a large gloomy bear sat in a cage.

The world's greatest doctor of acupuncture, Dr Wu Wei-ping, has his clinic in Taipei. When we called, Dr Wu was examining a patient – or 'listening to him', as he put it. Dr Wu was large, fortyish, and bustled energetically about a consulting room decorated with photographs of distinguished clients. By pushing fine needles into several of 365 points in the body, the body's energy can be controlled and corrected according to the theory of acupuncture. Cures for rheumatism, appendicitis and practically everything else can result. I said my right shoulder ached – could he do anything? Dr Wu confidently pushed two needles into it about an inch deep and another between my thumb and first finger. I felt a slight additional ache in my shoulder, nothing much. 'You would have to come here three or four times to be cured,' said Dr Wu. Patients poured in, all ages, both sexes, poor or well-dressed. They lay down bravely and Dr Wu inserted needles gently and without fuss. He pushed two into the mouth of a man with a paralysed tongue. A group of French acupuncturists looked on, admiring the doctor's deft fingers. Dr Wu's cure rate, I was told, is very high. He has treated Lon Nol, the President of Cambodia, for a stroke.

Modern science is also Taiwan's forte: the engineering and electronics departments of Taiwan's university have unusually high standards. The day I went there I was shown a $400,000 computer and sat in on a seminar on Chaucer. Chaucer in Taipei? Chinese boys and girls ploughed through *The Book of the Duchess*. This was, naturally, the Advanced English Lit. course. 'What will you do with Chaucer afterwards?' I asked a young man. 'Oh, teach, sir, I expect.' Most people want to be technicians: better money and opportunity for going abroad. Once there, a fair percentage stay, and Taiwan suffers a brain drain – worrying, but not disastrous.

Still, for all their liveliness there's something missing in Taiwan's students' lives: an almost total political apathy grips the campus. Admittedly there's a state of near war, at least one of emergency, on the island because of Peking's proximity. But the police control of student thoughts, the suppression of debate or discussion on Government policy is pitiful. The fine university library contains no books on Communism.

About Taiwanese nationalism no one breathes a public word. The Taiwanese Independence Movement – the movement among the 12 million original Taiwan inhabitants to be quite separate from mainland China and to end the domination of Chiang's 2 million mainlanders – is not now much of a physical force on the island. But it is a very strong feeling, latent now, likely to surface later if repression falters.

In essence, the TIM wants recognition of the fact that Taiwan has been an independent state for twenty years, the evacuation of all Taiwanese from Quemoy and Matsu (which the TIM says belong indisputably to mainland China), recognition of Taiwan as independent and its seating as such at the United Nations, and self-determination for all 14 million on the island. With that, of course, would go proportional representation for the Taiwanese in the highest institutions of Government. This is blatantly denied them. 'We are all well aware of our different backgrounds,' say the Taiwanese members of the island's population, 'but we share a desire for peace and we do not want to be governed by Peking.' That's basic and vital.

In fact, what the Taiwanese fear more than anything astonishes a newcomer. It is that the ruling mainlanders – even with all their hatred of Maoism, their history of bloody struggle against Communism in China – will do a deal with Peking that will turn Taiwan into some kind of closely associated province of Mao's successors. There have been rumours of such a deal for a decade. Nothing, most agree, while the Old Man, the Gimo, Chiang Kai-shek is alive. But the old guard ultra-conservatives can't have long to go. Behind Chiang is a more 'progressive' group, headed by Chiang's probable successor, his son Chiang Ching-kuo.

At sixty-two the son is no youngster either. But he supported the reform of the Assembly that the blindly selfish old guard scotched in March. He is very bright, if retiring. The younger Kuomintang (Nationalist) ruling party men are with him, and he has powerful backing in the armed forces and intelligence services. This group is trying to chip away the old, rigid, unrealistic, we-will-return-by-force-to-the-mainland dogma that Chiang stubbornly clutches. 'Realism, pragmatism' are the new watchwords. Chiang Ching-kuo has a Russian wife. Rapprochement with Russia is currently on the cards. So, after old Chiang, could rapprochement with Peking be on the cards? Such a thing might save Taiwan's non-Communist integrity. It would not allow for what the Taiwanese want – complete independence. But Chiang Kai-shek, by adherence to the 'One China' idea, has sacrificed that Taiwanese aspiration to his own old dream. Taiwan could be sitting beside Communist China in the UN today if Chiang had not stuck to that untenable principle.

This is the cause of indigenous Taiwanese anguish. True, young

Taiwanese and mainlanders are growing together. Young mainlanders reject their fathers' idea that Taiwanese are inferior. In time, Taiwanese superior numbers will prevail over the mainlanders. But will there be enough time? Today, no one can say.

Cut off from debate and political activity, isolated on their island, do Taiwanese feel claustrophobic? I put this to a Taiwanese. He smiled brightly and replied: 'I have a very large radio set.' But Taiwanese can and do meet foreigners. They are never happier than when they can entertain them. If you go there – anyone who can go there *should* – visit the Taoist temples of Tainan, particularly that of the Jade King. Here, amid incense and the intense ritualistic activity of a medieval place of pilgrimage, dragons and gold, black and red images seem to lean down to embrace you. Simple Taiwanese load altars with gifts of food and rice wine to propitiate the evil spirits that threaten their dead relatives. The wild women in trances rolling their heads and moaning, watched anxiously by small groups of men and women, are trying to find out what offerings other angry spirits require of their clients. A seedy, piratical 'priest' flicks a whip and blows blasts on a curved bone horn, chasing off bad spirits and summoning the good. Another, with a knocked-about face, traces cabbalistic signs with his foot. An old man with a hare-lip is carrying miniature paper houses, paper furniture, even bicycles of paper, to a small furnace; relatives bring them so that their dear departed will be well-housed, be able to get about, in the Other World.

Here is one Taiwan: old, superstitious, courteous. Another, newer Taiwan effervesces on street or campus, under the eyes of Chiang's old cronies, his police agents and unimaginative information officials: energetic, young, welcoming but never obsequious. Rather anxious now as the friendly foreign consuls are yanked rudely out. Abhorring all totalitarianism, particularly Mao's, though accepting the last years of Chiang's dragooning *faute de mieux*. And courteously inviting you and me to explain why in God's name they – with more people than Australia or Belgium – should not be helped to live alone and do nobody harm.

Paradise Murdered

Despite frequent efforts by the international community to end the unnatural division of Cyprus, nothing has changed since the Turks invaded and occupied the Northern part of the island in 1974. Turkey remains adamant. The leader of the Turkish Cypriots has even proclaimed an independent Turkish entity in the north. It's a sad situation that grew out of years of violence between Greek Cypriots over the issue of ENOSIS – union with Greece. EOKA men were ready to kill fellow Greeks for that.

NICOSIA, 15 SEPTEMBER 1974

Last spring, walking with friends in the wilder hills above Kyrenia, I came across a strange phenomenon: a woman's handbag suspended on a string from the branch of an ancient carob tree. Quite soon we discovered ourselves in groves hung about with other objects: an elderly umbrella, a plastic shopping bag, a stone, a shoe. Far from the neat, antiseptic villas of the British tourists on the shore below, far from Greek Orthodox and Muslim Cyprus, Cypriot peasants were still scrupulously striving to propitiate the spirits of this antique island as they had done for thousands of years.

In Cyprus again now, in a new version of peace, one does not have to be as superstitious as those poor peasants to feel that something has been killed here. Among those groves, now shrivelled to charcoal by the shelling, the spirits of Cyprus may be dead for ever. Talk here of speedy recovery and reconciliation – there is some – rings utterly false. And by a hideous irony the murder of Cyprus has been committed by two races, Greeks and Turks, vehemently protesting their love for it. But you see the wreckage of this exceptional place and realize that it is only mindless nationalism rooted in God-knows-what psychological disorder masquerading as love. What else could account for the mad, murderous Greek officers' coup against Archbishop Makarios that started it all? Of the horror of the second Turkish offensive? Or the shameful trading of mass murder accusations last week?

One wonders if the acting Greek Cypriot President, Glafcos Clerides, and the Turkish Cypriot leader, Rauf Denktash, can see anything but intermittent war ahead. During eleven years of weekly talks between 1963 and 1974 they pitifully failed to agree on how Greeks and Turks could live happily together on this beautiful,

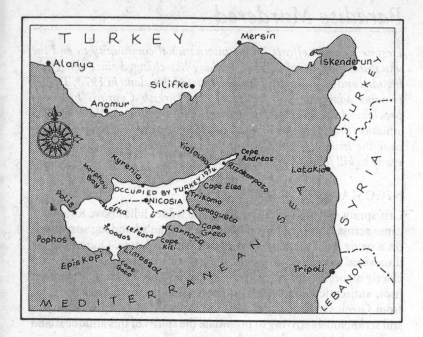

uncrowded and fruitful island, and now, in Nicosia's Ledra Palace Hotel, stare at each other for the 500th time over a green baize negotiating table.

For this time, the short, ex-EOKA, ex-RAF navigator Greek and the stubby Turk with the face of an ebullient potato – Tweedledum and Tweedledee – face each other amid the human debris of an island paradise and incalculable racial bitterness. Cyprus is never going to be the same place again: that much is certain. The question is simply whether, for its inhabitants, it will ever be much more than a confined region of almost unendurable fear, erupting regularly in waves of political and racial thuggism and murder. The destruction of human relations, in fact, far outstrips the purely physical wreckage.

Taking a new look at the island, I drove through Turkish Army lines to Kyrenia. At the fortress on the hills over the little harbour a sign in Turkish and English said: 'Don't start forest fires.' All around, as far as the eye can see, the hills, recently green with trees, were black as burnt toast. Two large British-owned houses stood gutted on crags. Nearby, two bluff, brave British women, both ex-majors in the ATS, showed me how, as they watched the Turkish bombing, the fire lapped their garden, then almost miraculously stopped. They will stay; Turks and Greeks are all one to them. 'Keep your head down and your chin up,' they called cheerfully as I left them. We exchanged the thumbs-up sign.

Kyrenia stands largely intact. The harbour is still full of foreign yachts. Turks have boarded up the looted main street shops and you can't go down it. Greek signs are painted over. A bust of Atatürk has been unveiled with grotesque goose-stepping military ceremony next to the Dome Hotel, once favoured by elderly foreigners (and so nicknamed 'The Doom'). Kyrenia is full of squat Turkish soldiers in flat helmets, with faces the colour of reddish clay and empty, moronic eyes, as dangerous as cobras. Their commander has flogged some and is holding others and Turkish villagers for rape and pillage.

I found a middle-aged Greek I have known for some time detained with other Greeks in the Dome. He shook my hand. 'We are all right,' he said weakly, glancing at the listening Turkish police round us. 'Do you think we'll be able to go home soon?' I could only say I had no idea; that's politics and nothing has been decided.

At Bellapais, under the Tree of Idleness by the great ruined abbey, white-moustached men and scores of Greek women hang about with their children waiting for something to happen. Their husbands have been carted off to Turkey as 'prisoners of war', though most were not carrying any weapons when the Turks arrived. 'They are probably EOKA terrorists – anyway, they could be,' Turkish officers told me. The women crowded round asking for news. 'Of course we want to go back to our homes – even under a Turkish Administration,' they cried in a wild chorus, plucking my sleeve, tugging my shoulder, all trying to make some personal point to someone who was not a cynical Turk, who might have a fevered memory of gross Greek bullying of Turkish Cypriots ten years ago, when a hundred or more Turkish villages were laid waste and 20,000 made refugees.

'We sleep on hard floors here,' the Greek ladies said. But they have a doctor and a sympathetic Turkish police sergeant called Khalil who is tireless in trying to stop looting by Turkish villagers and soldiers. 'I went into my house and saw a khaki-clad leg under the bed,' an elderly British doctor said irritably, but he had remained throughout the bombardment and had dug out his medicines again to treat the villagers.

Last March I almost bought a house in a handsome little Greek village called Trimithi. Today Trimithi is a corpse. Above the battered main road, past a villa called 'High Heaven', scooters, a doll in a pink dress and a pram littered the lane. The village is deserted, looted and eerily silent. A gutted tank stood outside the little church, the garage door creaked, flies buzzed round stale food, two mules, with no one to feed or water them, tugged at a vine.

'A dead place,' I said to my Turkish officer guide.

He nodded glumly. 'Dead place, yes.'

Near here one Christmas Eve Cypriots had laboured in darkness and pouring rain to repair my car. Cypriot friendliness is unforgettable. Now those men are dead or destitute refugees. Back in Kyrenia, I watched the Turkish commander in Cyprus, a strong little figure, in a phalanx of guards touring the castle where last winter Greeks and Turks had happily watched Peter Sellers and Spike Milligan filming in a crowd of extras at the Greek-owned Dorana Hotel, dressed as pirates.

Hassan Tahsin, the young Turkish barman of the Harbour Club, stood at the door of the hotel with a satisfied grin on his face and a pistol in his belt. I said, 'Hello, Hassan. Have they made you a colonel?'

He said, 'No, I am running this. I'm keeping the place warm.'

'Where are the owners?'

'I don't know.' He didn't, and for him from now on Kyrenia is as Turkish now as Brighton is British.

Up in the sharp peninsula of north-east Cyprus, Greeks have stayed in their villages and their Turkish neighbours have behaved well. But the Greeks are overcrowded because lots of Greeks from Britain were there on holiday – including a man ('Call me Nick the Greek') who worked at the Embassy Club in London for over twenty years. There's no electricity now and a water shortage. Faraway men in uniforms and suits and ties in Ankara, Athens and Nicosia will decide whether they get electricity and water, and even if they can stay where they have lived for generations. Local Turks there seem reasonably tolerant to local Greeks. 'Let them stay. But we are the bosses now. We shall take the best jobs,' Turks say to me. And they add, 'Greeks made us suffer for eleven years. Well, things are reversed now.' A hefty dash of vindictiveness is evident too.

The whole business of regrouping the two populations of Cyprus is paramount, particularly with 220,000 people on the run from their homes. The problem is rooted, of course, in politics. But opinions on the ground are going to matter, too.

I drove to Limassol to see the surrounded, outnumbered Turkish population. A Turkish doctor in the hospital thumped a table. 'We are at the mercy of the Greeks,' he shouted. This is strictly true, and although I saw the Turkish detainees in a pleasant school under the charge of a pleasant Greek Cypriot captain, there are nasty rumours of village slaughters in the hinterland, uncheckable just then. The furious doctor was the first Turk I heard in 'Greek' Cyprus who insisted on moving out. 'One hundred per cent, we want to go to the Turkish areas in the north,' he thundered, 'or our Army will take over all Cyprus.'

'What has backward Turkey got to offer a lively place like Cyprus?'

'We are stronger.' A depressing reply.

In Paphos, the harbour front was disgracefully bombed by Turkish planes. Nothing more military was destroyed than a series of houses, small bars and restaurants, including one that housed an elderly pet pelican – the only thing not blown to smithereens. Priceless antique mosaics were badly damaged. Yet Paphos never posed the remotest threat to the overwhelming, if somewhat incompetent, Turkish Army operations at the other end of the island.

Mr Murat, a Turkish leader of the 2000-strong Turkish community in Paphos, tripped up to me in a narrow street, the slightest bit tipsy. In his living room, he produced beer and pistachio nuts under the eagle eye of a portrait of Kemal Atatürk in a wing collar.

'On 21 July,' he said, 'Greek soldiers said that if our Air Force machine-gunned them they would destroy us all, even our cats, everything. They were EOKA B men. We were saved by Coldstream Guards of the United Nations. And – I admit it frankly – by a Greek officer who told the EOKA youths, "History will judge you if you kill unarmed people."'

But some did die. A Turkish woman teacher in Mr Murat's room said, with tears in her eyes, 'I saw four students killed in front of me. Boys I had tried to bring up as civilized young men. . . .' She couldn't go on.

I asked, 'Will you stay in Paphos after a peace settlement?' and a small storm of passion broke around me. Mr Murat pointed dramatically, 'See this gentleman? He's a Member of Parliament and rich. He cannot even go and water his farms and orchards. We want to leave everything and go.'

The teacher began speaking agitatedly in Turkish to Mr Murat, who waved his arms. 'She says we'll leave our very clothes here rather than stay among Greeks any longer.'

The anguish was there all right – never, I think, to be exorcized from these people's minds. Any more than it will be erased from the mind of Andreas, the twenty-year-old villager from a small hamlet near Polis in the north-west, whose family I met last year. During the invasion this immature peasant was shooting at Turkish planes made in America roaring in over the island, and he thinks he shot one down.

'Lose many friends, Andreas?' I said.

He sat, head in hands, shaking with the memory. 'Very many,' he said.

What now?

'I'd like to leave Cyprus, go to London maybe, or Australia. Well, why must we wait here for the Turkish Army to take us all over next year or the year after?'

'They probably won't do that,' I said.

'But do we have to live wondering if those barbarians will or will not?' he suddenly shouted. 'For God's sake help me to leave.'

Barbarians is the word both races hurl back and forth at each other. Security is another. In a Turkish hill village near Polis I found 700 Turkish peasants still armed. They have not been required to surrender. In the Mukhtar's small stone-floored house we ate walnuts and grapes under the cut-out wall decorations of Turkish film, pop and football stars, and Atatürk again, this time in uniform.

'For eleven years we've had no security,' he said, and other villagers nodded in unison. 'We paid our taxes, but we were given no electricity in return, no village telephone. From time to time neighbouring Greek villagers blocked our road to market so as to get there first.' An old white-headed woman said, 'Of course we shall leave' – leave, she meant, to the rich, newly Turkish region in the north.

From the window I could see citrus trees withering for lack of water. Why? Lack of petrol to work the water pumps, they said. But why water trees you are going to leave to the enemy? I suspect they just weren't bothering. And there is the other great danger for Cyprus: that in this distracting time tracts of land will die. It takes years to grow an orange plantation. Will there be years of peace to grow them in? In many parts of Cyprus today, including Nicosia, the disaster has left people punch-drunk. They feel nothing as positive as despair, even, or hate. 'We may have some music in our bar soon,' said a usually jolly Greek. 'But not bouzouki. It's too soon. So many deaths.'

But there's plenty of hate, too. The mainland Greek major in Polis, dark, taciturn, could hardly speak for the hate in his throat. For him – he was here for the anti-Makarios coup and has not been replaced –

the Greeks are blameless. 'Outsiders did this. Why can't they leave us alone? The Americans want bases here. The Israelis want America to have bases to help them from. Britain has bases. Russia would like one. China next?'

Then came a pillar of current Greek belief: 'The Turks could never invade without American help.'

But was the coup against Makarios wise?

'Let's talk of the future, not the past.' His Cypriot lieutenant, speaking good English, added passionately: 'ENOSIS is the future. If it means war again in twenty years, okay, why not? It's in our souls.' The window of the little office looked across a counterpane of dark green trees to the perfect sea. It seemed an almost unbearably dire statement.

It was a statement repeated with inebriated gusto by a cheerful rabble of Greek youths I met latish one evening in a Nicosia restaurant. Beards matted, hair wild, uniforms anyhow, they proudly proclaimed themselves EOKA B. Among the clashing wine bottles, the litany poured out: Pan-Hellenism, anti-Communism, ENOSIS, blaming the Americans.

'Nicos Sampson was a leader: that's what we want,' they cried. 'If the Colonels in Greece had not resigned, we should have defeated the Turks.'

Myth after myth.

'All right, the coup against Makarios was a bad miscalculation. But now all we have to do is unite and fight in the hills.'

A war every few years?

'Why not?'

The romantic, brutal voices rang out into the night, rising in excitement as the wine was poured. They might have reached the school notice boards down the road with their pathetic lists: long lists of names of those still missing, shorter lists of those recently found.

A Greek Cypriot lawyer-politician said next day, 'EOKA is over-rated. More and more people realize that ENOSIS cannot be achieved now.'

Maybe so. It is true that the EOKA men did not plan and start that fatal coup. It is also true that those who did are still – many of them – alive and well and living in Cyprus. Partly because of them, the wall of mistrust between Greek and Turkish Cypriot now is a thousand feet high. Nothing can eliminate that pathetic fact, which means federation or something very like it, a separation of the communities.

An extra dimension to the Cyprus tragedy is that the world is full of places made hopeless by famine or cyclones or racial and religious conflict. It could have done with what Cyprus was beginning to be: a prospering, peaceful, unaligned oasis, outside the swirl of East–West rivalries. Now it's probably all up. Turkish arrogance and insensitivity and the zany Greek pursuit of the old Pan-Hellenistic will-o'-the-wisp may well have reduced paradise to a place of permanent fear and vendetta.

Only one recent incident here has given me any hope for the future – and it was a bizarre one. One night, on the 'Green Line' that separates Greek Cypriot from Turkish Cypriot fighters, the few meaningless shots in the air died away and the regular exchange of invective began. There were one or two shouts of 'mass murderers'. But they gave way to half-affectionate taunts: 'Hey, Andreas,' (from a Turk). 'Your mother left her slippers under my bed. When are you coming to collect them?' And then suddenly a Turk began a Cypriot song in Greek and soon the Greeks joined in. For a few minutes across the barbed wire, the burnt-out cars and scarred trees in a tiny sector of this utterly unnecessary battlefield, a score or so of young men were no longer Greek and Turks, but Cypriots.

Italy under Siege

'[He] paid a ransom for his father . . . and then found they had fed him to the pigs. The pigs eat everything . . . even the bones.' For the rich in Italy, life in 1979 was a waking nightmare compounded of political terrorism and the constant fear of kidnap. Now, by 1987, the Italian police are more or less on top of Red Brigades terrorism and Mafia kidnapping. Bravery and moderation have paid off.

ROME, 31 JULY 1979

'Anyone could be waiting for us here,' Anna says with a shaky smile. 'That's the truth, I'm afraid.' The swing door of the apartment block closes behind us with a sigh. A short black driveway glistens with the evening's rain. It is easy to imagine kidnappers with their guns in the deep shadows under the trees by the front gate. The near silence is bad for the nerves, too. In the street outside, the headlights of an occasional car sweep past but disappear almost immediately round a bend towards the autostrada. 'No buses stop near here. And the porter died three days ago. So you see . . . ,' Anna says.

Anna is beautiful. She is separated from her husband. She is also well off. She is very well qualified to show me how it feels to live in Rome in 1979 with the day-to-day fear of kidnapping or her children being kidnapped. Of being murdered. Of being minced up, *after* the ransom money has been paid, and fed to somebody's pigs.

It feels worse in the concrete underground garage, like Hitler's bunker, where she has to park her car every evening. There, the silence is total. 'See this damned iron grille? I have to open it and close it every night,' Anna says. The metal concertina shrieks when I tug at it, and an elderly woman in a fur coat, locking her little Fiat, looks up terrified. We clack through the concrete pillars to Anna's small blue car. 'You could yell your head off down here, and no one would hear a thing.' I have no difficulty imagining four figures in windcheaters and balaclava helmets, the smack of gun butts on my skull, the eventual wakening, bound and bleeding, God knows where. Or the shots meticulously splintering my thighbones, smashing my kneecaps.

For beautiful Anna, daughter of a millionaire industrialist who would certainly pay the ransom as the others have done, it would be kidnapping rather than kneecapping. Kneecapping is a sick retribution – there's no money in it. It's the political version of infants torturing cats. Kidnapping is big business: it has set up illiterate Calabrian goatherds or Sicilian garage hands in luxury for life.

Anna is a brave woman. She would drive her son, eight, and her daughter, six, to school next day on her way to work at a publisher's. A neighbour would bring them home. She would get back well after dark, to brave those shadows, the empty lobby and lift, and to wrestle with the iron grille in that terrifying underground bunker. As I leave her, she says, 'I'm not sure I can stand being alone here much longer. I hate running. But at least I have to find a flat I can share.'

The precautions make good sense. The five-year-old wave of terror in Italy shows little sign of abating. Twenty kidnappings in the first five months of this year: by the Communist Party's count, more than 5000 incidents of political terror in the three years from 1976 to 1978: murders, shootings, firebombings; attacks on police stations, trade union offices and the headquarters of political parties – and over 300 kidnappings during the same period, most of them non-political.

The precautions are also often complex and expensive. Soon after arriving on a recent visit to Italy, I was driving along the coast north from Rome with a man who must be on every terrorist list, a very prominent public figure. Also, it seems to me, a totally unflappable one. Nevertheless, his car is an armoured Fiat 130. The roof, engine, sides and floor are lined with steel plates, heavy plastic and wire mesh. The 400 kilos of extra weight make it a little heavy on the steering. It has two tall aerials, a radio, a telephone with a push-button switchboard, a siren, and – in case someone tries to set us on fire – a James Bond gadget that can instantly cover the outside of the car in anti-fire foam.

I tap on a windowpane as thick as my little finger. 'Can anyone break that with an iron bar?'

He smiles. 'I'd be disappointed if a bullet got through it.'

A gun?

'I don't have one. No point in becoming a slave of a gun. He has one.' He nodded towards the trim young driver in a smart dove-grey suit, who at that moment was thrusting the Fiat through Tarquinia. 'We are in radio contact with the Carabinieri posts along the way. Did I tell you my No. 2 at the office is on the latest Red Brigades' list of people to be killed?'

'He's married?'

'Two children.'

'That's no joke.'

A thin smile. 'No joke at all. One mustn't spend too much time thinking about it.'

There is, after all, plenty to think about in your car when a vehicle swings in front of you, or walking towards a figure by the gate, or in bed when a window swings in the wind.

You can almost divide the Italian terrorist industry down the middle. On the one hand, shootings, murders and bombings are political, carried out – and proudly claimed – by one of four or five extreme left-wing groups, now and then by a right-wing group.

By far the best-known and most feared left-wing organization is the Red Brigades, *Brigate Rosse*, whose brilliant planning frustrated the frantic efforts of the entire Italian police system for fifty-four nightmare days between the kidnapping and killing of the king-pillar of Italy's political establishment, Aldo Moro, the President of the Christian Democrat Party.

On the other hand, the kidnappings are 90 per cent non-political. They are the work of professional *banditti* – little Mafias of Sardinians, Sicilians, Calabrians, some foreigners. They plan meticulously, spending months checking on potential victims' habits, friends, servants, movements and character.

Anyone with extremely wealthy relatives may be grabbed anywhere at any moment. The youngest *rapito* (kidnappee) so far was sixteen months old; the oldest was an eighty-six-year-old chemist who was never returned, despite payment. And those payments range from about $1 million to $6 million. In February this year Maria Sacco, one of Italy's rare women jockeys and daughter of a wealthy Milan contractor, was released after 107 days, much of which she spent blindfolded. No one outside the family circle knows for sure what ransom was paid. Almost $2 million was asked: then, in line with official policy, the police confiscated $1 million that the family intended to pay. When the release came, the family announced that no ransom had been paid. . . . In May, a millionaire textile wholesaler, Franco Casillo, paid $180,000 for the release of his twelve-year-old daughter. In April Marco Gatta, twenty-two, the grandson of the founder of the Lancia motor company, was released after his family paid almost $1 million.

The world of kidnapping is a world apart. A world of luxury, fear – and strange relationships between kidnappers and victims, like those formed between soldiers of opposing armies.

Evening in the Via Condotti. I sit in a plush office behind showcases gleaming with expensive objects in leather and gold. Sleek girls, like models advertising *la dolce vita*, glide about enveloping customers in heady clouds of Guerlain's Shalimar. When I say yes to a drink, someone puts in front of me a bottle of Chivas Regal and a bucket of ice. J. pours some whisky into two glasses, and sits down. He is the boss of this smart shop. J.'s brother was kidnapped last year; it took $7 million to spring him. J. is a large, courteous man and his watchful face tells you he knows how to bargain. He did bargain – for weeks – on the telephone with his brother's kidnappers. Offering money for a life.

J. says: 'They were extremely efficient. Not educated, but certainly far, far from stupid. Can you believe that, despite what they had done to my brother, we became almost like friends after two conversations? Very polite, too. They, after all, can only deal with you. You are the buyer. They need you.' A smile. 'We became just like business partners.' He looked steadily over his glass. 'And the police became the enemy. The police could come between us and what we both wanted. You find that strange, I dare say.' J. is not optimistic about Italy. 'It's like the Weimar Republic. Soon it could be like Lebanon. But Italy is too beautiful to leave. It's reality, too. Where would I go? I find places like Geneva really intolerable.' There are quite a few rich Italians who have found that, to adapt a phrase, 'Perfect fear casteth out love.' But most agree with J.

Next day, I stand at the tall window of a magnificent flat high above Rome. Below me, flesh-and-peach-coloured buildings splashed by the winter sun. Pigeons tumble in sunlight over domes and palazzos, the railway station, the Bank of the Holy Spirit. I watch a huge silver dirigible with the label 'Goodyear' floating over St Peter's. Behind me on the sofa a teenage girl with blonde, shoulder-length hair falling over a high-necked sweater is agonizing over her kidnapping.

'They kept me in a box two metres long, two and a half metres high and a metre wide for seventy-one days. Tied by an ankle chain. The isolation was terrifying.' She sucks compulsively on a cigarette, simultaneously chewing gum. 'It happened one evening . . . I drove up to our villa with two boyfriends. A little van pulled up and three masked men leaped out with guns. I knew immediately what it meant. They smashed the windows and just pulled me out. My boyfriends sat paralysed. I was punched and manhandled into the van. They hand-cuffed me and jammed tape recorder earphones on me so I couldn't hear their voices.' She fumbled out another cigarette. 'I was two and a half months in that box. One day – it's unbelievable – the police searching for Moro knocked on the door of the little flat where I was hidden. My kidnappers kept quiet and the police went away.'

Politics?

'No, they kept saying, "we're not political. We do this because – well, because it pays better than work." ' It paid them about $1 million in cash.

This girl, the Italian press said, had had a passionate affair with one of her captors.

She said: 'I hate Italian journalists. It wasn't like that. The whole experience was utterly unreal, like a nightmare. I was scared and weeping a lot. One of the gang was a Frenchman. I could tell by his accent and on his windcheater I saw a label "Marseilles". He sometimes talked to me gently. I even held his hand. He was a bit on hashish, I think. He told me mad stories of how his grandmother had bicycled round France with a machine gun robbing banks. But you've no idea what a comfort that gentleness was.'

What now?

'Now I want to finish my studies and go . . . anywhere. To a place I don't have to wake up in the middle of the night wanting to crawl into my mother's bed. Here I cringe if someone runs past in the street. I'm lucky. A friend of mine paid the ransom for his father in Sardinia – and then found they had fed his father to the pigs. The pigs eat everything . . . even the bones. The son is a big, grown man, but he weeps when he talks to me about his father.'

If a loved one is snatched by Sardinians it is certainly time to prepare to weep. Their brutality is a byword. In the 1950s the Sardinian and Sicilian Mafias began kidnapping people – or even sheep – to finance restaurants or businesses on the mainland. The Calabrians joined in, too. Soon, these poverty-stricken southerners migrated to Milan and Turin in the rich, bourgeois, industrial north. And to Rome where drugs were all the rage. Kidnapping is easier and far, far more profitable than robbing banks.

Police reports say many of these kidnapping gangs may be linked into a multi-national crime syndicate bossed by a secret 'cabinet' of Goldfingers – small Napoleons of empires so brilliantly run that prisoners can be cached almost indefinitely. These Mafias are unconnected with the Red Brigades and politics, although on occasion the Red Brigades, in need of operational funds, may hire a professional gang to get some. (Moro was kidnapped not for money but to blackmail the Italian Government into releasing imprisoned Red Brigades 'prisoners of the class war'.)

Political terrorists use bullets and bombs. It is not their aim to get rich quickly, but to scare industrialists and capital out of Italy, to bring about the collapse of the economy and the state: to cause anarchy. The Mafias wouldn't want that at all: anyone worth ransoming would have vanished.

This twin-headed threat to life and limb makes for strange political bedfellows. Gianni Agnelli, the head of Italy's great Fiat empire, lives in a building belonging to a billionaire Communist, has bodyguards, flies around in helicopters, and is rumoured to secrete a poison pill in a hollow molar to bite on if the kidnappers close in on him. I am told that Luciano Lama, the boss of the Communist trade unions, moves with cars and bodyguards fore and aft, has guns, electric gates, the lot.

This fortress existence is a bizarre experience. I am invited to stay with a rich family – eminently kidnappable – in the deep country. The drive there in armoured cars is swift and there are no stops. One has a cosy feeling when the electric gates to the estate purr shut behind one. That night, risking the electrical alarm system, I step into the garden and find a huge guard dog staring at me. I stare stupidly back. It whines and slinks behind a tree. At 5.30 a.m. heavy barking begins in the middle distance. I check my bedroom shutters. Later, we go out bicycling in the woods. A young bodyguard, bald and named Vittorio, wobbles along behind us. Later, when other guests are in the sauna, I talk to Vittorio. Under his baldness he has a cheerful moon face, a close-cut beard, a white cardigan over an open shirt. He is twenty-nine, from Turin, an ex-paratrooper with seven years' experience in the Special Service of the Carabinieri. He volunteered for this private job.

Vittorio has an accountant's diploma and has studied law. He is stocky with plump, muscular hands. He is a judo Orange Belt. I ask how his karate is.

'Good enough to kill,' he smiles back.

I ask about the armoured cars.

'You'd need dynamite or a mine to get into one. Perhaps some kind of heavy machine gun might penetrate.' I ask if the bodyguard business has lost glamour since Moro's guards were wiped out. Vittorio registers mild scorn. '*Non erano professionisti. . . .* They were sloppy. First, Moro's car was not armoured. Second, you keep your guns at the ready. Moro's men put them under the seat. They were shot through the windows like clay pigeons.'

(Moro left his home in two cars – his own blue Fiat 130 for himself, his chauffeur of twenty years and one bodyguard; and an Alfa Romeo 130 (Alfetta) for three bodyguards. The fusillade from the gunmen disguised as Alitalia pilots who stepped into the road when a Red Brigades car pulled up in front of Moro's car, and from gunmen behind in three other cars, was devastating. Only one of Moro's bodyguards managed to open a door. He was almost cut in two. A passer-by covered his face with a newspaper. The whole incident lasted a minute.)

I say to Vittorio. 'Dangerous work.'

A grin: 'Better than sitting in a bank all day.'

Vittorio has two guns. From his right hip he pulls a snub-nosed but nicely weighted Smith & Wesson 3.57 Magnum carrying eight expanding bullets. His second gun is a kind of pocket Big Bertha – a long Remington 12-gauge, eight-shot, semi-automatic pump gun, firing large lumps of lead at tremendous velocity. It has no stock: you blast away from the hip.

I say: 'Remove a man's face?'

Vittorio smiles pleasantly. 'Take off his head, you mean. With a few rounds from this I've disintegrated a car.'

Bodyguard agencies are booming. 'If you want a guard,' Vittorio says, 'I'll fix you up for $5 an hour.' Some agencies charge outrageously – $25 an hour. And watch out: 'Some will even shop you to the terrorists.'

Susanna (Suni) Agnelli, the sister of the great Gianni and author of the best-selling story of her early life, *We Always Wore Sailor Suits*, told me once she knows of people who have ten bodyguards – 'an army'. Suni is imperious, tall, fiftyish, with white flowing locks. She has the noble profile of a grand matron of Ancient Rome, giggles and likes to call a spade a spade. 'A lot of women reporters come and ask me to talk about the kidnapping scene. I tell them to get stuffed.'

She was elected mayor, with Communist help, of the coastal resort of Santo Stefano. She is a Republican (Liberal) Member of Parliament. She travels economy class on planes. She is scornful of very, very rich Italians who pack themselves, their children, even their nannies and chauffeurs onto Concorde. 'No wonder they get kidnapped,' she says derisively. There are many, she admits, who pay far too little income tax. A Roman dandy I met, ostentatiously clanking gold bracelets, a gold watch and gold cufflinks, replied, when I asked him if he wasn't scared that someone might pinch all that obvious expensive ornamentation: 'Well, let them. It's easy to replace, my dear.' Such people, Suni Agnelli says, give kidnapping a good name.

Suni Agnelli knows that someone might have a crack at her one day, but I think she is fearless. 'You should go to Milan,' she tells me. 'In Rome we have tourists, the Pope, and fewer rich families. Milan means industry. Ready money – the sort kidnappers like.'

Milan. The golden Madonna on the cathedral watches a Santa Claus in an ill-fitting beard watching schoolchildren kicking the pigeons in the piazza below. By coincidence Mel Brooks's film *High Anxiety (Alta Tensione)* is playing. The first man I meet, a jeweller with handlebar moustaches, says, 'Here everyone is in shock.' A woman eating chocolate mousse at a plush party says, 'My sixteen-year-old son went out yesterday to buy a ski jacket without his bodyguard. I was distraught.' The tension must be catching. I find myself asking if the waiters handing round the drinks are armed. 'Well, I doubt if the actual waiters. . . .' The flat door, I notice, is steel-plated like the inside of a safe. No one at the party stays late.

Tension – and bravery. Next day another rich mother says, 'At first, we sent our kids out to Lausanne. They begged to come back. It's better to face reality despite the armoured cars and the guards. Although one daughter, eighteen, did try to take an overdose of pills.'

The following day the streets are full of yelling left-wing students. Traffic stops. Hefty bus drivers lean frowning on their steering wheels, looking as if they'd like to get a good swipe at those teenage bottoms. Round the corner I hear the crash of plate glass. A white-helmeted traffic cop hares down the street pursued by a knot of youths. But in half an hour life goes on as if such empty ugliness had never been.

I lunch with a twenty-year-old girl who was kidnapped, then rescued by the police after forty-seven days. She tells me she is getting more kidnapping threats on the telephone. Leaving her building is an unpleasant ritual. I wait on the pavement; she stays behind the front door; her friend brings the car to the kerb and releases the special locking device. I look up and down the street. Then I rush with the girl into the car, the locks click back and we speed away.

In a large factory, behind electric gates, guards dressed like Texas Rangers with slavering alsatian dogs. I had coffee with a middle-aged industrialist who had got on quite well with his captors. He identified one of them as Calabrian, another as a Moroccan. They respectfully called him 'Doctor'. When he told them, 'I am terrified, I don't know why. But I am,' they gave him cigarettes and whisky, saying soothingly, 'Take it easy, Doctor. We are thieves, not murderers.' At Christmas they gave him a ball to play with. Even so, they warned him, 'If you see any of us, Doctor, sorry, we shall have to kill you.' And he was kept blindfolded for seventy-one days. All the kidnappees I talked to spoke of the high quality of the food, an indication that crime certainly can pay. These kidnappers ate *foie gras* and caviare. They often produced champagne – particularly to celebrate holidays. (After a ransom payment or just before a release, the atmosphere, I gathered, can become quite jolly.) They explained, 'We're making up for the poverty of our youth, Doctor.' But their youthful poverty had clearly not made these men Socialists or Communists.

On the contrary. A rich, left-wing woman told me in rueful bewilderment that she tried her damnedest to start up a kind of cosy, Socialist workers' seminar by assuring her captors that she understood profoundly how capitalism had driven them to crime. All she got in reply was the obscene Italian gesture that consists in slapping the left bicep with the right hand while jerking upwards a rigid left forearm and clenched fist – 'Up yours, mate!'

The Red Brigades members, who of course *are* political, don't waste time with kidnappings or caviare. They prefer a clean, no-nonsense shot through the heart – or, if you're lucky, through the legs. I met a lucky man. Indro Montenelli, founder and editor of *Il Giornale* of Milan, is able to stand up behind his desk and shake hands, in spite of the four bullets that tore into his thigh and groin as he crossed the Piazza Cavour one morning on his way to work. I found him, sixtyish, in a bottle-green corduroy jacket, his handsome face recognizably that of the young Lieutenant Montenelli in Abyssinia in the 1930s in the photo hanging on the wall of his executive office.

After three weeks in hospital, he went straight back to that office. 'I *could* have given up my crusade against this infantile left-wing violence before they shot me, possibly. Certainly not afterwards. One has a certain sense of dignity. . . .' He is pessimistic and explains why with a quiet intensity. 'Our rabbit-brained politicians have dismantled the state security system, because someone whispered that it contained Fascists. Now we cannot fight terror. We just have to get used to it.'

Mention politics and Montenelli does a good though unconscious impression of Vittorio Gassman. 'Christian Democrats and Communists – all criminals and crooks! Italian political parties are Mafias, not parties. This paper was founded to encourage a strong Centre Party. We failed. We Italians have a real genius for anarchy. Our rule is: don't trust anyone, only your father or your son. Do everything for yourself. A society with a solid national conscience, as in England, doesn't exist here. It's all family here – family and the Mafia.' Leaving for lunch, he stepped into the middle car of three: bodyguards piled into the other two. 'Luckily, Italians are survivors,' he smiled through the bullet-proof window.

A day or two later, in Rome. Pope John Paul II is to lay a wreath in the Piazza di Spagna. I push through the crowd with two tiny, eminently kidnappable girls, pretty in long Alice-in-Wonderland hair and white stockings, who skip excitedly around their mother and grandmother. Vittorio, the bald young bodyguard, follows us. His well-cut grey herringbone overcoat is hanging open over his dark suit. I notice he hooks his right thumb into his trouser pocket so that his hand has only a few centimetres to travel upwards in order to draw the Smith & Wesson on his hip. The Pope appears, large, genial, white hair shining like a halo above the cheering crowd. Vittorio is looking intently at the crowd, not at the Pope. I wonder what on earth will happen if someone starts shooting in this mob.

Presently we leave, packed sweatily into the armoured Fiat. Vittorio in front next to the driver. In a traffic jam – a thing terrorists very much like to catch one in – we are gently bumped from behind. The driver shoots a look into the mirror, swings the Fiat out fast, and we flash like a tadpole through the oncoming traffic and through the gates of the Borghese Gardens.

Then we all relax. The girls happily chat to their housekeeper on the car's emergency telephone. 'We saw the Pope up close . . . *molto bene* . . . *si* . . . *ciaò, Giovanna.*' Vittorio hangs the receiver back on its cradle. He reminds me, in his gentle, heavy concern for the children, of Nana, the dog-nanny in *Peter Pan*.

It is difficult for an outsider to judge the strain of this life. It is based on strict rules. To break them may cost you your life. Imagine it. If you see a strange face by your door, you don't go home. You keep in constant touch with friends. You never take the same route to work. You look out of the window before going into the street. In the car, you keep your eye on the mirror. Will your children return from school today?

What can be done? Efforts to lock up the assets of people who want to ransom their loved one and so deprive the kidnappers of their motive do not seem to work. Desperate people will find money *somewhere*. Oddly, no one seems to be urging the death penalty. Most think prison sentences are outrageously light, which they are. The best solution seems to lie in unifying and modernizing Italy's police; better police pay; harder sentences; international exchanges of data on terrorism. As for the political terrorists, hundreds are in jail today. Many are bourgeois intellectuals who seem far nearer the Khmer Rouges of Pol Pot's Kampuchea than the stodgy Italian Communist Party. Their empty anarchism repels the workers. They are not likely to give up yet. But they are not succeeding in their objective of dismantling the state.

Whether to be rich is good or bad, there are brave people in Italy. As beautiful Anna told me, half-laughing: 'I take my children to school – alone. I go to my office – *alone*. I don't want to live in my own country as a guarded recluse. I live a normal life. I am very scared.'

'Will Those Argies Come Back?'

12 DECEMBER 1982

There was no Task Force to accompany us to the Falklands. We were content with three albatrosses, and several birds which the second officer described dubiously as dusky fulmars.

Eleven days of South Atlantic swell and 3000 miles out of St Helena island, the little Royal Mail ship *St Helena* – whose modest owners, Curnow Shipping, of Porthleven, Cornwall, might have been designated by an early American advertiser 'the greatest little shipping line in the West' – dropped anchor in Stanley harbour, bringing a good deal of cargo, beer, seventy-five British servicemen and myself to the islands which the Argies surrendered six months ago this Tuesday.

As we slid through the narrow entrance to Stanley harbour, the second mate, Jeff Pearce, a Cornishman, was on the bridge singing, 'I 'ad 'er, I did (it cost me a quid), goin' up Camborne Hill, comin' down.' However hard the next four months' work to build a better and Argie-proof Falklands is going to prove for these new arrivals from Britain, we had a light-hearted landfall.

But it happens that the islands are going through a continuing period of tension and excitement. Their future – in the form of £31 million to be spent by the British Government on agriculture, roads and other projects recommended by Lord Shackleton in his report last September – is very much in islanders' minds at this moment. And for new arrivals, there is excitement of another kind in the amazing scene in Stanley harbour. A narrow sheet of water bordering a small, low township like an English seaside village is dwarfed by four seemingly immense ferries and passenger vessels which dominate this diminutive place as the *QE2* would dominate, say, Cardiff. On the surrounding yellow-green headlands are protective missiles. Above, the racket of continuously shuttling Sea King, double-rotored Chinook, tiny Rowdy Scout and Wasp helicopters, and the occasional Harrier or Phantom jet. At lower levels, the largest and cruellest-looking gulls I've ever seen squawk and glare like the guardian spirits of the islands. Luckily the wind is sharp but not very cold; the long johns I wore on Cape Horn in August stay in my bag.

Are the islanders reacting badly to this military hubbub – the trucks, the wandering soldiers, the speeding jeeps? A stroll down Stanley's narrow streets – badly chewed up by military traffic – gives an almost instant answer. Outside Victorian façades of Jubilee villas, the post office, the garden gates of two-storey dwellings with names like 'Sparrowhawk House', island man and women unfailingly smile and say 'Good day' or 'How do'. Smiling, they help you in shops, smiling, they invite you home and make you tea. Where, I began to wonder, is the islanders' alleged rage against all this? I'd read British newspaper reports from Stanley of a grudging, surly acceptance by the islanders of the British military. Well, where is all this resentment? It seems important to know this, considering the number of servicemen who are here to stay – about 4000 of them. Important too, in the light of the envisaged developments over the next six years.

The islanders I probed for the answer were fiercely forthright. 'Tripe!' snapped Graham Bound, the blunt-speaking editor of the island's newspaper, the *Penguin News*. 'That thing about the islanders' sullen resentment against the British forces – tripe. Relations with the forces are very good. I'm sick and tired of people from Britain coming here saying things are in a mess. That shops have put up their prices to cheat the troops. That Des King at the Upland Goose Hotel has put his prices up to £20 a night for the troops when we all know that his prices are unchanged for two years. It's lies, bloody lies.'

Strong words, but not isolated ones.

A sheep farmer from Bluff Cove, a former lawyer from London, Kevin Kilmartin, said, 'That resentment, it's the jaundiced view of journalists rather than of the people here,' and a young Californian artist, Duffy Sheridan, added, 'The British Government has to maintain troops here to protect the islanders. People realize that and accept them. And they are happy to do so.'

Dire prediction after the war that local girls would inevitably be raped by sex-starved troops are similarly dismissed. All agree that the soldiery has, so far, behaved admirably despite the lack of 'suitable entertainment'. Take the town's librarian, an ex-headmaster, unlikely to condone untoward military goings-on: 'I've heard nothing of that sort,' he assured me. 'And I would certainly have heard in this place where, if someone at one end of the town should only breathe once and he breathes twice, everyone at the other end knows about it in a flash.'

Confirming this, other islanders point out the fact that most families in Stanley are willingly boarding two or three servicemen – despite their small houses and the children to look after. It is not compulsory to do so. Nor is it a way to get rich.

Again, a few months ago it was said that disgusted Stanleyites wanted to move the capital from Stanley to a site farther north, away from the noisy military and the ubiquitous mines scattered by the fleeing invaders. I've met no one who takes that suggestion seriously. The mines and booby traps were, of course, a major menace, but today they are not scaring islanders away from the capital or the islands.

'The mines, though thick in places, are under control, I think,' Kilmartin says. 'Beaches are still out of bounds. But people adapt. You get used to not going to certain places.'

I found Major John Quin, the bulky, genial commander of the Royal Engineers bomb disposal squadron, surrounded like a museum curator by shelves of the devices he's retrieved. Some 27,000 have already been exploded – 155 mm shells, anti-tank and anti-aircraft missiles, grenades. 'Our Number One problem was to stop the kids picking things up. So we displayed all these horrors in the schools and we enrolled kids who reported suspicious objects as "deputy bomb disposaleers" and encouraged them with highly coloured certificates and badges.' The certificates included a solemn promise Not to Touch – only report to Quin. Contrary to early fears, not a single child or adult civilian has been injured by such infernal machines. 'Stanley is as clear now as any part of the UK,' Quin told me. Only a very confident man could say that.

Clearing mines is something else, however. Major John Baker and his stocky Gurkha Engineers have lost one man killed by a Sam 7 missile, and three others were wounded by a booby trap on a hillside the day I arrived. (The one Gurkha is the only mine death.) I visited two of the wounded Gurkhas in their hospital beds surrounded by flamboyant 'get-well' cards from British soldier friends and watching a sugary Indian video love story in Hindi. 'Go back to our unit soon,' they said to me happily.

Minefields are being plotted and fenced off; this will be completed in two months. The actual exploding of the mines may take two years or so. Thus, certain hills round Stanley will be unapproachable for that time. This too the islanders have accepted. But today, across by far the greater part of the sprawling Falklands hillsides, sheep may safely graze and men may safely walk.

Echoes of that astounding time – the Argie occupation – hang about the islanders, for whom, one of them tells me, it all seems as unreal as a fantastic film, once seen, never forgotten. Don Bonner is the Governor's major-domo and driver of the red London taxi that is Sir Rex Hunt's official car in toy town. Bonner recalls General Menendez, the

Argentine commander, strolling through the downstairs corridor where disapproving portraits of the British royal family from Queen Victoria to Prince Charles stared down on this uniformed intruder, standing pensively under the well-lit, full-length portrait of Queen Elizabeth II, and murmuring: 'What a fine family. So much respected.'

The Argentine staff officers ate off china stamped with the royal cypher. It was the young soldiers who went hungry. Bonner remembers the pathetic private who moaned, 'I want to go home to mother' (the conscripts from school spoke some English). He had lost a brother in Bluff Cove, he said, and his father had 'gone down, glug glug, in the cruiser *General Belgrano*'. Later Bonner found this young soldier dead from shell blast in a shed in the garden.

A macabre touch. An islander in Stanley's post office says that letters still arrive from Argentina, sent by parents of missing soldier sons they think – they hope – may be in the Falklands. But there are no living Argentines here. There are dead ones, however – and a living scandal to be laid at the door of the Government of Argentina. New bodies are discovered continually by British soldiers searching for mines on the hillsides. The British want to return the bodies for proper burial in Argentina. Yet every attempt to arrange this meets with a dusty answer from Buenos Aires. Presumably the generals there don't want to stir their compatriots' emotions any further.

I wandered about the Stanley cemetery with Monsignor Sproggan, the Catholic priest here, a Geordie who had buried some of the Argentine dead at ceasefire time. 'We had an Argie padre here and some prisoners to help and it was done most properly. A Welsh Guards bugler sounded Last Post and Reveille. After the ceremony the Argies came up to me and said, "*Muchas gracias*".'

Simple wooden crosses litter the area of the cemetery nearest the petrol dump. I read some names. 'Carlos Alberto Benites . . . Roméro Raul'. A plastic flower lay on each grave, and usually a rosary was entwined round the cross. Some graves were more like collapsed trenches – a muddle of stones and mud, no names, no crosses. Bluebottles buzzed around these crude graves dug in haste by their beleaguered comrades. These bodies could be returned to their next-of-kin if only the word came from Argentina. Otherwise they will be reburied here in new war cemeteries. There will be many crosses marked 'Unknown Argentine Soldier'.

The Army Air Corps flew me to West Falkland. At Chartres, Bill and Pat Luxton, the only islanders to be expelled by the invaders, own

150,000 acres of sheep grazing. This is not an exceptional acreage in the Falklands. Here farming is a feudally organized business. It has also been stagnant for a hundred years. It needs new blood and the enthusiasm for work that ownership inspires. Luxton's father farmed Chartres before him, and his grandfather before that. You might think he has every reason to resist land reform. Not a bit of it. Luxton says: 'This farm's too big for us. I'd like 8000 sheep here on 25,000 acres.' Speaking of the Shackleton report, he adds: 'The end was in sight for the old life anyway.'

I also found young and middle-aged farmworkers in favour of land reform – many want to buy and farm their own land. So are people in Stanley in favour of it. So is Sir Rex Hunt. He heard the news of the British Government's pledge of aid for the Falklands late on Wednesday afternoon – at the time I was watching him standing on his head in his full-dress uniform for the amusement of some island children, although this ebullience was not directly linked to Mr Francis Pym's statement.

Later he told me: 'I am delighted. That the British Government has committed itself to paying out £31 million should reassure the islanders a good deal. It means we'll be able to implement most of Shackleton's recommendations.'

But though Shackleton, give or take a few of his suggestions, obviously embodies most island aspirations, there was a certain dismay that the Foreign Secretary's announcement ignored a cardinal recommendation in the report, something paramount in any consideration of the future of the islands. This is that the British Government should buy up all farms owned by absentee landlords – and by the Falkland Islands Company – as a first step towards resale to islanders or 'suitable outsiders'. Many islanders see Mrs Thatcher's silence on this point as a dismal sign that, because of doctrinal Tory opposition to Government takeovers, she cannot and will not act on this recommendation, one that is most dear to Falkland hearts and minds. It is on this point that resentment could flourish.

Graham Bound and others here were once reported as feeling dismay at Rex Hunt's return to the Falklands after the Argentine surrender. Last week Bound told me, 'I think now that Hunt is absolutely the right man for the job.' Bound goes much further than most other islanders in wanting, I think, an independent island (though how this is possible now with such financial dependence on Britain, heaven knows). Still, others would like to have greater participation at the top by the islanders and they may well get it. Hunt is a man who knows the islands intimately, and the islanders know he is accessible and that he listens.

Nevertheless, when the people of the Falklands read the British press and listen to the politicians, anxiety creeps up on them. They have seen suggestions concerning United Nations trusteeships, and judge such things to be betrayals. They've seen offensive proposals to pay every family here a whacking sum of money to go somewhere else, as if they could be bribed out of what they consider to be their homeland. To this suggestion, an islander said to me: 'How can you justify going to war, if then you pay the people whose rights you died for to get lost?'

At any rate, Kevin Kilmartin believes that 'people are more Falkland islanders than ever: "This is ours," they say. No one I know wants to leave.'

And in Chartres, one of Bill Luxton's older men – a Hampshire man out here for thirty years, who has only been to Stanley four times in his life – stood with me looking up at the long chain of hills, the 50,000 acres that Luxton has leased to the British military as a firing range for £1 a year ('the cheapest training ground in the world'). 'Oh, no, I'd never leave. Isn't it peaceful? We had some of them Gurkhas living in our house, the wife and I. Never fighting each other, always clean and smiling. We'd like some more British troops out here.' A pause. 'Do you think those Argies will come back? Will the British Government give us up, do you think?'

It's waiting for the answer that has given the friendly Falkland islanders the new sort of drama, the almost palpable tension, with which they live now.

The Condemned Playground

A report from a Crown Colony in crisis.

HONG KONG, 2 NOVEMBER 1983

Typhoon rain has covered Hong Kong like a funereal veil. Is it a sign from above? Ten days ago, a bad hailstorm told superstitious Chinese that some disaster was near, and soon, like a k.o.'d boxer, the Hong Kong dollar slid to the floor – 40 per cent down on a year ago, over 10 per cent down in twenty-four hours. 'My God!' an American Old China Hand said to his tenth gin and tonic at the Foreign Correspondents' Club. 'It's like the fall of Shanghai.'

The analogy with Shanghai in 1949, when the Communists came in, is dubious. But conscious of the peril implicit in the stalemate between Britain and China in their talks over Hong Kong's future, there is now a very grave, almost palpable, unease here, verging on panic. Hong Kong's British and 5.6 million Chinese feel they are reliving the last hours of the *Titanic*. Things are as bad as that. That the Chinese will take Hong Kong back in 1997 is not in question any more. What this population, largely formed of refugees from Chinese Communism, worry about is whether Mrs Thatcher and China's leader, Mr Deng Xiao-ping, can agree on the form of post-1997 Hong Kong, and Britain's role in it, if any. If they fail to agree very soon, according to bankers and businessmen here, confidence in Hong Kong as a viable international centre of commerce and finance will fail, and this place of gleaming promise will very swiftly become a ghost city, a desert. To avoid this, these people say, Britain and China must work something out very soon.

Confidence is the nub. Mrs Thatcher wants to retain a British presence – perhaps a Vice-Governor – in Hong Kong after 1997 to make sure China adheres to undertakings to allow the combination of capitalistic practices and the basic freedoms – including that of the judiciary. 'Nonsense!' retort the Chinese. 'What's all the fuss? We have as much interest in capitalism flourishing here as anyone. Hong Kong's lifestyle is assured. But let's have no more colonialist talk of a British presence. A few British advisers is as much as we'll allow after 1997.' Then the sinister words: 'If they behave themselves.'

Minds are not meeting. According to Peking, Hong Kong Chinese will run the newly 'liberated' territory. Chinese representatives here

91

make distinctions between 'patriotic' Hong Kong people and 'non-patriotic' people. Guess who they believe the real Hong Kong people to be. Unrealists abound. Mrs Thatcher speaks of her moral obligation to the people of Hong Kong, although there is no question of self-determination here. This is not a democracy. The Chinese have the final say: 'If there's no agreement on our terms, we realize Hong Kong will be reduced to an urban desert. Too bad for all of us. But at least it will be *our* desert.' That may be a huffing and puffing ploy for negotiating purposes. But they are chilling words.

The British are silent. Behind a principle of 'confidentiality' they say nothing. This in itself swells the general unease. 'For God's sake say something, even if it's only goodbye,' is the prayer to Mrs Thatcher and Governor Youde. And the alarming thought intrudes: maybe they've got nothing good to say. The Governor himself, in any case, is a man so self-effacing that it might be said that when he leaves a room it seems as if someone has come in.

Hong Kong is not one city, like London or Paris. There is, for example, the European Hong Kong – rich, some would say filthy rich. Its gold, silver and ivory high-rise offices and flats climb up from the harbour's edge like imperial dragons' teeth. That is where the billions of dollars are. The sun washes over the snouts of Porsches, Mercedes and pink and yellow Rolls-Royces in the parking bays (a good number belong, admittedly, to ultra-wealthy Chinese). Filipino servants polish the silver. In the harbour are the yachts, in the streets the absurdly inappropriate Savile Row suits and the booming accents from Bromley and Weybridge. Here, you can smell the profits and the dividends – although less so now that the outrageous property boom has collapsed, and rich sharks, with no other commitment to Hong Kong than to milk dollars out of it, have begun to cut and run. It is very British, this Hong Kong; very un-Chinese, and very conservative. You meet people at parties who say perish the thought that they should ever return to 'the UK'. They say: 'Tony Benn will be our first Communist Prime Minister in a few years.' Although Maggie's their woman, if they leave Hong Kong it will be for somewhere like the Algarve.

If Hong Kong does collapse for lack of trust in Peking's word, what of this lavish world? It strikes me, as I contemplate this lotusland of lolly, feasting and fun that I may well be looking at – with acknowledgements to Cyril Connolly's famous book – a condemned playground. It is the voice of rich high-rise Hong Kong that, in the main, will be heeded by Mrs Thatcher, and even Deng Xiao-ping.

After all, if the businessmen go away, the international business goes away too. Probably most British businessmen spend years here without once saying hello to a Chinese – except perhaps to Sir Somebody Somebody at the Jockey Club.

In a way, the Chinese of Hong Kong are the invisible men. Imagine their plight in this crisis. Many have been refugees before. Many have swum from the mainland, risking the sharks, to escape what now is unavoidably closing in on them again – a Communist regime. A quarter of all the Chinese in their twenties arrived here in the past few years. They don't like the British. My friend Sergeant Lim of the Royal Hong Kong Police is blunt about it: 'We hate the British for many historical reasons.' Yet at the individual level Chinese are warm and very friendly. I have never experienced the slightest personal hostility here, even in the sleaziest back streets.

An incident last week is illuminating. A film from Peking has been packing Chinese audiences in at four cinemas in Hong Kong and Kowloon. Called *The Burning of the Summer Palace*, it showed in gory detail British nineteenth-century invaders massacring and mutilating Chinese of both sexes and all ages. British firing squads mowed down Chinese by the score – too slowly for the British general, who ordered, 'Use artillery!' The packed audience sat mute. No one cheered or shouted in outrage. No one jostled me going out. Evidently it was just an historical film to the Hong Kong Chinese – and made in Peking at that. The Hong Kong authorities had hesitated to let the film in – they need not have worried. I sat through it with my Chinese friends Wei Kuen and Ah Po and their wives. They live in dim flats about half the size of the top of a London bus, and all work in factories here. From time to time during the film they nudged me, grinning and whispering 'English! English!' That was all. Our friendship remains intact.

Wei Kuen's concern for his penurious future is nothing to do with democracy and voting. He and Ah Po have no vote under the British here anyway. But their wives are from Shanghai – I met them there last year – and the freedom they cherish here is the freedom to work overtime, to earn more money, to spend that extra money on better clothes, a good school, the cinema, and to be able to save for their children's future. And perhaps to travel – some time. An older friend of theirs whom I met in Shanghai, and again here, suffered whipping and a terrifying humiliation during the cultural revolution before getting out. He says: 'In Hong Kong you can have tea houses, restaurants. In Shanghai there's nothing to do. So boring. I like to read – you can't get many books there. And Communists always interfere. How beautiful and calm Shanghai would be without them.'

There are many people here, rich and poor, who know by experience what he means. 'We are patriotic Chinese,' they say, 'but we don't want a Communist society. Why else are so many of us here?' Quite simply, these people are trapped. They have no money or passports. They have nowhere to go. Even Sergeant Lim is denied a British passport (only 10,000 Hong Kongers have them), although he serves the Queen in a dangerous job. The rich, naturally, will buy their way out: the great poor majority must stay. At a Chinese banquet in Kowloon last week, Lim suddenly burst out in anguish: 'For God's sake, get me out of this bloody colony!' Ah Po said: 'In our factory, no man wants any change.' But Lim cannot get out, and the change is coming, whatever Ah Po and his workmates want.

Of course, Peking's representatives try to allay these fears. Over oysters at the Foreign Correspondents' Club – under blown-up photographs of Vietnamese suffering in the Indo-Chinese War – two of them produced a reassuring list of good intentions. There would be no Communist cadres from Peking running things in post-1997 Hong Kong, they said. A Hong Kong Chinese would be the Governor: perhaps not even a Communist. The colony would be granted 'special administrative and economic status' within China. Capitalism could carry on regardless. There could even be horse-racing, mahjong and . . . yes, girls. More still, freedom of the judiciary would be guaranteed, and the freedoms of speech and the press. 'We would even allow a Taiwanese newspaper.' I asked about a possible forcible takeover of Hong Kong by the Chinese Army, if things went badly. That was not, I was told, on the cards – (pause) – for the time being. Further to emphasize their goodwill, the Chinese representatives stress Peking's aid to Hong Kong over the past several years. Peking supplied much-needed oil in the oil crisis of 1973. China provides fresh water, pigs, fish, rice – and, not least, 91 per cent of Hong Kong's toilet paper. All this is true.

The trouble is that, while the Chinese urgently press their promises to respect their own solemn undertakings, few think that these promises are enough. International businessmen are a canny lot. They say they need a tangible guarantee – some sort of British or international presence here after 1997. China says no. This central fact is delaying an agreement – even perhaps making an agreement forever impossible. Yet the short-term agreement is vital to restore and maintain confidence in Hong Kong today, as well as to tide things over until 1997. If such an agreement is not reached within a year, the business community says: 'The whole thing will slide down the tube.'

That is the short term. The long term has its own set of snags. A major one is that, even if Mrs Thatcher and Mr Deng agree, exchange loving toasts at a banquet in Peking, and all seems set fair, 1997 is still a long way off. Mr Deng, for all the reports of his daily 10,000-pace walks, is eighty years old. Even the indomitable Mrs Thatcher is unlikely to be Prime Minister in 1997. New people will be in control. Who can say if they will honour the agreement they didn't sign?

And sceptics have yet another strong card to play. The Chinese, they say, promise freedom of speech, assembly and the press for Hong Kong, but all those freedoms, although they are written into the constitution of China, are in practice ignored there. To this, the Chinese eating oysters with me at the Foreign Correspondents' Club replied that, in effect, times (and China's thinking) have changed. Hong Kong, they repeat, is a special case – it is as much in China's interest as Britain's that Hong Kong flourishes after 1997, and because the Chinese are intelligent enough to see that liberal government is the *sine qua non* of prosperity, liberal government is what Hong Kong will get, and once again, after this, comes the reminder that, if China's word on this is not accepted, rather than give way to bullying China will take over an urban desert.

If negotiations do fail in the next few months, what vision of the collapse of Hong Kong, the profiteers' playground, leaps up to appal the eye? It would be swift. ('We have seen, with last week's lightning fall of the Hong Kong dollar, just how swift,' a banker told me.) Business would disappear, and with it jobs and money. There could be workless thousands rioting and looting, and a destitute Government no longer governing. The police force would disintegrate. The Europeans, of course, would leave *en masse*. The Chinese would be obliged to cower helpless, jobless and fearful – or to scramble to greet the advancing Chinese People's Liberation Army and grovel for positions in the Socialist administration. Thousands of the rest of the 5.6 million could turn into a new wave of boat people, but such a wave as might make the Vietnamese exodus look like a ripple on the surface of the South China Sea. Who would suffer? Not Britain: the Foreign Office tells us we get very little out of Hong Kong beyond the landing rights at Kai Tak airport – about £100 million a year. China could survive, too, of course, and the rich British and Chinese of Hong Kong would have followed their money to London, San Francisco, Los Angeles and Sydney. The sufferers would be, as always, Wei Kuen and Ah Po and their families, waiting with their goldfish bowls and TV sets in their tiny flats. And policeman Lim, pensionless, at the mercy of the people from across the border whom he now thinks of as 'rubbish'.

Of course, it may not come to this. 'Surely, in 1983, statesmen are big enough and strong enough to agree on things like this?' someone said this week. But even in 1983 it is still easy to underestimate the brutal persistence of utopian ideologies, and the stultifying import-ance which politicians attach to saving national 'face'.

Marshes on My Mind

22 MAY 1977

I wish all young people who long for adventure could have the luck that made me pick up that old London newspaper in 1952. (It was covered with lizard droppings, I remember.) 'When the moon has waxed and waned thrice,' an article said, 'the great Arabian explorer, Wilfred Thesiger, will paddle his canoe to the two lone palm trees on the Tigris. There, under the Mesopotamian stars he will find two faithful Marsh Arab tribesmen awaiting. . . .' The article gushed along in that vein. And suddenly a thought exploded in my mind: 'My God, this is where my life will change!' I had picked up the paper, by chance, from a pile on the floor as I slumped gasping in the humid heat of a jerry-built bungalow I shared with two other shipping clerks in Basra, the Iraqi river port at the head of the Arabian Gulf.

The newspaper was running a series on Great New Elizabethans: Wilfred Thesiger was Number IX, I think. I had heard of Thesiger. He was a famous name to Arabists, even then, long before *Arabian Sands*, his classic book of desert exploration, appeared. The last of the great explorers of the region – there is nothing left to explore in today's Arabia of Cadillacs and oil sheikhs – he is one of only three Europeans to have crossed the vast Empty Quarter (the sand seas of southern Arabia) on foot and camel; and *he* chose to cross it twice. During the war, he raided behind the German lines in Libya with the Special Air

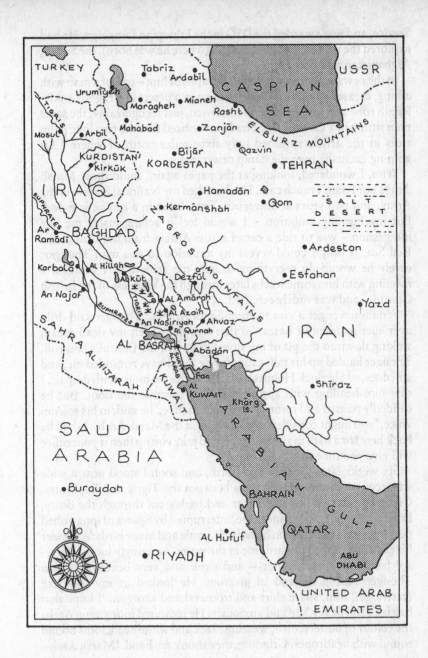

Service, and was awarded the DSO in the Ethiopian campaign. He had explored the wildest parts of Ethiopia (where he was born), the Sudan, Afghanistan and Persia.

In the newspaper I saw two photographs of him – one of a man with a long, creased, sunburnt face, standing in a desert in a ragged ankle-length robe and turban; the other showed, just recognizably, the same man sitting in a Chelsea flat. I had also noticed that the two lone palm trees in the article sprouted only sixty miles north of where I sat gulping excitedly over the damp newsprint.

Who, I wondered, looking at the paper again, could those Marsh Arabs be? I didn't much care. I had finished my National Service in the Army, and two years at university. True, I was in a romantic mood. But my burning ambition – I would feel it aching inside me like indigestion – was to ride a camel across Arabia from the Gulf to the Red Sea. If only I could reveal my ambition to this man Thesiger, surely he would do everything to help me achieve it. I wangled a meeting with him some weeks later through the kindness of the British Consul – and was rudely rebuffed.

'You'll never get a visa to enter Saudi Arabia,' Thesiger said drily over suet pudding in Basra. So that was that; I felt my dead dream sinking down to the pit of my stomach to join the Consul's jam roll. Thesiger hauled up his tall, gaunt frame (he always reminded me, and still does, of Sherlock Holmes) and, through eyes moist with despair, I saw him heading with apparent finality towards the door. But he suddenly paused and turned. 'As an alternative,' he said, in his solemn voice, 'you might consider having a look at the Marsh Arabs. I shall be back here for a bath in six weeks. I could take you up then if your office will give you time off.'

Six weeks later I took a taxi north, and soon I stood near a wide watercourse in the great flatness between the Tigris and Euphrates. Green swathes of rice and sugar and barley cut through the dusty, brown Mesopotamian landscape, interrupted by figures of long-robed people, one or two men on horseback, cattle and many birds. A slender black canoe dipped towards me in the water, amazingly long – thirty-six feet, I discovered later – and sleek and very beautiful. I saw Thesiger raising a hand in greeting. He looked at my tiny bag (cartridges, film, spare shirt and trousers) and shotgun. 'I hope that bag isn't too heavy,' he said anxiously. He indicated four young Arabs the colour of butterscotch, wearing black and white headcloths bound round with headropes. Grinning, they shook my hand. 'Marsh Arabs.

They'll look after you,' said Thesiger. 'Step in the centre of the boat or you'll have it over.' I sat cross-legged and too terrified to move in the flat bottom of this work of art, this wonderful boat, so delicately balanced and so low in the water that it seemed bound to capsize. The four Arabs plunged their paddles in unison into the pale brown stream, and we shot away.

That first night we slept on the edge of the Marshes in a house I could never have imagined. It loomed large, golden and quite alone on a fork of the waterway; built entirely of reeds – a great hump-backed reed house like a reed church. Men wearing bandoliers, men with bolt-action rifles, and some in gold-fringed cloaks took in our bags through a high arched entrance. The curving reed columns of the house – it was the guest house of a sheikh – were turning honey-coloured in the afternoon sun. On the water's edge, black and white kingfishers dived from willow branches after fish. 'The Marshes are just over there,' said Thesiger. I couldn't see the first reed beds; they were a little too far away. But, at the age of twenty-two, I felt plainly enough that this was the beginning of a high adventure. I forgot about the camel and the desert there and then.

Next morning, we reached the Marshes proper. Our water channel frayed out into a deep water, and a palisade of twenty-foot-high reeds stretching as far as the eye could see closed behind us like towering, soundproof screens. Like Alice in Wonderland, we had plunged into another world. It was a world to be lost in. I liked that.

During the next week, Thesiger told me about the Marsh Arabs and their history. In the beginning, 5000 or more years ago, the Tigris–Euphrates basin begat ancient Sumer. The Sumerians invented writing, and without doubt were among the most gifted people the world has seen. They lived in the long, narrow stretch of watered land between Baghdad and the Marshes, which in those days tapered off directly into the 'Sea of the Rising Sun', as the Sumerians called the Gulf. Not even the Nile Valley and the plains of Greece left treasures more dazzling than the ones unearthed by archaeologists – including such famous Britons as Sir Leonard Woolley, and, in our day, Sir Max Mallowan (Agatha Christie's husband) – in Mesopotamian cities such as Ur, Uruk, Nippur and Eridu. The original story of the Flood came from ancient Sumer, where the Marsh Arabs now are: it was written out in a great epic poem 1500 years before Homer. And the Creation, according to the Sumerians, came about when their great god, Enlil, 'built a reed platform on the surface of the waters', just as the

Marshman does today. The great civilization of the Sumerians threw up city states on the dry land around the Marshes. But their cylinder seals, stone vases and bowls show that the brilliance of the Sumerians was not matched by their looks. They were generally potato-faced, stocky and thick-necked, with protuberant noses and large round eyes.

A Sumerian – or a Babylonian – could probably be transported without too much shock to his nervous system into the Marshes of today. The panorama of rivers, reeds, date palms is the same now as then. Plonked down, for instance, into a high-prowed Marsh Arab canoe, or onto the threshold of a reed house completed last week, he would be at home. Sir Leonard Woolley found the silver replica of such a canoe in the ruins of Ur. You can see it in the superb museum in Baghdad; it is thousands of years old.

This February day in 1952, the canoe men sped our boat along at a tremendous pace with deft and gentle strokes. We burst out of reed forests into dazzling sunlit lagoons. We saw Marshmen in the prows of other canoes of the same immemorial design, bending against the curve of reed puntpoles or poised with their fishing spears. Others seemed dressed for the warpath; clutching World War I Lee-Enfield rifles and with daggers in their belts, they paddled fast and strong with a grim, preoccupied air. The larger war canoes carried twelve fully armed men.

We stayed in humble Marsh villages with no special food, no boiled water, not even insect repellant (the fleas and mosquitoes made the most of that), because Thesiger believed that such artificial aids to comfort made breaking down barriers of race and upbringing that much harder. The beauty of the place was hypnotic. Snow-white pelicans fished the lagoons, clusters of storks arced overhead; there was always at least one eagle in the sky. The reeds we passed through trembled or crashed with hidden wildlife: otters (my friend the late Gavin Maxwell, author of *Ring of Bright Water*, found his famous otter Mijbil here), herons, purple gallinule, and the huge and dangerous wild pigs.

I had been thrown into this natural paradise by a chance newspaper cutting. Spiritually, I haven't cut adrift from it yet. This first, early 1950s' part of the adventure lasted about two years. The second started when I returned there in 1973 on a voyage of rediscovery after an absence of twenty years; there is a good deal about that in *Return to the Marshes*, the book that brings my adventures there up-to-date.

Soon after that first week with Thesiger I chucked up my job in the Basra shipping office. I had to – I could think of nothing but the Marshes and the friendly, if wary, people living in that almost lost world, in hard, raw, but vivid surroundings. After a time I mastered enough of the local Arabic dialect to get on well enough without having to travel with Thesiger. A Marsh sheikh gave me a canoe almost as fine as Thesiger's. I took on a Marsh Arab crew of my own: Ajram, Hafadh, Hasan, Chethir. They were all strong as acrobats, zestful and alert; full of humour, some of it ribald; full of mischief held in check by their tribesman's sense of what is fitting. They owned little beside the clothes they wore and the daggers in their belts. In a sheikh's house, they could behave with as much dignity as if they were sons of sheikhs themselves. They were brilliant boatmen – after all, they had 5000 years of experience. They were the descendants of those untamed people who had preyed on the sumptuous caravans of Ancient Greeks, Persians and Turks.

There were no doctors in those days; certainly no clinics, still less hospitals within easy reach. We carried medicines to repay the extraordinary, automatic hospitality of poor people: there were diseases galore. And blood feuds and tribal vendettas sometimes splintered the quiet of it all with fusillades of bullets. So, because there were a score or more of largish tribes, it was important to keep track of their alliances and enmities.

The Marshes cover about 60,000 square miles. And the thousands of Marsh tribesmen lived off the reeds (to make houses, and mats for sale), their water buffaloes (for their milk), and by fishing the lagoons with their five-pronged spearheads mounted on six-foot-long reed stems. Some cultivated rice. Each house in a village perched on its own tiny island; to visit a neighbour you needed a canoe. There is no dry land in the Marshes, although huge floating islands of tangled vegetation could seem like land.

We travelled continuously, getting to know the extent of the Marshes and the way of life of its unusual people. It was a sort of paradise; but it was not – thank God – a blandly perfect place. Its occasional acute alarums and discomforts kept one's senses alert. The climate varied amazingly. In the extreme heat of summer, when you felt you were breathing damp air from a steam bath, people let up flaps in the house sides to encourage the breeze; but often there was no breeze. Of the birds, only the herons and cormorants stayed. In winter the duck and geese, greylag or white-front, swirled down from Siberia.

It was nearly always English-summer perfect. Usually the mornings were diamond-sharp, but sometimes sudden gales struck down from the mountains of Kurdistan and Pusht-i-Kuh. Instantly, the Marshes disappeared in a raging, icy whirlwind. If you were caught in a canoe in the middle of a lagoon, you would almost surely be capsized and drowned.

Apart from doctoring, we did the Marsh Arabs a favour by shooting the wild pigs that attacked them and ate their rice. They were enormous beasts, as big as donkeys, measuring three or four feet at the shoulder, and as numerous as rats in a farmyard. Sumerian carvings show men hunting them with nothing but spears – a fearful risk of being smashed down into the mud and then either rolled on and savagely bitten (by a sow) or ripped up the belly by a boar's razor-sharp tusks. I see them in my mind's eye – shaggy hulks galloping through walls of spray; the dark shapes forty yards away raising their snouts and sickle tusks and wheeling head-on to charge; the obscene weight of a sprawling boar, suddenly revealed at one's feet in high reeds, the split-second terror of him, the end of terror as boar and gun sight spring up simultaneously and the high-velocity bullets smother his charge just in time. Many people in the Marshes have been killed by pigs; many more have been crippled or scarred by them.

The ancient Assyrian kings hunted lions on the Marshes' edge, and Sir Henry Layard, the excavator of Nimrud and Nineveh, saw Arabs shooting them with matchlocks. But they disappeared shortly before World War I. By then, the Marsh Arabs had probably assimilated some Babylonian, Greek, Mongol and Persian blood. Muslim warriors of the Arabian desert had installed themselves and their language in Iraq. There were now many more straight Arab noses and finer features round the Marsh Arabs' evening fires (every European who passed through the region from the sixteenth century on raved about the beauty of Marsh women). Desert Arab codes of conduct and battle took hold. In 1915, the British and Indian troops of Generals Maude and Gorringe advancing against the Turks upon the Tigris and Euphrates respectively took a battering from the tribes en route.

I returned 'home' from each long expedition round the Marshes to the village houses of Ajram, Hafadh, Chethir or Hasan and their families, and sometimes to the house belonging to Amara, a friend of Thesiger's. Weddings, funerals, marriages, deaths and a variety of adventures enlivened succeeding months. Then, I moved on; sadly, but one couldn't spend all one's life in the Marshes. Phase One was over.

The farewells were not easy. 'I'll come back soon,' I said, and handed over my gun to Hafadh as a present.

But I did not go back soon. The revolution in Baghdad came two years later, and from 1958 to the early 1970s travel to the Marshes was impossible. None the less, their memory haunted me. And when, in 1973, I could go there again, I went – despite warnings that going back to places one has loved is one of life's great mistakes. On the road south from Baghdad my nerve almost failed me. I thought: after nearly twenty years all my friends may have emigrated to the towns or died; the Marshes may be drained. I knew the sheikhs had gone and that the house in which we had slept on the first night out in 1952 was no more.

But that evening, amazingly, I found myself sitting round a fire with an astonished Amara – his house on the edge of the Marshes proper was nearest – and an excited crowd of old friends. We talked and talked, under the same swarm of stars, in the same warm breeze, in the same amazing space. And next day Amara and his neighbours brought a fine, long canoe, and we set off to look for other friends, and for the old excitements. We found both. Phase Two began; it had been right to go back. A new prosperity, the old friendships superimposed on the drowsy landscape of Old Sumer rounded off a twenty-year span of adventure, born quite casually from a glance at an old newspaper. If only all young adventure-seekers could have the same good luck.

The Marsh Arabs Go to War

In 1980, a war broke out between Ayatollah Khomeini's Iran and President Saddam Hussein's Iraq. Fighting became particularly intense around the Iraqi port of Basra as the Iranians tried to break through to Kuwait. So the Marsh Arabs, for centuries secure in their reed fastnesses, were drawn into modern warfare.

MAY 1984

'You may not find any of your Marsh Arabs there,' someone said in Baghdad the first evening. 'All fighting probably. Or dead.'

'Well, someone must be milking the buffaloes and planting rice.' But my fear instantly doubled. It had driven me back, this fear, after four years away from the Marsh Arabs of southern Iraq: fear (more like terror) of what the Iranian Ayatollah Khomeini's 'martyrs' had done to a beautiful place and to a unique people I had known intimately since the 1950s.

Since the new offensive in March, in kamikaze style the frantic Iranians have been throwing human waves against the Iraqi defence line in the Huweiza Marshes, seeking to split Iraq in two, to seize Basra, Iraq's only port, and the Rumeila oilfield beyond. Seeking much more, in fact: to overturn the West's allies – Kuwait, the Gulf States, even Saudi Arabia – for the glory of Khomeini's retrograde brand of Islam. It's Arabs against Persians again. Regardless of a grotesque irony – and the horrendous cost of life – Khomeini's Shia Iranians had hurled themselves against co-religionists in the Shia Arab region of Iraq. (Iraqis, Christians apart, are equally Sunni and Shia Muslims; the Marsh Arabs are Shias.) Television had shown sickening pictures of rotting bodies and smouldering reed houses. Hell in the Garden of Eden.

It wasn't quite all catastrophe, thank God. I found, for example, my friend Bani, a good-humoured Marsh Arab if ever there was one, with strong hands calloused by work in the reeds and sun-darkened face, dressed casually in tousled headcloth and sweat-stained ankle-length Arab shirt, relaxing with young friends on the island – it looks rather like a coot's nest – on which his reed house stands. Chatting over small glasses of sweet tea, he grinned at the Kalashnikov automatic rifle across his knees, 'When the Persians get out of Iraq, we'll shoot wild boar with this, eh? Like old times.'

On other islands the familiar hump-backed reed houses lay, golden in the sun, like ungainly craft afloat on water as flat and blue as the Mesopotamian sky. Men and women skimmed silently about in slender canoes identical to the gondolas built in Ur of the Chaldees 6000 years ago.

Suddenly it seemed less timeless now. And menaced, far more than ever it had been by the old invaders, the Assyrian King Sennacherib, or Nebuchadnezzar the Babylonian, Alexander the Great, the Turkish *walis*, or even the British Army in the 1920s. Audibly menaced, too. For across the reed beds that hemmed in Bani's village like a stockade drifted an awesome sound. The Iraqi Army's heavy guns, grumbling like water buffaloes with fearful indigestion, were chewing up human fodder, the concentration of young boys and greybeards which Khomeini's officers kept pushing forward.

Bani and his friends were soldiers, only home for a few days' leave. I was lucky to catch them. Bani had survived the two furious Iranian offensives in the eastern Marsh. Others had died – 'Fadhil, Haji Ahmed's eldest, and Falih, and his cousin Daoud – remember them?' In his doorway I could see Haji Ahmed, a friend of thirty-three years, pale, mourning, staring blankly at the water. I had found the war.

In Baghdad, there were few signs of it. No blackout, no curfew. Lights blazed from the ultra-modern monument to the Unknown Soldier to the ancient Khorasan Gate through which the camel trains once passed on the Golden Road to Samarkand. Baghdad's night life seemed to have taken over where Beirut's had collapsed in rubble. The streets were full of cars; the bazaars were well stocked. Iraq's Arab neighbours had dutifully rallied, syphoning in food and fuel.

But the truly amazing thing was Baghdad's new look. I found a city transformed almost out of recognition. In 1979 I explored it from top to bottom for a book on the cities and landscape of Iraq. Since then, in only four years, these flyovers, massive hotels, splendid Government buildings, housing estates, monuments had sprung up like dragon's teeth. Miraculously, during a severely debilitating war. I could still find old Saadoun Street with its Ali Baba Restaurant, the Babylon Cinema, the Sindbad Café. But the strange tomb ('worth a detour') of the Caliph Harun al-Rashid's wife, for example, the domed shrines of Kadhimain, the medieval caravanserais and hammams of Harun's 'dim-moon' City of Peace, now had to be searched for. Yesterday's ramshackle city is suddenly and startlingly a modern one, something that represents an extraordinary effort of organization on the part of the Government of President Saddam Hussein. Perhaps that's one reason why twenty-foot cut-outs of him, in uniform, or a suit, or an Arab headdress, smile so proudly at one at such frequent intervals throughout the city – indeed throughout the land. 'Everyone loves the supreme leader,' the captions say. (Another reason, naturally, is an unprecedented cult of personality to match that of Khomeini.)

Presently, a journalist from a Baghdad newspaper came to my hotel to ask if I knew that the Marsh Arabs were now national heroes, defending Iraq's front line against the Iranian invaders. Their women too, he said. I told him I was glad they were considered heroes. For years, I joked, people had thought me slightly mad for spending my time with an unreliable people they saw as poor and backward, unhealthily inhabiting a squalid and undesirable swamp. I added (not too sententiously, I hope) that I had always admired the virtues the Marsh people had inherited from the eighth-century influx into Mesopotamia of pure-blooded Arab Muslim tribes of the Arabian desert. The virtues were: thrift, hard work, courage, simplicity, generosity, reverence. Not virtues universal in big cities. As for women, I said, they had always been a back-parlour power in the Marshes.

I saw the newspaper with this interview in it two days later down south in the hands of a ginger-moustached Iraqi major. It helped the security-minded officer to grasp why on earth a foreigner might be heading into a vast swamp on the rim of which Iraq's Army was battling for the survival of the nation.

'My sergeant-major is a Marsh Arab,' he said unexpectedly. 'He says you circumcised him thirty years ago.'

That wasn't me, I said. It was Wilfred Thesiger, the British explorer, who brought me to the region in the days when there were no doctors. But he let me go on.

First, I came to the house of Sayyid Sarwat, a place, I suddenly realized, that had become of outstanding significance today. For here some of the most respected Shia *sayyids* of southern Iraq live in a cluster of houses on a tributary of the Tigris, in the path of an Iranian offensive. *Sayyids* in Arab Iraq are the equivalent of *ayatollahs* in Persian Iran. Revered as descendants of the Prophet Muhammed, they rigidly eschew alcohol and all immodesty. They are founts of religious wisdom. Their spiritual influence can halt tribal conflict and much more. They draw inexhaustible religious inspiration from the Iraq cities of Nejef and Kerbela, where the shrines of the holy martyrs of Shia history, Hussein, Ali, Abbas, infinitely sublime, raise their golden domes above the desert. Here, across the centuries, countless Shias have been buried in Nejef's Vale of Peace in the shadow of the tomb of Ali, the Prophet's son-in-law. Before this war, Nejef received a million pilgrims a year from Arab countries, Iran, Afghanistan and Pakistan.

Sayyid Sarwat, most revered of *sayyids*, died here three months ago aged eighty-six. He was not merely my close friend. He personified all that was finest in Iraq, in Arabs, in Islam. Tall, and powerfully built, he was the opposite of fanatical. He was warm-hearted and humorous, not even a prig. Killing and cruelty were anathema to him. He was firm with religious offenders but he always reminded exasperated suppliants that Allah is 'the Generous One'. His own generosity was unbounded. When he told me, 'My house is your house,' he meant exactly that. The magnificent war canoe I have travelled the Marshes in since 1973 was his present. Muslims say 'In the name of God, the Kind, the Merciful.' I wondered if Ayatollah Khomeini would have shown such unstinted friendship to a non-Muslim.

Now the war had come to this peaceful place, and soon old Sayyid Sarwat's youngest son, Abbas, stepped, grinning, out of a taxi from Basra. 'I heard you were coming,' he said. 'So I got leave.'

I hardly recognized him. Abbas is a *sayyid* himself, but now he wore the khaki battledress of an army lieutenant and a pistol on his belt. He'd been in action more than once. After the usual embraces, he showed me a badly treated wound – a shattered kneecap, a patchwork of clumsy stitches, a bony protruding lump. 'The first doctor wanted to cut it off,' he smiled.

'Better take it to Baghdad or London,' I said.

'Well, after the war.' He showed me two medals for bravery from Saddam Hussein – eight-pointed stars with crossed swords in gold and a black-red-black ribbon. 'Let me tell you about my father's death,'

Abbas said. 'Two hundred thousand people came to his wake – from Baghdad, Basra, Kuwait, even Bahrain. All the tribes here came, the Shaghanba, the Fartus, the Suwaid. . . . We killed dozens of sheep. My father sent for you when he was dying.'

'Yes, the message came too late.'

Near the stream, workmen building a shrine for the old *sayyid* kissed Abbas's hand. The shrine would have a large tiled dome and marble walls. 'Many pilgrims will come here. Of course, my father's tomb is in Nejef.

'Is a Christian allowed to visit him there?'

'We'll go together.'

Abbas told me that all the Marsh tribes had sent men to fight in the army. 'The war made my father sad. He never talked about it. Two of his nephews were killed in the fighting near Abadan – my cousins.'

'Keep away from the front, Abbas, with that knee. You've done your bit.'

'Oh, if the republic needs me, of course I shall go back.' It almost sounded like a rebuke.

To tease him, I pointed to an aerial: 'Listening to Tehran Radio, Abbas?'

'Ha! No, only Baghdad and London.' (In Baghdad just then the Iraqi press was fulminating against the BBC for harping – unduly, they thought – on Iraq's human rights record. 'Why does the BBC concentrate on Iraq now? What about Iran?' Abbas frowned. In their old walled embassy on the Tigris, British diplomats in Baghdad were asking the same question.)

Recollections of the past grappled with this unsettling present. I stood with Abbas, as so often before, under the willow trees, gazing at kingfishers diving into the stream, at the flat Mesopotamian landscape interrupted only by clumps of trees, distant villages, long-robed figures, a man on a horse, sheep, a green swathe of sugar. But the guns dyspeptically grumbled along the eastern horizon.

Yet even the present, I found next day, was not all bad. Since my last visit, it soon appeared, Saddam Hussein had been as busy here as in Baghdad. When the *sayyid*'s canoe took me into the Marshes proper, it turned out to be powered by a Johnson outboard motor, no longer by young men with paddles. We puttered briskly along the familiar reed corridors, past swimming buffaloes, barking dogs, waving women in black cloaks over rainbow dresses, and reed houses with old friends scrambling onto their humped roofs to shout, 'Gavin, ho!' On those same roofs, for the first time I saw TV aerials. And refrigerators in reed doorways: 'Whatever next?'

The Marsh Arabs with me laughed. 'Saddam Hussein had promised us this,' they said, and I thought: 'Extraordinary. An Iraqi Government has kept its promises.'

At Bani's village, his father Sahain said: 'Can you credit it? A motor canoe at every door these days. Soon, the Government will pave the lagoons and we'll all have cars.'

A joke, but it explained something unknown for many years – respect for a Government in Baghdad. In four years, Sahain said, Saddam Hussein had given the Marsh Arabs electricity and piped water (before, we had made do with marsh water); ice factories and Government-subsidized motorboat transport to markets that had greatly increased local income from fishing (a large fish in Baghdad costs £10 these days); new factories buying reeds for paper. All this and doctors and clinics, too.

Sahain explained how this had stopped the drift of young men to the cities that had imperilled the very existence of the Marsh life. Young Marshmen had always preferred to live on the lagoons, in the familiar reed houses, hunting boar and wildfowl – their traditional life, in fact. Now, Sahain said, they could enjoy modern innovations as well. No need any more to go to noisy cities to be pushed about by men in suits.

Baghdadis used to consider Marsh Arabs unreliable. Now they thought of them as heroes. And so they were. Here was Bani resting between battles. And Khanjar, who now punted me out with Sahain and other friends to drink tea on a reed island in a favourite lagoon, had been in the war zone of Majnun, scene of the one local Iranian breakthrough (the Persians still occupied part of an island oilfield on the frontier), where the bodies had lain thickest. Kharaibat, now pinning cigarette packets to reeds as targets for our shooting match with Kalashnikovs (ammunition, apparently, galore), had been in fierce fighting east of Basra. We joked in the sun; heron flapped overhead; coot swam across the waterways. But these men, and others, would be returning to the front in a day or two.

Jabbar, an older man who had travelled with me in Sayyid Sarwat's war canoe in the seventies, told me of the human-wave attacks. 'The Persians sent small boys like my nine-year-old son. Unbelievable. Some carried tape recordings of shouting voices to make us think they were more than they were. They had been given false maps, too, showing holy Nejef only 200 yards into Iraq, although it's more like

200 miles. Ah, but we stopped them.' Jabbar, like all Marsh Arabs, talks of 'Persians' – a disparaging word that recalls the great Arab victory of Qadisiya in AD 637 which swept the Persians out of Mesopotamia for good.

'Being Marsh Arabs,' Jabbar said, 'I and my friends could slip a canoe right up to the Persian positions.' He laughed. 'Like stalking wild geese.'

But it was not all laughter and boasting. There were missing arms and legs, too, and men on crutches. And there were the dead – most of them known to me. All already buried in Nejef, at Government expense. I muttered condolences to fathers, mothers, brothers.

'In God's hands,' they murmured back.

I drove south, where the armies faced each other. To the east of the roadside tomb of the Jewish prophet Ezra, the marshes were beaten down: villages were a desolation of burst sandbags, destroyed reed or mud houses, craters of filthy water, where packs of dogs snarled and fought. Crows picked at buffalo bones. Of the population some were dead; most had fled. There were refugees near Adam's Tree in Quirna, a reputed site of the Garden of Eden. Near a ruined school, a booted foot stuck out of the mud. The area was a mass grave, smelling too full and too shallow.

'It was hand-to-hand here, like Vietnam,' a confident Iraqi general said. 'Loss of life, as in any war.' Deftly, he took an awkward question. 'Gas? We've not used it, but we are certainly prepared to, to defend Iraq. Wouldn't you have, if Hitler had invaded Britain? Well, wouldn't you?'

Who knew? I'd read that Churchill considered using it at the time of the V2 raids in 1944. (In Baghdad, diplomats said they were sure the Iraqis had used gas in some areas. They based their belief on United Nations reports from Iran.) Iraqi soldiers carry gasmasks in the south – and explain it's in case the Iranians use it. 'Americans covered Vietnam with napalm, which is worse – what hypocrites!'

'We expect another human-wave offensive,' the general said. In anticipation, the Iraqis' tanks and guns form a metal wall twenty or thirty miles long, backed by bunkers, trucks, tents and barbed wire all the way to Basra.

Basra, Sindbad's city, was being shelled at random by the Iranians – about fifteen 175 mm shells came every day. The first crash came at about 7 a.m. – a useful wake-up call, people said. It reminded me of London under those V2s. Life went on. The bazaar was full of strolling

110

window gazers, though odd shells had dropped there. Cafés were full. I found my old shipping office, crumbling but still busy. A new sign on it said, 'Dr M.S. Naama, Specialist in Skin and Venereal Diseases'. A man I asked about the shells said, 'You only have one death.'

War took shape in guarded bridges, and in the motionless line of cargo ships stranded for months in the Shatt-al-Arab River. Iranian shells had shattered an old mosque door; blown up parked cars; killed women and children in their houses; destroyed students' lodgings. Yet the university was open. In a large, cheerful girls' school they sang, 'If a million Iranians come, they'll never win.' Although some girls wore mourning black, classes went on normally. In a night club, a young man feverishly pinned banknotes to a dancer's dress, shouting that he was off to the front next day. A pastrycook in a restaurant said, 'Welcome. But why Mrs Thatcher sell to Iran?' (I replied: 'She needs the money.') Basra seemed full of foreign workers – Filipinos, Dutchmen, Koreans, Scotsmen, a Nepalese. Cheerful Egyptian workmen were building a new cabaret behind my hotel. Evidently the little city was not yet on its knees.

Back in Baghdad, an Iraqi friend asked, 'Why doesn't Western Europe stop selling spare parts to Iran?'

'And to Iraq as well?'

'Oh, yes. Stop selling to both. According to Western moral standards, isn't it correct to stop profiting and help negotiate an end to this war?'

Yes, I said.

Others said, 'America and Israel want the war to go on, so both sides are destroyed, no?'

I said that was perfectly possible.

At a musical party on a bank of the Tigris a well-known Iraqi musician drew, from the tiny one-string Arab fiddle called a *joza*, the sad-sweet far-off music that sounds like an echo of Sumer or the glorious Baghdad of Harun, the Peacock of the World. It is as popular in Saddam Hussein's new housing estates as it is in Bani's reed house. It seems to say that wherever Mrs Thatcher sells her spare parts, or whoever prolongs this war, old Mesopotamia is indestructible – unlike Western interests if those fanatical Iranians reach Kuwait.

The experience of my last day conveyed a similar message. I took a car to Nejef, the Shia pilgrim city. Young Sayyid Abbas in his uniform, and his bigger brother, Motar, met me at sunset at the door of their father's tomb in the Vale of Peace. Prominent among a million others, the tomb's dark green dome glowed with one perpendicular neon light. Inside, a portrait of the venerable *sayyid* was flanked by photographs of his two nephews killed by the Iranians – young, moustached, serious. The one old body, the two young ones, lay in brick niches in a vault below. There, Motar and Abbas lit three incense sticks and leaned against the wall, choking, tears oozing through their fingers to the dust floor.

Presently, Abbas prepared to drive back to his unit. He buckled on his pistol, showing me the inscription: 'A present from President Saddam Hussein for a defender of the nation.' Kissing me on both cheeks, he said, 'Come back very soon. You'll find me waiting at home – your home. . . . Or here in Nejef.'

'Let it be alive at home, Abbas.'

'Well, it's as God orders.'

The sublime dome of the Caliph Ali rose above the city so yearned for by Khomeini's juvenile soldiers – floodlit, a perfect shimmering golden bud. Abbas glanced at it, and back once more to the tomb of his father. Then, with a wave, he drove off, refreshed, smiling.

Samoa: The Fatal Impact

JULY 1986

The Pacific Ocean, that remote region of blue lagoons, hurricanes and Sadie Thompson, out of the news for decades, is back in it – thanks once again to fresh wickedness from Europe. The French are to blame this time: French nuclear tests on Mururoa Atoll, the French Intelligence Service's ham-fisted (and murderous) sabotage of the Greenpeace protest ship *Rainbow Warrior* in Auckland harbour, the inter-racial violence that threatens New Caledonia with a smaller repetition of the Franco-Algerian War.

Not for the first time – far from it, alas – defenceless islanders are being grievously disturbed by intrusive Europeans. Has a fine book called *The Fatal Impact*, written some twenty years ago by the late Alan Moorehead, been forgotten? If so, what a pity, because its theme was the corruption – and in some cases, destruction – of Pacific island peoples and cultures by European or American adventurers in the

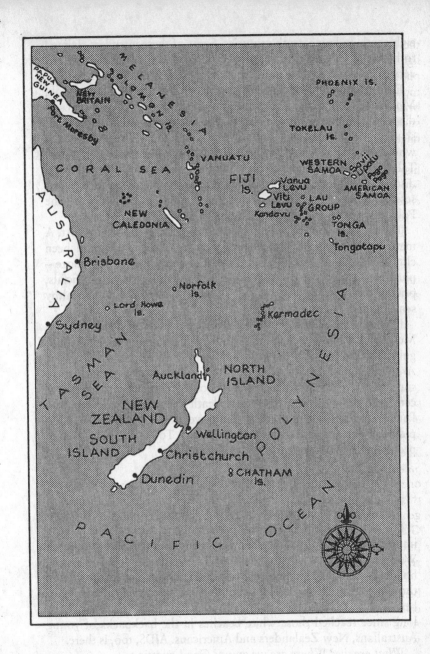

eighteenth and nineteenth centuries. Some of these intruders claimed to be acting in God's name; others, impious scallywags, denied His very existence. For their native victims it made little difference.

Even that high-principled Yorkshire navigator Captain Cook, Moorehead told us, let it all come in: tuberculosis, smallpox, venereal disease, gunpowder, booze and blackbirding (the Pacific version of slavery) – things hitherto unknown in the islands. A measure of the whole disaster was that, a mere sixty years after Cook's arrival in Tahiti, a visitor was able to report, 'In the slovenly and haphazard and diseased inhabitants, it was vain to attempt to recognise the prepossessing figure of the Tahitian as pictured by [Cook].' Even their fine Polynesian teeth were rotting, thanks to European food.

The pure-blooded Marquesan islanders actually ceased to exist. A mere eighty years after the coming of the French, they had been eliminated from the earth's face by the familiar diseases and booze – plus life-extinguishing prohibitions imposed by French officials, priests and *gendarmes* against singing, dancing and a healthy semi-nudity.

It was the same story all through the islands of Polynesia and Melanesia. Famous eye-witnesses have left testimony to it all: Gauguin in his diaries and paintings like *Where Do We Come From? What Are We? Where Are We Going?*; Jack London, Robert Louis Stevenson and Herman Melville in their books. Recent events have concentrated the world's attention on death by nuclear pollution, and Pacific islanders are now to be found wearing T-shirts stencilled in pidgin: '*Nuclear him killim iumi evriwan.*' Today the old Tahitian prophecy seems more fearfully apt than ever:

> The palm-tree shall grow,
> The coral shall spread,
> But man shall cease.

But our nuclear tests are only a part of the story. A much more immediate threat to island cultures and peoples is the steady inflow of Western high-rise, junk-food 'culture'. Tourist hotels already disfigure hundreds of island skylines, casting their monstrous shadows over those big lagoons. Reefs and the marine life dependent on them have been dynamited to make way for runways for Jumbo jets. Drugs have long since reached those white beaches in the backpacks of young Australians, New Zealanders and Americans. AIDS, too, is there.

What are we? Where are we going? Good questions.

I first spotted this cultural mushroom cloud on a visit to Western Samoa in 1982. The visit fulfilled a dream I had had as a boy reading Robert Louis Stevenson's letters from Vailima. (Neighbouring American Samoa is a United States territory, on which those Samoans who have not scampered off to California cultivate waterfall moustaches like Charles Bronson, wear baseball caps and drawl: 'No way, man,' and 'Ya bedda believe it.') Western Samoa, independent of New Zealand since 1962, holds grimly on – just – to its *fa'a Samoa*, its traditional and dignified way of life.

Inside the reef at Apia I stared from the rail of a little Tongan freighter at a shallow horseshoe bay lined by low wooden buildings, a white double-spired church and a woody hillside that the map said was Mount Vaea with R.L.S.'s tomb on its peak. Happily I lugged my suitcase down the road to Aggie Grey's Hotel.

Through Aggie's son, Alan, who runs the hotel, I soon met a variety of Samoans, pure or half-caste (*afakasi*), traders, politicians or pastors, successors to the nineteenth-century missionaries who saved the Samoans from their gods and goddesses. ('Samoa is founded upon God' is the national motto now.) Then I rented a car, packed a bag and drove off down the coast.

The road ran through some villages of traditional open Samoan beehive houses, thatched and pillared, half buried in flowering shrubs and bright-leaved trees. There were frequent cool white churches. Handsome young men and women strolled barefoot in vividly coloured *lava-lavas* – the elegant sarongs of Samoa – scarlet hibiscus blooms in their thick black hair. Older people held up open parasols against the sun and half-naked elders reclined on mats and cushions, visible through the open sides of the houses.

Where the road became a rough track I met my first Samoan family, Tolu's. A girl ran out of a house calling, 'Come in, come in' – Tolu's eldest daughter, Emma – and in a moment I was drinking coconut milk with Manino, her mother, and Fili and Isaia, her brothers, who fanned the mosquitoes away from me with a banana leaf. The house was small and very ordinary; a few chickens, a single chestnut horse tethered to a clump of bamboo outside. In the next few days I got to know the family pretty well.

At sunset Tolu himself arrived, sweating from his plantation, and took the sight of a tall white stranger in his stride. A large, strong, overweight man, heavily tattooed from waist to mid-thigh, Tolu is a *matai*, one of the 10,000 elected chiefs who run life in Samoa, representing the 'extended families' (people have literally dozens of uncles, aunts and cousins) as well as the villages and districts of the islands. The *matais* are the backbone of the age-old democratic system of *fa'a Samoa*, and in a firm but remarkably thoughtful and tolerant way take care of everything outside Apia from law and order to agriculture, cricket and adultery. *Fa'a Samoa* itself – a culture as well as a guide to conduct, and still sturdy, persistent and respected (the missionaries trimmed it somewhat, but left the roots intact) – gives the Samoan's life dignity and meaning.

The days passed. We fished in the glassy waters of lagoons. Tolu whacked cricket balls into distant thickets for his village team (twenty players). Fili worked in the family plantation. Isaia did his homework – 'Simi said she is not a tall nurse. . . . He is not a noisy teacher.' In an oven of hot stones, Manino cooked huge meals of cowries, cockles, spotted crabs and green pigeons. We climbed Mount Vaea, and the Samoans draped themselves on Stevenson's tomb in unconscious imitation of the pallbearers who had carried him there.

It was not unlike Tennyson's 'land in which it was always afternoon': people with glossy, butterscotch skins laughed and sang, worked and played. It was not Lotos-land: the taro, coconut and banana plantations required constant hard work. But what counted was the pride and self-sufficiency: those plantations were their own, there was plenty of land and it was fertile. You only had to put a seed into the earth and – bingo! – something green would spring up. There was peace. No social conflict. No class; no tyranny. What more could anyone want?

Serpents lurked in this Eden – human serpents, of course. They were the 'mushroom cloud factor'. Strange, wild creatures were abroad in the streets of Apia and, to a lesser extent, in the villages. They were Samoans, but unlike other Samoans I had seen – their hair tangled, their eyes bloodshot and their faces spotty, grey and puffy. They wore grubby jeans and T-shirts. They smelled of booze. They stood on roadsides thumbing for lifts and then harassed the drivers kind enough to stop for them. They threw stones and beer cans at those who didn't.

A couple who pestered me were certainly drunk, drugged or both, and proudly showed me tattoos on their arms that said, 'Deported from New Zealand'. Other Samoans told me they were indeed deportees from New Zealand, but the tattoos were self-inflicted – to have been abroad (however they might have returned) gave them, they thought, kingly status among stay-at-homes like Tolu and his family.

Tolu, Manino, Emma and Fili deplored these human disasters. 'Very bad,' they said, making disapproving faces. But what was to be done? A couple of thousand Samoans went to New Zealand every year. Thousands stayed there, hard-working and sober; hundreds of others ended up like this. 'Tut, tut!' was Tolu's comment. But his family, too, hankered after New Zealand. One day I sat on a perfect beach with Emma on a perfect lagoon and heard her murmur, 'Oh, I do wish I could go to Auckland.'

'Why, Emma?'

For the money, of course, she said. She would send it back to her father, Tolu, for the family plantation.

'Why not stay here and teach?'

She was silent, gazing eloquently towards the horizon beyond which lay El Dorado – money, bright lights, video: Life.

On my second, and very recent, visit to Tolu I found he had enlarged the little house and added a small thatched guest house. His brother-in-law had sent money from New Zealand and Fili told me, pointedly, how cheap the return air fare was from Western Samoa to Auckland. Would I help him . . . ? No, I said irritably. Down the track the Methodist pastor's son had been found dead drunk by the roadside at four o'clock the previous afternoon. What *was* all this about New Zealand? I thought I had better go to Auckland and see for myself.

Auckland is an attractive, low-rise little city sprawling like bits of a jigsaw puzzle around bays and inlets. 'A magic town,' Kipling called it, passing through in the 1880s. 'Soft and lovely in the sunshine.' (He had intended to visit Stevenson on Samoa, but the captain of the fruit boat that would have taken him was so 'devotedly drunk' that he made a beeline for India instead.)

I saw no sunshine even in November (early summer down there). On the contrary, it was damp and chilly. Fifty thousand Samoans live in Auckland, and every year about 1500 leave the islands to join them: how could they stand this climate? When I met my first Samoan-in-exile I wasn't sure they could. He lived in a district improbably named Ponsonby – a name I associate with majors in the Guards more than a rather 'gentrified' working-class Polynesian suburb. His house was a large bungalow like many others, with a tiny cropped lawn in front of it, adequate furniture and a huge, twin-speakered radio sitting on its doorstep. He was stout, friendly and middle-aged with cropped grey hair, a thick shirt and a jersey (which he needed) and trousers of some strong material held up by a wide belt. He had been a naturalized New Zealander for many years, he said, but he took his shoes off in the house, Samoa-style, and he could still speak Samoan. 'There's no place like home,' he said, and hoped to return to Apia before he died. Touching to hear. The only thing was he didn't look much like any Samoan I had seen before. He had a dull, grey-skinned appearance apparently quite unrelated to the rich, brown, healthy gloss and glow of Tolu's kith and kin. Unnatural. It was a first impression that would recur.

Technically, it was not hard for Samoans to leave the golden sands of Samoa, the intelligent young Consul-General of Western Samoa told me next day. You needed, of course, to be convinced that this rainy, European city was El Dorado and Xanadu combined. 'After that,' the Consul-General said, 'you only have to have the air fare, be less than forty-five with no more than four children, and have a valid job in Auckland, arranged by a member there of your extended family.' Samoan labourers were much sought after. 'They don't malinger. They only have to behave themselves and they can stay forever and become naturalized.'

An obvious question: wasn't this annual exodus a tremendous manpower drain for Western Samoa and its diminutive population of 160,000? 'Oh, yes,' the Consul-General admitted. 'It is. Of course, they send money back to their families.' That would be well earned and well spent if it went into improving the plantations and the islands' economy.

But already I knew the dusty answer to that. 'Sad to say, much of it goes on buying sprees in Apia. On the cinema. On tinned, imported food from New Zealand and Australia.'

Two films Samoans could do without had been playing in Apia on my last visit: *Commando*, starring Arnold Schwarzenegger, and *Rambo* with Sylvester Stallone. The shops were full of tins of imported corned beef and pineapple. What was this other than the Fatal Impact (Cultural and Economic Divisions)? It seemed to me to turn the Samoan labour drain to New Zealand and the remittance of money to Samoa into a most vicious circle: Samoans left Samoa because of the 'stagnation' of agricultural life there, yet the money they sent home actually became the islanders' alibi for less and less work on the plantations. The easy development of the good rustic life is neglected for *Rambo* and bully beef.

'About a thousand Samoans are deported from New Zealand every year,' the Consul-General went on. 'Some overstay their permits. Others can't cope with the freedom, the dance halls, all that. The grog, too; the drugs.' So much for the tangled hair, the red eyeballs in Apia: Fatal Impact, again.

Consciously isolated in an alien culture, Samoans in New Zealand cling desperately to their own island traditions – their *fa'a Samoa* and to their churches, Methodist, Congregationalist, Catholic, Mormon or Anglican. Like anxious bees they swarm round their churches for social, as well as spiritual, life. It is a question of a proud people's terror of losing identity and self-respect. Yet there are snags even in this. A Methodist pastor said: 'Remember, people come here principally to save money. They are mostly poor manual workers, even if some are teachers or work in offices. Their financial obligations are severe. Perhaps they send back half their pay. But they are also responsible for members of their extended family here. Then they must contribute to their local church. On top of that there's rent and taxes, food and clothing.' Life was often an exhausting search for a salary. 'Some are really struggling,' the pastor said. And when I came to meet social workers, they mentioned slums.

Actually slums – as I have seen them elsewhere – are what there were remarkably little of in Auckland. In Otara, one of the city's poorest Polynesian suburbs, the houses are low, wooden bungalows not unlike those of the rest of far-flung Auckland. There are pediments over the flaking lintels and occasional panes of stained glass, as in the windows of cheap English seaside boarding houses, and little patches of grass. Nothing remotely like the ghettos of New York, Paris or Brixton in London. None the less there is poverty, and there is certainly overcrowding.

At the Otara Social Workers' Centre, one of several affable Polynesian workers (this one from Tonga) had sad tales to tell of overcrowding that led to delinquency – glue sniffing and teenage boozing. Gang warfare, too. On a nearby bus shelter I had seen graffiti two feet high saying: 'Sons of Samoa'.

'We have gangs, yes. There are Samoans in the Stormtroopers. And in the Headhunters. The King Cobras – well, they are more a youth club, even though one Cobra was beaten to death with a baseball bat in broad daylight a short while ago. At night, gangs hang around pubs – there's a roughish local here, for instance, commonly known for obvious reasons as the Flying Jug.' As we talked he was called to another room – three teenagers were asking for a handout. The banks were on strike, they said, which was true.

'Hi, boys,' said the social worker breezily.

'Hi,' they answered.

'Why do you need the money?' I asked one of the boys wearing old jeans, scuffed shoes and a lumber jacket with the collar turned up like Marlon Brando in *On the Waterfront*. They were all about sixteen. With the wide eyes, high cheekbones, flattish noses and wavy dark hair of Samoa, they looked like a trio of Polynesian Artful Dodgers.

'For the pub,' the boy said. He rubbed his shoulder and groaned. 'I feel real bad. Real bruised.'

'Fighting in the pub again, eh, Raymond?' the social worker laughed.

'Yeah. Four against one.'

'You don't look like a brawler,' I said.

'He's a terror with his knees and feet,' a second kid said proudly. They were cousins, they informed me, living nearby with the family. Lots of relatives; few rooms. They dossed down in the garage, and their sisters slept in a caravan 'out the back'. 'When it's cold we all push into the caravan.'

'Overcrowding,' the social worker said when the boys had trotted off grinning, pleased with a couple of quid. 'A major problem. They'll be drinking and fighting again. You see, to make enough money, the mothers go to work. So no discipline at home. Kids take to the streets, the pubs. In Samoa, mothers stay at home, make sure the children go to school.' An irony: here the island women found themselves 'liberated' (i.e. free to slave in a factory); but the children went to the dogs. If Tolu's wife, Manino, came here perhaps Fili and Isaia would become corner boys while she crept to work each frozen dawn. God knows what might become of Emma and her sisters.

What would stop Fili taking to drink? Polynesian drinking is a special phenomenon: I have seen that from the Solomons and Tahiti, on ships and ashore. Perhaps it's because they are so big, they can take it in gallons. Some say that in this respect Samoans, when grog is around, are the Irishmen of the South Seas. At about nine o'clock at night, with the seventh pint clutched in his massive fist, a Samoan friend suddenly looks much less friendly than he did at 7.30. In Auckland, police officials agreed that most Polynesian crimes were 'drink-related'. A sensible police sergeant (a Fijian) agreed that 'The Polynesians tend to bash it along a bit in a pub.' But they maintained there was no Polynesian *crime* problem, as the local press kept on claiming. After all, there were vicious white gangs, too.

In Samoa, the *matais* keep drink out of the villages, and in any case there is little time to waste on drinking. Everyone has land to work. Frank, a New Zealand–Samoan schoolteacher, once a youth gang hooligan but who now lives respectably with his wife and children in Otara, told me how he had visited Samoa and loved it there, but 'It was like a slave camp,' he laughed. 'Everyone toting bags of coconuts in the plantation all day. Everyone so strong. No hanging about idle. Healthy outdoor work. That's good.'

Like many Samoans, Frank takes God seriously. Photographs of his children at their first communions hung on his wall. A vivid wall hanging depicted a brightly haloed Virgin Mary blessing kneeling shepherd boys and girls in vaguely Hungarian garb. It is wrong to imply that all – even most – Samoans go to the bad in New Zealand. On Sundays, the white-clad congregations – men in white shirts and *lava-lavas*, women in wide, floppy hats and gloves – crowd into morning prayers as they do on the islands. Even if the young go to church less or respect tradition less than before, Auckland is certainly not all booze and brawling.

There are five hundred or so hard-working students, for instance. Some turn not to booze, but to racial problems. I met a 'radical' girl student who warned me that, as a white, I should find her 'intimidating'; she read, she said, coldly arrogant, nothing but books by American Black Power feminists of the 1960s. I found her irrelevant rather than intimidating, since twenty-year-old dogmas of American Black Power have nothing much of value to say to Samoans in the tolerant New Zealand of the 1980s. New Zealanders no longer jeer at Samoans tripping over their new shoes in the street, calling them 'coconuts'. True discrimination is hard to find. This is a story of seduction, not of repression.

I visited houses with cars at the kerb in largely Samoan areas, where respectable people squatted on their living room floors among the armchairs and plastic-topped tables and played innocent games of cards, ignoring the American movies that flickered on the telly for the benefit of the children. I attended wedding parties that might have been in an island but for cement walls instead of coconut fronds – parties at which the traditional presents of fine-woven mats were exchanged, and long, formal speeches rolled on and on until the young people began to yawn.

Samoans are as musical as Welshmen. A quintet of richly successful Samoan pop singers called the Five Stars invited me to the grand house their profits had bought them, where their father and manager – who spends his spare time rescuing Samoan street boys from self-destruction – laid out a barbecue and jugs of beer. Music and speeches alternated throughout the night until the invited *matais* – all long resident in Auckland – turned red with drinking and orating. The songs were in Samoan and one at least carried a moral from American Samoa:

> All you island girls,
> I never thought you were so stupid –
> Boys from the United States come here,
> So you put on all your lipstick and shoes,
> And now the sailors have all gone away
> And left you on the roadside with a headache. . . .
> *Sha la la! O lia papa é, O lia mama é!*

Here were Samoans who had made many a happy transition into exile, however much I – or they – would have preferred a background sound of surf on a reef rather than of cars accelerating up the asphalted street outside.

Still, the song – as these young men who wrote it knew very well – had a point. As valid a point as a song I had noted on my first visit to Apia. That one addressed Samoan deportees:

> You come back so pale and white.
> You've gained nothing, and you're just a fiery barrel of trouble.
> Forget all about these motor cars and that la di da English.
> Time is precious. Do something useful. Get to work on your banana
> > plantation.

'Pale and white' – I had never seen such a physical change in exiles in any part of the world. Whatever could be the cause? The cold climate and lack of sun?

'That's it,' some Samoans agreed. 'And the bad European diet.' Others put it down – angrily – to the daily urban grind (coming from a village society *guaranteed* suffering): the getting up in a thousand clammy dawns to go to the factory – or to traipse round looking for a job. Others blamed it on the anxiety of poverty. Leftish intellectuals flatly stated that it was the mere fact of living in a European country. (New Zealand – where Polynesians are 15 per cent of the population – should be run as a Polynesian country, they argued, as if history could be switched into reverse like a dodgem car.) Whatever the reason, Stevenson's 'walking gods' have not survived the trip across the sea. How can this be anything but tragic?

The insidious spiritual deprivation is another thing: the nagging awareness of the slow death of a proud identity. A well-educated Samoan of thirty-five whom I shall call Jonathan put it like this: 'Those who come here have eaten of a Forbidden Fruit – nothing is ever quite the same after that. I am not the same Samoan who left Western Samoa. I enjoy the material things success has brought me in New Zealand – but I'm two-sided. I *must* practise *fa'a Samoa* – or a modified form of it – because in my deepest feelings I'd feel like a stranger's adopted baby if I didn't. Otherwise, I'd be like a Hawaiian – a rudderless canoe in the ocean.'

Why not return to Western Samoa?

'I've two involvements, do you see? Actually I am dying to get back to Samoa. But my children are ... well, New Zealanders. I must *sacrifice* myself for them now. They're at home here. So I must stay, and cling to what *fa'a Samoa* we have here to save my sanity.'

> The palm-tree shall grow,
> The coral shall spread,
> But man shall cease . . . .

Across the world of the South Seas people like Jonathan – or Tolu or Fili – are seduced and shrivelled like moths by the pitiless lights of the white man's El Dorado. Eat the Forbidden Fruit; suffer the Fatal Impact.

The Walled City of Kowloon

1986

Stretching out my arms to their fullest extent I could touch both walls of the alley without difficulty. Oozing with damp, they felt leprous and unwholesome. I edged my feet cautiously over an uneven cement floor made slippery by drain water – or sewage.

It was decidedly creepy. Hong Kong's Walled City, I thought, was more like the depths of the criminal East End of Victorian London than the Kowloon of the 1980s. This would have been the time for Sherlock Holmes to whisper, 'Better have your service revolver ready, eh, Watson.'

As it was, Police Inspector David Hodson's cheery voice came to me from the gloom ahead: 'If anything falls from above, for God's sake don't pick it up. It might be something – er – very unpleasant.' It would certainly be unpleasant. Round the next twist in this sinister warren we might be going to stumble on the secret headquarters of that emperor of crime fiction, Dr Fu Manchu. One might bump into anything here.

The Walled City is, you might say, the Casbah of Hong Kong; a sordid anomaly within a larger, grander one. By now everyone knows how overcrowded this last, condemned fragment of the British Raj has grown over the years since World War II – any postcard of Hong Kong shows you the older forests of high-rise buildings in Kowloon and the new ones that are pushing up into the green hills of the New Territories. These teeming outposts of the poor are the reverse of a golden coin on the face of which is the Hong Kong of Western or Chinese bankers, merchants and speculators whose multi-million-dollar office blocks and luxurious housing march like imperial warriors in gilded armour up the slopes of Hong Kong island that face the harbour. It is not the fault of Hong Kong's British governors that overcrowding exists – how can anyone force the Chinese to stop breeding? Yet, even in terms of cheek-by-jowl, semi-slum housing, the Walled City is something special – a place to make you keep glancing around you, alert for heaven knows what. Certainly no place for the nervous or sufferers from claustrophobia.

In fact, because for some time I had been hearing that this unusual place was *so* unusual, I was determined to see it, and I consulted David Hodson, a Cantonese-speaking friend in the Hong Kong police. When he agreed to take me on a tour I quickly dug up the bare bones of the city's history from Kowloon's local government offices.

The Walled City's troubles (the records said) started in 1898 at the signing of the Convention of Peking, whereby Queen Victoria leased what is now the territory of Hong Kong, including Kowloon, from the rulers of China for ninety-nine years. The Walled City area, then the imperial Chinese administrative centre in Kowloon, was, at Chinese insistence, exempted from this British takeover. A Chinese presence of some sort was a question of 'face'. Thus a mandarin and a detachment of Chinese imperial troops remained isolated there, like an untreated boil, to the irritation of the British – who, however, did not put up with the boil for long. The infuriated mandarin and his outnumbered garrison were summarily ousted – though without bloodshed – the following year, and through succeeding decades British Hong Kong swiftly sprang up like an uncheckable fungus around the Walled City. Despite this, no Government in Peking – Imperial, Nationalist or Communist – admitted Britain's right to administer it. So there it uneasily sat, a sort of urban no-man's-land.

Recently, with talks afoot between Britain and China for the 1997 handover, the Hong Kong Government started to improve conditions in what for years had been a shunned and untended slum. Sanitation, electricity, water – up to now practically non-existent – have been minimally introduced: an overhead electric lamp shines dimly here, a communal water tap drips there. Even so, not much has changed. The seemingly impenetrable maze of ramshackle buildings has ensured that the Walled City remains an area of mystery, a sanctuary for a variety of local villains and for the illegal fugitives who still sneak in on dark nights from mainland China. Tourists are advised to steer clear of it.

To start our tour David Hodson met me in Wan Chai, the flamboyant district made notorious by the fictional bar girl Suzie Wong. In casual plain clothes he came to my hotel, the Luk Kwok, once part of Suzie's beat and now a pleasant Chinese hotel. 'Ready?' He introduced his sergeant: 'Meet Sergeant Hon Yu-ki,' and I held out my hand. Sergeant Hon has since become a friend; he is ebullient, good company, with one eye wide open for the girls, the other on Canada as a possible bolthole before 1997 lets the Communists in. I see, now that I know him, that many Chinese in Hong Kong do not view the prospect of a Communist takeover in 1997 with anything like the easy optimism of British officials. But all I saw at that first meeting was a stocky, square-jawed Chinese with heavy black eyebrows, whose stiff black hair fitted his head like a helmet, and who wore a gun on his hip under a white cotton shirt that was not quite loose enough to hide it.

'Let's drive to Kowloon.' Hodson's driver swung the police car towards the cross-harbour tunnel under the bay, leaving Wan Chai's neon-lit hubbub, its Hi Fella Sea Food Restaurant, the Crazy Horse Saloon, the Pussycat Topless Bar. The wider streets of Kowloon have a similarly garish look, but we shot through them and pulled up at a large, grand, yellow-tiled temple on its northern edge. It was equally noisy here, though Kowloon's noise is different from that of Wan

Chai. For one thing, the international jets interminably scream down over Kowloon to Kai Tak airport like maddened eagles, their wingtips scything menacingly close to the pathetic washing on the roofs of cheap high-rise housing estates. But there are other, pleasanter noises, too.

Before the temple's crimson pillars, dozens of Chinese of both sexes and all ages stood shaking pint-sized wooden cups full of numbered fortune sticks, anxiously seeking the future. Striking the sides of the wooden cups and each other, the sticks whirl about like a roomful of infuriated rattlesnakes. When at last a stick falls to the ground some excited suppliant snatches it up and bears it away to a grey-headed seer in a nearby booth who reads out the fortune corresponding to the number on the stick.

Hodson said, 'Every Hong Kong Chinese wants to know the future. Particularly with 1997 in the offing. Hard-headed businessmen you wouldn't think cared a damn about such mumbo-jumbo burn a joss stick or two here for luck. So do drug smugglers hoping for a successful "run".' As he spoke, ecstatic middle-aged women fell to their knees near the temple steps. 'At St Paul's Cathedral you wouldn't see quite so many people consulting the spirits, would you?'

'They'd be in the pub reading "What the Stars Foretell" in the evening paper.'

'Too true.'

The temple's collection boxes bulged with the cash donations of the devout. Would a percentage go to help spruce up the seedy jumble of high-rise flats across the road? We aimed for one such slum block now.

'Let's go up,' Hodson said, pointing at a dark, Dickensian doorway.

In a second-storey flat, containing nothing but a makeshift shrine, six Chinese crones sat in a semi-circle like the witches in *Macbeth*, lighting joss sticks with shaking fingers. On the next floor up, a group of children huddled on a single low bed, and an adult's bare, skinny legs hung over the side of a hammock. The sickly smell of the joss sticks floated up the stairs and out onto a narrow balcony where an emaciated old man sat on a three-legged stool peering at a mynah bird in a wicker cage. He opened his puckered mouth in a smile when Sergeant Hon stooped and opened the door of the little cage. The mynah hopped along its perch, head cocked on one side, inspecting us all with an eye as bright and black as the head of a hatpin.

Hodson looked anxious. 'Careful now, Hon. It'll fly away and we'll spend the rest of the day arranging compensation.'

'Oh, no,' Hon said seriously. 'It will not fly. It born here and will not leave.'

'Talk to it, Sergeant Hon,' I said.

'Three months older it will learn to talk. Now it too young.' He took out the bird on his finger and stroked it. The bird turned up its big orange bill to get a good look at him. It seemed to want to say something, even if it couldn't. 'Good bird,' Hon said to it, and gently returned it to its cage.

We climbed more seedy stairs. The roof of the building was littered with refuse and afforded a good wingtip view of the aeroplanes landing. As we stood there under the washing lines, a China Airlines jet skimmed in at what seemed like touching distance between two banks of buildings. An amazing forest of old-fashioned television aerials hemmed us in. Pigeons swirled overhead – the pets of poor tenement dwellers everywhere – and on a neighbouring rooftop in the forest of TV aerials three or four boys were feeding a cageful, pushing small lumps of rice through the wire netting. But our tour had hardly begun.

'Down to the real Walled City now,' said Hodson, and we descended to a street full of dentists' shops. Displays of dental plates like flayed mouths, plastic fangs and flesh-pink gums snarled and grinned at us from their windows. Through a doorway, I glimpsed a man supine in a dentist's chair and someone in a white coat thrusting his fingers into his mouth.

Here Hodson suddenly disappeared. Looking about, I spotted with difficulty the only place he could possibly have got to: an alley so narrow that it was a mere crack between two palsied buildings. Into this Hodson had vanished like Alice's White Rabbit down the rabbit hole. I squeezed in too and could see him dimly in the gloom ahead, stumbling over the uneven surface of the alley floor of a passageway as murky as any hideout of Bill Sykes or Fagin. The distant sky above was reduced to a thin, grey ribbon by the walls of houses that leaned closer to each other as they rose higher. The windows giving onto the alley were barred or crudely stuffed up with cardboard or broken bicycle wheels, old rust-eaten paint drums, strips of corrugated iron and parts of wrecked perambulators.

Dense cat's cradles of dusty, refuse-laden telephone wires writhed overhead, increasing the gloom which was deep enough in places to make walking here quite dangerous. One could have had a nasty fall on a switchback cement floor glistening with the overflow of drains. So with Hodson in front and Hon behind I crept cautiously along, ducking the loose wires that plucked like malevolent fingers at our clothing and poked into our eyes.

It was then that David Hodson called out, 'If you see something coming down between the houses, get out of the way as quickly as you bloody well can. Ten to one, it'll be a lump of shit wrapped in paper. Don't, for God's sake, stop to pick anything up – or try to throw it back!' I heard Hon laugh behind me, and then bark angrily in Cantonese and stop to scrape something off his shoe on the lintel of a low opening so dark it might have opened onto the Bottomless Pit.

I shouted to Hodson, 'How does the postman find his way in all this?' – not thinking for a second that any postman would penetrate in here. But Hodson replied, 'Actually we do have a government postal service here,' and soon he added proudly, 'Electricity, look.' A sturdy overhead electric light standard – one of perhaps three I saw all morning – was another sign that Hong Kong had not entirely forgotten the Walled City.

To be fair, there were other signs too. Twisting into a cul-de-sac, we blundered into the gate of a temple flanked by stone dogs and carved scrolls. Twisting some more, we bumped into a huddle of buildings that resolved themselves into a small clinic and a public sitting room where old women sat watching a TV soap opera. This refuge for the elderly was run by some evangelical Chinese church, and it crouched there dwarfed by its surroundings. The high-rise tenements around it seemed to make reluctant room for it, and craning my neck to look at their uppermost windows I saw a surprising number of air conditioning units. I had wondered how so cramped a population survived the sweltering hot Hong Kong summers. The windows were small and heavily protected by bars and metal grilles, but at least there were *some* luxuries in the Walled City.

In strict truth, 'Walled City' is a misnomer – the little city no longer has a wall. In old photographs a very thick and solid stone one surrounded it, and it could only be entered through massive stone gates. Evidently Peking's old mandarin had held court in a fortress outpost before the British so rudely expelled him. That ancient wall was only finally demolished during World War II by the Japanese, who used its venerable stones to extend the runway of Kai Tak airport. Now it exists only in the imagination of mainland Chinese, who still see the city as a precious sanctuary, worth risking drowning and sharks to reach.

128

To reach . . . what? Can this malodorous rookery really be anyone's idea of Eldorado? The answer – as pathetic to us as it is plain to those driven frantic by the political repression, sheer boredom and economic ineptitude of Communism – is yes. Europeans may laugh. But the misery of Asia knows no bounds.

Of course, the Walled City has perfectly legal, uncriminal residents, too; people who enjoy the low rents and rates. I asked David Hodson what the total population is, and he said, 'About forty thousand, likely more. No one quite knows.'

You would never know it. Those forty thousand residents – legal or illegal – are exceedingly elusive. The sordid back alleys of Cairo or Calcutta, for example, are full of people. You may feel overwhelmed by noise and smells, but you are in the midst of shouting, scurrying, jostling life. But here – where on earth, I thought, *was* everybody? The Walled City's tucked away silence was sinister. From time to time the odd human shadow slipped by; sometimes someone stopped and looked at us with a furtive alley cat curiosity. Once a man carrying a rat trap murmured something that might have been hello. But to come upon an occasional bright, well-lit shop was a relief. Even sounds of human activity had this furtive quality – they were mechanical sounds rather than vocal ones. Once I heard – from where? – the muffled, rhythmic clash of what must have been a printing press – turning out subversive or pornographic pamphlets, counterfeit banknotes, an unlicensed newspaper? Elsewhere, a textile loom rattled in some hidden basement like a pair of skeletons dancing in a tomb.

It was impossible to tell behind which walls such sounds originated. Now and again dim figures were silhouetted through a subterranean 'factory' door, and over another a painted sign said 'For Import and Export' (in English, but for whose benefit?). In a sunless shop three steps down, blank-faced men in dirty singlets silently rolled fishballs on a wide, flat tray, and in the alley the stink of the fish mingled with an overriding smell of urine. Yet not everything here was lifeless and inhuman. In an arched room like a wine cellar, four skinny boys with pallid churchyard faces, wrapping sweets in small twists of coloured paper with squirrel-fingered intensity, looked up all of a sudden to see this monster – a six-foot Englishman – staring at them through their doorway, and, unafraid, straightened their hunched shoulders, grinned and called: 'Bye-bye.'

Given a romatic turn of mind, it was easy in the Walled City to recall the stews of Edwardian Whitechapel – and that hidden fictional world where criminal masterminds like Sax Rohmer's Dr Fu Manchu ('the yellow peril incarnate in one man') held sinister sway; where lascars of fiendish aspect lay stupefied by opium fumes in Thames-side hovels while, in heavy Asian disguise, Sherlock Holmes lurked to the outrage of Watson ('Holmes! What on earth are you doing in this den?'); where police informers were fished, hideously mutilated, out of the river ('My God, it's Odgers, poor fellow!' ejaculated Commissioner Nayland Smith. 'Let's hope he didn't suffer!'). Is it surprising that the Walled City is not listed with the aquarium or Aberdeen's floating restaurants as a prime Hong Kong tourist attraction?

David Hodson said, 'In my days with the narcotics branch, we found a factory here once – a heroin factory. The owners hid the stuff by pushing it through loose bricks in the walls. But the houses are so irregularly built, and the place is so like a rabbit warren, that it took us half a day to find the *other* side of a particular wall.'

'Could you ever track a fugitive down in here?'

'Difficult.'

'Bodies?'

'Sometimes bodies turn up. More in the harbour, perhaps. Hard to identify, too, if they are drowned swimming from the mainland.'

I knew something of bodies in Hong Kong harbour. A couple of years before I had spent a chilly night in a Hong Kong Marine Police patrol launch searching in the fog for clandestine swimmers from China – men and women who had waited months for this moment, risking death to cross Deep Bay at the mouth of the Pearl River below Canton. Lured on by the magic lights of that Eldorado – the loom of Hong Kong's neon against the clouds – they had watched patiently, night after night, for a fog, for a moonless sky.

The young British officer in charge of the launch said that about one in every hundred swimmers drowned. Eventually their corpses were washed up, bloated and stinking, to pollute Hong Kong's beaches and frighten the holidaymakers. Or they just floated about the harbour. Not easy, the officer explained, to yank a rotting corpse out of the sea, even if you use slings and sacks. In any case, Chinese constables hate touching a corpse. 'Superstition – spirits and all that,' the young officer said. With all those bodies bobbing about, it should be easy enough to slip one more into the harbour: someone you had knifed or garrotted, perhaps, in a rat-infested basement in the Walled City. No official figures cover that sort of death.

David Hodson and Sergeant Hon headed for the entrance to an

alley, and soon, like mice emerging from a hole, we came into the light of a normal side street. There a young, ginger-haired British police officer and two Chinese constables stood staring at a young Chinese civilian in handcuffs who in turn stared expressionlessly at the ground. Hodson gave the officer a nod and said to me, 'It looks as if they've caught an illegal immigrant.'

A few steps further on a pimply Chinese youth with long, tangled hair and bedraggled clothing slouched by, clutching a can of 7-Up. He cheerily hailed Sergeant Hon, who laughed back at him.

Surprised, I said, 'Hippy friend, eh?'

Hon smiled: 'No hippy. Kowloon CID.'

So the good old days of Holmesian disguises are not dead.

The car and driver were waiting for us outside the dentists' shops. Through plate glass the pink, plastic gums and the false molars grinned wickedly at us like the flayed relics of a secret society massacre. I've no doubt they will still be there in 1997, grinning with ironic glee as the red flag with the yellow stars of China goes up over the rooftops of the Walled City – and those seamy alleys and the secret basements of Dr Fu Manchu's domain return at last to their former owners.

Notes on the Orient

FEBRUARY 1986

Odd, but there's a feeling of tranquillity just now about the world east of India. It's unmatched, it seems to me, since the Vietnam War ended nearly eleven years ago. A fragile tranquillity perhaps. The Philippines may go up in blood and flames any time soon; Lee Kuan Yew's 'miracle city', Singapore, is struggling through its worst economic crisis in twenty years; thousands of Vietnamese boat people are compelled to raise their children in prison camps in Hong Kong; and the ageing Communists in Hanoi still refuse Cambodians the freedom of their own country.

Nevertheless, there's a tranquillity. . . .

When, next week, most Chinese hail the new Year of the Tiger, only

Hong Kong people will think, waking or sleeping, of the next twelve months as 1997 minus eleven. The Chinese takeover of Hong Kong in 1997 lies ahead as inevitably as death, yet Hong Kong, I think, is still a goodish place to be. Far better than in 1983 before the Anglo-Chinese Joint Declaration on the territory's future was signed. That year, appropriately, was the Year of the Pig, and there was a distinct feeling of the Last Days of Pompeii. Amidst lethal typhoons and hailstorms that looked to superstitious Chinese mighty like premonitions of disaster, the Hong Kong dollar slid to the floor like an anaemic boxer, and Hong Kong's rich wondered whether the time had come to do a quick bunk to the Algarve or the Bahamas. A weird year, 1983. A turning point: the year the countdown to 1997 really began.

It's better now. For one thing, relations between the British and Chinese of Hong Kong have mellowed. Some of the Raj-style smugness has gone out of the younger *gweilos* (white ghosts=Europeans). It has done them good to face the fact that the skids are under them. The ordinary Hong Kong Chinese are even friendlier than before. Here we are, trapped, they seem to say; so why not smile? No soul living has the remotest idea of what will really happen in 1997. All one can see in the present is a monotonous pattern evolving. Monotonous, and in some ways soothing.

One after the other, elderly Chinese emissaries of Deng Xiao-ping troop down to Hong Kong like bespectacled headmasters, display mouthfuls of indifferent teeth to the photographers, make delphic, vaguely reproving remarks to deferential British officials (the head prefects), and depart. Each set of remarks contradicts the ones before, so they cancel out. The Hong Kong Chinese-in-the-street shrugs, sneers in Cantonese: 'One day, one word', which means roughly, 'Sez you', and gets on with earning a living. Many Chinese, like my friends Lim and Wei Kuen, have more or less decided that 1997 for them – though not for the British or the richer Hong Kong Chinese – will be something akin to the fall of Saigon. If they carry on for now quite calmly, like men living on a hefty dose of Valium, it is not Valium that has sedated them, it is fatalism.

What the state of the nerves of Hong Kong's 10,000 non-Chinese minority people (mostly Indians and Pakistanis) may be, heaven knows. They will not get British citizenship – that is the clear message from Whitehall – and the British Government has helpfully suggested that they become citizens of China instead. Four hundred families whose menfolk fought for King and Country in World War II are similarly advised – the sort of end-of-Empire recommendation that some call betrayal.

Lim, laughing, tells me that mainland Chinese tourists have been seen here spreading their arms wide to embrace the neighbouring skyscrapers, banks and neon-lit night clubs like American billionaires, proudly announcing to their children, 'All this will be yours one day, my sons.' So it will. In the meantime, the mainlanders charge down here on shopping sprees like marauding corsairs. Wei Kuen's mother-in-law was here recently from Shanghai, bullying him into squandering far more than his meagre salary as a fork lift operator with Esso on hi-fi equipment, several tape recorders, five gold rings and no fewer than twenty pairs of shoes for her to take back. To keep his wife and baby he has had to suspend his weekly 'horsey-horsey' (off-course betting) – a most painful sacrifice.

The Hong Kong dollar now looks firm – unlike the old rupee I read about recently in P.G. Wodehouse's autobiography. P.G.'s father, after many years' hard slog in Hong Kong, was obliged to accept his pension in rupees. 'A thoroughly dirty trick,' his son remarks, 'for the rupee was then the last thing in the world with which anyone who valued his peace of mind would wish to be associated.' Rather like the Hong Kong dollar in 1983, it never stayed put for a second, usually going down. As family expenditure had to be regulated in accordance with its mood, 'Watch the rupee!' was the constant cry in the Wodehouse family.

P.G. Wodehouse spent two years in the Hongkong and Shanghai Bank – 'the most inefficient clerk whose trouser seat ever polished the surface of a high stool'. A simpering menace in Outward Bills, he became a historic disaster in Fixed Deposits. 'Wodehouse is at a loss. He cannot cope' – the whisper soon went about. And shortly thereafter he found himself at liberty to embark on the life literary.

The spirit of Wodehouse popped up at a recent party in Raffles, the grand old hotel in Singapore, for Raymond Flower, the author of a splendid new illustrated history of the hotel celebrated by Kipling, Maugham and Coward. Mr Flower, a genial man with a jolly, rubicund face under a white thatch, recalled as he autographed his book that Plum Wodehouse had dreaded the sort of people who held up a book to be signed, gushing, 'Oh, *please*. Not just your *name*. Write something *clever*.' Wodehouse claimed (no doubt tongue-in-cheek) to have taken in self-defence to inscribing his books with the legend:

You like my little stories do ya?
Oh, glory glory hallelujah.

He had to admit: 'It sometimes goes well, sometimes not.'

What forever goes well is old Raffles – a Bertie Woosterish name in itself. There is a most pleasing irony in this. *All* the ultra-modern, over-pricy hotels in Singapore are now desperately trying to entice tourists into their echoing rooms. Most hoteliers offer 50 per cent discounts. Some have taken to mothballing whole floors, like surplus warships in peacetime. It's hard to believe, but two new monster hotels, resembling ill-designed Babylonian tombs, will open their doors quite soon. They, I predict, will fare no better.

This satisfying tragi-comedy is partly due to the recession which resilient, brainy Singapore will no doubt survive. But surely it is significant that, alone amidst the wringing of expensive hotel executives' hands, unmodern, comfortable, creaky, friendly, beautiful old Raffles is having the time of its life. Now that the raunchy alleys of Bugis Street, for decades a wonderfully colourful kaleidoscope of noodle stalls, prostitutes, transvestites, sailors and tourists from evening to dawn, are nothing but a bare, dead rectangle of ground waiting for some planner to stick an underground railway station on it, it has taken Raffles to show once again that, given a chance, people will not pay just anything to stay in smart and boringly identical international hotels – and that nostalgia is alive and well and packing them in.

We must all pray that, now they have got all the supermarkets they need to look 'progressive', the non-Communist countries of the East will throw off any vestige of the ridiculous shame for the historic past that spiritually castrates so much of the Third World.

I have always admired the crafty Thais. Thais *know* that their culture is, quite simply, the best. They remind me of wary yet gluttonous golden hamsters, joyfully packing their cheeks with exciting foreign tit-bits. Unshakably proud of their semi-divine king, their Buddhism, their temples and their own beauty, they gobble up all they covert from the West or Japan without giving a cultural inch – except for the odd McDonald's here, a Kentucky Fried Chicken there. It's always good to deal with people who feel superior to you; it's the inferiority complexes that spell trouble. Of course, new Bangkok is a nightmare of tourists and traffic jams, but I believe the Thais have half-sacrificed it deliberately – as a sop to the American Cerberus ('Make a mess of the city, if you must. The rest belongs to us.')

In twenty years the Thais have survived a great deal: a *coup* or two; a serious threat from Communist insurgents; ten years of American 'occupation' (hairy, raucous Gullivers in a smooth-skinned, decorous Lilliput); a globe-shaking Communist victory in neighbouring Vietnam; an influx of Cambodian refugees fleeing, first, the genocidal Pol Pot, and now the Vietnamese Army. Thailand has become what the United Nations calls an NIC (a newly industrialized country), and has inherited economic problems thereby. Yet the glossy Thai hamster smiles as sweetly and imperturbably as ever. It's nice to see character prevailing.

Nowadays Bangkok's invaders are newly affluent Japanese rather than American servicemen. They flock in like ravening wolf packs, leaving their golf clubs at the airport to be collected on their way home, so as not to be too blatant about the sexual purpose of their trip. This detail I read in *Behind the Mask: On Sexual Demons, Sacred Mothers, Transvestites, Gangsters and Other Japanese Cultural Heroes* – a most serious and entertaining book on the fiercer social quirks of Asia by Ian Buruma, Cultural Editor of Hong Kong's *Far Eastern Economic Review*.

Mother worshippers to a man, these Japanese. Did you know that the kamikaze pilots one imagined screaming '*Banzai!* Long live the Emperor!' as they crashed their planes into American warships were really shouting, at the tops of their terrified voices, 'Mummy!'? Tired Tokyo businessmen adore tiny bars called Mother's Taste or simply Mother. After unburdening themselves there, over whisky and soda, to attentive ladies called *mamasans* – about their nagging wives, their unkind bosses – Japan's economic warriors stagger hiccuping home, 'jumping on and off each others' backs, and shrieking with the sheer joy of being eight years old again'. Evidently there will never be a Nipponese Woody Allen to mock the Great Japanese Momma.

Things are carried to odd extremes in Japan. Ian Buruma told me of Japan's *nopan kissas*, meaning 'no pants coffee shops', a new and lucrative entertainment gimmick. Tokyo's Bond Streets, Regent Streets, Mayfairs and Piccadillys all have one or two. The visitor is courteously received by two plump girls, naked apart from minuscule skirts and two dainty ribbons round their necks like Christmas presents. 'Welcome inside,' they pipe in perfect unison.

Inside there's quite a production. The usual pin-ups on the walls, porn comics on the coffee tables, beeping, buzzing invader games for those who might get bored with staring at waitresses' legs, and suspended from the ceiling a dozen or so condoms inflated like balloons at a children's party. The walls are further embellished with various articles of women's underwear. . . . All this for a cup of expresso.

The coffee costs $7 – and the effort needed to endure groups of Japanese men giggling nervously and bobbing their heads up and down like yo-yos each time the girls bend down to serve it. The climax, says Buruma, is an auction of one of the girls' panties. The winner is allowed, for a considerable sum, to slide the panties off the girl's goose-pimpled legs. Then these besuited makers of the Economic Miracle spring up and make for the door.

But wait! – there's a last delight: 'One of the girls stands by the exit and one by one the men are invited lightly to squeeze one of her breasts, almost brushing the cash register, *just once*.' All the girls bow and chant, 'Thank you for patronizing our shop.'

The oddity of it all, of course, lies in the behaviour of the men. ('But the men did nothing, Holmes.' 'Precisely, Watson, that was what was extraordinary.') To this boyish voyeurism has the noble geisha tradition descended. Manners and decorum reign supreme even at the summit of sexual exploitation. And there is further incongruity in the revelation that, despite ubiquitous strip-tease shows of the most eye-boggling kind, a small army of Japanese schoolboys and old ladies are employed part-time in Japanese customs offices deleting with ink and razor blade the slightest hint of pubic hair from imported publications.

Japan and China both benefit from the nostalgia quotient in another sort of imported publication. The airports of the East – the world, indeed – are awash with best-selling paperback books with gong-like oriental names – *Tai-pan*, *Taikoo*, *Shogun*, *Dynasty*, *Mandarin*, *Manchu*. Now come *Shanghai*, *Comprador*, *Jade*. Probably *Canton* and *Macau* will soon follow. *Tai-pan* is being filmed at this moment, and last week I spotted Madonna in 1920s garb on location up a back alley in Macau. Nostalgia, nostalgia. Where will it all end?

I am seriously thinking of getting into the act before all those romantic oriental titles are used up. It may mean resorting to the kitchen. I have already planned a domestic comedy set in modern Hangkow to be called *Chop Suey*. Next will come *Spring Roll*, a tender tale of adolescent love in Yunnan. The third – the one that might easily put paid to the genre for good and all – will be a thousand-page swashbuckling historical drama of the South China Sea. Naturally it will be packed with lust, blood, opium, white slavery, pirates in sailing ships – and (as book blurbs darkly promise) *much more*. I shall call it quite simply: *Junk*.

Past Masters Lost Leaders

The Dream World of Ian Smith

In 1974 a General Election took place in what was then still Southern Rhodesia. The guerrillas of Robert Mugabe's Zimbabwe African National Union (ZANU) and Joshua Nkomo's Zimbabwe African People's Union (ZAPU) were already on the warpath to win majority rule for nearly 6 million Africans. Their next door counterparts in Frelimo – the Front for the Liberation of Mozambique – were similarly armed in pursuit of independence from the Portuguese, and were threatening to cut landlocked Rhodesia's rail and road outlet to the port of Beira on the Indian Ocean. Despite this, and the imposition of sanctions against his regime by Britain (only partly effective), Ian Smith, Southern Rhodesia's Prime Minister, could still assure his white Rhodesian Front audiences, 'The Front will never hand over the reins of power to a black majority.' Nevertheless Southern Rhodesia became the independent African state of Zimbabwe in April 1980, with Robert Mugabe as its first black Prime Minister.

SALISBURY, SOUTHERN RHODESIA, 8 AUGUST 1974

'Every vote cast against the Rhodesian Front is a joy to the Organization of African States and the Communists.' Lean, prim, oddly spinsterish, Ian Smith lisped that appealing message to white Rhodesians and won a famous election victory this week.

Smith's speeches have been pugnacious, sententious and utterly banal. They have also been sprinkled with apparent untruths, as, for example, 'Africans come here by the hundreds of thousands because they know it is better in Rhodesia than in their own countries.' If they did come, the Smith Government would not let them in. Sometimes he puts back his head in the terrible dry laugh of the mirthless man, and you wish he wouldn't.

Only just over 1 per cent of all Rhodesians voted for Smith, but as it is only whites who count in elections, Smith won hands down. Indeed, after a few days in this white dream world you feel you are living in some perpetual whites-only Club Méditérranée, unconnected with any real world.

Sir Roy Welensky, in retirement, and Dr Arhn Palley, the courageous liberal defeated by only three votes this week in a partly Asian and Coloured constituency, agree that white Rhodesian ignorance is 'fantastic'. Why? Partly at least because in this country of the blind the one-eyed box is king. *Peyton Place*, Billy Graham and endless fifth-rate soap operas fill the television screen, punctuated by commentaries supplied by Rhodesian Front spokesmen. The daily *Rhodesia Herald* censors itself out of fear of prosecution. Perhaps even more amazing, last Sunday's midday radio news bulletin, in a longish programme that took in Peru, Uruguay and elsewhere, managed to avoid any mention of pregnant events in Rhodesia, Portugal or Mozambique at all. Films are prissily cut by censors who might be covered with confusion at the sight of a corset on a clothes line. *Playboy* is banned (a paperback edition of Synge's *Playboy of the Western World* I brought in had a customs officer in a momentary dither). The official forty-two-page booklet of banned publications includes J.P. Donleavy's *The Ginger Man*, Jules Feiffer, Germaine Greer, Martin Luther King, Norman Mailer, Mary McCarthy, Edna O'Brien and John Wells. Rhodesian Doris Lessing's *Golden Notebook* has just been restored to legality.

Rhodesia is staggeringly beautiful. You can easily see why the whites want to hang on to it. The problem is 5,700,000 blacks, and when it comes to them urban white ignorance excels itself. A Catholic bishop here estimates that fewer than 10 per cent of whites can speak to an African in an African language; less than that have the remotest notion of the customs that dignify the African way of life. Inter-racial mixing is minimal. At the university, in fact, it is less than ever before. Whites eat and walk with whites, blacks with blacks. Even in sport there is hardly any mix-up: blacks play soccer, the whites rugger. 'There is no trust now for whites,' Mr Machingambi of the students' union says. 'It's too late.' The head of the university law faculty, Dr Christie, says lack of advancement opportunities and lack of recognition weigh on African minds as much as seats in a white-dominated Parliament. But indignant white parents have stopped efforts by bank directors to place black clerks next to their daughters working in the banking halls: there might, they say very seriously, be rape among the ledgers. Many municipalities have reversed a law permitting mixed swimming pools. Blacks cannot drink in a bar in Salisbury city after 7 p.m. Two worlds.

Ewan Campbell, head of the Standard Bank here and a former much respected Rhodesian High Commissioner in London, says: 'Ninety per cent of businessmen here are very worried.' He says that when Frelimo finally closes Rhodesia's outlets to Beira and Lourenço Marques in Mozambique, the problem of exporting and importing vital supplies will be dire. Salisbury today looks sleek enough. Sanction-busting has been a spectacular success. But militarily, things are already strained and getting more so. The situation is not critical yet, thanks partly to an influx of about a thousand South African police, a stringent call-up, the raising of a second African battalion and the purchase of French helicopters.

ZANU guerrillas, entrenching themselves after entry from Zambia, have attacked farms north of Mazoe, twenty-five miles from Salisbury, and some have been picked up there. In the north-east, at least twenty farms have been attacked, and white farmers crouch at night behind steel shutters, rifles and sub-machine guns on the table with the whisky bottle, floodlights on the garden. Dust roads are regularly mined. Security officers admit that the effects of ZANU cadres (some women) in 1973 to 'subvert' Africans inside Rhodesia have succeeded. Hence the regrouping of 60,000 Africans forty-five miles from Salisbury into the sort of fortified villages that failed in Vietnam. Official figures say 354 ZANU men (called 'Ters', short for 'terrorists') have been killed. Army losses are around fifty. But no one denies that it is going to get worse, rapidly. Ian Smith was obliged at one election meeting to admit that young men were leaving in sizeable numbers to avoid call-up. And a Mozambique front will stretch Rhodesia's 5000-strong Army still further.

On top of all this, a Chinese stick bomb which exploded recently in a night club here has raised the spectre of urban terror. Security men claim to be surprised it has not started already, and say they are ready for it. If bombs began to explode in Salisbury, old Rhodesian settlers would stand firm. The post-war newcomers would very likely bolt. Whites in Angola, Mozambique and South Africa have a deep sense of local nationhood. Only the old settlers have it here.

Every non-Smith man waits now to see if Smith, from his pinnacle of electoral might, will astonish them by offering Bishop Muzorewa's African National Council (the ANC, which is the moderate nationalist movement) a substantial parliamentary bone. Only parity in Parliament and a ministry or two would mean much, the bishops says. And Mr Sithole, the bishop's recently detained colleague, would have to be released with about a hundred other ANC officials.

But many Africans, including intelligent men in the ANC, are beginning to think seats in Parliament are a trap, a sort of tranquillizer, an irrelevance. Smith will never give majority rule, they say. In the election campaign, one of Smith's Ministers said, 'The African does not want political power in this country because he knows he will not benefit from it.' (He was not addressing a black audience, naturally.) He added: 'The Front will never hand over the reins of power to majority rule.'

But that is the crux of Rhodesia's problem. Many white Rhodesians, I find, desperately want a 'settlement' with Britain because they sense enormous dangers impending as they feel nakedly alone. But the ANC cannot accept what little inadequacies Smith would give them without being denounced by the forceful men of ZANU in the hills. So there's stalemate as the time fuse splutters.

I asked Bishop Muzorewa: 'How long until African patience runs out and you moderates can do no more?'

He said: 'Two years from now. By then the opportunity for peaceful agreement will have been lost.' And he added, sadly: 'And really everyone is in favour of a peaceful solution.'

African colleagues of the bishop and liberal whites believe two years is over-optimistic. This week I watched at an African polling booth as blacks voted in an independent ANC candidate. The man with me, Gordon Chavunduka, a senior ANC man and a university lecturer, watched too. From beyond the wire fence and low hut of the polling station, beyond the streams of Africans bicycling back to work in the gleaming steel and glass white man's city, it was not difficult to feel the vastness of Africa and its black populations pressing in.

'Believe me,' Chavunduka said unsmiling, 'this is the last white-run election in Rhodesia.'

The Shah

'Padshahs [kings] stand more in need of the advice of intelligent men than intelligent men of the proximity of padshahs.' Sa'di of Shiraz, Rose Garden *(AD 1258)*

16 NOVEMBER 1975

The Shah of Iran is one of the world's few Really Important People, and as complex as the polyglot empire he rules. (The Shah is 'Imperial Majesty' because, apart from Persians, he rules 10 million Turko-mans, Kurds, Baluchis, Assyrians, Armenians and others.) Some would say Lord Curzon's description of an earlier Shah is still apt – 'impetuous, diligent, and fairly just'. Yet many young Persians would furiously reject that 'fairly just' and substitute 'tyrannous' and even 'murderous'.

He can appear gentle and humorous – 'What a nice man', you think, emerging from an audience. Yet the Shah's secret police force is among the largest and most repressive in the world. He can seem almost humble, yet he arrogantly describes Sheikh Yamani as 'that fellow Yamani' when the Saudis oppose his oil policy – and Yamani is not alone in calling him a megalomaniac.

I first met the Shah, His Imperial Majesty Muhammad Reza Pahlavi, Shah of Shahs, Light of the Aryans, one winter's night in 1963 when, because it was the royal nanny's evening off, he and I helped the Queen to put the Crown Prince to bed. The Shah's police had helped me cross from Iran into Iraqi Kurdistan to visit Mullah Mustapha Barzani's rebels – the Shah was helping them in those days – and as a *quid pro quo* he wanted to have a chat about the Kurds of Iran – 'my Kurds' he called them.

I turned up after dark, as arranged, at a rather rickety palace (since abandoned) in central Tehran. In its grounds Imperial Guardsmen, greatcoated from chin to ankle and carrying rifles with monstrous bayonets, loomed in and out of the shadows. Inside a curiously empty, echoing palace, a major-domo led me to a small, rather shabby room in which the Shah sat alone among furniture half covered by dust-sheets. A whistling draught froze our ankles as he said, pleasantly: 'Will you have some tea?'

Despot or no, he sat quite relaxed in his rattling mansion, apparently likeable, smiling and talking softly – though not for long.

The door crashed open and a furious small boy, obviously the Crown Prince, dashed into the room. He was followed by a very beautiful woman, the Queen, crying, '*Please* help me to get him to bed!'

'Excuse me a moment,' the Shah said to me, getting up as the Crown Prince deftly whizzed a child's brick between us. An energetic game of catch-me-if-you-can finally forced the Prince upstairs, where he dug in behind a low barricade of toys. In the end, the Shah pulled a *coup de théâtre*. A revolving globe of the world stood in a corner. Casually, the Shah began to twirl it, murmuring in French: 'Where is your country, *chéri*? I can't see it. How terrible, it's disappeared! Quick, find your country for me!' Sidling up, his face relaxing, the Crown Prince peered intently at Nasser's Egypt (then at daggers drawn with the Shah), then jabbed a tiny finger on the largest bit of green – Saudi Arabia. 'No, no, no!' The Shah reproachfully shifted the finger east-north-east: 'Here!' In a trice he had grabbed the boy and thrust him under the covers, and we were heel-and-toeing it down the corridor. We finished the tea and I left.

That year, 1963, like so many since the Shah's accession in 1941, had been turbulent enough. The Army had crushed serious rioting by urban poor and ultra-religious groups. But a tidal wave of change has swamped Iran since then. Today, no foreigner – and very few Iranians – would be permitted to see the Shah in such an 'ordinary' setting. Perched aloof and imperious on the Peacock Throne, he has no time now to play hide-and-seek among the palace furniture. He is far too busy taking day-to-day decisions designed to turn a semi-desert nation with an uneasy, backward population of about 34 million (one third peasants, 60 per cent illiteracy) and an annual income of £22 billion into the world's fifth most powerful industrial state by 1990.

So, when I saw the Shah on a recent visit, it was in the day-lit, chandeliered grandeur of the Saadabad Palace in a suburb of Tehran on the slopes of the Elburz Mountains. Knots of courtiers stood about in the drive, bodyguards checked credentials, and Iranian television men were setting up equipment in the garden for some royal evening function. From a reception room window, I saw the Shah's helicopter clatter down into the palace grounds and the Shah himself step briskly out of it wearing military uniform. Someone explained that he had been addressing cadets at the Military Academy.

Surprisingly soon I am shown into a smaller room and find him, the civilian again, standing facing the door, hand outstretched, a slender, neat figure with grey wavy hair, a grey suit and a pink, gold and brown tie. By coincidence, he begins talking of the Crown Prince, who is fourteen now, and, I am told, a cheerful, football-playing, French-speaking, averagely bright boy. 'I don't want to impose a rigid education on him,' says the Shah. 'Why send him abroad? We have the right kind of school in Iran, and none of those evil influences we see in Europe can dominate him here.' (The Shah despises Western 'decadence'. He favours Outward Bound-type schools and scouting.)

Chandeliers sparkle overhead. Persian carpets glow underfoot. A telephone with a tiny gold crown stands on a marble table at the Shah's elbow. The Shah himself sits upright, managing to look both very alert and very relaxed. A soft voice and the occasional flash of humour come unexpectedly after the solemn, hawk-eyed portraits one sees staring down from office walls all over Iran. I get the impression of a rather gentle personality sheltering under a, by now, well-controlled range of royal facial expressions. (He was the sickly son of an ogre of a father – Colonel Reza Khan of the Cossacks, who shouldered his way to the throne by force.) But then he begins talking of Iran's golden future – his Vision – and he moves perceptibly into a sort of emotional overdrive, and his words blend into an alarming monotone, almost as if he were programmed.

'We Iranians are entering a great era,' he says, staring at a point rather high up on the wall. 'My country will become the second most sophisticated nation in Asia after Japan. My people's cultural maturity and intelligence is going to put this country up with yours. Iran will be one of the *serious* countries in the world.' (The Shah is fond of using the word 'serious'.) 'Everything you can dream of can be achieved here – in culture, sports . . . this . . . that. . . .'

As he speaks you can see that, for him, the Vision is as real as the wall he is staring at. 'Every Iranian will be *guaranteed* security until the day he dies,' he says, as if there can be no possible doubt about it. He has forgotten you. An obsession has taken over.

The need to protect that obsessive dream from any conceivable attack is the grim, inhuman, reverse side of an essentially humanistic vision. Hence the great spider's web of the Shah's brutal police organization; hence his extraordinary, almost absurd, military build-up – an extravagant collection of non-nuclear weaponry which already makes Great Britain, say, look puny, but, as the Shah keeps on spending about £2 billion a year expanding it, will soon leave us behind and out of sight.

There he sits, like his son that evening years ago, behind his barricade of wonder-toys – Croesus, Dr No and Goldfinger combined. At the moment he has on order a £200 million Ibex electronic intelligence-gathering system from Rockwell International which, it is rumoured, will be able – among other tricks – to monitor people's secret conversations from the Indian Ocean to Syria. They are the sort of things the CIA and Israeli Intelligence, both of which have close liaison with the Iranian Intelligence Service, will find useful, too. A British ordnance factory projected for Isfahan would make Iran self-sufficient in a variety of armaments and could cost £800 million. The British are also providing a Rapier missile defence system.

The Shah's Air Force – the élite arm – already has 100 F-4 Phantoms and 100 F-5A fighter-bombers. It is taking delivery of 70 more Phantoms, 140 F-5Es and 80 swing-wing Grumman F-14s, and will soon collect 300 light attack jets. So, by 1981, the Shah should be sitting on a fleet of 800 ultra-modern combat aircraft.

On the ground, the build-up is similarly formidable. Fifty years ago, the Persian Army consisted largely of 3000 Cossacks commanded by the Shah's father, a Swedish-trained and somewhat lackadaisical gendarmerie, and a British-officered force called the South Persia Rifles. Today, the 260,000-strong Imperial Iranian ground forces have 760 of Britain's superlative Chieftain tanks and will take 1200 more in the next few years. (British Tank Regiment officers are training Persian tank-men in Shiraz.) They already have 860 American M-47s and M-60s and British Scorpions. Thus, by 1980, the Shah will have at least 3000 super-modern tanks – probably more like 5000. The Army, supported by 640 helicopters, will travel swiftly and grandly in six Boeing 747 Jumbos.

At sea, the Shah already has the world's largest hovercraft fleet, capable in theory of landing 1500 men in, say, Kuwait or Qatar – should they become threateningly radical – in next to no time. He has bought three submarines and six missile destroyers from America. He is forging a naval alliance with South Africa, and by 1980 will have the biggest fleet in the Indian Ocean after India.

It is not stressed in Iranian newspapers that paying for all this – and a mighty industrialization programme, too – is suddenly a problem. Despite that $1 billion a month from oil, the Shah will have to *borrow* abroad at least $1.25 billion by the end of this year (some bankers say $4–5 billion. No wonder the Shah gets tetchy with 'that fellow Yamani' when the Saudis try to keep oil prices down. Nor is it stressed

147

in Iran's press that for the foreseeable future all this hardware needs about 50,000 American (many ex-Vietnam veterans) and British technicians to train Iranians. Nor are estimates that, without American assistance, only a smallish percentage of those tanks and planes could fight for longer than five days without grinding to a halt. (But five days might be enough to force a stalemate with, say, Iraq.)

Despite that – and very close American involvement with his secret police organization – the Shah boasted to me, 'We are no one's lackeys.' And he has shrewdly won Russian tolerance for a regime that Moscow not so long ago did its utmost to subvert, by piping Iranian gas across the northern border in exchange for Soviet armoured personnel carriers and heavy artillery.

What next – nuclear bombs? Iran has signed the Nuclear Non-Proliferation Treaty, but in September the Shah told his officer cadets that 'if every upstart in the region acquires atomic bombs, then Iran must have them as well'. (The use of the word 'upstart' reveals the Shah's enormous pride in the antiquity and grandeur of Aryan culture. To him, modern Iran cannot conceivably be termed as 'upstart'. It is the 2500-year-old issue of the great Achaemenid dynasty of Cyrus and Darius.)

The Shah's Army and Air Force are not deployed to face the northern mountains, from which a Soviet invader would come. Nearly all the tanks and guns and planes are in the south. Ranged in an arc through the cities of Hamadan, Kermanshah, Ahwaz, Shiraz and along the Gulf coast to Baluchistan (a vast naval airbase will be built there), the missiles, the jets, the guns of the Chieftain tanks point, if anywhere, towards Iraq, Afghanistan, Pakistan, the Gulf Emirates, Kuwait and Saudi Arabia. The Shah believes he can rely on the Americans to deter the Russians. But, terrified of being contaminated by 'radicalism' from other bits of the region, the Shah takes no chances. He blithely seized the Arab-owned Tumb Islands and Abu Musa in the Hormuz Strait in 1971. ('Those islands have nothing but snakes on them,' he told me, excusing his action, and couldn't understand why outraged Arabs didn't see it that way.) And he almost grabbed Bahrein before common sense (and world opinion) restrained him.

Insecurity, of course, haunts the idealist. 'Who can guarantee me the future?' the Shah asks plaintively, hugging his dream of Xanadu. And you see in your mind's eye an early photograph of him as a tiny, timid boy in short trousers on the knee of Reza Shah, the bully of the

Cossacks, a Shah who struck Ministers in public, frowning in fur cap, white high-collared tunic and jackboots. ('Proverbially in Persia, to get things done you must both reward and punish. My father ruled more on punishment . . . ,' the Shah says.) You think, too, of the decades of humiliating interference in Iran's affairs by domineering Tsarist and British ambassadors, the Anglo-Soviet occupation of Reza Shah's country in 1941 and the destruction of his Army, his enforced abdication, his death in exile in Mauritius, still clutching a souvenir handful of Persian soil; and then of the blatant and ham-handed Soviet attempt to annex Azerbaijan, and of the struggle with the obstinate British that lasted from 1951 to 1953 and ended in nationalization of the Anglo-Iranian Oil Company. The material for several complexes is there – and a massive insecurity is certainly one of them.

Iran's manic arms build-up is designed, of course, to exorcize that insecurity by protecting the flanks of a Great Plunge Forward relatively not much less dramatic than the Great Leap of Mao's China. Defence of the Vision also means huge investment abroad: £8 billion invested in a French project to supply nuclear reactors, in Krupp's steel, in Indian iron ore, in British industrial equipment, in the Suez Canal, in massive aid to developing countries. At home, the Vision means a landscape transformed. The encircled domes of Isfahan and Shiraz strain up desperately through new industrial suburbs like golden tulips in a construction site. A new cacophonous age has come to the sandy edge of the Gulf, tribal Baluchistan and the mountains and passes of Kurdistan and Azerbaijan, scattering watch-towers, concrete airstrips, pylons, nuclear reactors and steel mills. Petro-chemical plants poison the rivers. In relentless pursuit of the Shah's billions, European and American businessmen jumbo in to Tehran's cockeyed Mehrabad airport like briefcase-bearing puppets on an endless belt. They clog hotel lobbies and plunge into the petrol fumes and traffic jams, eager for contact.

Of this chaotic extravaganza, the Shah himself is producer, director and star – like a 1930s movie mogul, overbearing, booted, barking orders through the megaphone in his fist. The pettiest problems still end up on his desk. He is said to approve every Army promotion over the rank of major, to give a personal nod to every city road-paving scheme. When I asked him, 'Don't you get tired?' he replied cheerfully, 'No, I'm used to working. I sometimes think if I didn't it would be bad for me.'

Up at dawn, he eats breakfast alone – fruit juice, one piece of toast, one cup of black coffee – while he wades through a heap of newspapers – American, British, French in the original, Italian and German in translation. (He says he listens to, or reads, abusive foreign broadcasts or articles with interest and 'a sort of relaxed disdain'. He does exercises when he has time (he looks remarkably trim and fit for a fifty-five-year-old), drinks hardly any alcohol but likes a forty-five-minute nap after lunch. Mornings and afternoons he reads reports – including, I suppose, the police dossier on the day's arrests, trials, interrogations – holds audiences and carries out inspections, always travelling by helicopter. In the evening, if there is nothing official on, he dines with the Queen, then plays cards or watches a film with the family or a few friends.

A Shah is not a Caliph, like the former Turkish Sultans. Though a Shi'a Muslim, he makes no claim to rule by divine right, though he believes in divine guidance. 'In no way do I regard myself as the one true repository of knowledge and enlightenment,' he wrote in his autobiography. But neither – he claims – does he rely on a narrow circle of advisers – 'My father did,' he says, 'and they flattered him rather than telling him the truth.'

Profiting from that lesson, he keeps a grip of steel on the machinery of decision taking. In the first, and perhaps most important, place he holds regular *private* audiences with a mixed bag of top men, whom he fairly regularly changes, often without warning. These include the Intelligence chiefs, armed forces generals, the Chairman of the National Iranian Oil Company, the Governor of the Central Bank, the Dean of the University of Tehran, a few boyhood friends like ex-Prime Minister Assadollah Alam, now Minister of the Imperial Court, a handful of other high-born cronies, and (not least) his wife, the Queen (who is clever and broad-minded as well as beautiful and indefatigable in trying to curb her husband's illiberalism).

And there are regular Cabinet meetings, at which Ministers report and recommend to His Imperial Majesty. In fine Byzantine fashion, however, these Iranian Ministers must endure the relentless snooping of royal 'narks' – 'shadow' Ministers, appointed by, and reporting to, no one but the Shah. However important you are, in Iran you can be quite sure that Big Brother is watching you very closely indeed. While those varied and cunningly overlapping audiences provide the Shah with a major supply of detailed information about the country or individuals denied to any other person or group, this channelling upward is disruptive. Because of it, too few officials feel like taking responsibility. You can be driven almost berserk by the apathy that hangs around the less exalted Civil Service offices like a debilitating smog. I know people who have had to kill time in Tehran for three weeks on end waiting for some simple arrangement to be made by young Iranian dandies in a ministry, who passed the time comparing the splendour of their ties and cufflinks, drawling: 'Please go and wait in your hotel. We will telephone,' and then did nothing.

When something similar happened to me a year or two ago, I learnt a lesson. Finally exasperated, I drove to the palace office of the Minister of Court, Mr Assadollah Alam, a man as near as anyone to the Shah himself. In ten minutes Mr Alam achieved what three weeks' badgering could not elicit from a ministry. It was a dazzling perform- ance: after a series of quick flourishes with a golden pen, the ring of a tiny bell and the appearance of a competent-looking middle-aged male secretary who bowed with deep respect to Mr Alam, my requests to see various places and talk to various people, including the Shah, were unhesitatingly met. But then Mr Alam, a slim, fine-featured man of exquisite courtesy and needle-point intelligence, personifies centuries of Aryan culture. I was lucky to see him; hardly any Iranian can do so.

'I am much more accessible and much less forbidding than Reza Shah,' the present Shah has written. 'But,' he admits, 'it is one thing to issue an order and another to see it is carried out. . . . Remorseless following up is required.' The Shah is as remorseless an idealist as idealists in pursuit of a vision usually are; as remorseless as, say, Castro, Tito or Mao. Against odds, he is trying to build an Aryan Japan, not with the indefatigable, unquestioning and robot-like Japanese, but with an easy-going and underskilled Iranian workforce, a peasantry with nineteenth-century attitudes, and a deeply sceptical intelligentsia. He seems to be pleading *and* threatening when he says, 'Nothing at all can be done if I am not obeyed.' He rules with carrot- and-stick. He unhesitatingly fires the incompetent. ('I don't accept the oft-repeated refrain: "It's not my fault." ') He prefers to reward loyalty and buy, rather than punish, opponents. And he likes to show his awareness of the shortcomings of his minions. He enjoys, for example, telling the story of his father on an inspection tour of some notoriously corrupt Police Headquarters. Reza Shah stumped into a reception room crowded with gendarmes, stopped, clapped his hands over his pockets and yelled to his retinue, 'Watch your money!'

But when the jokes are over, when the rewards have failed and the golden carrot has been spurned, you are no longer left contemplating a humorous, if sternly paternalistic, scout master so painfully grown from that tiny figure in shorts on his father's knee. You are face-to-face with something as hard and forbidding as the great cliffs at Persepolis, and with someone as cruelly inflexible as the mighty Persian kings, Cyrus and Darius, when, 3000 years ago, they hacked out the empire of which Muhammad Reza Pahlavi claims to be, by God's grace, the natural inheritor.

The Shah's Police State

'Be neither so harsh as to disquiet the people with thee nor so mild as to embolden them.' Sa'di of Shiraz, Rose Garden *(AD 1258)*

The Shah can seem so open-minded and gentle that even shrewd people leave an audience feeling 'How undictatorial he is!' It is not all bluff. I believe this immensely complex man secretly nurses a love for democracy. But it is the hopeless, crossed love of one species for another, of a tiger (say) for a rose.

Thus, he yearns for recognition from the democratic West. Yet his Prime Minister (his mouthpiece) shocked a goodwill congress of Western politicians and intellectuals in Shiraz last September by shouting: 'Do you think we want the democratic mess you have in Britain, France and Italy?'

'Iran now is Mussolini's Italy, 1927,' says an Italian editor. Only after years, the Shah jettisoned a façade of party democracy. Now his one-party system keeps the lid on politics – but only with the aid of an immensely expensive police organization. Savak is an offshoot of the Imperial Iranian armed forces, of which naturally the Shah is Commander-in-Chief. The Army is the cornerstone of the regime and by far the most efficient bureaucratic machine in Iran. In positions of control it is all-pervading. No wonder the Shah lavishes so much care and attention on it.

The Army, for example, provides the generals who run the Sazemane Attalat Va Anmiyate Keshvar (State Security and Intelligence Organization), which is Savak's full name. It also controls the National Police, and the Passport Service, and has a large (and benevolent) role to play in the Shah's civic action groups – the

Literacy, Health and Development Corps, which build roads and schools and distribute food and medicines in emergencies. Generals have become Ministers and one is now Director of Civil Aviation.

The Shah keeps up the morale and loyalty of the armed forces, already gratified by an élitist position in the country although not overly popular, by higher and higher salaries, better and better equipment, by chanted parade-ground slogans like 'Khoda, Shah, Mihan' (God, Shah, Fatherland), and personal scrutiny of promotions above the rank of major. Favourite generals have regular, private access to the Shah. One such these days is General Nematollah Nassiri, sixty-eight, the present boss of Savak. He was a classmate of the Shah's at military academy and has been commander of the Imperial Guard. He is said, not surprisingly, to live quietly apart from the odd night playing cards with the Shah at the palace.

Savak is an enormous organization. Its full-time membership is hard to estimate – some say 40,000, some 60,000; but that takes no account of the countless paid informers, in the old familiar guise of waiters, drivers, guides, students and so on. Savak was formed, organized and trained by top CIA men in 1957 and retains very close ties with the CIA and the Israeli Intelligence Service, Mossad. But even General Nassiri's office is not the inner sanctum of the Shah's security structure. Other spiders lurk in other corners of the cobweb. When I asked him about the problem of being truly informed – a problem all dictators share – the Shah laughed and said: 'I have several threads. They can't gang up on me. I am not like Nasser, who was a pure dictator – I don't surround myself with a closed group. I talk to lots of people.'

Just as 'shadow' Ministers watch the nominal heads of Government departments, a super-Savak watches Savak. The boss of *that* – the Special Intelligence Bureau – is General Hussein Fardust, fifty-six, a former classmate of the Shah's, who as a boy accompanied him to the boarding school Reza Shah chose for him in Switzerland. The Special Intelligence Bureau, though nominally inside Savak, works separately and is financially independent. Its function is to duplicate Savak's work and keep an eye out for treachery. But even *that* bureau has, in turn, another watchdog called J2 – the Intelligence branch of the imperial armed forces – also directed by a general with access to the Shah.

These onion-skins of watchfulness have proved invaluable in the past. There have been only three bosses of Savak since the total

American reorganization of it in 1957: Nassiri followed quiet, donnish General Pakravan (relieved of his post and sent off as Ambassador to Pakistan for being too lenient), who had succeeded the sinister General Teimur Bakhtiar. Bakhtiar is a figure from an Ian Fleming novel. A graduate of the French Military School at St Cyr and a *khan* of one of Iran's most powerful tribes, Bakhtiar met a very old Persian end. The Shah sacked him from Savak in 1961, for apparent implication in horrendous student riots in Tehran. In 1962 he was ordered into exile and, after much coming and going in a sinister manner between Europe, Beirut and Baghdad, was shot dead by his chauffeur (presumably representing the long arm of Savak) on a hunting expedition on the Iran–Iraq border in 1967. Following his death, 'a massive plot' was announced in Iran and there were mass arrests.

There is no doubt that Savak is licensed to be rough and ready and on occasion, one supposes, to kill. Historically, a Shah's guardians have never been squeamish. In Reza Shah's day there were ugly stories of bear pits and political prisoners being thrown into them. Today the talk is of torture, execution and shootings 'while escaping'. In interviews, the Shah has never denied that torture exists in Iran. 'Every country uses it,' he says in effect. 'Show me the country which does not.' He has simply denied that certain specific and publicized cases are true. And those denials have been pretty vague. Foreign investigators – most notably from Amnesty International – are, on the contrary, very definite. They say that, if exact numbers are elusive, they know of several thousand prisoners of the Shah's jails whose treatment has been, or is still, 'very bad' and many others whose treatment has been shocking. They have documented lists of Iranians arbitrarily arrested, of people kept months without access to lawyers or family.

Studying Amnesty's evidence – the statements taken from prisoners' relatives, the eye- and ear-witness testimony of French lawyers and others who have glimpsed prisoners in jail and in Tehran's perfunctory military courts – it is clear that almost routine methods of torture include whipping with a kind of metal whisk, violent electrical shocks of the kind the world became grimly familiar with during the Algerian War (and which can maim for life), and – something new? – the toasting of prisoners on a metal table, heated red-hot, across which victims are stretched on a grill and then interrogated.

Torture is used, predictably, to obtain information, or – and Savak

154

is very keen on this – to induce recantation and public declarations (on TV if possible) of future loyalty to His Imperial Majesty. (The Shah's motto, you might say, is: if you can't beat them, get them to join you.) Irritated by inquisitive Europeans, the Iranian authorities no longer allow visits to the special courts (in theory, public) or the political wings of Tehran's Ghassr or Evin prisons.

But Amnesty has established that, if you are arrested in Iran – it will be on Savak's say-so – you will get a travesty of a trial with your sole defence in the hands of lawyers who are not lawyers at all but retired military officers, chosen by the court. Amnesty also claims that there have been about 300 executions since 1972. To this the Iranian authorities reply that the real figure is 239, mainly 'drug pushers, police killers, armed bank robbers'. They admit, too, that since 1970 fifty-seven Iranians have been killed in shoot-outs with the police. Perhaps the most alarming case recently was that of nine Iranian political prisoners, several on the point of completing ten-year sentences, who were officially pronounced 'shot dead while trying to escape' last March. It has been suggested that they were shot in cold blood or that they died while trying to escape. But would they risk an escape when release was so close? Why, if they *were* escaping, were there no wounded among the dead? To these questions General Nassiri vouchsafes no reply whatever, and his silence certainly encourages the worst interpretations. What is more, anything General Nassiri knows, the Shah himself must know, too.

Of course, dangerous enemies *do* threaten the Shah. Wild people *are* preparing an armed struggle against the regime: that much, prisoners – and their sympathizers out of jail – admit or even boast about. And, of course, the Shah indignantly stresses this point. He said to me: 'But you ask me "What about the people you put in jail?" "Yes, I say, but those people want to betray their country." Sometimes I have to laugh – liberals in Europe defend natural murderers who machine gun people in the streets. What have those men got to offer? If they come to power, how would they treat their present apologists?' The softness goes from his voice: he is talking of the hired guns stalking his Vision for Iran.

The Shah has first-hand knowledge of opposition: assassins have come very close to him. When he was an officer cadet a gunman put bullets through his uniform cap, his cheekbone and his shoulder. But his narrowest escape came in the early fifties when a rebellious nationalist Prime Minister, Muhammad Mussadiq, raised the masses like a new Messiah, urging a takeover of the 'imperialistic, exploiting' Anglo-Iranian Oil Company. Mussadiq was lampooned in the Western press for his public weeping fits and the interviews he gave wearing pyjamas in bed.

But, to poor, repressed Iranians, Mussadiq represented both reform *and* Iran triumphant over foreign exploitation. He became a national hero. Thus, he united the two extreme wings of Iranian politics – the ultra-conservative Shi'a Muslim fanatics and the Tudeh (Communist) Party – and even parts of the Army against the Shah. He was understandably very popular and he released a tidal wave of pent-up violence. Britons were killed by Tehran mobs, the Abadan oil installations were seized by force. The Shah – it is amazing to recall now – fled via Baghdad to Rome (in both places the Iranian ambassadors, thinking he was done for, refused to meet him at the airports). Dismantled statutes of the Shah lay in the dust of Iranian streets. But in a week he was restored by a curious combination of a loyal Army, the American CIA, and enormous pro-Shah street mobs largely organized by the muscle-bound inmates of the traditional *zurkhanahs* (gymnasiums) of Tehran who, down the centuries, have provided monarchs with a sort of rent-a-crowd service. Mussadiq was arrested by the present head of Savak, General Nassiri, then a colonel.

Without Mussadiq there might not be so much talk of White Revolution today. The Shah half admits this. 'Mussadiq might have been a great leader,' the Shah wrote in his book. To me, he called him 'that crook Mussadiq', but added: 'Yes, you might say I have continued some of his nationalism – without his fooleries.' In fact, he took not a leaf but a chapter out of Mussadiq's book. The White Revolution has twin aims – reform on the Shah's terms, and the defusing of opposition by the co-option of anti-Shah elements and recruiting by rewarding them. True, the Shah's White Revolution is not quite what it's cracked up to be, but it is certainly not just a façade. Things are planned, and money is spent, as the Shah says. Nobody alleges the Shah is personally corrupt (he is a billionaire by birth). The power of landlords *has* been broken and land distributed to scores of thousands of peasants; women have been to a relatively large extent 'liberated'; hospitals and schools have been built; a major health and anti-illiteracy campaign is under way. Workers *are* to get 49 per cent shares in major enterprises – surely a genuinely revolutionary step, that has some foreign investors worried. Thousands of highly placed profiteers are being arrested (as I arrived in Isfahan last month the mayor of the city was exiled to a remote province on the Afghan border).

You are likely to be bowled over, or asphyxiated, by the fantastic crush of Peykan (really Hillman) cars in Tehran; but look at their passengers and you see the new Persian middle class. It is an already sprawling, proliferating class, built on the earnings of the new generation of doctors, engineers, Army officers, pilots, oil drillers, entrepreneurs, contractors and skilled workers. The jostling foreign businessmen attest to the fact that Tehran is Dawson City in Asia — that the new Gold Rush is on.

Yet formidable flies lurk in the golden ointment. The White Revolution is threatened in various ways. First, there are the urban guerrillas. This year police have arrested several armed terrorists, who are said to have confessed to recent killings. One was the shooting of Savak Brigadier-General Zandipur and his driver as they travelled to work. Another was the double murder of American colonels Paul Shaffer and Jack Turner outside Tehran. One of the men who shot the Americans is an ex-economics student at Tehran University, an unfailing breeding ground of dissent. From time to time the Iranian police put a newly discovered arms cache on display. Now and again someone is shot in a back street or a grenade goes off in a bazaar, or the British Council in Shiraz or Meshed gets a bomb scare, or (as recently) a bomb.

Such activist opposition can be right- or left-wing. The Shah's most vicious opponents have often spawned in the murkier pools of Muslim Persia. They lurk among the Shi'a faithful swarming in the shadows of the great mosques in the shrine-cities of Meshed and Qom, faces pale with religious venom, fanatics to watch or avoid. Such men have assassinated the Shah's Prime Ministers, have tried to kill the Shah, recently shot dead the two American colonels. They have fought with appalling mob violence against rights for women, land reform, the growing American influence ('infidel, alien') they see threatening Muslim Iran.

'Islamic Marxists' is the name the religious rebels give themselves. Straight Marxist-Leftists, Maoists, anarchists and whatnot are active, too. At any rate, Amnesty International people have in the recent past talked to leftists in Iranian jails who *said* they were preparing armed struggle against the regime. And particularly important state functions — like the Shah's great banquet for world heads of state at Persepolis in 1971 — are heralded by waves of arrests, which give some idea of *official* estimates of hostility.

The lid is on. But another snag for the Shah is the really massive indifference of Iran's swelling student population. Unfortunately, despite cash encouragements to the students to take jobs with Government, many do so, as it were, with a big yawn – certainly with none of the Shah's own feeling of adventure. Student apathy could be fatal, because the White Revolution not only depends on the new educated generation, it is meant to be *for* it.

'You see, there's no hint of political discussion,' senior, obviously well-meaning, university professors say rather desperately. 'Things should be *explained* more. Perhaps we need student councils, but the Shah. . . .'

'Students turn their backs on the Chancellor when he walks past,' another professor told me. 'Yet he's a moderate man.' He is, but he was also Chancellor of Pahlavi University, Shiraz, when last year the police, on a ludicrous pretext, stormed onto the campus (illegally) and savagely beat to the ground anyone in sight – students, visitors, faculty members. The Chancellor happened to be out of town, so was Shiraz's excellent Governor-General. Who then ordered that barbarous attack? The students don't care any more – several are still in jail, untried. Once more the Shah's image has suffered an irreversible setback among the élite of his students.

I believe the Queen, who is humane and well informed, sees the point. In a TV programme that asked why students didn't debate issues, one official demanded irritably, 'Well, why don't they?' The Queen shot back at him: 'Maybe they're afraid.' That fear contributes to a chronic brain drain. And mixed marriages and money problems also keep Iranian graduates away from Iran. 'I want to come back here,' a young Persian doctor, visiting Tehran from Germany, explained to me. 'But the pay's good in Germany. There aren't so many hospital jobs here' (though, God knows, Iranians need doctors like him in or out of hospitals). His German wife had her own reasons: 'The schools here aren't good enough for my children, and social life in Tehran is stifling.'

Iran's inadequate labour supply is yet another snag that is causing the great plunge forward to fall short of the planners' targets. There are simply not enough Iranians capable of building an industrial state. The lack of foremen, supervisors, bank clerks, trained civil servants and electronics experts has slowed projects down by creating bottlenecks, just as bad roads have trapped mountains of supplies at too few ports with too few off-loading facilities. Yet still the Shah cries 'More,

more! . . . quicker! Quicker!' like the Red Queen in *Alice*. Today's hectic Iran often looks like a man on the edge of a nervous breakdown.

Even senior Iranians are grotesquely overworked. Prime Minister Hoveida told me he gets up at 5.30 every morning; Mr Jamshid Amouzegar, who is Interior Minister and the Shah's man at the OPEC meetings, said, 'Oh I work seventy . . . eighty . . . ninety hours a week. I couldn't keep count.' Hoveida has had to rush out in person to Tehran's chaotic airport to bang official heads together. But still the Shah invites in more foreigners peddling Metro systems or industrial complexes, more trade fairs, more conferences on education or Mithraism, more dance companies for more cultural festivals. All this means that the Shah is now flooding his proud Aryans with brash aliens.

By now you meet foreign workers everywhere, in the street, on internal flights, in the new supermarkets; mainly Koreans, Filipinos, Pakistanis, British and French. And of course, American. A few steps into the airport arrivals terminal you hear a familiar accent: 'This way all United States military personnel,' an American voice sings out. At the hotel, your radio picks up an American disc jockey dishing out pop over the local US armed forces radio network. Already a hundred or so American pilots teaching Iranians to fly Bell helicopters at Isfahan have revolted against sanitary and safety standards. (All American advisers are paid an extra 10 per cent on their salaries as danger money because of the risk of assassination.) Once more an ancient people and culture are being assailed by a strident American presence – soon to amount to about 50,000, with wives and kids, large cars, money to throw around. Already Tehran rents and wages for cleaning women equal those of New York. Elsewhere – even in wartime Britain – this has meant corruption and great resentment. When I put this to the Shah he said: 'In the past the Americans have been absolutely stupid here. But I need lots of technical aid very fast. What can we do without them?' – the dilemma of Iran: the Shah has set two worlds in conflict.

In beautiful Shiraz – the antique 'nest of singing birds' – the Old Iran of the poets Sa'di and Hafez, music and rose gardens, and nightingales (championed by the Queen, a former architectural student who fights for Old Persia as bravely as she fights to mellow her husband), struggles to survive alongside the new electronics centre and polluted water. Will the domes of Isfahan disappear in the clamour of seventeen industrial satellite towns that are to be built round the city?

There are so many cross-purposes. The Shah agonizes over his apathetic students, ignoring the unbearable price they must pay for his dream, failing to see them as birds in a gilded cage with clipped wings and stilled voices. Students, some idle and inadequate, doubt any royal tyrant's revolutionary sincerity – though certainly, whatever else the Shah is, he is sincere. On the right, a swarm of Shi'a Muslim fanatics spit on the Shah's liberalism and nurse their guns. On the left, the wild ones must know how much easier it is to kill the Shah than to ensure a pure left-wing succession. Abroad, the Shah's arms suppliers in the West are aware that one day some chauvinist pan-Iranian Colonel Gaddafi could take over that pyramid of super-weapons – and shudder at the thought.

Perhaps the Shah – moving too swiftly and with too massive a combination of willpower, brute force and money for his fragmented opponents – *will* create, whatever the human price, the Aryan Japan that he so desperately craves. Or perhaps, as some prophesy, the oil flow *will* stop, the petro-chemicals and the copper prove inadequate, the money run out. If so, an image looms of a Dali-like landscape littered with the shells of steel mills, half-built nuclear power plants, obsolete air armadas; of this Shah (or his son) become a space-age Ozymandias. Sheer fantasy, one might say. But today the Shah himself sighs, 'Who can guarantee me the future?' And out of the muddle and drama of modern Iran, no answer comes.

Indeed no one could guarantee his future. The Shah threw his loyal servants, Prime Minister Hoveida, General Nassiri and others, to their deaths at the hands of his enemies. That did not save him. He died in exile on 27 July 1980 and Ayatollah Khomeini ruled in his place.

India's First Family – Democrats or Dictators?

Sanjay Gandhi died in a plane crash soon after I wrote this. His mother, Indira, was assassinated by her Sikh bodyguards in 1983. Her second son, Rajiv, succeeded her.

In a tumultuous back lane behind the Red Fort in Delhi, a crowd of rickshaw wallahs stood outside a sterilization centre waiting for their work permits to be signed. Those who were sterilized by vasectomy had their permits signed first. But one ragged young man held up to the official a paper which said, 'I have only twenty-three years old. I am unnecessary for sterilization.' His fear was prudent. Although the campaign (with 7 million sterilizations in 1976) has been an unprecedented success, in their rush for instant achievement – and a cash reward – Mrs Gandhi's followers have sometimes swept grandfathers and pre-teenagers into the sterilization campaign net. There have been protest riots in several cities. Yet undoubtedly the *idea* of the campaign is not only admirable, it is vital. In some ways India today is a golden dream in search of an administration worthy of it.

More than eighteen months after Mrs Gandhi jailed opponents and stifled the press in a deft act of bloodless political repression, many Indians are still anxious to see if she has colleagues practical, capable and sensitive enough to remodel the old, suffering India. They know she has a whim of iron. That is still about all they do know.

This uncertainty is not confined to her enemies. Last month, a young Delhi newspaper editor (appointed, it is said, because he is 'pro-Mrs G.') smiled across his desk at me and said, 'Frankly – you want my personal opinion – I can't say if we're heading for the millennium or the Third Reich.' The last time I had been in his office, in 1975, that desk had been occupied by one of India's most admired editors, later fired, an early victim of Mrs Gandhi's clamp-down on the press. Now, this pleasant young man said, 'Mrs G. is not the stuff of which dictators are made.'

What about the censorship?

'You know, we had no calls at all from the censor here last month.'

But I had in my pocket a list of calls the Government censors had made to other newspapers, if not to his, during that month.

On the 6th (the list said), Mr K.B. Sharma of the Delhi Censors Office telephoned at 6.15 p.m.: 'Kindly do not publish any news about the strike in Dhariwal Mills.' On the 13th: 'All news, reports or comments about the American sale of arms to Iran will be subject to pre-censorship.' On the 22nd the deputy censor phoned to say, 'Please do not play up the Chinese players' participation in the Fourth Asian Badminton Tournament at Hyderabad. This includes photographs of the Chinese also.' In all, there had been sixteen calls from the censor. But not to this editor.

'Do you think that's because the authorities think of you as good and reliable?' I asked him.

He evaded the question by hamming: 'I no speaka the English,' he grinned, putting on a deliberately funny accent.

Of course, Mrs Gandhi and her rising son, Sanjay, have not yet inaugurated the millennium. But neither, despite the censor and the people in jail, is India anything like the Third Reich. True, in one magazine office I heard someone saying into a telephone, 'Oh, hello ... yes ... My God, how did you get away with that? Oh, nobody is within earshot, I see.' But he was half-laughing.

Later, as the Rajdhani express streamed through the night between Delhi and Calcutta, the steward brought curry on little folding tables into the four-berth sleeper in which two Bengali engineers (one of them a Government official) genially argued about the pros and cons of the Emergency, the new 'discipline', the way Mrs G.'s power proliferates like some man-eating plant. 'Prices are down. ... Fewer strikes. Yes, but bureaucracy is still a nightmare ... newspapers are damned dull.' A third man silently puffed a pipe.

'Aren't you uneasy, having public discussions like that?' I asked one of the Bengalis when we parted.

'Oh, it hasn't come to that.' He seemed surprised.

As it happened, the train *did* reach Calcutta's Howrah station on time, yet I gave up my ticket to a near-skeleton in a tatty semi-uniform, with no sense that I was in anything like Italy, 1927, or the Shah's Iran, 1977.

A Marxist writer and critic of Mrs Gandhi in Calcutta said, 'Lots of people were arrested, but there's not been much brutality. Very few cases of systematic torture as in, say, South Africa or Chile.' In Delhi, an opposition Member of Parliament revealed plans for a union of all anti-Congress parties under the veteran politician, Morarji Desai, who is still in detention, and said, 'Morarji has been kept in an old, modernized hunting lodge. He gets the censored newspapers, sees his family once a week. He's up at 5 a.m. doing his yoga exercises. He spends a lot of time teaching his policemen Hindi, Sanskrit and English.' Jayaprakash Narayan, the almost saintly apostle of non-violent grass-roots opposition to Mrs Gandhi, now released but gravely ill, told me he was treated 'quite well in every respect' – except that 'I was kept quite alone for four months' (a horrid form of mental torture, certainly). George Fernandes, the Socialist Party Chairman, has denied to journalists that he has been tortured in prison. I saw Fernandes handcuffed but apparently healthy, at a brief court hearing in Delhi attended by his lawyers.

Many people are still in jail, – about twenty-four MPs and 50,000 to 60,000 others, according to an opposition leader I met; not nearly as many, says the Government. Enough, anyway, to have disrupted the machinery of the opposition parties. Their enforced silence means that political Delhi is now a bit like a television programme with the sound turned off. In October, this unnatural silence was broken quite unexpectedly. Mrs Gandhi allowed public seminars to be held on drastic amendments she had devised for the constitution approved by her father, Jawaharlal Nehru. And these were reported uncensored in the press. Suddenly, the daily *Statesman* of Calcutta appeared with the headline 'Lawyers criticize amendment' over two columns, humming with anti-Mrs Gandhi-isms. I squeezed into a packed and sweltering hall in Delhi to hear applause for speaker after opposition speaker. Phrases like 'drastic and draconian laws . . . constitutional dictatorship . . .' boomed from loudspeakers into a hall downstairs where Mrs Gandhi's Congress Party was holding a similar meeting – far less well attended.

The free debate on the constitutional changes lasted about a month. The enthusiasm of audiences at the open seminars may have been a major reason why Mrs Gandhi postponed elections due this March. Another may well have been her twenty-nine-year-old son Sanjay, now a major – some say *the* major – force in the land. 'Is it more important to have the election or to have a stable economy?' he demands.

That question encapsulates the Government's justification for the Emergency. It was put in another form decades ago by Aziz, the Indian doctor in E.M. Forster's *A Passage to India*: 'Half closing his eyes, Aziz attempted to love India. She must imitate Japan. Not until she is a nation will her sons be treated with respect. He grew harder and less approachable . . . "We need a King, it would make our lives easier," said Aziz.'

The irreverent began to call Mrs Gandhi 'Queen of India' after June 1975. And since then the lives of too many Congress people have become too easy. But has India begun to imitate Japan? It has, and had done so before the Emergency. Now it is the world's ninth largest industrial producer; Indian factories make practically everything from

Worcestershire sauce to steel to whisky. India exports steel mills to Third World countries like Libya. It has a Department of Space, a space rocket range, an atomic research centre, and hopes to launch a four-stage satellite rocket quite soon. Eighty million industrial workers make tractors, trains, light tanks and computers.

What can Mrs Gandhi claim? Quite a lot. Taxation checks, a massive drive on smuggling (textiles, electrical goods, liquor slipped ashore by catamarans from Hong Kong, the Middle East and Singapore), and restrictions on foreign exchange, have reduced a 40 per cent inflation rate to practically nothing. Industrial production is up 10 per cent. The public sector of India's mixed economy has begun to pay largely because millions fewer man hours have been lost (strikes are not banned – 'Mrs Gandhi is not that crude,' my Marxist writer friend said, adding ironically, 'but the climate is against strikes.') Prices generally are curbed. Some dead-beat babus in the bureaucracy have been axed; a few whizz-kids have been given a chance.

In the countryside, miracles are harder to conjure up: minor land reforms; the abolition of peasant debts (although this has made necessary credit harder to come by); the abolition of bonded labour (although the British Raj had, in theory, put paid to that iniquity). Perhaps there is also a belief seeping through to India's poor that at last Mrs Gandhi intends to do something for them.

'We are racing against time,' said Mrs Gandhi's Law Minister, Mr H.R. Godkhale, the other day, excusing the guillotining of debate on the changing of the Constitution. Easy to see what he means, in a country where 1300 babies are born every hour of every day, where millions suffer from hunger every day from birth to death. Impossible not to agree with Ruth Prawer Jhabvala, the European writer married to an Indian – 'We may praise Indian democracy, go into raptures over Indian music, admire Indian intellectuals . . . but all the time I know myself to be on the back of this great animal of poverty and backwardness.' You look at the poor cluttered landscape of, say, Bihar, or West Bengal – and you seem to feel that great animal stir beneath you. How can one not believe passionately that something must be done? Something like Mrs Gandhi's justification for postponing elections – her 'dynamic socio-economic policy'.

It is not, after all, as if the opposition presented a positive alternative. It was riddled with dissension, corruption and shameful incompetence. J.P. Narayan, a great and good old man, said from his hospital bed in Bombay, 'The political parties are certainly not the path. They miseducate the people in far too many ways.' V.S. Naipaul, the West Indian writer, is correct when he says that if you support the rule of law in India you find yourself sponsoring some startling causes. The Jan Sangh Party, for example, the National Party of Hindu Power, clamours for nuclear weapons on the one hand, and on the other free fodder and good homes for ageing holy cows. 'It is not a joke,' Naipaul adds. 'It is the best organized opposition party.'

Though Mrs Gandhi is blamed for allowing her brash and far-from-universally loved son, Sanjay, to come blazing, like a particularly flamboyant comet, across the Indian political sky, one has to admit that his proclaimed *policy* is admirable. Mahatma Gandhi – no relation to Indira or Sanjay – could hardly find fault with a programme that urges everyone to plant a tree a year, to educate an illiterate every year, to limit families to two children. He talks of helping 'the poorest of the poor'; is hailed by the Congress press as 'the much awaited leader'; pilots his own plane, 'unleashing Youth Power'. He is right when he implies that the odoriferous hulk of the corrupt, self-satisfied Congress Party needs a ruthless overhaul. When I saw him, cool, balding, with sideburns, glasses, a loose white cotton shirt, he was saying with a faintly supercilious and utterly confident smile, 'I've never said the old members of the Congress Party should be *sterilized*' – (laughter from his companions) – 'nor that they should step aside. But I *did* say that they shouldn't stand in the way: that's different!'

Perhaps the impetuous Sanjay will actually beget the idealistic, youthful, grass roots movement that even J.P. Narayan insists is vital for India's transformation. Already he has clashed with Congress stalwarts like the Chief Minister of West Bengal, Siddartha Shankar Ray. Ray ordered some disorderly Sanjay Youth cadres to be jailed in Calcutta; but Mrs Gandhi supported her son. Now Sanjay's brash young friends have moved into banking, defence, internal security and other niches of power. The Communist Party of India, the only non-Congress party to support Mrs Gandhi's Emergency, has certainly scented trouble.

The CPI men I met in Delhi talked scornfully of Sanjay and 'reactionary developments in [Sanjay's] Youth Congress'. Not surprisingly: for Sanjay is against nationalization, and a declared anti-Communist. In a fury Mrs Gandhi has branded any Communist attack on Sanjay as an attack on herself. Sanjay is a product of the Emergency. But so is the burgeoning of the internal security organization, RAW, the Research and Analysis Wing of the Prime Minister's office. 'Oh, those files, those bulging files that Mrs G. has on all her opponents – and her colleagues,' an Indian friend said, throwing up his hands in mock fright.

Despite them, I received a passionate assurance from Mr V.C. Shukla, the Minister of Information – 'I want to repeat and repeat again that we are democrats!' If so, has Mrs Gandhi got herself into a muddle, half democrat, half autocrat? The quite unnecessary saga of the *Indian Express* makes it seem likely. For months its owner, Mr Ramnath Goenka, a shrewd, determined and spritely seventy-year-old businessman, has been absurdly harassed. Censors have deliberately badgered him; Government advertising and electricity have been cut off; presses have been seized by the police. Though the courts ruled for the *Express* and made Mrs Gandhi look both tyrannical and ham-fisted, the Government is still darkly manoeuvring to buy control of *The Statesman*. Yet the two newspapers are actually pretty tame, even if they do occasionally enjoy teasing top people by quoting Mahatma Gandhi and Nehru on press freedom.

All the more confusing, some critical weeklies are left more or less alone. 'Some words may be deleted,' a writer for the Calcutta *Marxist Review* told me. 'But without compromising our ideas.' The *Economic and Political Weekly* of Bombay is still lively. Of course, several major papers have been closed, and in December a left-wing review closed itself down in protest against censorship. Several foreign journalists are barred from India. The *Times* has no correspondent in Delhi, but the BBC has just been given permission to return after eighteen months. The *New York Times*, Reuter's and other news agencies are hardly bothered by the censors these days; the vultures' nest in a tree in the Reuter man's garden is therefore less of a black joke than in the days when expulsion seemed always imminent. Neverthe-less, the fracas over the *Indian Express* and *The Statesman* makes one wonder. Can this confusion reflect a tug-of-war among the self-professed idealists round Mrs Gandhi? Has she, among her colleagues, men in whom venom is stronger than dignity or sense – men obsessed with total control over everything in India, even to two rather staid and mutedly critical newspapers read by a minute fraction of India's 650 million people? For such bullying seems to be less the outcome of cool, long consideration by Mrs Gandhi than of panicky *ad hoc* decisions of her Cabinet.

One trouble is that, to some top Indians, criticism is regarded as subversion, probably encouraged from abroad. Up to a point, history justifies this paranoia. Unfortunately, it inspires verbal outpourings from close colleagues that diminish Mrs Gandhi's mystique as she relentlessly isolates herself – from non-Congress moderates, from Communist Party allies, even from elements of her Congress Party.

Mr Mohammed Yunus, one of her closest advisers, for example, sits a few doors away from Mrs Gandhi's office in the rose-pink masterpiece Sir Edwin Lutyens built for India's rulers. A bombastic orator, he proclaims triumphant lies: 'In some American States, women have no votes!' And: 'Elections? Britain did not have elections for eleven years during the war.' And: 'I talked to the Shah of Iran recently about what he did with prisoners and his reply was: "We do not have prisoners, we just shoot them."'

Mr Yunus is the Alf Garnett, more than the Enoch Powell, of Emergency India. But he is not simply a TV or a political grotesque: he is a chosen buddy of the Prime Minister. All the same Mrs Gandhi, that hard but strangely vulnerable woman, does not seem to aspire to total dictatorship. Perhaps her India is difficult to pin down precisely because she is not a Mussolini by temperament. (To play a full-blown Duce in such a vast and varied country she would have to bring the Army into the political act, and the fate of Sheikh Mujibur Rahman in Bangladesh – killed by Army officers – is fresh in Indian minds.) She *could*, after all, have sent the police to close down the *Indian Express* once for all. There *have* been several mass meetings recently criticizing the Government – particularly in the Tamil south.

Nevertheless, the brashly insensitive way the Family Planning campaign has been handled (how many Ministers qualify for vasectomy, by the way?) is the thing that worries many Indians, not the idea of it. And the dubious company Mrs Gandhi keeps in Delhi is another – particularly since the radical changes in the Constitution mean that, although Mrs Gandhi herself may not intend to use it, any later political smash-and-grab merchants will find the machinery of dictatorship conveniently parked and ready to drive away. Some Congress Party men are urging even more drastic changes. Why? There may never be anything like an Indian Third Reich if Mrs Gandhi can give the Indian people the merest glimpse of a millennium within – how long? 'Say, two years or three,' a sensible Indian journalist forecasts.

So the danger to Mrs Gandhi, and of the total demolition of freedom and hope in India, lies in one thing: the possible failure of men who, having dismantled the Constitution, find themselves – through muddle, fear, or even competence too ruthlessly applied – unable to deliver the goods.

'We need a King,' said Aziz in *A Passage to India*. 'It would make our lives easier.' It is difficult to say he was quite wrong. But one should keep a sharp eye on the courtiers.

The Iron-fisted Dandy

Oxford-educated Zulfikar Ali Bhutto was trying to drag Pakistan into the modern era – and upsetting many people in the process. Even old allies deserted him as he was accused of vote-rigging in the General Election of 1977.

1 MAY 1977

Even if Pakistan's elections were not rigged, I believe Zulfikar Ali Bhutto would have won. Not only because he had the electoral aids of Government transport, a controlled press, the patronage of power and lots of money. There is more to it than that. Quite simply Bhutto, like him or not, is by far the brightest and most forward-looking Pakistani.

He has held nearly every Government portfolio in his time ('Except Finance – I'd have ruined Finance,' he jokes). He is also expertly aware of what makes the international world go round (he could make an excellent Secretary General of the United Nations) – a vital asset for the head of a relatively weak, poor but crossroads-of-the-world country like Pakistan. And he is only forty-nine. All these things must have – or should have – counted for much with Pakistanis who think seriously.

The trouble with Bhutto – and the extreme fascination of him – lies largely in the clash between his own dandified sophistication and acute intelligence on one hand, and on the other the underdeveloped and psychologically repressed Middle Ages atmosphere of Pakistan – even Pakistan in 1977. The intense dislike he inspires in decent men like his arch-opponent Ashghar Khan is the kind that worthy, beta-plus schoolboys feel for a brilliant head of class who is also a bit of a bully. For Bhutto does not simply not suffer fools gladly – he doesn't suffer them at all. He has always been an alarmingly turbulent mixture of seething ambition and hard-shelled self-esteem. He has always known where he was going. At an age when many boys dream of becoming an engine-driver, he confidently announced his intention of one day being a Head of State. He was raised in a family atmosphere well suited to such lofty ambition.

Bhutto's ancestors were Rajputs, the Hindu warrior caste who lived among the romantic hilltop palaces of desert-bound Rajasthan, and whose chiefs – reflections of the chivalrous knights of medieval Europe – were often in the past sent by the Muslim Mogul emperors to govern the provinces of northern India. (There is thus a faint historical echo of this in Bhutto's latter-day lordship over what remains of dismembered Pakistan – a land that stretches from the Indus to the frontiers of Persia and Afghanistan.)

Four centuries ago one of Bhutto's ancestors converted to Islam. The family moved to and remains in impressive estates at Larkana in Sind, the desert southern state of Pakistan. Bhutto's father, an eminent Muslim leader, built a grand mansion in Karachi, amassed one of the world's largest collections of works about Napoleon, and was knighted for services to the Raj.

In his youth, Bhutto rapidly equipped himself with the essential paraphernalia of modern, intellectual, political man. He achieved lofty degrees in law and political science at Oxford and in California. Returning to feudal Pakistan, he practised law in Karachi. He left the law in 1958 to join the military regime of General Ayub Khan – a fact which is nowadays a point of attack for his critics, who say he was the most 'Fascist' of the Ayub regime, and that he introduced the iron-handed press censorship of those days.

Today Bhutto admits that Ayub Khan's Basic Democracy was a disguised form of something very like Fascism – but he quickly adds that at the time he felt that anything was worth trying which would end the political chaos that was humiliating Pakistan in the eyes of the world, particularly when contrasted with the stability of big rival India. He was Ayub's very young Foreign Minister in 1965 when the General signed the Russian-dictated Tashkent Declaration which ended the war with India, but which Bhutto thought intolerably humiliating to Pakistan. He broke with Ayub.

He suffered and gained much from that break. For some time he was harried, wooed and harried again by the Ayub regime. He was offered sparkling posts abroad: he refused them, preferring his estates at Larkana. Soon he launched his People's Party and openly attacked the dictatorship. Thugs – set on him by Ayub – disrupted his rallies (there's nothing new about this year's political violence). In November 1968 he himself – the elegant, young, reforming mandarin – was thrown into a cell with rats, bats and mosquitoes. When he emerged it was like a rebirth.

Jail – as it has done for so many other ambitious and rebellious men – made him a martyr. His 'Fascist' past was forgotten. A wave of popular support enveloped him. Quite soon, with his undoubted involvement, a student uprising overthrew Ayub. Even Bhutto's enemies cannot deny that he was the only political leader who had the courage to come out against what looked like an impregnable dictatorship.

Bhutto says he never expected Ayub's military successor – General Yahya Khan – to last ('second dictators are always weaker'). And it is not yet possible to unravel satisfactorily Bhutto's precise role in the tragedy of East Pakistan (Bangladesh), which deprived the state of Pakistan of 80 million citizens. He openly deplored the excesses of the Pakistani Army in East Pakistan. But wouldn't he, like Yahya Khan, have used force to break a rebellion fuelled by India, the great enemy, to dismember Pakistan? Very probably.

After the surrender of East Pakistan in December 1971, Bhutto really came into his own. It was a terrible time. Practically every prominent Pakistani was discredited in some way: 90,000 Pakistani soldiers were in Indian prisoner-of-war camps. East Pakistan had gone for ever, but the urgent danger now was that West Pakistan might fly apart too. In this fearful crisis, Bhutto became President – with the mission of saving the state.

He has ruled Pakistan ever since, later switching his title to Prime Minister, according to a new Constitution. From the beginning, Bhutto the brilliant politician had known exactly how to deal with his rivals – and importunate allies – on the scheming left and the elephantine, tricky right. Luckily, he had won the elections of 1970 hands down, partly through his catch-all slogan, 'Islam is our faith, democracy is our policy.' Democracy appealed to Pakistanis grown disillusioned with years of military rule.

Once in power, Bhutto soon disposed of all the 'scientific Socialists' who disapproved of him. Some are retired. Some are in Hyderabad jail. I don't know of any who are still around.

On the right flank, the old guard – generals, landlords, a rag-bag of corrupt blimps left over from Ayub – was discredited. When catastrophe finally handed the leadership to Bhutto, it meant an end to the most blatant aspects of the feudalistic dominance of a score of families, backed by strong-arm retainers and the regiment of crabbed religious leaders ('the grey beards', Bhutto contemptuously calls them) who sought to keep the clock back as far as possible, and the modern world at bay.

His Ayub experience had switched Bhutto towards Socialism. Some might call it 'bourgeois Socialism' (Britain's own Pakistani lefty, Tariq Ali, for instance), but at least it meant a bayonet charge against the Middle Ages mentality that was keeping a nation in purdah. Bhutto's main problem remains one of modernization. 'Pakistan is hidebound,' he says. 'I want Pakistanis to travel and bring new ideas back with them.' (Lots of Pakistanis travel, but equally lots of them never come back: among other natural ills Bhutto and Pakistan must face is a brain drain.)

'Give me time,' he pleaded in 1971. And since then there have been innovations. Nationalization, for example, of banks, insurance, cement, fertilizers; land reform, in the teeth of mighty landlords. National production has gone up 50 per cent. Pakistan is practically self-sufficient in wheat and rice. Soon, the $1 billion Tarbela Dam will be opened again (it sprang a leak last year).

Bhutto negotiated the 90,000 prisoners back from India. And his twenty years of top-flight international experience – from the heady, Bandung conference days when Nasser, Chou En-lai, Sukarno and Nkrumah 'founded' the Non-aligned Movement – helped him to make things up with India, achieved friendship with the Shah *and* the Chinese and friendly non-alignment with America and the Soviet Union. He is also – important for Pakistan – getting on well with President Daoud of Afghanistan.

But there are bluebottles in the ointment. His birth control plans have failed – traditional feelings scuppered them. So the 73 million Pakistanis continue to over-proliferate. Nationalization has alienated businessmen. 'There's too much of it,' some say. Others say, 'Bhutto puts in his cronies to run things and they don't know how.' Investment flags. Prices go up. Corruption in high places is admitted by Bhutto. From the left come charges that his land reform is a fraud – he of course is a big landowner himself. Above all, there is the accusation of high-handedness. Certainly the press is controlled to the point of inanity. Bhutto has not shown great flexibility, either, in dealing with incipient separatism in Baluchistan and the ever-restive Pathan-populated North-West Frontier province. He moved the army into Baluchistan, and bullets have flown and bombs exploded there. He imprisoned the fiery Pathan leader, Wali Khan, for sedition – though the prison is air-conditioned and relatively cosy.

I saw Wali Khan's wife, Nasim, vehemently campaigning in Peshawar, attacking Bhutto for political jailings, alleging intimidation and worse, railing against 'one-man rule', to the approving growls of tribesmen from the Khyber Pass.

One-man rule? Mr Bhutto, when I uttered the phrase, looked sternly at me. 'We have a constitution,' he said, 'adopted unanimously by all parties. So, really, it is not that here we have a banana republic with only one tree and under it Mr Bhutto is sitting.'

What about those political opponents in jail?

'We were dismembered. Some people here also want to break up West Pakistan' (Asghar Khan would deny this). 'People who want to create trouble might be in jail – there is a law of the land, after all. But you will find the least number of people in jails in Pakistan than in any other neighbouring country.' (Probably true up to the end of the Emergency in India.)

The crying lack of criticism in newspapers, then?

'That will gradually go. You see, when the fat is in the fire, the newspapers get a little yellow. With greater national confidence, greater technological self-sufficiency, with secessionist elements defeated, why should we not allow uncomplimentary editorials to appear?'

The unforced words fall from the sensuous lips in the handsome face. Smoke curls up from a Havana cigar. A backward nation needs discipline: that is the idea – not, by the way, an idea confined, on the subcontinent, to Pakistan.

It is difficult to avoid the thought that Bhutto, diplomat, clever politician, nobody's handservant, is not the best man to rule his difficult country. Equally difficult not to grasp the cast of his mind when he calls, languidly, the late Sheikh Mujibur Rahman, the first hero of Bangladesh, 'oppressively mediocre'. And of his dogged opponent, Air Marshal Asghar Khan: 'He turned to politics after leaving the Air Force, because he missed the panoply of power, you know, the brass bands, the salutes. He tried to imitate my political style. And, by slogging away at the political nets, you might say, he has become a cricketer – not a Denis Compton or a Hammond – but still . . . he has . . . become . . . a cricketer.'

Imagine how such light drawing room talk might translate into the day-to-day treatment of individuals, and you have some idea of the feelings of frustration and humiliation even his colleagues sometimes feel – leave alone opposition spokesmen struggling to be taken seriously. It is that aloof, donnish, know-it-all property in Bhutto that infuriates them. It would go better perhaps in England, a country which, although he led Pakistan out of the Commonwealth, he sincerely loves (he buys his clothes in London's West End. His Oxford days were sublimely happy.) Yet he is as brave as any ancient Rajput warrior. He is not afraid of physical contact with the masses, and in crowds of half a million or more, without the encircling police that Mrs Gandhi insisted on, he is down there in the pungent ruck, shouting his speeches, no holds barred, no further from his fans or a would-be assassin than an outstretched pistol arm.

In Lahore last winter I met an intelligent, well-born young Punjabi who for an hour and a half poured out his hatred for what Bhutto had done to drive his father out of politics – something about an arrest and a court case. Then, without pause, he switched to a wretched story of how medieval Muslim tradition in Lahore still makes it impossible to take his girlfriend to the cinema. 'She would be obscenely hissed and pushed around. . . .'

'But surely, whatever you say about Bhutto, it is he of all politicians here who stands the best chance of changing that sort of lunacy?'

'OK. Yes. I agree,' he said after a pause. 'That's the way things are here.'

Zia Gets Set to Hang Bhutto

To his opponents, Zulfikar Ali Bhutto was the Al Capone of Pakistani politics. It was probably true that few scruples restrained him in his pursuit of power. Enemies believed he had manipulated the voting results in the General Election of 1977 and accused him of the intimidation and murder of political opponents. Pakistan was in a sorry state at the time. Psychologically, Pakistanis still suffered from the humiliation of defeat by India in the war of 1971, as a result of which East Pakistan became independent Bangladesh. The country's economy was in deep trouble, neighbouring Afghanistan was increasingly threatened by a Soviet invasion, and the forces of fundamentalist Islam, hitherto dormant, were taking to the streets in huge anti-Bhutto demonstrations. General Zia al-Haq, Bhutto's own appointment as Chief of Staff, took over, and Bhutto, the cleverest Pakistani, was soon on trial for his life.

RAWALPINDI, 1 OCTOBER 1978

'There's going to be an important hanging here soon. They're going to hang Mr Bhutto.' Similar words have dogged me these past two weeks from Karachi to the Khyber. I have begun to believe them. I walked in the heat of 'Pindi, past the wall of the jail in which Mr Bhutto awaits the outcome of his appeal against a death sentence for murder. I was not allowed to see him. But nearby I stopped at the gate of the white, grandly pillared mansion where I last saw him in 1977. Then, the opposition had already started the demonstrations that drove this too-arrogant man from supreme power to the death cell.

Last week, General – now President – Zia al-Haq, the man running Pakistan like a learner driver wrestling with a secondhand Maserati, said to me: 'With his brain, Bhutto could have been President for life.' Now it looks very much as if, one morning in November, the cleverest Pakistani will be hanged for murder as shabbily as Kipling's Danny Deever, among the tree-shaded British-built cantonments and dusty military cemeteries. (Zia to me: 'If the Supreme Court says, "Acquit him," I'll acquit him. If it says, "Hang the blighter," I'll hang him.')

Yet if ever Pakistan needed the brains of Bhutto, it is now. With uncertain leadership, dangerously isolated, it suddenly faces an old, familiar menace. First, the kind of situation bedevilling the Shah in Iran is not impossible in Pakistan – extreme Islam (vintage AD 670) rebounding into extreme leftism. But much more immediately perilous – and it *is* immediate – is the jet-age revival of the Russian shenanigans that nineteenth-century British viceroys called the Great Game, and John Buchan heroes scrambled eagerly into disguise for.

I was made aware of the urgency of all this when the Chinese Ambassador in Pakistan, clutching a cup of vichyssoise at a party, having told me how grave the Shah's state was, earnestly added that he really believed the Russians were on their way to Pakistan. (General Zia to me last week: 'Afghanistan is now a proxy Soviet state. For good. It cannot be changed back.') Why should Zia or the Chinese be wrong? Across the petrified wave of the North-West Frontier, armed

174

Pathan tribesmen are being energetically rallied – or bombed – by Moscow's Marxist friends in Kabul. ('Kabul,' Zia told me, 'is full of troops and thousands of Russian advisers.') Kabul newspapers have recently renewed claims to chunks of Pakistan's frontier province.

Pakistan confronts this emergency with a half-cock Government. And this parlous state of things could drag on until October 1979, when Zia has promised elections. Meanwhile the new interim President has thinly disguised his military rule with a batch of conservative Muslim Ministers who spend much of their time like the Iranian mullahs propagating a basic medieval Islam. Every day acres of Pakistani newsprint forecast 'an Islamic order which will efface all evils', (or alternatively give a fine religion a bad name). Yet someone ought to get on and govern, or people might start to complain. Martial law is already becoming an irritant to many. For Pakistan is one of the most backward countries between Rabat and Rangoon: population 75 million, 80 per cent illiteracy, with a failed harvest and hardly two rupees to rub together.

In Karachi, to check on a possible swing back to seventh-century Islam, I climbed betel-stained stone stairs to a tiny third-floor office. There I found one of Zia's hot-gospelling Ministers, a leader of the extremist Jammaat-E-Islami Party. He was a slight, friendly man with a white, close-clipped beard. He told me there had not been a proper Islamic state for 1400 years. He went on to explain what that involved: 'No interest rates on money. No sexual relations without marriage. No drinking. (You may bring your own, Mr Young.) No gambling. Adultery punishable by death, but only if vouched for by three eye-witnesses with beards.'

Handcutting for theft?

'In theory yes. But re-education will induce total, voluntary discipline – so finally there'll be no theft to punish. No hands have been chopped here so far, incidentally.'

Re-education?

'Books, all TV, all films, will be educative and have an Islamic moral. There'll be no dancing, and no press reporting of murders, suicides and such things.'

A sort of religious police state?

The Minister smiled. 'Until people grasp the discipline. You see, Islam is not just between a man and God; it is a state. That's why the penalty for treason against Islam is death, too.'

The veil?

'Western people get that wrong. Women can show the forehead, cheeks, and chin, the hands, and the legs from the knees down. Isn't that enough?' His smile was almost naughty.

In need of fresh air, I took to the Murree Hills, north of Rawalpindi, to see the man who is probably Pakistan's Great Political Hope. Air Marshal Asghar Khan is a powerfully built, rather solitary, utterly honest, moderate man, who was also tough enough to lead the nationwide agitation that put Bhutto behind bars. I found him in a friend's bungalow near an old British mule depot at a cool 8000 feet, wearing a cardigan. From wicker chairs we looked across grey-green ridges, north-east to Kashmir, north to the invisible Hindu Kush.

Feeling a bit like someone out of *Greenmantle*, I asked if trouble was really brewing.

'Yes. Iran and Afghanistan could easily be bad trouble,' Asghar said. (He had just returned from China. Zia's foreign affairs adviser has just been there, too.)

Well out of sight below us, as far as Waziristan, I had been told, Pakistani political officers are busily warning 'their' tribesmen against Communism from Kabul. Further north, mullahs are talking of Afghan 'infidels'. But the tribes seem wary, waiting to spot the winner. (Zia to me on the Russians: 'The Soviets can now see their dreams come true – to reach warm waters. Through Pakistan.') To be more precise, through Baluchistan or the North-West Frontier Province. In fact, the recurring nightmare in Islamabad is that Baluchistan and the Pathans of the frontier might secede from Pakistan.

'That's not a danger,' Asghar said, 'if – *if* – we are left alone. But with the Soviets creating trouble here. . . .'

A day later, in Peshawar, the capital of the North-West Frontier Province, I heard the same view from the witty and warm-spirited Pathan leader, Wali Khan, who has the flowing white locks and Roman nose of a nineteenth-century Welsh preacher, and three years in Bhutto's jails behind him. 'British policy was always to stop the Russians on the Oxus and the Hindu Kush,' he said. 'Now the line is the Khyber, just up the road.'

Faced with these new threats, Pakistan feels acutely isolated and abandoned. A Pakistani brigadier told me sadly, 'Carter is interested in Japan, Israel and oil. That's all.' (Zia said, 'America has given up caring about us.') So despite the fact that the Chinese Ambassador, over his soup, said he hoped Pakistan would stay in CENTO (the

Central Treaty Organization, whose other members are Britain, Iran, and Turkey), Zia evidently feels it is hardly worth it.

But lonely Pakistan needs a club to join. Zia now fancies the non-aligned nations and the British Commonwealth. ('I told Mr Callaghan it had been folly to leave. Pakistan behaved like a stupid child – the credit to Mr Bhutto for that.') Naturally, India and Pakistan are still sulking over their past conflicts, and one can see them sulking still as the heavens fall on them both. So, Wali Khan says, 'China is the obvious pillar of our foreign policy.' And Zia from his sitting room sofa, said, 'The Chinese say that the security of Pakistan means the security of China. I agree. I don't necessarily expect the Chinese Army to march down the Karakoram Highway. But I don't rule even that out.'

Zia was unexpectedly short. I had been told about the barrel chest and three rows of medals, and that he looks fiercer in press photographs than he actually is, which is true. But he is not a military Bertie Wooster. He is not even Terry-Thomas (I had been told that senior officers call him that, and that he even has the same gap in his teeth. Perhaps he has had it filled in). He is likeable. He talks in a relaxed and surprisingly fluent way. Words like 'bastard' regularly shoulder their way in.

Zia gave me an interesting insight into Bhutto's mind. 'You know, Mr Bhutto brought me up to Chief of Staff from seventh in the list' – he grinned. 'I said, "I hope you've made the right choice." ' Later Zia told Bhutto he was going to remove him. 'And do you know what Mr Bhutto said? He said to me, "Look, I have a solution. We'll have new elections. If the opposition wins, you'll impose martial law. Then with my brains and your power, we'll rule Pakistan." I said, "My God. You can't go behaving like this. I mean to say." '

About the Islamic states, Zia says, 'These lashings. It was I who introduced them as a martial law measure. You know, "If a man rapes a girl or something, give the bastard so many lashes." But that's not Islam. That's myself.' He laughs.

But there's worse to an ultra-Islamic, 1400-year-old state than lashings. Censorship, for instance, and 're-education', the machinery of discipline used by 'religious' states like the Soviet Union. Zia – I thought – seemed to say: Communism is bad, so such machinery is unacceptable; Islam is *good*, so it's fine. Does he really want a kind of extreme Islamic dictatorship? He actually *promises* democratic elections.

Tough-minded political people like Asghar Khan look beyond Zia's promises. 'I think the Army – all those Punjabis – is in a mood to run Pakistan again.' The shame of the loss of Bangladesh has been blotted out by Bhutto's discrediting of democracy. We don't want these extreme Muslim measures. Those ministers of Zia's have the breadth of vision of a lot of frogs in a well. The people want a progressive society for the jet age.'

Wali Khan (and his intelligent wife whose political career has been affected incalculably by a recent shoplifting conviction in London) half-joked: 'Zia's ministers are like sandbags. Take agriculture. It's in a devil of a mess. The present minister couldn't tell wheat from barley, and if any critical bullets start flying they'll hit him, the sandbag, not Zia. Very convenient.' Wali Khan and Asghar and others have refused Government jobs. 'The Government has no mandate. We must have elections. If not, there'll be trouble.'

But for now, at the centre of things there is Zia – Zia happily sitting it out; President Zia, incongruously showy, perhaps, for a destitute illiterate population, in his white, bemedalled, epauletted dress uniform (as if the Queen wore her crown to a jumble sale); General Zia protesting from his sofa, 'I didn't take over for the heck of it. Only to restore political stability and have elections.' Will power change him? While Pakistan waits to find out, the frontier rumbles, the economy lolls and politicians stamp impatiently in the vacuum of Zia's martial law – which is based on a single fact.

That amazing fact is that Bhutto has achieved a mystique almost comparable to that of a voodoo witch doctor. Until he is out of the way for good and all, many Pakistanis in public life find it very hard to believe that he might not yet return to raise Cain. Bhutto's People's Party faithfuls, including his wife and daughter, Benazir Bhutto (a former President of the Oxford Union), hold their meetings round a chair on which Bhutto's portrait is reverentially propped, like a totem. What if he is acquitted (that is at least a possibility) and walks out of that jail free to stalk his enemies? What if his sentence is reduced to imprisonment and he is eventually released? If he is executed, some may fear his influence – through his still-powerful party – from beyond the grave. Such has been the impact of Bhutto on Pakistan. Clever, contemptuous Mr Bhutto would revel in all this mumbo-jumbo.

Mr Bhutto was hanged in Rawalpindi jail in April 1979. The Russians invaded Afghanistan the same year. By her political agitation Bhutto's daughter Benazir is indeed keeping his name alive.

Avuncular Sphinx

A review of In Search of Identity *by Anwar el-Sadat.*

4 JUNE 1978

President Sadat may have stumbled across his true identity as he wrote this book, but, if so, he doesn't reveal it. Much of the book might have been written by a dead-pan comedian. Can he really be as naive as that, one asks oneself at intervals, or is he having us on? What *is* the riddle of this cool, well-tailored sphinx?

Earlier this year, Sadat sat talking in a villa outside Cairo, jovial, pipe-smoking, everyone's favourite uncle. I asked him about the serious uprising last year with which Egypt's long-suffering poor protested against a rise in food prices in a society where opulent *nouveau riche* vulgarity contrasts with the poverty of everybody else.

'It was not fair,' said Sadat, referring to his most wretched subjects. 'They should not have burnt Cairo. They could have written to the newspapers about it. ....' But did he, the man in control, really not foresee popular fury over the price rise? If not, one might perhaps coin a phrase – 'culpable innocence'.

His book lopes along easily and amiably. His early years as a revolutionary conspirator read like a mixture of Dennis Wheatley and the Marx Brothers. In 1941 (we read) the British authorities in Egypt decided to disarm Egyptian Army contingents on the Western Front. Sadat was a signals officer at Mersa Matruh, busier plotting than signalling. He drew up 'the first plan for the revolution': all 'Egyptian units withdrawing from Mersa Matruh would assemble near the Mena House Hotel outside Cairo. From there they would march into Cairo and topple the British. ... 'In one stride, we were just outside Alexandria. The next day would see me at the Mena House Hotel, with the other units – to carry out our long-dreamed-of revolution.' But horror! No other units turned up at Mena House.

Sadat took the disappointment, he says, 'like a sportsman'. Soon, however, in order to smuggle an important plotter to Iraq, two of Sadat's friends ('excellent pilots') pinched a military aircraft. Only a few minutes after take-off, one of them turned off the oil pump instead of turning it on, and the plane landed on the top of a tree.

Presently another member of Sadat's clandestine Free Officers' Organization agreed to fly over the British lines at El Alamein to drop a 'treaty' guaranteeing Egypt's post-war independence for Rommel to sign. No one had told Rommel he was coming, and, because he was flying in a British aircraft, the Germans promptly shot him down. Sadat – you can't blame him for it – makes the most of his 'martyrdom' in jail. But in one British jail he had tobacco and newspapers, and kind Mr Hickman, the Governor, sent him collections of short stories. In another he was able to breed an army of rabbits. Later, he trained one Hussein Tewfik in grenade throwing (even so, Tewfik's grenade missed the Prime Minister, Nahas Pasha, by several yards). Sadat was Tewfik's chief accomplice in the murder of Amin Osman, Nahas's Finance Minister, but, soon arrested, he suffered no worse punishment than eighteen months in a very nasty jail.

Sadat nearly missed the 1952 revolution – he was in a cinema with his wife when Nasser gave the 'off'. But subsequently he had eighteen years of power at Nasser's right hand. Here the book reads more seriously but, even so, how he managed to remain so long at Nasser's right hand is something Sadat never really explains. Working alongside Nasser must have been extremely nerve-racking. Sadat describes him as 'trailing hate'; as a man with no friends, wary, highly strung, extremely bitter, suspicious; as a man prone to horrendous tantrums and a pathological believer in inaccurate tittle-tattle.

When Nasser's closest friend, the corrupt and incompetent Field-Marshal Abdel Hakim Amer, having made a hash first of the union with Syria and then the Yemen War, began a reign of military police terror, Nasser did not try to curb him, although, Sadat says, he realized how much ordinary Egyptians were suffering. All Sadat himself did, apparently, was to advise Nasser to have a private word about it with Amer, which achieved nothing. Yet Sadat loathed the excesses of Amer's police, he says, cherishing a profound belief in individual freedom that he had discovered in prison.

Sadat's book opens an interesting window here and there. He tells us how contemptuous, rough-neck Russian diplomacy systematically humiliated the great Nasser, a priceless Middle Eastern ally, finally alienating him. There are memorable vignettes, too. Of Amer in the

Operations Room on the morning of 5 June 1967, struck dumb as the news came through that the Israelis had just destroyed the entire Egyptian Air Force. Of Sadat himself, a few hours later, sadly watching Egyptians applauding 'the faked-up victory reports which our mass-media put out hourly', and wishing a second heart attack would carry him off. About Nasser in defeat, looking like a 'living corpse', Sadat says, 'Those who knew Nasser realized that he did not die on 28 September 1970, but on 5 June 1967.'

Then there is Sadat himself – the actor-manager – boldly uniformed in *his* ops room at 2 p.m. on 6 October 1973, calmly ordering a cup of tea and lighting a pipe, as the attacking Egyptian soldiers pushed their boats into the Canal shouting '*Allahu Akbar!*' – 'to explode forever the myth of an invincible Israel'.

Finally, the miraculous arrival in Jerusalem, and heavy jokes at the airport with Dayan and General Ariel Sharon ('If you attempt to cross to the West Bank of the Canal again, I'll put you in jail!' 'Oh, no. I'm Minister of Culture now!').

Of course, the Israelis have not returned Sadat's warmth. Those Israeli settlements on Arab land, always so many nails in the coffin of Sadat's peace hopes, multiply day by day. His Peace Initiative is dead, even if it refuses for the moment to lie down. Yet surely Sadat knew before he went to Jerusalem that the Israelis would not compromise on the occupation of the West Bank? Or did he simply want to expose Israeli intransigence? Again, is it wise to fanfare democracy and a free press in Egypt and almost immediately start muzzling critical politicians and journalists? Is it enough to urge Egypt's poor to write their grievances to the newspapers, like 'Disgruntled, Tunbridge Wells'? In brief, is Sadat naïve or shrewd, a hard man or a desperate chancer? All his book actually reveals is charm, a measure of humanity and a massive self-confidence. Across muddles, triumphs and disasters, the sphinx looks back at us, its smile still inscrutably in place.

I doubt if Sadat felt the ground under his feet after his military coup de théâtre in 1973 at the start of the war with Israel, and the subsequent heady and much publicized meetings at Camp David with President Jimmy Carter and the Israeli Prime Minister Menachem Begin. At Camp David Sadat certainly achieved the return to Egypt of the Sinai peninsula occupied by Israel in 1967. But for the Israelis the talks ended in real triumph – the neutralization of the one Arab nation capable of waging war against them single-handed. The second part of the agreement – positive steps toward ending the Palestine problem – came to nothing, as it was bound to. Sadat bought peace for poor, battered Egypt but for nobody else, and thus alienated much of the Arab world. At home he designed Ruritanian uniforms for himself, lavishly entertained the international jet-set, and overtaxed the poor. Essentially likeable and well meaning, this strangely obtuse man became many people's target. His assassination by Muslim extremists while taking the salute at a military parade in Cairo in October 1981 was a shocking thing, but it should have come as no surprise.

Vietnam

I arrived in Vietnam early in 1965, shortly before the first US Marines landed there – the advance guard of the American military presence that was later to swamp the country. Almost as soon as I arrived, I began looking for places outside the capital to visit – Saigon was interesting, but I wanted to find somewhere more purely 'Vietnamese'. A knowledgeable friend suggested I should fly up to Hué, the former imperial capital of Annam, in the north of South Vietnam. Thank heavens he did. Hué was little visited then by foreigners of any kind. I found a beautiful, largely unspoiled and strongly Buddhist city whose inhabitants, proud of their history and culture, took a profoundly independent, nationalist view of the war – they despised and feared foreign influences. They had fought, like so many Vietnamese, with the nationalist Viet Minh irregulars against the French colonial regime. They considered Communism barbaric and malign and Americanization degrading. In early 1966, egged on by a respected Buddhist leader, Thich Tri Quang, and other monks, the population of Hué and its sister city Da Nang, a major American base, actually took to the streets in arms, erecting barricades and firing on troops sent up from Saigon in American planes to put them in their place. The Americans simplistically labelled them fools and Communists, but all the rebels wanted was a free and fair General Election, a popular civilian Government and an end to the corruption for which the American-sponsored generals who ruled the country were notorious and which, the people of Hué correctly believed, was dangerously inhibiting a successful conduct of the war against Communism.

On that first visit to Hué I met a Vietnamese family and they became my friends. From then on, I tried to see the situation in Vietnam through their eyes and to translate what I saw into print.

Summer of Accusations for Vietnam

HUÉ, 3 MAY 1966

The turbulent central Vietnamese city of Hué – of which the enigmatic Buddhist priest Thich Tri Quang is spiritual master – was shaken the

187

other night by a series of shattering explosions. The ground quaked; people ran from their beds to see flashes in the sky. Clearly bombs were falling. By morning it was known that for the first time in the war there had been a mortar attack on Hué's tiny airstrip. There seemed no reason to doubt that the Vietcong were responsible. Who else could have been?

The mystery was, and still is, why the Vietcong chose this moment of – for them – healthy political agitation against the 'puppet' Saigon Government to bombard an unimportant airstrip within the historic walls of Hué's ancient citadel. The area is densely populated by poor Vietnamese families. A much more obvious target, the American airbase, is several kilometres away. Predictably the mortar demolished some civilian houses and killed four Vietnamese, two very old and two very young. The airstrip was untouched.

It is typical of Hué – and of Vietnam – that the obvious explanation of the attack, that it was a thoughtless Vietcong adventure, immediately became the subject of angry controversy among the Hué hotheads and of calculated, portentous doubt among local elder statesmen. But it did shed significant light on the convoluted nature of Vietnamese thought. It demonstrates also the prospect this summer of months of political myth making and bitterness as Vietnamese rival political groups move edgily towards elections in August. Vistas are opening of false accusation and counter-accusation; of the propagation of endless false reports for deliberate, tactical reasons, of 'this-is-the-last-straw' declarations heralding violence. They will come from extreme Hué Buddhists led by Thich Tri Quang, from Saigon Buddhist moderates led by Thich Tam Chau, from Catholics, Army officers and any other group with a political axe to grind.

Hué is comparatively small, and recent anti-Government demonstrations have shown that Tri Quang has a well-organized Buddhist movement, based on a very general desire for representative government. But even in Hué there is no monolithic unity of political views. The morning after the mortar attack I found a large crowd of policemen, soldiers, peasants in coolie hats, young men with scooters, and mothers and infants poking round the charred wreckage of one of the bombed houses. Orange-robed Buddhist priests, weeping women and neighbours moved in and out of a building next door where ritual bells tinkled over the dead body of a bomb victim. A friendly Vietnamese doctor in a Mercedes said: 'The Vietcong? It may have been them. Bandits more likely.'

Why bandits?

'That's who it was.'

At the seedy bungalow that houses the Hué Students' Union, a tall, tense-faced student leader said: 'Vietcong? No. This is a trap. I'd rather not yet say what sort. I suggest you ask the Americans what they know of that bombardment.'

Is it really conceivable that the Americans would have mortared Vietnamese houses in Hué? And for what possible reason?

The student leader said: 'I'm calling an immediate general assembly of all our "struggle" students. We may have to demonstrate.'

Against the Americans?

'I can't say now.'

In the Town Hall, a much more moderate adult 'struggle group' leader said: 'Yes, I'm fairly sure it must have been the Vietcong. I think we may have to condemn them for this attack in a public meeting. But one must be sure. It could have been people in that part of the town paying off old scores. You know, neighbours getting their own back for quite personal reasons.'

With mortars?

'There are a lot of arms about.'

There is no motor transport in Hué. I bicycled to the riverside headquarters of the vigorously anti-Tri Quang, anti-Communist Vietnamese Nationalist Party — the Kuomintang of Vietnam — that has a strong following in the countryside. I found wary young men with rifles in the garden. A group of middle-aged leaders inside said: 'It looks like the work of Buddhist "struggle groups".' A number of their supporters had recently been beaten up by Buddhist extremists. 'We are informed that General Thi's soldiers were responsible for the mortaring. They hoped to blame us. They need an excuse to destroy this office. We'll fight to the last.'

General Thi is the former commander of the Central Provinces and a Tri Quang sympathizer. His dismissal by Air Vice-Marshal Ky set the last few weeks' political upheaval rolling. He now lives in a borrowed house in Hué, and commands no troops any more. If he did, it is most unlikely that he would agree to bomb Vietnamese civilians in Hué for the sake of an excuse to hit at the Nationalist Party.

In the event, there was a half-hearted rally next day organized by the Hué 'struggle committee' to condemn the Vietcong bombardment. The moderate 'struggle group' leader attended discreetly, and so did a number of his followers. Two or three people made speeches saying that the Vietcong should not think they could exploit the people's aspirations to be free of Communism and American attempts to dominate Vietnam. It was not a big meeting. A number of soldiers in uniform were there, and two or three hundred children between the ages of eight and fourteen, who habitually are marched up in a neat crocodile whenever a meeting is likely to be under-attended. Few students bothered to come. Another large group, the trishaw drivers, blank-faced elderly men with hard, stringy brown legs who are willing material for mob organizers, failed to show up at all. And no major political leader appeared, because in Hué they prefer to retain their mystique by remaining unseen in their pagodas.

But for all this apparent indifference to Vietcong callousness, the war in the centre of Vietnam goes on. Army units in the region, after a few days of indecision when Thi was dismissed and the American advisers withdrawn as civil war threatened with Saigon, were carrying out military operations normally. The American advisers are back again.

The failure of the anti-Vietcong rally really demonstrates the immediate order of political priorities in many Vietnamese minds. Without being pro-Vietcong, they are obsessed now with this year's political evolution behind the battle front. The preoccupation is with who will come out on top during the next few months' struggle for control or influence in the National Assembly to be elected – if all goes well – in August. Any comparatively small incident, such as the mortar bombardment at Hué, may from now on be used by the various Vietnamese factions in any way that suits their book. Anti-American slogans, pro-American slogans, peace cries, accusations of Communism and of thraldom to foreign imperialism, furious impugnings of good faith – all such tactics will from now on and more and more frequently bedevil the political atmosphere. The truth behind individual incidents will become harder and harder to determine as the red herrings spawn. All this will be on top of an already traditional determination on the part of Vietnamese in all classes and religions to divine the most hideously Machiavellian plottings behind the most obviously innocent event.

Goodbye to All This

Just before returning home after my year in Vietnam (1965–66), I sent the Observer *some extracts from my notebook.*

JUNE 1966

It is hard to see how anyone could fail to fall in love with Vietnam and its people. (I exclude, of course, the American soldiers in the mud and the jungles.) One wonders, and doubts, if any European people could have held up as the Vietnamese have done in such a tiny country trapped by monstrous forces in a period of national disaster agonizingly prolonged – twenty-five years so far and no end in sight.

The Vietnamese seem imbued with a kind of Asian 'Dunkirk spirit', plus a smattering of fatalism. They may look like a race of fragile dolls, but they bend, not break. They are a sentimental but not hysterical people. At the same time, they are not the sort of strength-through-joy Asians who go around arrogantly smashing planks of wood with their bare fists. After all that has happened here – after the Japanese, the French and now the Americans – they have not given way to xenophobia. Heaven knows why. Among rising prices and falling bombs they remain hospitable, humorous, quick-witted and, I would say, gentle. Some people here see them as a race of tiny Genghis Khans and cite examples of torture and emasculation in the villages. In a war as bitter as this atrocities happen all right, but I would judge the Vietnamese by their urban population. One continually remembers the brutalities of Algiers not long ago, or Nicosia, or Elisabethville. One's spine refuses to tingle in expectation of a bullet between the shoulder-blades in Saigon's back streets. I have yet to be spat at or threatened, yet I must be assumed to be an American. Considering that the Americans can only be misfits in the small, sophisticated, quicksilver world of Vietnam, this says a lot for Vietnamese tolerance.

There seems to be a need here for a special American appointment: a sort of Dale Carnegie-to-the-forces. Example: a Vietnamese colonel, perhaps 5 feet 5 inches, stands with his junior officers near a helicopter pad in central Vietnam. An American helicopter drops down in a swirl of dust. The Vietnamese colonel's American adviser – also a colonel – jumps out and strides towards the Vietnamese. 'Hi, colonel. How we doing?' With a fluent, joyous gesture he sweeps the Vietnamese colonel off his feet and swings him round and round. 'We're real buddies, me and the colonel,' he cries. 'That right, colonel?' Regaining his feet under the, yes, inscrutable eyes of his staff, the Vietnamese colonel is suddenly convulsed by giggles – the Vietnamese refuge from shame.

The influential 'neutralist' monk, Thich Tri Quang. Going to visit him in Hué on a swelteringly hot day, I bicycle to his pagoda with two Vietnamese Buddhist students, stopping on the way at a small tea-house to drink iced coconut juice.

It is very quiet in the pagoda courtyard. Among the trees a bell tinkles. Pale novice monks with shaven heads and traditional top-knots glide about. Tri Quang has a large head and a white, cold and sensuous face. But he is not the horror to look at – Yul Brynner playing Dracula – he often appears in press photos. His hands flutter, he chews sweets, and he picks his bare feet. His eyes are quick and watchful. He is withdrawn and very proud. His humour is mischievous, and his attendants shake with sycophantic glee at every sally.

One can see that, with such a man, American appeals to postpone political agitation until the war is over – some Americans talk of from five to ten years – are most unlikely to wash. To himself, and many others, Tri Quang is an embodiment of Vietnamese sovereignty. Wait until the end of the war to extricate Vietnamese identity from a foreign-dominated shambles, and it may be too late to extricate anything. Five to ten years – what will be left of Vietnam?

There's something de Gaulle-like in all this – particularly the bitter wartime de Gaulle who fought Churchill and Roosevelt for the right to control the destiny of France. Perhaps Lyndon Johnson in his memoirs will echo Churchill: 'The greatest cross I had to bear in Vietnam was the Buddhist swastika.'

On my way out of the pagoda, an elderly monk approaches tentatively to ask: 'Please tell me – how is Hampstead?' He had been there visiting Buddhist friends a year or two ago.

The young American officers who have volunteered for field service with Vietnamese Army units are touchingly good. They feel they are fighting a forgotten war, because American correspondents tend to concentrate (or perhaps it's their editors) on the day-to-day small-town 'human interest' story of individual actions by *American* units – so minor, compared to the importance of Vietnamese morale and behaviour in the wider context of the whole war.

These young Americans are quite unlike their compatriots. They are unconcerned with 'improving the Viets', probably because they are in such close, life-and-death touch with them. They consider the Saigon of bars and brothels 'a can of worms'. They live and eat, despite their stomach troubles, with Vietnamese soldiers, and are happy doing it.

Watching Vietnamese make a river crossing – they look like puppies, with their over-large helmets just above water – an American lieutenant says: 'I've learned a lot from my Vietnamese officer. He's been fighting the war for seventeen years. I salute him and call him "sir" just as I would an American. There's one embarrassment, though. When we come under Vietcong mortar fire, I have a hell of a lot of trouble fighting off our Vietnamese soldiers. The five or six nearest will throw you down and pile on top of you to protect you from shrapnel. Makes controlling the battle kinda hard.'

Seventy-year-old Monsieur Ottavij has lived in Saigon since he left the French Army after World War I. He is small and upright, and his gentle face is as creviced and gnarled as a contour map of the Vietnamese Central Highlands. He is devoted to his Vietnamese mistress and smokes opium steadily but in moderation ('Fifteen or sixteen pipes a day, *monsieur*').

M. Ottavij would quite like to pay a last visit to Corsica and France, where he has relatives unseen for forty years – but it is not all that important. After years of invasions, riots and the sound of *somebody's* artillery booming across the river, he remains kind, wholly uncynical and monumentally resigned. 'If the French had judged the Vietnamese better,' he says unregretfully, 'their Army would probably be here today.'

As it is, the Americans are here. M. Ottavij has prudently implanted a few chattering Vietnamese girls in his crumbling hotel bar ('Call me Curly,' squeaks one girl in an American accent) and extended his restaurant. Clams marinière remain its speciality. 'We,' he says, dimly sipping his Algerian *vin du patron* and meaning 'We Vietnamese' – 'We have learned to live with circumstance.' He stares vaguely at the

GIs at the bar and ruminatively purses and unpurses his lips. M. Ottavij dabbles with spiritualism.

Despite 'liberal' rumours to the contrary, there is no sign that blacks are being drafted into battle out of all proportion to whites. I have seen white GIs – Southerners at that – quite happily taking orders from black officers and NCOs. 'Vietnam is where the white men call Negroes "sir",' a British correspondent has said.

In Saigon, black troops on 'rest and recreation' have turned part of one side street into a tiny Harlem. Whites hardly ever go there. Some blacks, off duty, wear black trousers, white socks and narrow-brimmed Sinatra-type straw hats. They supply the bar owners with records of the springy, soulful music they prefer. They swear they are not there because of discrimination anywhere else. They just 'naturally gravitate, man'. Late at night they engage in hilarious bouts of improbable story telling: '. . . so Ah said to this lil' Viet-nam-ese officer – "Hee-eey, dig *you*, captain baby." '

A negro paratrooper, his teeth gritted, his face streaked with sweat, blasting away with a machine gun as Vietcong bullets pang about him. Negro soldiers, with terrible, undefinable wounds, being dragged limply to helicopters in jungle clearings – surely this is the final answer to Governor Wallace of Alabama, Ian Smith and Dr Verwoerd.

In September last year, I took an Air Vietnam DC-6 from Saigon to Hué. The flight seemed endless. I had never been to Hué before; few, if any, journalists went there. I was going because I had heard of its beauty and because of rumours of impending political violence there. I watched the jungle humps of the Central Highlands slide past, and felt a touch on my arm.

'Have you been to Hué?' a light Vietnamese voice said in French. My neighbour had an unusual face: prominent cheekbones, a strangely lop-sided smile, and a nervous tic.

'No,' I said.

'My name's Vinh. I am a student. I have a very small house in Hué. Would you like to see it?' We talked until we landed. Vinh radiated the bounding puckishness of a music hall comic and that eager openness that instantly proclaims honesty. In Hué, through Vinh I met his best friend, Tam.

Tam's family asked me to stay with them in Hué. Mother, aunts, uncles, two sons, two married daughters and a nephew live in a dark, rambling, wooden-beamed house on Hué's High Street behind a clothes shop, where six teenage tailors stitch away twelve hours a day. The mother spent four months in the jungle as a volunteer with the Viet Minh years ago. She resented their callousness and contempt for family feeling.

Today the family's main immediate worry – apart from rising prices – is that political disturbances have disrupted examination schedules. One son and a nephew need diplomas this year. Another son has just returned from demonstrating in Da Nang with his Buddhist 'struggle group' friends. He was excited, but clearly glad to be home. He had hung onto his green 'revolutionary' scarf and his carbine, which his mother irritably tucked away in a drawer. 'What do you expect to do with that?'

It is perhaps a typical family of Hué. They are not opposed to the American Army's presence. They are worried about Americans behind the firing line 'pushing the Vietnamese about'. 'They're so bad-mannered,' the son, Tam, said.

'No, different,' an uncle corrected.

None of them much like Tri Quang, although their house is full of Buddhist symbols. They disapprove of monks in politics and think Tri Quang is too ambitious. Of the political agitation they ask: 'Where will this end?' They think Air Vice-Marshal Ky is too weak to 'stand up to the Americans', but they are very afraid of a Vietcong victory. Every evening at half-past seven the family rushes to the radio and friends are invited in. Hué Struggle Committee Broadcasts? No, the BBC. The family watches anti-Government demonstrations from a balcony, without great enthusiasm. Soldiers, police and student demonstrators march in groups, each carrying a banner of identity. A contingent of wrinkled crones shuffles by, mumbling imprecations through cannibal mouths blood-red with betel juice. 'Those are the fanatics. They believe the monks are gods,' someone says. 'They beat you to death with their slippers.'

Crisis without, crisis within. The family dog, Mimi, has eaten the chicken on the dinner table. The youngest daughter is sent upstairs for taking a second helping of rice without laying down her chopsticks first. The mother is worried about her son: 'Tam is twenty. So idiotic about girls. He takes after his father. I've warned Tam – one scandal, just one, and he leaves this house.'

I sleep on a wide mahogany bed with no mattress – even rich Vietnamese seldom use them. In one corner of the room is a desk piled with books: *War and Peace* in French, Camus in Vietnamese. In another corner, an old female retainer chain smokes, dangerously, under a mosquito net. Far away, the American guns rumble against the Vietcong.

I spend a long, interesting evening with the Rector of Hué University, in his lodgings. He is close to Tri Quang. He talks of Vietnamese culture. Vietnam, he says, is not everybody's primitive colonial possession. Communism is a foreign influence that must be resisted – but Vietnam must have a 'legal' Government and be able to raise a proud head to the world. Some Americans think the Rector is a Communist. To draw him out, I say that surely, from the perfectly understandable point of view of thousands of young Vietnamese facing call-up, any peace is better than war?

He looks astonished: '*Monsieur*, I must make you realize before you go the danger in what you are saying.' He pours out two more Rémy Martin brandies. Later, I hear from a friend that the Rector enjoyed our talk, but thinks I am a dangerous neutralist.

In Saigon, a newly arrived British journalist says to friends over drinks: 'Obviously the future of Vietnam is in President Johnson's hands. How can a backward people like the Vietnamese know what they want?'

One night this week I walked M. Ottavij home from the calm of his favourite opium parlour through streets still tangy with the tear gas that has broken up the day's Buddhist demonstrations. Outside his door, an American military police jeep stood near a struggling group of drunken GIs. The gutter was strewn with broken glass. A few Vietnamese looked on.

M. Ottavij only momentarily breaks off a story about a mystical encounter he thought he had once had with the Comte de St Germain, who died in the seventeenth century. Glancing at the heaving group he murmurs indifferently: '*Ça arrive . . . ça arrive.*' I thought he was going to add, '*plus ça change. . . .*' M. Ottavij's life could probably be

The Murder of Hué

HUÉ, 3 MARCH 1968

It is hideously unreal, yet you can feel real rubble underfoot; put a handkerchief to your nose and you can still smell the corpses. I visited Hué first in 1965, and came to know and love it. Now, between them, in the name of the people's salvation, General Giap and the US High Command have killed the flower of Vietnamese cities. Today Hué is no more the city I knew than a friend lying in a street, charred and ripped by a bomb, is the human being one talked or made love to. You can disguise it in whatever military terms you like but in Hué murder has been arranged.

Along the airport road to Hué, which I used to travel in a minibus full of cheerfully chattering Vietnamese, I was made to feel like one of General Patton's soldiers storming across occupied France in 1944. I came, of necessity, in a convoy of fifteen vehicles; huge petrol tankers, trucks full of GIs, lewd or comic slogans painted on the camouflaged covers of their helmets, crouching with Lucky Strikes clamped in dusty and unshaven jaws, guns at the ready for ambushes, tanks spewing up the dust, their drivers' feet stepping hard on the gas.

Fear of the enemy and the enemy's persistent power is everywhere evident. By little bridges, blown and hastily repaired, Americans crouch in sandbagged strong-points. Jets and helicopters scream overhead without cessation, airstrikes and artillery barrages send napalm and bombs down on the surrounding green countryside. Impassive Vietnamese villagers line the road in the dust and stare at the pandemonium, the clanking machinery, the big-nosed foreign soldiers. Are these the saviours?

Coming into Hué is like a dream in which you turn a corner expecting to see a familiar scene and find that it has undergone a sudden and hideous change. You twist and turn through deep mud roads between blighted gardens and skeleton houses and shops, looking for the makeshift pontoon bridge the Americans have thrown across the canals. Bewildered Vietnamese carrying bundles of possessions press into the roadside to avoid being crushed by the trucks. There are soldiers everywhere, Americans in helmets and bulky in flak jackets, tense Vietnamese fingering sub-machine gun triggers. Huge armoured personnel carriers are waiting down side alleys like gangsters in ambush. There is no transport; you walk, and that is better because you can escape with the Vietnamese from a military machine that is more and more irritable now that its omnipotence has turned to myth.

Always in the past I had stayed with a rather poor Vietnamese family who live in an old-fashioned, rambling building on the north bank of the Perfumed River between the river bank and the Citadel, where the North Vietnamese and Vietcong held American mobility and firepower at bay for three weeks. From the south bank it seemed as if they could not possibly have survived. The north bank area looked like the worst parts of London after the Blitz. Formerly, I had always hired a bicycle in Hué and ridden across the great-girdered bridge over the river. Now the central span plunges into the water, dynamited by the Vietcong who held it for a time. I had to push my way through a horde of Vietnamese struggling desperately across the one narrow gangway. When too many people force themselves on it you wade calf-deep. Machine guns and mortars cracked and thumped in the river bank trees not far away, where the Vietnamese used to take me on picnics. The Citadel has fallen, but the Americans are still fighting in Hué. The family's street is a blackened shambles of gutted houses. The market and teashops across the road on the river bank have ceased to exist. Miraculously, my Vietnamese friends were there, standing outside their door, running through the rubble to meet me. Their house is one of the very few that has not been razed.

They led me in excitedly. One or two were crying. They began to explain that they had gathered as usual in the house for the Tet (New Year) holiday, ten of them, uncle, aunts, cousins, sons and daughters, with two small babies and Mimi, the old dog with stubby legs. Since then they had had three weeks of unimaginable nightmare. The upstairs rooms no longer exist. They were torn apart by American fire during the Buddhist 'struggle group' demonstrations against the Ky Government. In 1966 I stayed in the front upper room and we watched the angry torchlight processions parading through the street shouting: 'Peace'. Now there are four walls and no roof. The floor is littered with broken tiles and burned beams. The American mortar bombs had thrown the family's little Buddhist shrine into a mass of coloured tatters in the dust; a piece of shrapnel had embedded itself in a French translation of *The Grapes of Wrath*; the braided, ceremonial uniform cap of the eldest son, who was shot in action last year, lay on the wreckage of the balcony.

We sat downstairs in a room pocked with bullet holes and a floor littered with tiles from the roof. There was a small mortar crater in the cement floor. Madame Dinh, a tiny, frail and very wise woman of about forty-five, who runs the house, explained: 'When the first fusillades began we were all asleep. The Vietcong were firing across the river at US headquarters. We thought it was like any other bombardment, and would stop. But then we all got up and came downstairs and saw the Vietcong in the street outside. There were about twenty of them, then sixty. They made for the bridge. The first ones to come wore shorts and khaki shirts and no caps. They were very young – seventeen or eighteen. They didn't come into the houses here because everyone had barred their shutters. I knew then that in the end the Government would drive them out. But I didn't know when, and I knew we would suffer.'

Madame Dinh has lost a husband and her eldest son in war. Tam, the eldest surviving son, who studies Government administration in Saigon, said: 'One Vietnamese soldier lay wounded and bleeding outside our door all the morning. Nobody dared come out and help him. Then one of a Vietcong patrol walked up and just shot him. He was harmless, but he just shot him.'

What about the bombing?

'That happened after the Vietcong had left – at least in this street. When the Americans shelled us the Vietcong had retreated towards the Citadel,' said Tam. 'Can you imagine, shelling twenty-four hours for fourteen days?'

For all that time this family huddled together with no link to the outside world except the radio. They listened avidly to the BBC or Saigon Radio. At US headquarters in Hué an American colonel, phlegmatically contemplating his artillery shelling a suburb, said next day: 'You know what BBC stands for? British Communist Broadcasting Corporation.' Only hawks are really welcome in the North now among the military.

Behind Madame Dinh's house, outside the colonel's field of vision, the teeming residential and commercial areas resemble something out of Goya. Whole streets are laid waste. Rubble chokes the sidewalks.

There are craters in the streets and blackened shells of cars. A truck is embedded in a wall. At two points I saw crowds who scrabbled and clawed at the grilles of stores where rice was being sold. The lucky ones – paying four times the normal price – quickly loaded the sacks onto bicycles and scurried away. They looked, if one approached too close, as if they would turn and defend the rice like famished dogs with a bone. The Americans had dropped huge bombs – 750 and 500 pounders – on what they imagined were the Citadel walls. Where they fell is one of the more fearful parts of a fearfully shattered city. It was a residential area packed with families like Madame Dinh's gathering for Tet. Now, like the Vietnamese, you walk there with a handkerchief to your nose.

A wispy Vietnamese teacher of French came up. He was trembling, and looked as though he might cry. What did he think of all that had passed?

'We don't think any more, *monsieur*. We are like dogs. We live by instinct. Instincts are all that are left to us.' He pointed to a monstrous pile of rubble. 'The man who lived in there was shot by the Vietcong. Now his house has been destroyed by the Americans. Curious, eh?' He stopped in front of another. There were plenty to choose from. 'There are thirty people under this one.' Vietnamese were digging in another mound of bricks and mortar. 'They are still bringing the bodies out of there. Two families, about twenty people, eight survivors.'

Here the stench of the dead was overpowering. In an open space between the houses mutilated corpses were being wrapped in sheets. Three men in nose masks dug graves. Women and children stood around keening, and shaking with sobs. A woman flung herself on a new mound of earth, hammering on it with her fist, and rolling on it in a paroxysm of grief.

We stepped through fragments of glass, pathetic muddied wrappings of Tet holiday gifts, filth and dead rats, to where a crowd of Vietnamese were passing under the great ornamental gate to the Citadel stormed by the US Marines. They shuffled through quickly, holding their noses because here three rotting bodies of Vietcong soldiers lie as yet unburied. The Citadel's solid walls are punctured by shells, and the gate itself riddled by everything from bullets to rockets. Inside the Citadel there seems to be no shop nor house that is not wholly or partially destroyed. The Americans used tanks here, after the airstrikes. The Vietcong and North Vietnamese used rockets from the camouflaged foxholes you see everywhere.

In a dazed way the people are friendly. There is no doubt they are glad the Communists were driven out – a number of civil servants live in the Citadel. In another quarter of Hué inhabited largely by Army officers and civil servants they are still digging up the bodies of relatives, men, women and children, who had their hands tied behind their backs and then were shot by the Vietcong. There are still many families missing. Mothers stand about weeping as the diggers work, and rush forward to try to recognize relatives as the bodies are taken out of the earth. This is in a secondary school garden used by the invaders as a command post. Thirty bodies have been recovered so far. But scores more may be there.

There are thought to be 300–600 Government employees buried in two mass graves somewhere in the city, but no one has been able to find them yet. In any event, Government here is like the city itself – in ruins. Officials have disappeared for the most part, kidnapped or killed. Official records were destroyed by the invading Vietcong and North Vietnamese when they occupied the municipal buildings, which are themselves in ruins.

No one knows how many civilians were killed. Perhaps they never will. Some were killed deliberately by certain Vietcong, others by American bombing and mortaring. Two French priests were shot by a Vietcong patrol at eleven o'clock one morning in a crowded street, and their grave now stands in the grounds of their house near the Collège de la Providence in West Hué. Yet other priests were not molested, the Father Superior told me. 'The North Vietnamese – they were from Tonkin – occupied the College. I would describe them as very well disciplined and ferocious.'

In the Citadel an old Vietnamese with a wispy beard said: 'They came into the house but didn't harm us. They said they were winning the war and we should support them. They were 40 per cent Tonkinese, the rest Vietcong from this region.' So they behaved well in some areas, badly in others.

In Madame Dinh's house one evening, a family came in which had had to put up with Vietcong units in their house for eighty days. 'They blew down part of our walls and fired out through them, and they knocked down walls into neighbouring houses all down the street, linking them all up,' said one.

A student called Minh said: 'They tried to organize young people like me to study their doctrines, carry arms for them. They sat about singing Communist songs.' He sang one to illustrate the point. The

Dinh family rocked with laughter, out of sheer relief that the worst is temporarily over.

The song was the souvenir of a monstrous experience. Did many young Vietnamese respond to Vietcong propaganda? 'Only a few spivs and the very poor – some trishaw drivers, people like that.'

What did students like Minh think?

'Well, the Vietcong told us they were fighting for the independence of Vietnam from the Americans. I don't like the Americans, but I don't like the Vietcong either. I am sure some students went with the Vietcong, but, believe me, not many.'

These student attitudes are extremely significant. All the student friends I have made in Hué were militant 'struggle group' members in the days when Hué and Da Nang rebelled against the Government of General Thieu and Air Vice-Marshal Ky. Minh and Tam both took carbines down to Da Nang and manned the barricades against Ky's troops. They wanted then – and they want now – an end to the Thieu–Ky Government and really free elections, which can throw up, they think, a representative Government with which the National Liberal Front would bargain. They say they are true nationalists. They feel the Vietnamese nationality is being swamped by a massive American presence, which rules Vietnam against its better interests through unrepresentative people like the Generals. They did not even like the Buddhist monk, Thich Tri Quang, who played a leading part in the struggle movement. They suspect he might be playing along with the Vietcong. They did like the dynamic General Nguyen Chanh Thi, who commanded the Vietnamese armies in Hué, where he was born, and was opposed to Thieu and Ky, and who is now living in Washington where the Government exiled him. All this Minh and Tam and other students have explained to me in Madame Dinh's house many times. They did not want the Vietcong. They wanted honest government. They did not want American domination. Yet few American officials in Saigon have ever been convinced that the struggle movement *en masse* was not pro-Vietcong. They thus approved Ky's dispatch of troops to Hué and Da Nang, and the bloodshed that followed.

But now the battle for Hué has highlighted something of considerable political significance. The Vietcong occupation of Hué provided the ultimate test of the students' real feelings. Since Tet they have had every opportunity to go with the Vietcong. Apart from an extreme left-wing minority, they did not, even when it was much safer for them to go than to stay and risk a bullet from angry Vietcong soldiers. Perhaps now the Americans will realize their grave political misjudgement over the struggle groups. In any event the Vietcong, too, must have had a sharp surprise.

Another student in the Dinhs' house that night lives in a suburban area where the Vietcong tried to organize a temporary administration. 'A tailor down the road was appointed chairman for youth. Only a few peasants were enthusiastic,' he said. And several friends were obliged to carry Vietcong wounded up into the hills during the fighting. 'We were sixty – four of us to each wounded man. We marched at night because the Vietcong officers said we must get past the villages and US flares and helicopters before dawn. We must have gone fifty kilometres, with no food and no water. They seemed to have no medicine. They did not seem to know the way very well either. At certain crossroads we had to stop and wait for other soldiers to come and show us which track to take. We didn't wait long, there were lots of Vietcong soldiers coming and going. When we got to a rough shelter on a hill we were made to sign a paper saying that we had delivered so many wounded for the soldiers of the National Liberation Front – they got very angry if anyone referred to them as Viet Minh or Vietcong. In my village they shot one man for saying "Viet Minh". Then they asked each of us to stay with them, saying they had already won in Hué and everywhere else, and that now was the time to make a choice. But we said we would go home. And we went all alone back through the dark.'

Not every Vietnamese in Hué was so lucky. 'Before they left our village they took a lot of young men with them,' I was told. And Madame Dinh's chief concern is to get her sons and nephews out of Hué in case the Vietcong return and take them off. In one quarter of Hué hundreds were led off with bandaged eyes and hands tied.

'They seemed to think that because we were Buddhist students and were in the struggle movement we would welcome them here.'

I asked my student what his attitude and that of his friends was now.

'I think you know what we have always told you. That has not changed. We think – I mean the educated people, more or less, from university and secondary school, like us – that the Vietcong is no good; that the Americans are not good for us, because they destroy our houses and our souls; that the present Government is no good because it doesn't represent anyone much, and its Army destroys whole streets because of four snipers.'

Once I said to them in Madame Dinh's shattered living room, while she and some women friends were playing cards: 'What a catastrophe for you.'

Tam leaned forward intently: 'Not a catastrophe,' he answered. 'It's normal, it's war, and this is normal. . . . Well then,' he cried, with a rising note of great anguish unusual for a Vietnamese. 'Well, we must have peace, mustn't we? Oh yes, yes, yes!' At that moment a violent explosion rocked the already weakened building and a shower of loose tiles fell into the room. I discovered later that it was a US ammunition ship blowing up after two direct hits from a Vietcong mortar. It was about 600 yards away.

Because things like that can happen, and are likely to continue to happen for some time, Hué is almost totally isolated from the outside world. The Vietcong are strong on both sides of the river that is Hué's main lifeline. The airport is open only to military aircraft. The road south is hopelessly insecure. With an almost non-existent local Government, the refugees, about 30,000 of them officially, are likely to get only the bare necessities for the time being, and their numbers are likely to increase. This week I watched thousands more scrambling to safety from a thickly populated suburb in which there were said to be Vietcong snipers and which the Americans and Vietnamese preferred to mortar rather than invade. Shops are still largely closed. Prices are up and there is a black market. Many families have suffered from the looting, of which there are unending complaints. The Vietnamese Army units undoubtedly took what they could, wherever they found it. Nor are the US troops above suspicion. A local French resident says he found his house denuded after US troops had occupied it. The safes were blown open, he claims, and everything that could not be taken was destroyed, including his desk.

So far American aid to the chief of the Vietnamese province is stymied because of a lack of men who know the region's problems. Perhaps twenty to thirty Americans were killed in Hué – nobody will say – and certainly several were taken off by the Vietcong. The local US Administrator, a man of long Vietnam experience, is now, it seems, suffering from nervous exhaustion and can hardly be much good on his own. Most American civilians in the northern sector work in a cloud of foreboding. It is obvious that pacification and development programmes are in ruins. Today there are large American, Vietnamese, and North Vietnamese and Vietcong forces in the neighbourhood of Hué. Military casualties are heavy and still rising. I watched US jets striking with napalm and rockets a few hundred yards away from Hué's stadium. American dead were being brought in there, wrapped in green plastic shrouds and loaded into helicopters. Cartloads of captured Vietcong weapons, many as good as anything the Americans have, were being stacked. There was a growing pile of uniforms of American dead, their water bottles, rifles, pathetic letters ending, 'With love, and try and write soon, Mom.'

And what has the battle of Hué meant? Tragically, it has symbolized the entire war. The people have been raped by two forces which they have come to distrust and fear. The Americans have regained Hué at the cost of destroying it. They will be blamed for that. General Giap's men thought they could win over people they wrongly considered ripe for conversion, simply because they have opposed the Saigon Government. In the main they, too, have had to learn that there are three political forces in South Vietnam, not two, and that the third one, the one that rejects the big-stick images of Hanoi and Saigon, is both large and, when opportunity arrives, courageous. Militarily, the holocaust that enveloped this beautiful city and its thousands of Madame Dinhs, Vinhs and Tams has ended in stalemate after the initiative with the North Vietnamese and Vietcong. Neither side has won any appreciable number of Vietnamese hearts and minds.

And standing in the stench of Hué's streets, contemplating the ruins of the university and schools – there will be no education in Hué for upwards of a year from now – and foreseeing the inevitable exodus from this cultural centre and former imperial capital of central Vietnam when travel from it is again possible, one can see only one thing very clearly: that a criminal act has been committed here since Tet. One is tempted to refer to other ruined cities: Warsaw or Budapest. But there is only one Hué, victim of cynical ideologists who talk with unctuous arrogance of nationalism and democracy from their loudspeaker vans and who between them have destroyed perhaps the most purely nationalist city in either North or South Vietnam.

Madame Dinh said one evening: 'You know, during the bombardment I sat thinking, "Suppose President Ho Chi Minh and President Johnson visited Hué at the same time and saw all this, and they said to each other: 'Why are we doing this?' and shook hands." ' She added shyly: 'You think that's very stupid. Of course, I am not serious. It was only my dream.'

A Peaceful Tet in Hué

HUÉ, FEBRUARY 1972

The North Vietnamese offensive, much predicted by the Americans here, did not come this week. It had been forecast as usual to coincide with Tet (the New Year festival) or with President Nixon's arrival in Peking last Monday. Even Madame Dinh in her little house under the Citadel in Hué thought the Vietcong would come.

'You have come just at the right time,' she said, smiling, on her doorstep. 'I hear they will come into Hué tonight.' She was partly joking. Her house was mostly destroyed by American shells in the 1968 Tet offensive. Then she had had Vietcong soldiers actually living in her poor home for days, trying to teach Communist songs to her sons, nephews and nieces, and urging them (in vain) to go off to the hills with them 'because victory is here'. She knew that if the Communists did come back tonight her street would be reduced to rubble once again. And that, ten to one, I, if captured, would be killed. There were no illusions left in Hué.

In 1968 Madame Dinh and her family huddled together for three weeks as mortar shells came through the roof and machine gun bullets through the shutters, and the young, black-dressed Vietcong knocked holes in the walls to communicate with neighbouring houses. Outside, at the same moment, hundreds of Vietnamese Government servants, students, priests, civilians, women and children were being murdered by the North Vietnamese and buried in mass graves. Few foreigners, even doctors, were spared. Some were buried alive. Most Hué people abhor the Americans but, particularly since 1968, they hate and dread the Communists, too.

The second son, Tam, said, 'They may come in from across the river from the villages. Now's the time for this.' He handed out a bottle of Japanese whisky and tiny glasses from near the family's Buddhist shrine.

I had forgotten, after an absence, what a habit Vietnam is: how accustomed one becomes to the casual unending noise of gunfire – of rifles, machine guns, mortars, artillery. The American pull-out has not lessened the horror of combat for Vietnamese. It has not changed the noise either. The Americans are still there, mightily armed, above you now in the sky. The same old flares wobble down the night sky. The same hideous clatter of helicopters echoes from Hué's Perfumed River.

This week we sat in Madame Dinh's house, once more waiting for something unpleasant to happen. A cement patch now filled in a mortar shell hole made during Tet 1968. The house has a new roof.

A nice Vietnamese major drove me to a base nine miles away to see the Vietnamese divisional commander, General Phu. But he does not see people he is not sure are '100 per cent pro-Government'. So I saw his tiny number two, a colonel, confident in starched fatigues, in a room full of maps. Hué is surrounded by such Vietnamese firebases. Could they 'abort' a full-scale attack?

'Well, they couldn't take this base,' the Vietnamese colonel said.

'They couldn't take any defended compound,' said the equally confident American aid boss of Hué, comfortably ensconced in his sandbagged compound in the city, where his staff was preparing to show a movie about drug addiction in America.

'Yes, the VC *might* come in tonight – though I rather *doubt* it,' he said.

He looked pleasant, dapper, unimaginative. He offered me a small tin of mosquito killer, a thoughtful gift because my hotel would be full of night-time mosquitoes, but no billet – though I didn't ask for one – in his womb-like compound.

Back in the city, Vietnamese in white played tennis at the Cercle Sportif on the river. With Vietnamese friends I was whirled out on a scooter to visit the tombs of Vietnamese kings, the girls' silken *ao dais* floating out behind them through the trees. Amid a good deal of giggling we ate shrimp and drank beer in a grove near one of 1968's mass graves. There were unidentifiable shots close upriver, yet no one looked alarmed. We went to a wedding ceremony in a fine old Hué house deep in a fruit and banana garden. The men wore traditional long black silk gowns and black round hats, and presents were handed solemnly back and forth between parents-in-law, while the bride wept and afterwards the young men gulped beer or orangeade and the older people drank brandy until their faces turned red. An aged man with a Ho Chi Minh beard recited a poem. And at last the younger people sang modern Vietnamese pop songs with an electric guitar to a flushed, happy audience.

How unfair if the Communists come in tonight, I thought. Yet the nightfall seemed ominous. My small, empty hotel was shaken with bomb explosions. Some thumps were heavy, and one imagined deep craters. After curfew descended at 11 p.m., I heard hoarse shouts repeated angrily like challenges, and sudden bursts of machine gun fire close by and across the river. But the Communists did not come that night.

Next morning, I scootered with the same Vietnamese friends to the two or three Buddhist pagodas – those hotbeds of politicking in the fiery, rebellious days of 1966, when Hué students, my friends included, took carbines to the barricades against the Americans' protégés, General Thieu and Air Vice-Marshal Ky, vainly demanding elections and negotiated peace. The tree-lined courtyards were quiet now. Under the yellow and red temple hangings, under the Buddhist swastikas, bells tinkled and hand drums clicked, and smiling monks said, 'Many people go to Saigon.' I knew why. General Thi, six years in exile in America, was due back at last. He is Hué's favourite general and one of Vietnam's best – tough, ebullient, exuding charisma. . . .

[But Thi was turned back at Saigon airport. Alone in a Pan-Am Jumbo jet built for 400, he was carted back to America on the order of President Thieu. So an anti-Communist general, one of Vietnam's few honest ones but highly critical of Thieu's conduct of affairs, was refused amnesty (granted even to Communist defectors) in this year of 'reconciliation'. The action typified the stupidity of the Saigon regime. Hué was outraged.]

. . . Evidently the city that suffered most in the great Communist offensive four years ago, and did not go Communist then though given the opportunity, is still not trusted by General Thieu in Saigon: that is how the message of Thi's new expulsion was read in the northern provinces this week.

With Tet over for another year, Madame Dinh's family has once again scattered to schools, to jobs further south, to Army camps. The family gets smaller with time – one soldier son killed by a mine last year, a nephew shot, two cousins missing. Friends go, too. 'Many people are running away to southern cities now – just in case,' says Madame Dinh. 'But,' adds that strong woman, 'my home is Hué.'

In 1968 we had stood together in the rubble of the city, handkerchiefs to our noses, trying to shut out the stench of corpses. And Madam Dinh had said: 'I had a dream. President Johnson and Ho Chi Minh came here and saw all this and said why are we doing this and shook hands.' President Nixon is in Peking now talking to Chairman Mao. Mao admittedly is at one remove from Ho Chi Minh and those other stubborn minds in Hanoi. But can this mean that at last Madame

Dinh's dream of reconciliation is very, very slowly beginning to come true?

Vien Goes to War

SAIGON, MARCH 1972

A Vietnamese friend called Vien stopped me the other day in a Saigon street. I had not seen him for some time. We had first met when I went, six years ago, to a Saigon pagoda to see if I could interview the leading monk there, Thich Tri Quang, the turbulent, so-called neutralist priest who was giving the Americans a lot of trouble – he wanted to get rid of them and negotiate peace with the Communist North. Vien had been sitting at the entrance to the pagoda as I waited. A skinny young fellow, his English was bad, but he was friendly in the inevitable Vietnamese way. He invited me to meet his family. They lived in a tiny house crowded with relatives near Cholon, the predominantly Chinese quarter of the city. Vien himself was at school – at least in theory. His father was a very minor civil servant. An elder brother was in the United States, learning to be a jet pilot.

Now here was Vien again, grinning, explaining that now he was an Army captain, married for two years. Next day he came to see me at my small hotel. He carried his tiny daughter, who clutched a large red balloon.

'I killed two Vietcong last night,' he said.

'Killed? In Saigon?'

'Yes. I was patrolling the streets with my security platoon at 3 a.m. and there they were.' The curfew started at 1 a.m. 'When I saw these two men in soldiers' uniform on a motor scooter, I shouted to them to stop. But they didn't stop, so I opened fire and we ran up the road. They fired back and my major was grazed on the wrist. But we killed them.'

In the middle of town? Or on the edge of Saigon?

'No, in So-and-So Street – not very far from this hotel,' Vien grinned. 'My major say I very good captain, okay.'

His daughter struggled and let go of the balloon. It floated up to the ceiling, far out of reach. We looked at the baby, worried she would begin to howl, but she didn't.

I was packing to leave Saigon for the Delta, and Vien saw a tie I had put out. 'Number one. Can I have that?'

We went down to the street and he threw a leg over the saddle of his scooter, one arm round the baby. 'Petrol *very* expensive now,' he said, smiling in a way he intended to be disarming. So I gave him 500 piastres, not much. 'I'll pay you back,' he called, driving off.

A few days later I had returned and he came to see me again, this time without the baby. He kicked off his boots and lay down on my bed without asking. One of the two Vietcong men he'd stopped and fired on had not died – had only been mildly wounded, in fact. 'I've spent all day today interrogating him,' said Vien, yawning and stretching. 'Very tiring.'

Well, what had he confessed?

'He confessed he joined the Vietcong when he was twelve. He's twenty-five now. He comes from the north of South Vietnam, and went with his family to North Vietnam some years ago. He's been in a military officers' school up there. Earlier this year he came down south through the Ho Chi Minh trail, through Laos and Cambodia.'

Did he say all this quite freely?

'Well,' Vien grinned, 'not quite freely at first.'

'What did you do – pull out his fingernails?'

'Oh, no. We attached his fingers and feet to the electric current and switched it on now and again. Sometimes we poured water down his throat.'

'I see. And what else did he say?'

'He's been living in the An Quang pagoda in Saigon. You know the monks are very loving people. Anyone can go and live there – me, even you,' Vien smiled. 'No need to have proper identity cards. He told the monks he was from Hué and they accepted that. And, of course, he said he was a soldier because he appeared in uniform. Very clever, the VC.'

Did he admit to any specific objective?

'He had orders to blow up two bridges in Saigon. He carried a Chinese pistol and some plastic – enough to blow up a bridge or two.'

I wondered if his plan was part of a general attack on Saigon.

'That's what I must make him tell me tomorrow morning,' said Vien. 'I told him I'd be back tomorrow morning and that he'd get a bad time if he didn't tell me.' Vien left then, but soon popped back. 'You know what? My general has sent a message he wants to see me on Monday.'

'What for?' I asked. 'To make you a major?'

'No, no, I am only just a captain. No, but I think he is very pleased with me.' Vien's excitement was shining into the room. 'I think he'll give me money. Oh, I don't know how much. But he must be pleased that I caught those VC.'

'That's good for you,' I said.

'Yes, thank you,' grinned Vien. 'Oh, by the way, could you lend me another 500 piastres? I'll pay you back on Monday. Sorry, but I spend money on girls too much.'

His grin didn't look sorry at all, and of course he is married, but I gave it to him. And he threw out a dinner invitation from his mother. Of course I accepted.

Not long ago, I remembered, Vien had been visibly upset when, as he left a café, a dog was run over by a scooter in front of us and badly mangled. His parents' little, overcrowded, mosquito-ridden house was destroyed by American bombing during the 1968 Tet offensive, when the Vietcong came into his part of Saigon. They got compensation for that – perhaps because his brother is a pilot and trained in America. Vien used to like to visit the zoo. He was rather short-sighted, on the shy side and gentle.

Now he's a captain, goes after Vietcong for a living, and the money goes on girls. At least he adores his baby girl and buys her a balloon every day.

Two weeks ago Vien was sent for by his major and told to go to the extreme northern city of Quang Tri, which was captured by North Vietnamese troops this week. 'Pick up some North Vietnamese prisoners who have decided to defect and come back,' said the major.

Excited, Vien came round to my hotel. He sat on the bed and screwed up his face in mock tragedy. 'I must go to Quang Tri,' he wailed, rocking miserably back and forth. 'Many, many VC there. Maybe I die.'

'Maybe you get a medal,' I said.

'No want a medal,' wailed Vien. 'Want to stay in Saigon.'

'Maybe they make you a major,' I said.

'No want to be a major. Want to be captain – even lieutenant – and stay in Saigon.'

He seized my arm. 'When I tell my mother and father I go to Quang Tri they cry very, very much.' He ran his fingers down his cheeks indicating tears. Even so, he was half grinning. 'I know – maybe I give my major some money not to go to Quang Tri. But I haven't enough money. Could you . . . ?'

'No,' I said.

Vien shook his head. He stood up, polished his stars of rank before my wall mirror and walked over to put his hands on my shoulders. 'I will not say goodbye,' he said in mildly tragic tones. 'That's bad luck. So – see you soon.' He made a consciously slow, sad exit, backwards.

Three days later he came again to see me, bounding in, full of life and pride. 'It was nothing,' he said happily. 'Now I can go to Quang Tri any time and not be afraid.' It seemed he had brought back a North Vietnamese colonel and a major among other soldiers of Hanoi's Army who had been captured and then defected.

'Do you think the North Vietnamese will come all the way down to Saigon?' I asked him.

'No, no, no . . . impossible. We cannot have North Vietnamese in here. No good. No good,' said Vien indignantly.

'But you are North Vietnamese.' His family, I knew, was originally from the North.

'Yes,' Vien grinned, 'but I am good North Vietnamese. I believe about Buddha. Hanoi is like you, not believing.'

A week later, back he came to my hotel. 'I'm off to An Loc.' He looked unhappy. 'No want to go,' he said.

An Loc is about sixty miles north-west of Saigon and has been the scene of a furious battle involving tanks and infantry for three weeks. I thought this sounded more dangerous than his mission to Quang Tri. I had been ambushed on the road to An Loc the same week. But I didn't say so to Vien.

'I am going to collect more prisoners. You think I will die?'

'Of course not,' I said.

A few days later he was back. He fell, beaming, into the room like a puppy with a bone. He might have taken the whole North Vietnamese Army on single-handed and routed it.

'Phew! You know An Loc full of VC,' he said. 'When we came down over An Loc in our American helicopter I saw all those soldiers sitting on tanks in the streets. Some were drinking soft drinks outside shops, and I think they must be our men. But my major says no, those are all North Vietnamese. I am so shocked and so scared, I fall out of our helicopter on my head. Very painful.' Vien laughed and rubbed a large lump on his forehead. . . . 'Sorry, must go,' he said soon. 'I must go to see prisoners – I brought back thirteen. Then I go to hospital to see my brother.' Vien's brother was shot down recently and lost his left hand – something Vien accepts quite unsentimentally.

I think Vien is typical of many South Vietnamese trapped in this appalling impasse. He is not urging an end to the war at any price, though he very much wants peace. He does want the moderate General 'Big' Minh to be President, and thinks the Americans' friend, General Thieu, too dictatorial and too corrupt. But for now he is plodding on with his military life, hoping to be a major, periodically scared stiff and periodically proud.

Not all South Vietnamese soldiers – we all know this by now – are the best in the world, and after all these grinding years of war, why should they be? Some run away and some do not; but, significantly, on the whole they do not desert. There has been panic here and there in the face of oncoming North Vietnamese tanks these last weeks, but no units have gone over to the North Vietnamese, although opportunity was certainly knocking. I believe this is important – and it should always be remembered, whoever wins this war. It means the Communists are not winning the hearts and minds of the South Vietnamese despite the corruption and incompetence in Saigon.

There is a striking calmness about many Vietnamese soldiers in the field – the calm of Buddhist fatalism, perhaps. Not long ago, I was crouching in an inadequate trench with North Vietnamese mortar bombs dropping here and there. I looked up to see a small, round, laughing face peering down at me, a face almost extinguished by a huge helmet: a Vietnamese soldier. Between his teeth he gripped a small, gold-coloured Buddha that was attached to a thin chain round his neck. He was far more exposed than I was, but he was calmly motioning with his hand for me to take care and get down further; he might have been my affectionate friend. Whenever I think of the Vietnamese Army I think of people like him and Vien.

A Major Prize in Hanoi's Grasp

The North Vietnamese Army launched a large-scale offensive into the South in early 1972.

SAIGON, 4 MAY 1972

The worst thing that could happen in the north of South Vietnam is, barring miracles, about to happen. Hué, the once glorious capital of Annam, the jewel of central Vietnam, seems ready to fall to the North Vietnamese Army. If they are lost to the South, the two northern provinces are most unlikely ever to be retaken. The provincial capitals, Quang Tri and Hué, will have gone for good and will be Communized by force. The terrain rules against recapture. To the north is the Demilitarized Zone and North Vietnam itself, to the west the convenient and attack-proof mountains that slop over into Laos and enfold the tentacles of the Ho Chi Minh trail. To the south a great mountain ridge blocks the way to Da Nang, the last great American airbase.

At the very beginning of the present North Vietnamese offensive, in early April, I sat in Saigon talking about the prospects on the northern front with a sensible British military observer. It did not seem too bad then. 'If Quang Tri falls,' he said, 'that's bad, but it would not give the North a particularly powerful edge over the Americans and South Vietnamese at the negotiating table. But Hué, now. That's a different thing. That's a major prize. The North could negotiate with Hué.'

The North Vietnamese may not negotiate on the crest of the wave – they may go for more and more spectacular things, aiming perhaps at a final, tumultuous break-up of the entire South Vietnamese Army. But short of that Hué is a stupendous prize. That is why the Americans sacrificed so many men to retake it in Tet 1968; it is the second city of South Vietnam. With Hué and the two northern provinces of Quang Tri and Thua Thien gone, and Binh Dinh and Quang Ngai virtually lost in the centre, even Da Nang, the place that because of its size somehow symbolizes the American presence more than any other city in Vietnam, Saigon included, will be threatened and isolated. If Kontum falls, almost the entire northern third of South Vietnam will have been lost.

It will be argued in Government offices in Saigon, no doubt, that the vast bulk of the population lives in the Mekong Delta and green areas around Saigon. This is true. But Saigon and the Delta are still a mere rump of Vietnam. And it is impossible to exaggerate the psychological effect on the rest of South Vietnam of the loss of the northern provinces. The impact on the Army alone is unfathomably great. The people of Hué of course have sons, brothers, uncles and husbands in Army units and offices all over South Vietnam. Their despair will be immeasurable. Will it induce the spirit of Dunkirk or lead them to give up the military ghost? The latter, very likely.

But whether Hué falls or is saved in the nick of time and lingers on under siege, how has the North Vietnamese advance been so successful? The heads of generals are beginning to roll – the commander of the two northern provinces, General Lam, and the commander of the Third Division, General Giai, whose responsibility it was to defend Quang Tri and Dong Ha, are both reported to be dismissed and facing investigations into their professional conduct. In the case of Lam action has come rather late in most observers' estimation. He has never impressed foreign onlookers. General Giai has. I remember him as a colonel in Dong Ha two years ago. Tough, no-nonsense, one would have said, a calm and confident refugee from North Vietnam. But now Quang Tri is in ruins and ashes, let alone Dong Ha, an unappealing little town at the best of times. General Giai is rumoured to be missing, though some reports say he made it back to Hué.

But who is to blame? Why not blame, for example, the American advisers and their ultimate boss-on-the-spot, General Creighton Abrams? The state of morale in South Vietnam's Army is not perhaps their responsibility, but did they fail to predict the inability of American shelling and airpower to halt a conventional North Vietnamese advance down a flat coastal plain without benefit of air cover? It seems that no one could predict that rather obvious development. So, out of Vietnam's agony and a spectacular débâcle is a new military truth about to be born? That bombs and shells cannot halt a determined offensive without adequate ground forces acting aggressively in cooperation with the gunners and airmen? Or was that known before – in which case how does one account for the manifest optimism in high military and ambassadorial quarters in Saigon since the offensive began? Once more over-optimistic field reports in Vietnam seem to have bamboozled American staff officers in Saigon and, by extension, in Washington. Mr Ellsworth Bunker, the American Ambassador in Saigon for the last five years, was confident (or that was his assumed expression) in making his prediction last month that the offensive would run out of steam after six or seven weeks. That would mean it should collapse about next week. Yet the Northerners are steaming ahead.

It is true that some of the human material found fighting in northern units near Quang Tri was of surprisingly low calibre – farmer's boys, lost and bewildered. Perhaps the North, too, after these dragging years of war and casualties, is scraping the bottom of the call-up barrel and this is the last desperate fling. The South Vietnamese lost 1150 men killed in the week of President Nixon's 'bombing Hanoi' speech, and 1000 the week before. These are official figures, and they match the worst days of 1964 to 1965. The true figures are probably higher. The North Vietnamese casualties could be higher still. But the world and the leaders in Saigon and Hanoi are accustomed to, perhaps even blasé about, such figures now.

And it is by now quite unrealistic to underestimate North Vietnamese endurance and invention. Throughout this war, and particularly in this present offensive, the Northerners have consistently outsmarted the South Vietnamese and American officers by the use of something that hardly seems to exist in Saigon – *imagination*: that is Hanoi's secret weapon. In the battle that has swirled for three weeks around the provincial capital of An Loc the Americans tried using napalm for a while. But the Communists were a match for them. As soon as their soldiers saw the deadly canisters of fire falling onto them they plunged into foxholes, pulled small portable sheets of corrugated iron over their bodies and held their breath. Not all survived, of course. But enough lived to carry on the battle. Overwhelming technical advantage, when matched against simple old-fashioned human grit and resourcefulness – and imagination – is a good deal less than overwhelming. That fact, of course, is the major lesson of this war. And it very likely will be the death of Hué. For if the Communists come this time, Communism may never be eradicated. The North Vietnamese regiments are coming now with sophisticated weapons – and something more deadly: the single-minded party men, the indefatigable cadres, the interrogators, the persuaders. You can rebel against Saigon and fail, but try again and succeed. There will be no rebelling against Hanoi. Will the royal tombs be disfigured with heroic Communist slogans? Will the beautiful six-tiered riverside pagoda among the trees above Minh's house be draped in hideous 'educative' banners?

At all events, this takeover against a people's will is going to be strong-arm stuff. Occupied in the Tet offensive of 1968, Hué spurned the opportunity to embrace Communism, which is a permanent thing, as it has rejected in its heart the rampages of the Americans and General Thieu, which are not. Perhaps all is not up quite yet. Perhaps some miracle will save this city that only wants – like all Vietnam – to be left alone and be itself. But today that seems too much to ask, and Hué's agony has no visible end.

The single-minded party men, the indefatigable cadres, the interrogators, the stony-faced persuaders have long since overrun Hué and all South Vietnam. If the royal Annamese tombs have not been daubed with heroic signs, if the six-tiered pagoda has not been draped with banners, the slogans and the banners are all around. Hué is a profoundly sad place. Many ordinary people have spent years in 're-education camps' with hard labour; many more have become boat people; uncountable numbers languish in gulag-style New Economic Zones. How many have died? The agony of the city which only wanted to be left alone has no visible end even yet.

Now That the GIs Have Gone . . .

From Saigon after the first week of the American withdrawal.

1 APRIL 1973

At last, the great American khaki wave has trickled away. The uncouth, hairy horde, so loud, so short on dignity, has vanished like another age. Lilliput – the small, beautiful, mercurial world of Vietnam – has re-emerged. Poorer, grubbier, but too old to be deeply changed.

No one who loves Vietnam more than some political dogma should feel less than joy now. The ceasefire may not be perfect, but a holocaust has been halted. Normal life seeps painfully back like feeling returning to a damaged limb. At last you can travel. Touch wood, even the Government's lyrical tourist posters, once so grotesquely inappropriate ('Big Game Hunting at Dalat', 'Yachting at Nha Trang') may be valid fairly soon. In a Saigon drawing room a European wife said to me: 'I hear the VC are quite friendly.' She spoke tentatively, like

217

someone confiding a belief in ghosts. But at last, indeed, you can meet the Vietcong.

I had waited eight years to meet the armed Vietcong with a bullet-shattered arm and the grave face of a worker-priest who the other day walked across a field and shook my hand. To get to him there was first a drive from Saigon, then a walk, led by villagers, across flat, hedgeless, cultivated land. Here, people work in mollusc hats in bean and melon fields. A boy passes carrying two rats in a cage. Buffalo carts creak through the dust and an old man says: 'Walk in the cart tracks in case of mines.'

In the shadow line between Government and Vietcong territory, a solitary reed stands up in the dust bath. It has a message tied to it, like an arrow in Red Indian country: 'Soldiers, let us put aside vengeance. We need reconstruction now, and friendship.' A little further on, another one in childish peasant scrawl: 'Soldiers, please do not shoot at us and frighten our animals.' As we read, a salvo of heavy mortar shells crashes out from an army post we can see silhouetted on the road. We duck, and the shells whirr overhead and explode a few kilometres beyond. Peasants crowd round to complain of frequent harassing Army fire designed to keep the Vietcong out, even though this is one of the few zones in South Vietnam permitted, in theory, to the Vietcong.

The Vietcong arrive silently, six men in single file, in dark green uniforms, guns balanced on shoulders. Their officer gives me a thin, priestly smile. He wears sandals, a black-and-white check scarf and a pistol slung round his neck. He shakes hands. The others grin. They look in their late twenties. I ask the youngest what his medal is for. 'For killing twelve Americans,' he says.

Their leader has been in the National Liberation Front for seventeen years. Captured in 1958, he did eight years in prison. He has been three times wounded. He was once a primary schoolteacher.

'The Army makes sweeps through here regularly,' he says. 'When they come in, we move out. Then we come back. The Army drops tracts telling us to respect the Paris ceasefire agreement. But we don't attack. Here we are politically strong. Trouble comes only when the Government tries to extend its area.'

It is obvious that here and elsewhere Government control is formidable – where most of the people are.

Even so, he seems quite optimistic. He speaks of 'President Thieu's indiscipline' and 'truce violations', but adds: 'Some soldiers are less hostile than others. If we can stick this period out, perhaps conciliation will grow.' That remark means hope.

(Peace takes getting used to, like war. In some areas, Vietcong have started the shooting: helicopters have been brought down. Later, I met a Government district chief who said: 'Drink tea with the Vietcong? My orders from Saigon say no fraternization. If the VC come here, I shoot them.' But others are less inflexible.)

As we talked, the gunfire swelled. Finally, rifle fire came from a nearby field. Too near. The Vietcong moved silently away.

We plough back to the Government-held village on the road, and sit sweating at a tiny stall where two girls sell soft drinks. A policeman, sipping Coke, points to the countryside we've just left, and says: 'Don't go out there. Very dangerous. *Beaucoup VC.*'

In Saigon, President Thieu's wife is opening a new hospital. We stand in heavy heat: journalists, diplomats, Vietnamese Ministers, their wives, Vietnam's heavy brigade. A band plays 'In a Monastery Garden' with an exaggeration of tubas. Soldiers, ordinary people, stare at the great slab of steel and cement from across a street.

An hour late, the President arrives, dapper, relentlessly smiling. His helicopter swoops down onto the roof of the hospital, its airstream throwing up a small tornado of dust, paper bags, cigarette packets. After Madame Thieu's careful speech, the solemn crowd jostles damply into the building. Security guards step on journalists' feet to keep them out. Various foreign Governments are said to have given money for the hospital. Diplomats had an impression it was for the Vietnamese man in the street. They come out baffled. 'There seems to be only one public ward. All the rest are large private rooms. Damned if I know who can afford it, or who will staff it,' someone in the British Embassy says. Is there a serum against official myopia?

Up in Hué, in the American military compound, the few remaining GIs sit around their makeshift air-conditioned bar drinking up the remaining cases of liquor. Prices are special – 1.5 pence for a Scotch. No one has anything to do. There is no possible way for these men to be drawn back into battle here. A tawdry, end-of-term look has begun to encroach on the nearly abandoned buildings, the ramshackle cinema with its 'Perfume Picture Palace' sign, the sandbags on the roof where I saw an American colonel direct mortar fire into Hué in the 1968 Tet offensive. The end of an epoch.

Not far away, the front rooms of Madame Dinh's house on a bustling Hué street are rented to a tailor. A small army of apprentices pedal away at their sewing machines. The upstairs rooms have been repaired since they were shelled in 1968 and the Buddhist shrine there destroyed. In the dark back of the house, with its sparse, dark furniture and the bullet holes in the walls, Madame Dinh, a strong, tiny woman, stitches a bow for her grand-daughter.

'Is it really going to be peace?' she asks. 'We'll see. How can one trust anything?'

At night, the hard wooden Vietnamese bed with nothing but a wafer-thin reed mat on it is as uncomfortable as always. But for the first time there is no sound of bombs and shells, no flares trickling down the sky.

Next day, Madame Dinh talks about her eldest son, killed in action in 1967. I remembered him, fat and jolly. 'He died so far away, near Quang Ngai. I went down there to bring him back for burial here. It was very difficult. He was so . . . scattered.' She was near tears. 'The Army gave me a plastic shroud. In the end I still couldn't find one arm.' We visited the tomb with Madame Dinh's two daughters and the grand-daughter in her new bow. The tomb is one of many in a soldiers' cemetery. Under the yellow Buddhist swastika, an inscription says simply: 'Died for his country 7.6.1967.' Madame Dinh lit some incense sticks, put her hands together and bowed several times to her dead son. Then we came away.

Bitterness hangs in Vietnam's air like tear gas. With an old friend called Chinh, I walk through a camp of a quarter of a million refugees driven out of Quang Tri province by the North Vietnamese offensive last year. The squalor is terrible. Nine families crowd into one stench-filled hut. Once American soldiers used it. On the door is an old stencil mark: 'No Vietnamese allowed in this hut.'

Chinh has a sad, gentle face. He is a dreamer, and works with munitions in the Army. His family is nearly penniless. I look at the refugees and say: 'Incredible.'

Chinh says with great force: 'What's incredible? Only foreigners are shocked by these refugees and beggars and cripples. Vietnamese feel no shock or horror or anger or even pity any more. They don't worry if one man is worth more than another or more in the right than another.' He added: 'My brother was killed last year, as you know. Did you know we couldn't find a single fragment of his body? Perhaps these wretches are the lucky ones.'

I take a minibus to a smallish seaside town. There people talk non-stop of three things: soaring prices, corruption, the possibility of war again.

In one long back street of tiny shops only two tradesmen say they are making ends meet. One is a photographer, his head draped under a black cloth, taking the portrait of a small girl who sits before a backdrop of a vast modern mansion, a red American car and something like Lake Geneva. The other is a Buddhist coffin maker sawing a plank among his oblong, swastika-covered boxes.

A sack of rice costs £10. An Army lieutenant gets £17 a month. A cyclo driver takes home about 25p daily. Hence corruption.

An old, calm-faced man with a Ho Chi Minh beard offered chrysanthemum tea in a room behind his shop of ceramic elephants and lacquer ornaments. He lost his eldest son five years ago, when an American jet crashed onto his shop. After six months, the Americans offered him £500 compensation and he rejected it.

He said: 'Strange. We have an authoritarian Government under Mr Thieu, but no national discipline.'

A middle-aged writer, who teaches for his living, said: 'Crime. Your watch is snatched from your wrist in the street. You ask a policeman to chase the thief. He says, "Do it yourself." Ask anyone. All agree that our national police is in league with the criminals, the heroin traffickers.'

A doctor told me: 'Look, if you come back, just bring me two things, if you don't mind. Some English pipe tobacco, and some medical journals. If they come through the post, someone steals them and sells them to other doctors for cash.'

Officials have two or three jobs. An army of unemployed haunt the streets since the Americans pulled out. Near the empty Cam Ranh Bay base, a whole township of Vietnamese are stranded, their livelihood gone.

Disparity in wealth is a yawning gap. Outside my little French-run seaside hotel, young Vietnamese with harsh faces said: 'Give me fifty piastres.' Inside, in shorts, a Vietnamese Intelligence major sat at the bar, his tennis racket in an airline bag. Farther down, an American construction man is saying loudly: 'They serve really nice lobster and steaks. Real big. Twice as big as I can eat. It's a real high-class place. Real high-class meat.' Americans talk about food as the British go on about the weather.

Another night we sat in the doctor's garden rubbing on mosquito repellent. He said: 'Look, the counter-appeal to Communism must be material or moral. But on the one hand, there are rising prices, unemployment. On the other, corruption, no real democracy; above all, no real patriotism.'

'Doctor, apart from the need to please the Americans, does there have, in principle, to be democracy here?'

'Well, democracy is written into the Paris Agreements, you notice – freedom of speech and so forth. But if the Government takes away some freedom and provides efficiency in its place, well and good. Do you think this Government can do that?'

Great American investment and development – a great Vietnamese hope, except for the left. The Communist position is militarily and politically so weak today that leftists can only hope for breakdown, economic collapse. It would involve the average Vietnamese in a new nightmare. But it might end with the left-wingers on the top of the pile. In that lies one danger for Vietnamese hopes of peace.

Another is connected with stubbornness and face. The sort of thing illustrated by the district chief's refusal to fraternize with the Vietcong. The sort of thing noticeable, too, the other day near Quang Tri city during a prisoner exchange. I crossed the river that divided the Communist-occupied part of this South Vietnamese province from the totally destroyed city itself. Both sides had set up thickets of flags, tents and loudspeakers. One side blared music at the other. Prisoners of both sides splashed through the shallow water, shouting, embracing their comrades-in-arms once they reached the friendly bank. Vietcong officers stood in khaki sun helmets and baggy trousers, watching or accepting huge, unwanted cigars from American colonels of the Joint Military Commission. North Vietnamese officers in peaked caps looked on, too. Guns pointed across the water, but nobody fired. An amazing spectacle. A young Vietcong officer (though he confessed to being North Vietnamese) said in English: 'I think perhaps our meetings with the Saigon people can go on. We talk. They listen. They talk, we listen.'

'Well, that is some sort of progress,' I said to him. 'Look at all these flags and guns. And in between them the empty rubble of a once beautiful, happily populated city. Both sides destroyed it. Doesn't that symbolize this war?'

His smiling face went dead, like someone unplugging a TV set. He turned away.

In another town, a Hungarian officer of the ICCS said: 'Vietnam is just as I was told.'

'What were you told?'

'Oh, that the fruit and flowers are very beautiful.'

'What did you find here in the way of the military situation, people's attitudes?'

His face went dead. 'Sorry my English is too bad. I cannot understand your question.'

Later he said: 'I don't dare to go to London. The Army shooting and bombing in the streets.'

'I'll take you. You'll see it's nothing like Budapest in 1956.'

'Many lies were told about 1956. It was a simple matter.'

At some levels South Vietnamese soldiers and Vietcong are getting on moderately well, though the scars of war are indescribably deep. The one overriding danger is connected with face – the face of non-South Vietnamese of any faction. If the leaders in Hanoi decide that they cannot live with failure – they have not won here, as they assure their people they have – the temptation of yet another offensive may prevail. Too much stubbornness in Saigon might encourage them. So might attitudes from extreme left or right elsewere, including America.

I returned to Hué and went out for a picnic. I watched Madame Dinh and her daughters walking by the river. Here, among vivid green fields, water, temples, the royal tombs of Annam, is something much nearer the essence of Vietnam than the loudspeaker vans of Hanoi or Saigon. Something indescribably valuable, that conveys, I believe, to the Madame Dinhs and the Chinhs: 'Peace and conciliation are all that matter. Here among this beauty is common sense. All the rest, from North or South, is a corruption.'

This face of Vietnam persists. But I hear it may be doomed. It has no political power. It is as intangible as smoke. It may be crushed again between armoured forces of inexorably selfish international idealists of right or left, whose idealism can lead to the machine gun burst in someone else's stomach, and to a woman on a remote battlefield scooping chunks of her son into a plastic bag.

A Family at War

A memoir of the Vietnamese family I stayed with in Hué while I reported a war that tore them apart. It was written when the news came of the fall of Saigon to the Communists.

25 MAY 1975

A dire and familiar curtain is falling on Vietnam. I remember my friends there sorrowfully, not sure whether to mourn their deaths. Did Madame Dinh take cyanide as she threatened? Was her only surviving son, Tam, killed in Da Nang? Did Vinh's family survive or was their helicopter shot down? Did the Communists shoot Chinh in the Army uniform he hated so much?

These were my friends. I don't claim they represented all Vietnamese. But, like millions of their countrymen, they were trapped between two forces they had no time for: Communism, and the corruption and repression of America's protégés in Saigon. Now the quicksands are lapping their innocent heads.

It doesn't seem like ten years since I had met Vinh in the Air Vietnam DC-6 from Saigon. And I remember how I lost him temporarily in the turmoil of the arrival at Hué.

In the next few days, with the help of a Vietnamese-speaking English professor at the university, I began to discover Hué. It was as beautiful as I had been told – more than just the capital of Annam, where two great Vietnamese, the historic hero Le Loi and Ho Chi Minh, had been born. Hué had something more than beauty: an antique pride, faded but beguiling. A city of pleasant buildings astride the Perfumed River, its two halves linked by a slender modern bridge cluttered with trishaws, coolie-hatted peasants and women in the floating white national dress, Hué had seen better days. Hué people knew this, resented it and clung for consolation to a pure nationalism.

Not surprising, then, that Hué was out of bounds to American troops. Neutralism was stronger here than anywhere in South Vietnam. Its population, led by Buddhist monks in saffron robes, teachers and students, had boiled out into the streets to help bring down the Catholic dictator, Ngo Dinh Diem. By the time I got there, agitation was bubbling up again, centred on Hué University with its 3600 students. The students were likeable, humorous and, like most Vietnamese, small, bright people. They had little money; some had one prized possession, a transistor or a scooter. They were sentimental. They loved music and the cinema. They scrubbed themselves and their clothes relentlessly. But they often had foot sores and were ill at ease in shoes.

Hué's intense resentment zeroed in on two men: General Thieu and Air Vice-Marshal Nguyen Cao Ky, now in California and about to become a college superintendent. Even then, Thieu was described by the contemptuous people of Hué as 'the man of a thousand mad ambitions'. Soon I was watching a Government 'rally' in Hué's principal cinema. The hall was packed, mainly with students, sceptical, mildly good-humoured. Almost provoking them by his presence, the Prime Minister, Ky, then the darling of the American Embassy in Saigon, lolled in the front row of the stalls, suave and black-moustached. (Thieu, then styled President of the National Committee of Direction, became the American favourite a little later.) The occasion was the presentation 'to the people' of some citizens of Hué recently arrested for clandestine Vietcong activities, and some Vietcong defectors to the Government. Choral singing began the proceedings. The defectors delivered their *mea culpas* to loud applause from the students – a clear sign of general lack of sympathy for the Vietcong, however great their hatred of the war itself. The traitors were greeted with light applause – no hisses or boos. As a propaganda exercise, it had mixed, Hué-like results.

When we all trooped out into the street, there was Vinh. He stood, waving joyfully, next to a stocky student with thick, bellicose eyebrows, who turned out to be Tam. 'Come home,' Tam said.

Madame Dinh made us tea. 'If you knew how fed up we are with the kind of propaganda you saw in that cinema,' Tam explained, and Vinh, his tic working overtime, prompted Tam's French. 'Look, I demonstrated against Diem,' said Tam. 'We fear Communism, and we want peace. And what we have is a Government of corrupt generals, utterly subservient to the Americans.' A legal Government freely

225

elected, of civilians capable of standing up to the Americans – only that would reassert Vietnam's identity in the world. In the next months I got to know Madame Dinh, who presided over the household, determined to make both ends meet. She was fortyish, and tiny, with a small, round, pale face and the strength of character of ten Tams.

In 1968, during the Tet holiday, the infamous holocaust devastated Hué. For nearly a month the North Vietnamese and Vietcong roamed the streets of Hué, fought from its houses, defended the Citadel against American Marines as American bombs fell around them on houses packed with ordinary Vietnamese, who could only crouch there and hope for the best.

The Americans were still fighting in Hué when I got back there. The stench of bodies forced you to put a handkerchief over your nose. My heart sank to see Tam's street a blackened shambles. But among the gutted shambles, miraculously, Tam and Vinh and the others stood grinning, and skipped through the rubble to greet me. They led me in to see Madame Dinh, some weeping and laughing at the same time.

She happily brought out tea and a meal and sat up that night playing cards with some women as if nothing much had happened. Yet among the remains of the roof, in the room with a mortar crater in its concrete floor and bullet scars on the walls, balcony gone, the family had sat out three weeks, while the Vietcong soldiers in their house shot back at the Americans, and American bombs buried their neighbours by the score. Jokes and stories of the siege made a kind of end-of-term atmosphere. But the strain had been immense. And what did the battle for Hué mean? It seemed to me – seems to me still – to symbolize the entire war. The Vietnamese people had been raped by two forces which millions of them had come to fear and distrust.

The next time I went to Madame Dinh's house she had more mouths to feed – refugees she had taken in. Three-ply wood replaced walls shattered by the Tet bombing. And I met another Vietnamese of about Tam's and Vinh's age – perhaps the most remarkable and lovable of all. I shall call him Chinh.

Madame Dinh had adopted Chinh's penniless father and mother as part of the family. The old man (people said he was a bit soft in the head) sat in a white smock rolling cigarettes on the pavement outside the tailor's shop, where the teenage tailors stitched away making name tabs. Chinh's mother served cheap, fiery rice wine to the cyclo drivers. Chinh had a long face that was saved from ugliness by its sad gentleness: a mixture of A.A. Milne's Eeyore and Dickens's Smike. He was gangling and bony, and he noticed things and thought about them. His shyness concealed affection and a surprising passion.

We often walked in the great greenness outside Hué. And if Vinh was in Hué he joined us, and we visited a deserted pagoda in a garden on the river and drank beer or tea there under the trees. Chinh would sit silent for minutes on end. When he thought his silence was impolite, he would shyly touch one's hand and smile a slow, clumsy smile of apology. One day, he jolted me into the most unbearable awareness of what it was like to have been born and grown up to twenty-one years old in the loneliness of the violence and the death of friends, uncles, cousins. He said dreamily: 'I wonder what the world is like?' And he quoted: ' "*Est-ce que le globe terrestre est beau? Ah, oui, très beau.*" Camus wrote that in *Sisyphe*, I think.' He paused, 'I shall remember it until I die.'

Whenever I left Vietnam, letters came once in a while from Hué. Tam wrote: 'We must write often because we are so far away from each other. . . . I will enrol in a School of National Administration: but a few months later I have to go to the Army. It is hateful. But it is obligatory. Chinh has also had to join the infantry. . . . Vinh is just leaving agricultural school as an agricultural engineer.' Later: 'Both I and Chinh are, by chance, in parts of the Army where we do not go to combat. So we are not forced to kill anyone, and that gives us great joy. We are lucky. Vinh is luckier still. He is working on an agricultural project near Qui Nhon. Perhaps, dear brother, we are really the most lucky ones because we are not obliged to bomb our own people.'

I saw Chinh, in a hopelessly ill-fitting uniform, at Da Nang. He was set to computing the number of shells in the armouries. He giggled about it when he told me, because we both knew he couldn't add two and two. But at least he was safe there: 'Unless I drop a shell!'

In 1972 Madame Dinh and the family had to leave temporarily. A North Vietnamese Army invasion captured Quang Tri, north of Hué, smashing it to powder. It was a dreadful time to be in Hué, almost as bad as Tet. A nightmare of violence, panic and misery erupted in the streets. Fleeing South Vietnamese troops, half dressed, desperate with fear, sometimes drunk, fought with each other in the market and set it ablaze. Refugees and their babies from Quang Tri clogged the roads, jostling across the bridge that had been rebuilt after Tet and forcing their way south to Da Nang. I found Tam's house deserted for the first time: a sinister omen. Drunken cyclo drivers struggled with each other outside; some dragged angrily at my shirt in the red glow of the burning market.

Madame Dinh soon wrote saying she had been obliged to evacuate the household to Na Trang, a long way south. 'I am alone with my unmarried daughter and my grand-daughter. If my only dear son is killed, I don't know what I should do. We think now this terrible war will never end. It is a kind of life for us now. My poor country. My poor children.'

But, a miracle! The next year, 1973, after the ceasefire that led to the American withdrawal, turned out to be the best time of all. The peace was like a sudden, glorious spring. 'Perhaps, at last, at last, the shooting is over?' laughed Madame Dinh, clapping her hands, back in the house at Hué.

Now Vinh was married from his little house on the river. The evening before, his friends hilariously celebrated on a sampan. Tam and Chinh and the rest played guitars and Vinh, twitching happily, sang through the night, and people swam in the warm water, and bought tea, beer or food from small floating stalls whose owners paddled them alongside. We landed again as the sun came up. We smiled at each other in something near heaven.

Yet there were insistent grimmer things: Tam's cousin visited the house on parole from prison. He was a paratrooper, and had deserted from the Laos invasion by clinging to the underside of a helicopter. He was doing twelve months. Madame Dinh, typically, was sheltering his wife.

Chinh and Tam had been changed noticeably by the war. At Da Nang, Chinh borrowed a jeep to drive me to an inadequate camp overstuffed with Quang Tri refugees. Among the shacks, Chinh suddenly burst out at me: 'The refugees congratulate you!'

Startled, I said, 'I'll bet they do.'

Chinh stared rigidly ahead: 'All foreigners, even British – you are only tourists here!'

'Please, Chinh, I don't feel a hero being here.'

His mouth was trembling. But he braked the jeep and quickly seized my arm. 'Of course you don't. I know that.' For a time we sat there looking at each other, recovering. Vietnamese like Tam and Chinh are astonishingly resilient. But the unfairness of the years of killing and maiming, and the squalor of refugees and of profiteers, embittered them in the end. They were not the sort of Vietnamese to be buoyed up by the American-invented 'revolutionary' cadres, who wore black pyjamas in imitation of the Vietcong and sang songs called 'Let's Build a New Life Hamlet' or 'Advisory Team 54'.

They were better than that. And even in 1973, it was too late, after all, to believe much in miracles. So when Tam and Chinh and I hugged each other goodbye at Da Nang airport, I think we were all numb with misery. Chinh asked me to bring him some books by Heinrich Böll; he could hardly get the words past his shaking lips; Tam ran off with both hands over his face. I haven't seen either of them again.

Of course, heaven had not arrived. Of course, the war went on, taking hundreds of thousands more lives. I am told that Madame Dinh, with her daughters and grandchildren, made it to Saigon before its fall. Vinh, with his tic and comic face, is there, too, trying to keep what's left of his family together; his father and other relatives are missing; his mother is dying of cancer.

Madame Dinh's last letter to me is distraught: '. . . all is lost. My dear, my only, son Tam was in Da Nang. I can hardly imagine he is not dead, do you think? We live from minute to minute now. How can I express it to you? . . . My poor Tam. My country, my poor country. Perhaps this is the last letter I shall be able to write to you. Adieu, my dear, good friend. . . .' I believe duty to her family will prevent her taking the cyanide she threatened to swallow in her despair.

Chinh, like Tam, was cut off in Da Nang wearing that damned uniform. None of them would have wanted to flee the country: they prided themselves above all things on being Vietnamese nationalists.

What now? Although the victory was total, South Vietnam is a mouthful to swallow, even for organized Communists. But within months or a year or two, I suppose it will be digested. Massacre or no massacre, the Southerners will probably be fitted, in time, as the North Vietnamese have been, with those meaningless, waxwork, political smiles that mean death to real friendship. So only a searing memory remains.

Again and again I think of Madame Dinh, that staunch woman, in the horror and ruins of Tet 1968, telling me how she had prayed that President Ho Chi Minh and President Johnson would say to each other, 'Why are we doing this?' and shake hands.

If only the politically self-righteous would permit such dreams to come true. But the curtain is falling on tiny Madame Dinh, and Tam with his beetle brows and infectious giggle, Vinh and his lop-sided grin with his tic, and Chinh with his sad, long, affectionate face.

I shall never forget them – any more than Chinh will forget the beauty of the terrestrial globe, of which he has only seen such a pitiable corner.

Among the Ghosts, a Pause for Quiet Tears

A return to Vietnam ten years after Saigon became Ho Chi Minh City, and the discovery that the anniversary is unearthing many graves.

28 APRIL 1985

Abrupt Vietnamese voices bark military-style commands under the trees in April drizzle. Between the towering red-brick cathedral and the former presidential palace columns of women and children are rehearsing their march-past for Tuesday's anniversary celebrations. Ten years ago on Tuesday, the Communist forces of General Van Tien Dung entered the shattered chaos of Saigon as the last distraught Americans scrambled into US Marine helicopters on the roof of their embassy – the only place in the whole of South Vietnam left to them to land on after thirteen years' total military involvement. That was what American power had been reduced to. Hardly surprising that the present Vietnamese Government wants to make a big thing out of it ten years on.

Liberation and unification are the official watchwords: that is what the celebratory banners will say and what the excited speeches will echo. They are the words with which I have been bombarded *ad nauseam* by my 'guide'. (Hanoi provides guides to all visitors to translate, to 'smooth the way' through a nightmare of restrictive and tangled Socialist bureaucracy, to make sure we do not stray and get up to mischief.)

No doubt official organization will provide adequate cheering crowds on Tuesday. No doubt it will be a colourful spectacle. No doubt many Vietnamese present will indeed feel happily liberated from the Americans and the 'puppet generals' who ruled here all those years ago. And there will certainly be many who do not. Many who were numbed by the events of 1975 – and who feel numb even now.

Many who have been destituted because of their connection with the former regime – an intimate or a haphazard connection, it makes little odds. Many who find no work, who blame the administration for economic mismanagement and can say nothing.

But it will probably be a fairly jolly affair for one overriding reason. It is the reason why I and other foreigners who were in Vietnam in the war chose to come back now after years of longing for just one more look – the magic of the irrepressible South Vietnamese *joie de vivre*, the humorous and unimaginably resilient character of a little people who somehow survived thirty years of all-out war and who are now facing year after year a dire, penurious peace.

No important guests are expected. The Socialist bigwigs of the world will be absent – Fidel Castro, for example, will be represented by his Foreign Minister. Jane Fonda is invited, but she seems utterly irrelevant here now. This April has had an oddly all-in-the-family property about it.

A bizarre relationship has been struck between the overwhelmingly Hanoi-born officials, ferrying people like me about the country, and foreigners who were here before in the war. In Ho Chi Minh City I find myself better acquainted with the place than my guide, Mr Thai, who, because he studied at Reading University in the late seventies, I nicknamed Mr Thai Reading.

There are plenty of Communist bloc technicians and a few delegations around. Byelorussia has 'adopted' Hué, Leningrad has twinned with Saigon (as many Vietnamese still call it). Large Soviet men and large manly women lumber about my hotel, eyeing Westerners lugubriously, envying us our dollars. But of two hundred or so foreign journalists whom Hanoi elected to invite, Americans form by far the biggest part. The TV networks have come in like Marines storming ashore once more, no expense spared, charting planes to carry hundreds of metal cases of equipment, zapping the Vietnamese all over again – but now with cameras poked in the face and heavy hands on shoulders – and above all showering the Communist conquerors of America's armed forces with hundreds of thousands of dollars (estimates reach a million or more) which hit the poverty-stricken Vietnamese with something near the psychological force of a B-52 strike. The rivalry is intense. Last week NBC: they imported a 'dish' – a portable earth station that transmits sight and sound via satellite live to the United States. 'Wonderful,' said Thai Reading, standing in the lobby of my hotel watching CBS lugging boxes and complaining that

ABC had a whole floor and they only had five rooms. 'How did we win the war and they lose it? Live television. Wow!'

I landed in Hanoi two weeks ago and have since travelled to Hué, my favourite city, and Da Nang. There was a lot to learn there. And a lot to mourn. But this weekend belongs to Saigon. The anniversary is unearthing many graves. I stood, after twelve years' absence from a country I knew well for nearly nine years, at a high window in the Caravelle Hotel in central Saigon and looked out – as so many times before – across the night-time city. Thunder rolled like gunfire. Lightning whitened the ocean of grimy rooftops. How could one not think of the time when flares swayed down the sky and from the suburbs of Cholon or towards Tan Son Nhut airport the rockets roared. On the river near a floating restaurant mined by Vietcong sappers twenty years ago, I looked past the rusty hulks of Vietnamese freighters that seemed destined never to sail anywhere again, at the clutter of hovels on the far bank. In the old days, Vietnamese pointed at them and grinned, '*Beaucoup VC.*' Now the 'VC' were here, in the person of Thai Reading saying, 'Come on. Lunch. Let's have a beer first.'

There are good ghosts and horrid ones. M. Ottavij, the old owner of the Royale Hotel, beckons from his doorway ready to recommend the Algerian wine bottled here on 10 February over the one labelled 5 March, and to predict a war in the Middle East at a distance of five years – 'Nostradamus has foretold it all, Monsieur Yoong.' But M. Ottavij has 'passed over' after a life that I always thought could have been measured in the tear gas canisters and drunken bodies of American roughneck construction workers that lay in the gutters outside his wonderful, unsmart bar that is now a printer's shop.

There is the corner where I unwisely halted one holiday evening in the Vietnamese New Year. I had entertained a young Vietnamese officer – captured by the Vietcong, heroically escaped, terribly wounded, decorated – and his new wife to dinner. In the market we had bought flowers. A last drink before parting? We hesitated on the kerb waiting for traffic to pass – I and this beautiful couple. A jeep pulled up by the girl. One of the American civilians in it – fat, drunk, cigar in his teeth, leaned towards her. 'You wanna fuck?' She smiled, not understanding. But her husband understood and that was that. His face went blank and pale. He took her arm and hurried her away. I never saw them again. It is a pleasure to celebrate the absence here now of such unquiet Americans.

Outwardly – but only outwardly – this city is much the same; poverty is a grand preserver of cities. But hundreds of thousands of people have no work though they would love some. They are obliged to live on their wits as Vietnamese so often have, and luckily these are people who have learned to do that rather well and even to smile and practise their scraps of English on you while they do it.

That is why this celebration will be viewed with a wary scepticism by a considerable part of the long-suffering population of Saigon. The city is down and out, there is little work, very little money, a good daily dollop of boredom and a motivation quotient that must be somewhere very near zero. It is hard to realize that the war has been over ten years. You would think it was more like twelve months. Yet one can say for Saigon that even after ten years it retains its spirit. That is more than you can say for Hanoi, which is more beautiful – perhaps one of the most delicately beautiful cities in the world – but where thirty years of wartime discipline and the relentless severities of Marxist–Leninist guided 'democracy' have flattened out the Vietnamese character as a steamroller flattens out the bubbles in hot tar.

The Saigon shops display shelves of books about Lenin – though there is no statue of him here yet to match the fifty-foot monster going up in Hanoi – and paperback novels that look horribly like Vietnamese versions of *The Love of Two Tractor Drivers* (though tractors are not much in evidence in the countryside of the South. Perhaps a better title would be *The Love of Two Water Buffalo Drivers*.) These bookshops are dreary places, hardly patronized. The men of Hanoi are irritated by this southern lack of politico-literary seriousness and have recently begun to say so in newspaper articles. Their articles have also attacked a southern hankering for kung-fu movies, disco dancing and immodest displays of slap and tickle on South Vietnam's beaches.

Another sign that humanity still breathes in Ho Chi Minh City is the extraordinary universal display of good humour and affection – not too strong a word – for foreigners. Everyone waves – construction workers from rooftops, girls in mollusc hats on bicycles (this is a city of ancient bicycles), red-faced men in cafés, peasant soldiers, rascally cyclo drivers and their passengers. 'Ooh,' they cry, 'What's your name?' It is not that one is taken for a 'liberating' Russian comrade (Russians are considered boorish, humourless and, above all, distressingly stingy). I announce my Englishness and the smiles widen still further. Away from the nursemaid fussiness of the official 'guides', I and other Westerners are enchanted Gullivers once more in a deliriously friendly Lilliput.

It must be said that our official hosts from Hanoi are doing their best to be genial within the confines of the paranoiac anxieties characteristic of Socialist countries. It is the many ordinary English- or French-speaking Vietnamese who have learned to give foreigners unaccompanied by a 'minder' a wide berth. You see them hovering, tempted to talk, then sidling away. Like my friend with the pale face, like the priests, like the monks, they have been warned. So being here is infinitely touching and infinitely sad.

'Liberation,' this week's loudspeakers will quack, reminding the people that the anniversary is about the death of capitalism. Not everyone will want to make merry over that. But anyone can celebrate Vietnam's liberation from thirty-five years of war. That is certainly most worth celebrating. Unification, too – Vietnam's North and South are certainly unified, even if the geographical unification has been matched by an imposed ideological unification that the Vietnamese would most likely reject if they were offered a choice.

But choices are things of the past now. You can only choose to go or stay – and conform. So there will be very many worthy Vietnamese missing from the crowds of onlookers on Tuesday – Vietnamese as patriotic as anyone in the country today, Vietnamese who won medals as Vietminh jungle fighters against the French colonialists, even some who fought the Americans in their way. Even 'Big Minh', the last President of the South, who ordered the laying down of arms ten years ago, is far away in France. Exiled groups, a senior official told me, can send representatives to the celebrations. But I am afraid these celebrations will be a time for secret tears more than for joy.

A postscript after the Tenth Anniversary Parade

At the celebrations last week about 20,000 Saigonese out of 4.3 million turned out to watch the parade. No one waved a flag, no one cheered the ageing Soviet tanks or the beautiful marching girls. On one side of the street the elderly, bemedalled Communist officials relentlessly smiled. On the other, across a spiritual chasm, the Saigonese masses silently stared. The Communists were having a party all to themselves.

How can one explain the extraordinarily touching displays of ecstatic affection for Westerners in Saigon last week? The universal whispers of 'Russian bad, English good' – or even 'American good'?

234

What next? Hanoi longs for a rapprochement with America – and with its dollars. But the Vietnamese want the dollars and to build a sister regime in Kampuchea, too. And why should the world bring cash and sympathy to a Government that goes on ladling out so much fear to its own people, leave alone Kampuchea?

Do we have to wait for a younger generation in Hanoi to replace the old men, heroes in war, cruel, ideological stick-in-the-muds in peace, who have won a great victory and yet seem to hate all the world – even their own people?

Poor Vietnam – mangled in war by colonialists, lobotomized and pauperized in peace by Communists. In Saigon last week I fancied I saw a lot of loveless ideologists dancing on a grave.

Vietnam: Casualties of Peace

5 MAY 1985

'I saw some smiling pilgrims at a pagoda yesterday,' an Australian diplomat confided soon after I arrived in Hanoi. 'That just shows how people aren't too unhappy under Communism.' An odd judgement, I thought. He might as well have inferred from seeing a couple of pilgrims sharing a sandwich that the economy was booming. Yet Vietnam is one of the world's poorest countries.

At any rate I was happy to be in South Vietnam after an absence of twelve years. Besides, I had old Vietnamese friends to find. I wanted to know how Madame Dinh and her family were being treated in Hué, or wherever I might find them. After all, by now I had known them intimately for twenty-one years and if Madame Dinh's smiling sons, daughters and grandchildren were still smiling, that would say something about the new Vietnam.

I had longed for, and dreaded, this return. But during the first days in Hanoi I let nothing depress me – not the rain on potholed roads, not the ramshackle transport, not the absence of soap, not toilet paper so rough you could have smoothed knots out of planks of wood with it. I was unrattled by the ham-fisted search of my luggage in my hotel room which left prickly-heat powder over everything. I was calm in the face of aggressively barking customs men at Hanoi's cock-eyed airport, who shouted, 'Open that – open that –' in what seemed like barely controlled rage that passengers should have come to Vietnam at all.

In retrospect, the airport 'welcome' was a portent. It revealed a contempt on the part of some officials for just about anybody they dealt with, and it was demonstrated most vividly in Saigon a little later. There, the press department officials of the Ministry of Foreign Affairs arranged for two hundred TV and newspaper journalists, mostly American, a visit to what they claimed was a political re-education centre for former 'criminals' of the old Saigon regime. With its swimming pool, little lakes and sleek buildings, the place was obviously a new tourist centre. After three weeks of official evasions and deceptions this, many thought, took the prize.

But that was still to come. During the first week, full of hope and accompanied by my official guide Mr Thai, I sat with my knees around my ears in a threadbare Russian plane, without overhead racks or oxygen equipment, on the way to Hué. In this beautiful city, once the imperial capital of Annam, languidly sprawling along the banks of the Perfumed River, I had first run into the Vietnamese who later became part of my life. Were they still here? Applying for my visa in London, I had specifically stated that my reason for going was to see what had happened to these friends. I had heard nothing of them since the disintegration and chaos of 1975 and the Communist occupation. No letter – no smuggled message. I would surely have heard from them if they had safely emigrated as boat people, so either they had been among boat people who drowned in the South China Sea, or they were somewhere in Vietnam.

My visa came after more than a year. In Hanoi I repeated my reasons for wanting to go south, and smoothly courteous officials asked for the names and addresses of my friends. I had no wish for the security police to stage-manage a meeting, so I said that I wasn't sure of their full names; perhaps their addresses had changed. They were small, unimportant people anyway.

The press department people nodded and smiled vaguely. They obviously found my request tiresomely eccentric. To see old friends – what for? Nevertheless, here I was with Mr Thai bounding across the familiar bridge over the Perfumed River, turning right, heading for the little doorway in which I had found sanctuary so many times in the nine years I had spent in Vietnam. There Madame Dinh stood staring at me in an almost empty room. I was shocked. She seemed to have shrunk. I looked around – there were two small girls in the room, neither of them hers. Unsmiling, as if dazed, she led me to a bare table where we sat facing each other in silence as if it were visiting time in jail. After a while she whispered, 'This is too dangerous.' She kept glancing fearfully about her – particularly at Mr Thai. 'The Communists . . . the terror,' she said into my ear. I felt I had stepped into a nightmare. I think even Mr Thai felt pity.

He moved away, saying, 'Have a talk,' and I asked her at once, 'Where's Tam?'

'In Saigon,' she said, her voice barely audible. 'Tam was seven years in a re-education centre. Chinh too.' She looked as if she had come to the end of her tether.

They typified two types of Vietnamese. Tam was an extrovert – forthright, humorous, talkative. Chinh was quite different. He had a long face with a crooked grin, saved from ugliness only by its extreme gentleness; he had always reminded me of the drawings of Smike by 'Phiz'. I remembered his long silences and his sad thoughtfulness. There was a little about him of the poet. He bought translations of *The Grapes of Wrath*, Camus, Heinrich Böll. If anyone had told me then that Chinh – or Tam for that matter – would be shut up for seven years in a camp for war criminals, I would have told him he was crazy.

At that time the Buddhist students of Hué, including Tam and Chinh, were in armed revolt against the growing American influence and the regime of General Thieu and Air Vice-Marshal Ky. Hué's streets were barricaded; the city was declared off-limits to American troops. The students were demanding free elections and an honest, representative, civilian government that could negotiate peace with Hanoi from a position of moral, as well as military, strength.

Soon there was shooting by and at the students, and tear gas in the streets. The Saigon generals managed to put down the revolt by force, but it had been a significant event. It had vividly revealed the intensely neutralist nature of Hué's people. The Communist officials had no monopoly on patriotism, however much they claimed it.

Unfortunately, like millions of their countrymen, Tam, Chinh and their friends were trapped inextricably between two remorseless forces they had no respect for – Communism on the one hand and, on the other, the Americans and their corrupt, unrepresentative protégés in Saigon. Tam and Chinh felt that by taking carbines to the barricades they were making a stand for a true Vietnamese nationalism, untainted by foreign ideologies from East or West. They carried out this protest against hopeless odds, and I sympathized with them.

Madame Dinh frantically glanced this way and that as if the house were haunted.

I said, 'And how is Tam?'

She said, 'Tam is destitute.'

'What does he do?'

A pause. 'He is . . . a coolie.'

'I shall see him in Saigon.'

She started. 'No, no. It is too dangerous.'

But, I said, he has served his time in a camp – he has paid for his so-called crimes. He must be free by now. She only repeated, 'Too dangerous, too dangerous.'

I had another thought: Communist re-education might have turned him against a capitalistic Englishman like me. 'Perhaps he doesn't want to see me.'

'How can you say that?' Madame Dinh demanded, and began to cry. 'The emotion,' she said, apologizing.

Our shared past lay about us – there was the break in the floor where a mortar bomb had fallen during Tet 1968.

The following day I passed the cemetery where Tam's brother lies buried, when Mr Thai and I went for a last look at Hué's beautiful royal tombs. I remembered Madame Dinh in the early 1970s holding her grand-daughter's hand and walking through clouds of butterflies among the lotus water tanks, the broken palaces and terraces of the old kings. It seemed monstrous that Madame Dinh could not come with me now.

I had a hard time explaining to her that Mr Thai's presence was an official guarantee that the people I was allowed to visit openly would not come to harm. At last she agreed to give me Tam's address in Saigon. I left her now where after the ordeal of Tet I had seen her standing, a tiny, birdlike figure, smiling. She was not smiling now.

I went on to Da Nang, a giant American base in the old days, hideous with the din of jets and trucks. Here in the early 1970s I had once found Chinh called up at last – even he couldn't evade the draft – and remembered how he had told me he was meant to be counting the shells in an armoury. He had giggled, because we both knew he was a daydreamer and would lose count. 'At least,' he said, 'I am not forced to shoot people.' Tam, he told me, was working at some job in the administration of Quang Tri province. Thinking of that piece of information now, so many years later, I said to myself, My God, that's why they got seven years.

Again I flew with Mr Thai – this time to Saigon. Before he even began to inquire about Tam's whereabouts, I bumped into Tam himself in the street. Like his mother, this once ebullient man stood staring at me as if he had seen a particularly terrifying ghost. 'Mr Gavin?' His face was pale, rigid.

'How are you, Tam?'

Like his mother, he kept glancing around him, scrutinizing each passer-by. 'It is forbidden in the People's Republic of Vietnam to talk to foreigners.'

'I know. But look.' I quickly gave him the name of my hotel and my room number. I assured him that a Government official would be in touch with him and that we had seen his mother. 'Perhaps,' I said, 'we can meet for dinner very soon.'

His face was almost a parody of fear. I had never encountered anything quite like it. I took a cyclo and left him. This, I thought bitterly, was the week 'Liberation' was to be celebrated.

Mr Thai waited at the hotel for Tam to appear with his family at five o'clock two days later. By six no one had arrived. Mr Thai gave up and left me. Tam came, alone, at eight. He told me he had been told to come at eight and so had done so. I didn't, for Tam's sake, want him to be alone with me for long. I left messages for Mr Thai and took him up to the hotel restaurant where he ordered a beer and a steak. He looked uneasy here too, although now he managed to smile. Undoubtedly the cashier and a waiter or two paid us some unusual attention. Presently, leaving the steak unfinished, Tam said, 'I'm going now. It's better.'

But by that time I had learned two important things. First, Chinh was a few miles outside Saigon in another province. Terribly poor, Tam said – could I possibly do something for him? He was ruining his already poor health working on some agricultural project as a labourer. No books by Camus or Heinrich Böll there, I thought. Tam said that he and Chinh had both escaped from Da Nang but had been picked up by the Communists from the house in Hué three days after the surrender on 30 April 1975. Seven years in a re-education centre near Hué had meant rigorous hard labour as well as continuous lectures on Marxism–Leninism and 'correct thinking'. But no torture, he said – no physical abuse – only back-breaking labour month after month, year after year. The food was inadequate, he said, but his wife had been able to visit him every two months for fifteen minutes, and to bring him a small food parcel.

Tam told me that he wanted at all costs to get his family out of

Vietnam. There was a programme by which it was possible to leave legally. But Vietnamese needed sponsorship. 'I'll look into this at once,' I said. Three times I asked him how he earned a living now – three times he promptly evaded the question.

First he said, did I remember his friend Ngoc? He had escaped to Australia by boat. Then he said, 'Oh, and Vinh tried three times to take a boat out, was caught three times, and jailed three times.'

'But where are you working, Tam?' I asked yet again. 'We have been friends for twenty years. Aren't I your elder brother? You used to say so. Even if you go down the sewers every day – even if you sleep down there – I shall understand. There's no shame now.'

Very painfully he said, 'I buy sweets in the market. Small packets. I resell them. The profit is very small, too.' For a moment I thought he was going to break down in front of the inquisitive waiters.

Sweets were better than sewers, I said, and at last he laughed. A few days later his wife, his two small sons and his sister were allowed to come to dinner at the hotel – a dinner supervised by Mr Thai, of course, who insisted on eating in a newly opened and almost empty night club. We had a joyless, indifferent meal under the tawdry decorations. Rats ran under our feet while a violinist played 'Red Sails in the Sunset' several times over.

With Mr Thai's consent, we discussed what could be done. Tam's family evidently had no future in Vietnam. Not after the stigma of re-education. The family was marked apparently for life – they had a police dossier. There could be no decent jobs now, no places eventually in the university for Tam's or Chinh's sons. 'Please help them find a life abroad,' Tam begged me when Mr Thai left for the men's room.

I knew by now that I could only try to get them into the Orderly Departure programme. It is a dignified way to jettison one's country, although not an easy one. Vietnamese began leaving their homeland legally in mid-1979 under the ODP, as opposed to the disorderly departures of the wretched boat people. The new programme would enable the Politburo in Hanoi to be rid of compatriots without incurring the odium attached to the shocking flight of the boat people – a flight that still continues ten years after 'Liberation'.

Eighty-one thousand Vietnamese have already left under the ODP. About 80,000 more are waiting for host countries to agree to receive them. A larger, unknown number have applied for exit visas from the Vietnamese Government – no steps can be taken without those exit visas. I was told they can cost several thousand dollars in bribes to

Vietnamese officials. Only a few thousand people are able to leave each month, so the wait to escape can last five years. It is a matter of painstaking screening by the Vietnamese authorities and by host Governments. Officially, priority is given to those seeking reunion with relatives already abroad, to inmates of re-education centres (though they cannot qualify at the moment because of the political impasse between Vietnam and the United States), and people released from re-education centres. Tam and Chinh, of course, may qualify for the last category.

But who will take them? America takes the most refugees – some 200,000 in 1984 – Canada, Australia and France come next. Britain's attitude to fugitives is comparatively frosty. But perhaps wheels might be set turning on behalf of my friends. I had, I thought, to see Tam again, at least so that he might give me details of his family's ages, marriages and so on. But a note appeared in my hotel mailbox the next day simply saying, 'Too busy to see you. Tam.' Obviously nonsense, this drove me wild with worry. How could Tam be too busy?

His future might be in my hands – such as they were. What was the Government up to? Mr Thai was expressionless. When I asked him to go to see Tam, he said sharply, 'No.' When I threatened to go to Tam's house on my own, Mr Thai said, 'I advise you not to, not for your sake, but for Tam's.'

'What about those papers for the ODP?' But Mr Thai had turned away.

I never saw Tam again. I was not allowed to see Chinh at all. I imagined a thin, worn, gentle face, and pictured myself talking to him about the passage from Camus's *Sisyphe* which he had quoted to me years ago in Hué: '*Est-ce que le globe terrestre est beau? Ah, oui, très beau.*' Now that he was in ill health, weary, and in a loneliness that must seem without hope, I wanted to say to him, 'Look, there is hope, after all this time I am going to try to help. Perhaps at last – who knows – you will see the *globe terrestre* that Camus told you was so beautiful, and you will know that he was right.'

I got the papers after all. Not everyone is heartless in Communist Vietnam. Mr Long from the Ho Chi Minh City press office listened to my last-minute pleas for someone – anyone – to retrieve those documents without which I could do little or nothing to get any Vietnamese out of anywhere. I told him I was leaving for Bangkok the next morning. It was now or never. I wanted to leave presents and some money. Mr Long nodded. He took the presents. And he returned with a manila envelope that contained all I needed to apply for the OD programme.

Mr Thai had lent me a booklet in Hué. It was called *Whose Human Rights?* and it was the Hanoi Government's reply to the flood of international protest on the subject of the re-education camps. A passage in it read:

Re-education and not punishment – such is the fundamental difference between our system and that of other countries which condemn the prisoner in court. By sparing him this conviction, our system spares him a stained police record which would follow him throughout his life and would even influence his children . . . a re-educated person could return to a normal life.

Tam and Chinh are 're-educated'. But can selling sweets and doing grinding agricultural labour be a 'normal life' for them? Are deliberately imposed fear and penury normal? These questions kept going through my mind throughout the last ten days of my visit to Vietnam.

'With malice towards none, with charity for all' – Abraham Lincoln's words would have no place in the new Communist Vietnam. I saw no efforts to reconcile the nation; no effort to bind up the nation's wounds. When I asked a senior official of the People's Committee in Saigon why in the much-talked-of battle to rescue Vietnam's abysmal economy every human resource was not drawn upon – Communist or non-Communist, re-educated or not re-educated – he simply evaded the question.

This article of mine will be thought regrettably 'negative' in Hanoi. The Communist regime has done good work in combating illiteracy, in curing drug addiction; recent agricultural production figures are said to be encouraging. If there are no tractors apparent, the peasants are working in their cooperatives and collectives with no fear of bombs or napalm or of brutal 'pacification' schemes thought up in Washington. That said, Vietnam after ten years deserves more than just peace. Since the victory, too many people have died, are or have been in camps, or have left (and are still leaving by the thousand) out of fear or the simple horror of living in a place incompetently ruled by privileged cadres, where there is no incentive, no chance to question authority, and above all no forgiveness.

People and Places

True or False?

NEW YORK, 5 JULY 1962

The space age has led to a boom in a number of major industries in the United States. A minor industry is also benefiting – the manufacture and sale of wigs to the nation's top women. 'Women these days haven't the time to go to the hairdresser's too often,' one of New York's top coiffeurs told me. 'After all, it is no longer the jet age, it's the missile age, and women are affected by this.'

One Fifth Avenue salon resembles a Hollywood Napoleonic set. At top prices (the director refused to reveal exact figures, for fear of competition) clients come for wig fittings, massage and facials in surroundings of pale gold and cream offset by dark red carnations and bowls of multicoloured bonbons. A special feature is 'pampering à la Pompeii' – hot, perfume-impregnated baths fitted with 'agitators'.

French vies with Mayfair English as the *lingua franca*. Male assistants in tight tunics glide over yellow carpets like ballet dancers. The establishment can afford to keep clients waiting (and does) without even recognizing their presence until they're 'due'.

'Oh, but *everyone* is wearing wigs today,' the publicity woman told me. 'I'm feeling rather lost frankly at the moment. I've stupidly left my wig in Paris.'

Most women wear wigs nowadays for evening parties and travel. They have little to do with baldness, of course. 'The menopause does lead to baldness in some women. For them wigs are an absolute salvation,' I was told. All the wigs are of human hair – from live people 'in northern Italy and such places' – which is inserted by hand into a net foundation. A lot used to come from Czechoslovakia, but no longer. They are light and easy to slip on, varying in colour and shape. They fit just behind the frontal hairline and are undetectable; when I was shown a selection of photographs of model hairstyles, two wigs I detected turned out not to be wigs at all. Rain does the wigs little harm but they should be cleaned – not washed – quite often, and set about once a month.

'I know women who wear the same wig seven or eight times,' said the publicity woman. 'Oh no, there's no trading in of wigs. That would be unhygienic. Many women have four or five.'

This establishment caters for Gracie Fields, Joan Fontaine and a bevy of names like Niarchos and Gulandris. Not, however, Jackie Kennedy. 'Her hair is so badly cut, don't you think?' I was asked acidly. In fact Jackie Kennedy goes to Madame Lillian Daché's on East 56th Street. Madame Daché is a plump, ebullient woman who has just been made an honorary Kentucky colonel.

'Whatever will my husband say?' she chuckled. 'But I sure get a kick out of it. I must be the only woman Kentucky colonel.' (She isn't.)

Jackie Kennedy sometimes gets the Daché service at the White House, otherwise she calls at the New York shop. 'Of course I don't like to advertise the fact,' says Madame Daché with a straight face, adding: 'Of course, I've got a wig. In fact I've got five. I wouldn't think of going away without them. I even sleep in mine.'

With a wig to slip on afterwards, a woman can swim all afternoon and go straight to a party. Wigs cannot be detected by feel, and will resist the strongest tug if properly attached. But women are not embarrassed to admit wearing them. One wig-wearing client said, 'As we all are wearing them, why be bashful? I'd admit it at once.'

'Do the men object?'

'Not a bit,' said Madame Daché. 'We get husbands coming to help their wives select their wigs. What's more, we make some wigs for men too; that's harder, of course. They've got no front hair to hide the seam. Still, more men are brushing their hair forwards these days – that helps the poor things.'

Madame Daché is married to a Frenchman. She agreed with her assistant Miss Borgia – a petite fifty-five-year-old whose hair (wig?) looked like a beehive of golden thread – that blue rinses are going out of vogue. 'No, it's gold these days in general, although a streak or two of grey is all right.' A number of illusions go out of the window in the heated, perfumed atmosphere of Madame Daché's tiny office. In a corner of the room a half-lifesize statue of a goat-legged satyr in a morning coat leers knowingly down on her clients.

A White House Musical

Asked what happens to United States Presidents when they retire, ex-President Herbert Hoover once replied: 'We spend our time taking pills and dedicating libraries.' This is the idea behind the next big new American musical, called *Mr President*. The show opens a four-week work-out in Boston on Monday, will then go to Washington for a special benefit before President Kennedy, and will finally reach Broadway – as a major theatrical event – in October.

The show will be lavish. Irving Berlin, now seventy-four, has emerged from twelve years of 'retirement' to write the music. The book is by Russell Crouse and Howard Lindsay, who produced such hits as *Life with Father*, *Call Me Madam* (also with Berlin) and *The Sound of Music* (with Richard Rodgers). This week the veteran director, Joshua Logan, has been enthusiastically urging the cast through final rehearsals. Watching from the stalls, Russell Crouse said: 'Imagine what it's like to be President one day and a private citizen "out to grass" the next, probably in some smallish country town. There's pathos in the situation, isn't there? When Berlin said he wanted to get back to work, we got to grips with it.'

Logan and Peter Gennaro, the dance director, were putting the chorus through its paces in a scene in the White House ballroom. Robert Ryan, who plays the President, strolled in – tall, loose-limbed, sweat-shirt, old trousers, dark glasses, and Logan cried: 'Let's go back to "Oo da da da oo da da da" ...'

'Bob's never done a musical before,' said Crouse. 'We had some trouble convincing him he could. Josh Logan had considered Henry Fonda and Fredric March. We had to have an actor who looks as if he could be a President. Bob does, and he's great. He really sings a song.'

Ryan, the most recent of a series of straight actors – Rex Harrison, Richard Burton, Robert Preston – to take to musicals, has a sensitive, pleasantly rugged face and a thoughtful look. His voice is deep mid-Western. 'I've always liked music,' he said. 'I sing a good deal at home after a few beers.'

The action of *Mr President* covers the last days in office of a middle-aged President at the end of his second term. No actual President, living or dead, is caricatured. There is little satire – except for a hilarious number, 'The Washington Twist', lampooning the manipulation of power and influence in the capital. The 'love interest' concerns an affair between a White House secret service man and the President's lively daughter, who is simultaneously pursued by an Arab diplomat. There's a strong line of unpretentious humour. And Nanette Fabray, as the President's wife just returned from a world tour, has a song and dance number called 'They Loved Me', which is going to be famous. Scenes include the President's White House office, his country house, a rural fair, and the inside of a Boeing 707 which moves up and down when taking off and landing. Wall decorations will be attached to the scenery with magnets – a new device.

It seems a pity that there'll be no part for director Joshua Logan, a bulky, white-moustached dynamo with a foghorn voice. 'You're turning your back on the audience over there – what's your name? Sterling. OK, Sterling, you're turning your back. Come down stage, won't you. Mary dear, I think you'll be able to use your *own* hair – yes, you know, done up a little. Now listen everybody. Listen! Quiet *please! What* is that goddam noise – rain?' (It was a neighbouring lift.)

The Arab diplomat told the President's daughter: 'I come from the Middle West. . . .'

Logan registered Homeric despair. 'No, no! Middle EAST! My *God*!'

Later he explained: 'Let's not exaggerate the sentiment in this scene. Theatre is an exchange of effort between audience and actors. Emotion is created between them, like a sex thing – you know. The actors shouldn't do it all themselves. It's give and take.' He stopped a duet to complain. 'This song looks as if it might go on all *night*. We'll have to vary the tempo, showing it's got form. The end of it didn't come over. What happened to the *end*?' Shading his eyes, he peered round the darkened theatre. 'Is Irving there?'

Berlin, a small intent figure in horn-rims, popped up in the back stalls. They conferred. Berlin wrote 'Alexander's Ragtime Band' before World War I; his last musical was *Call Me Madam* in 1952. He is short, birdlike, suffers from insomnia and looks ten years younger than he is.

'When I retired I found I had no hobbies,' he said. 'It was tough. So I decided that I'm simply an old ham and I went to see if Lindsay and Crouse had any ideas. I've been working on the *Mr President* music for over a year now and I feel good about it. I'll go on adding to it, and perhaps cutting it, until the New York opening. I wrote the best song in *Call Me Madam* after we'd opened in New Haven. And I always write my own lyrics, always have.' He said no one can know if a show is any good until an audience judges it. 'And an audience doesn't give a goddam if the composer is twenty-four or seventy-four, or if it's taken ten minutes or ten years to write. That's as it should be.'

Berlin's music for *Mr President* is simple, wistfully melodic or compulsively bouncy. 'I don't think I've been influenced much by recent trends. *My Fair Lady* is the finest musical I've seen in fifty years. I like its simplicity. Simple tunes – like my "White Christmas" – last longest.'

Logan called: 'All right, everyone. Now tomorrow's Sunday. Can you all get your church bit done early and be here by eleven?'

Mr President may not contribute anything revolutionary to the musical theatre. But it will make a lot of people happy and it should reassure President Kennedy that there's more to look forward to than pills and the dedication of libraries.

America's Respectable 'Pinks'

NEW YORK, 8 OCTOBER 1962

The news that the Russians will not participate in the 1964–65 New York World Fair has come as a blow to the organizers and the State Department. In only one quarter is there likely to be a feeling of relief – the Manhattan headquarters of Pinkerton's National Detective Agency. The Pinkerton men are to provide the security for the massive fair, and the absence of a Russian pavilion will mean one less responsibility.

Pinkerton's is the oldest detective agency in the world, and its World Fair commitment is a sign that it has moved with the times. It has had a romantic history. Readers of Sherlock Holmes will recall Pinkerton's from a climactic episode in *The Valley of Fear*. The scene is a bleak Pennsylvania mining valley. Boss McGinty and the members of a murderous secret society called the Scowrers crouch tensely in a lonely house awaiting the arrival of the famous Pinkerton detective Birdy Edwards. Edwards, unknown by sight to the gang, is inexorably on their trail and must be disposed of. The trap has been arranged by a trusted Scowrer of three months' standing named McMurdo. At the appointed hour for Edwards's come-uppance nothing happens, and the formidable Boss cries impatiently to McMurdo, 'Well! Is Birdy Edwards here?'

All at once McMurdo undergoes 'a subtle change'; his eyes shine with 'fierce excitement'; he has become a 'visible leader of men'. 'Yes,' he says slowly. 'I am Birdy Edwards!'

With the 'roar of a wounded bear', the Boss plunges towards the door to be met by the levelled revolver and stern blue eyes of Captain Marvin of the mine police. The reign of the Scowrers is at an end.

Conan Doyle's story was based on fact. The original of Birdy Edwards was an Irishman, James McPartland, one of the agency's top operatives. Under the name McKenna he was sent in 1869 to penetrate an Irish secret society called the Molly Maguires, who fought a murderous war against the coal operators of Pennsylvania. He succeeded in gaining acceptance in the top councils of 'the Mollies', and their leaders were finally trapped and hanged. McPartland was obliged to drink so much bad whiskey to sustain his undercover role that all his teeth dropped out.

But Pinkerton's was founded long before 1869. The original Pinkerton (Allen) emigrated from Scotland in 1850. He became the first detective in the Chicago police force and then began freelancing. He met Abraham Lincoln and, during the Civil War, formed the first Federal Secret Service. He saved Lincoln's life in 1861 by uncovering a Southern plot to assassinate the President-elect as he travelled by rail from Baltimore to Washington. Thanks to Pinkerton, Lincoln changed his schedule and his route.

Since then the agency has been run by three generations of Pinkertons. The present President is Robert A. Pinkerton, the great-grandson of the founder. The 'Pinks' became the scourge of desperadoes all over the USA very early on. They hunted down Jesse James and numerous other 'bad men'; they almost always got their man. Pinkerton's discovered the Gainsborough portrait of the Duchess of Devonshire in Chicago twenty-five years after it had been stolen from Agnew's galleries in London. Dashiell Hammett, the detective story writer, was said to have started life as a Pinkerton operative, although the agency says it is believed he was a clerk in their Baltimore bureau.

With the formation of the Federal Bureau of Investigation, Pinkerton's role as a criminal investigation organization quickly waned. Today, most of its work concerns the investigation of insurance claims, the patrolling of factories, office buildings, museums, exhibitions and racetracks. It won't touch divorce, but it will secretly photograph applicants for disability pensions as they throw away their crutches outside court rooms and jump nimbly into their cars. The agency once had an undesirable reputation for strike breaking; as a result, Pinkerton's today will have nothing to do with trade union investigations. It supplies elegant operatives in white tie and tails to guard the jewellery at society balls. And it works in close collaboration with the police.

Pinkerton's gave the expression 'private eye' to the world. The agency's symbol used to be an ever-open eye over the motto 'We Never Sleep'. But there's depressingly little glamour attached to the agency now. Today it has forty-five offices all over the USA and Canada, and its head office is in a gleaming glass skyscraper near Wall Street, complete with air conditioning, fitted carpets and potted creepers. It looks regrettably like any prosperous business office.

The popular conception of the private detective as a tough, seedily handsome extrovert with a bottle of rye in the desk drawer, obliging blondes for a fat retainer, withers in this clinical atmosphere. Pinkerton's today has about 13,000 employees – uniformed guards, investigators and supervisors. Their starting salary of $80 a week wouldn't keep them in silk shirts, Hispano-Suizas and large vodka martinis for long. Guard duties involve a lot of standing about, but not in bars or casinos. Eighty per cent of Pinkerton employees wear uniform. In New York they are not allowed to carry badges or call themselves private detectives. If they want to pack a pistol they can, and it's usually a Colt .38, but they must get a licence like everyone else. And if they use it they are liable to instant prosecution.

At the World Fair, the 'Pinks' will be on the lookout for pickpockets, drunks and thieves; they will sell tickets and collect lost children. And although some of the glory has departed since Birdy Edwards's day, business is booming. Allen Pinkerton started over a hundred years ago with only nine men. In 1959, the turnover amounted to $28 million.

A Conversation with Mailer

26 APRIL 1964

Norman Mailer's latest work is a novel called *An American Dream* which is being serialized by *Esquire* magazine. It cannot be judged adequately yet, since Mailer, like Dickens or Thackeray, is writing it instalment by instalment: so far four have appeared. It tells of a New York university psychologist who murders his wife, from whom he has been separated for a year after a violently tempestuous marriage. He drops her body into the East River from an apartment in Manhattan's smart Sutton Place. He then makes love to the maid before calling the police to report 'a frightful accident'. There are involvements with Italian-American mobsters and a blonde night club singer.

Over quantities of Old Grandad bourbon on the rocks, I talked to Mailer the other day in a restaurant in Brooklyn. I asked what had happened to the 'great' novel announced in *Advertisements for Myself*.

'That big novel,' he replied, 'may yet be 3000 pages long and could take five, ten or fifteen years to write. This implies some financial independence. I've lived a life I don't recommend to many. The practical issue of the last fifteen years is that I'm obliged, quite properly, to pay for my past, pay literally. I've got to earn $30,000 a year before I can spend a cent on myself. I'd been out of fashion for years – now I had the good luck to be sufficiently back in fashion to get a generous contract for this novel. The gamble existed in this fashion: I would write a novel in eight months, in eight instalments, which would be sufficiently good to stand proof against the advertisements I had devoted to myself, against the enemies I had made and even against the expectations of those who were ready to like my work most. As I see it, the question is not therefore why am I writing a novel for money, but can I bring it off in such a way that I'll not be depressed by myself to get back to the long novel? I don't think I'm at all the same man who wrote *Advertisements*. At the time I was sufficiently vain to consider myself a potentially great writer. Now, I'd be obliged to think that I'm a professional writer – and one of the best professional writers in the country – but, of course, considering the slimy, wet-egg face of American letters, this is virtually an apology . . . your health!'

An old waiter called Marcus came up with more Old Grandad. Mailer diluted it with a little brandy.

I remarked that a lot of people had criticized the sex and sadism in the *Esquire* novel.

'Sadism,' said Mailer, 'will remain obsessive until someone has something new to say about it. That's the nature of obsessions — great pressure which results in nothing but the repetition of the old idea. Patriotism is usually an obsession, so is sex, so is violence. The average man usually ends up saying: "Oh, God." '

'What would *you* like your reader to say?'

' "Where the hell is Mailer leading me?" ' Mailer grinned, downed his bourbon, pulled on a fawn raincoat, and we went to look for a taxi to take us on a tour of Harlem bars.

I jotted down Norman Mailer's remarks on the back of five menus at Foffe's Restaurant in Brooklyn. Despite the quart or so of Old Grandad we got through, I managed to read most of my scribbles next morning. When Norman looked over the modest piece I wrote from them, he asked me to cut a remark he had made at Foffe's that was critical of his fellow novelists. It went: 'If this [An American Dream] is not one of the five best novels written in the United States in the last ten years, then I just consider it a thorough-gone failure. Not just because this novel is so good, but because there just haven't been so many novels in the last ten years.' And he objected to the word 'fawn' to describe the colour of his raincoat in the last paragraph. He said it made him sound like a fag. It was a good evening.

In Search of Napoleon

A Visit to St Helena

16 JUNE 1985

The barman on the RMS *Centaur*, bound for St Helena from Cape Town, was short and round, and two things about him puzzled me. He was dark without looking Indian, Latin, African or Oriental. A name tag on his lapel proclaimed 'Brian Bar'. An unusual name.

'I'm a Saint,' he said. 'Not, I mean, that I'm saintly, of course.' He laughed. 'But from St Helena Island. That's what people from there

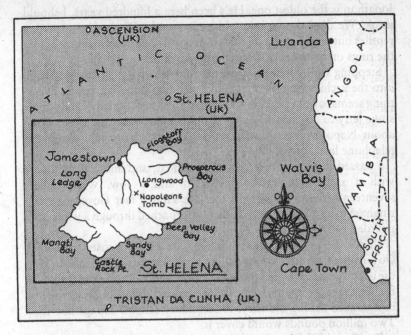

are called.' He spoke with a soft, attractive burr like that of Devonshire or Dorset.

'And Brian Bar is your name?'

'Well, Brian is my name, sir. Bar is my place of work.' He tapped the hard wooden counter between us.

'Nice piece of wood you've got here.'

'It *is* good. I am a cabinet-maker by trade, sir. Like all Saints I like to travel.'

'Will you ever go back to St Helena now you've seen the world?'

'Oh, yes. Very few of us leave the island for good.'

'It must be a good place to visit, then.'

John Massingham, the Governor of St Helena, stood with me in the paddock that lies on the other side of the gravelled driveway outside Plantation House, his handsome residence. He regarded the tortoise at his feet speculatively. It lay there like a large boulder.

Massingham is a bustling man, whose utter lack of pomposity made me feel at home at once. 'They're all Seychelles tortoises, I believe.

Jonathan is the oldest one. He's been here a hundred years, I should think. We don't know how old he is exactly. We had an expert in reptiles out and he said you can't date them. You can't measure age by the rings on their backs or anything like that.'

Stepping ashore in the tiny port of Jamestown is not just a step back into the architectural past, it is like stepping into Toy Town. Everything seems to be at peace and in miniature. There is a small and simple stone jetty to disembark at. In the main street you could shoot a film about Napoleon's exile without doing much more than remove a telephone line or two.

I passed through a rampart, over a moat, and into a little square with a spired church on the right and a low, whitewashed, seventeenth-century castle on the left. Here I met Governor Massingham in his high-ceilinged office, approached through a white arch guarded by brass cannons.

Under the royal portraits Massingham said, 'It costs the British Government, oh, about four million pounds a year in subsidies to keep the island going. We need things here very badly. A new power station, for instance – the system is overloaded now. A reservoir. A reorganized fishing industry. A secondary school. Things like that. Two million pounds would cover it.'

People said 'Mornin'' as we strolled slowly up the main street, running through a narrow valley with steep sides. Few of the two-storey buildings looked as if they had been built much later than the early 1800s. The police headquarters, for example, had been built in 1817; the prison, an attractive (empty) building of thick stone walls with a pleasant first-floor balcony, in 1827.

'We're not simply living on Napoleon,' Massingham said. 'I do all I can. I've dropped the "His Excellency" from my title. I give old islanders lifts. Try to be human. Unstuffy. I'm devoted to the people here, but the Government at home . . . ,' he stopped, frowning, in mid-stride. 'You've no idea. Look, that reservoir we need so much. The Royal Engineers have taken seven months – *seven months!* – to submit a report on it. It's intolerable. No civilian contractor would stand for that. I write to the British Government saying, "For God's sake, let's get a civilian set-up." If we were Afghan refugees or from Zimbabwe or somewhere. . . . But St Helena has no political clout in Britain. I shout and scream on the islanders' behalf – I may be sent to Outer Mongolia next!' (In fact he has now gone to Guyana as High Commissioner.)

256

'Trouble is, the Saints have been used to very pompous Governors who made themselves practically unapproachable – wearing dinner jackets at dinner, all that sort of thing. Plantation House is a fine place, but it isolates me. Sir Hudson Lowe, Napoleon's Governor, lived in it, of course. By the way, I should go and see our archives if I were you. The Napoleonic ones, I mean. And there's the museum and so on at Longwood House.'

The Duke of Wellington once stayed on St Helena as Arthur Wellesley, on his way home from India.

'Not being a licensed premises,' Mrs Yon announces at her café, 'adds greatly to the quiet and homely atmosphere that prevails.' She provides a twenty-four-hour electricity service of 230 volts and a 'good variety of Mineral Waters (Tonic, Soda, Ginger Ale, Bitter Lemon, etc.) are manufactured on the premises'. The heavy drinking is done, I soon discovered, at the Consulate Hotel ('Patrick G. Joshua, Licensed to sell by retail wine, spirits and beer'), which has a beautiful yellow stone façade and graceful iron pillars supporting its balcony. Up Napoleon Street lie such venerable establishments as Darling's, Truebody's, Miss Short's School and two pubs – the Crown and Anchor, and the Victoria.

The island's archives are in the fort overlooking the rampart to the Atlantic. 'Ask for Mr Maggott,' John Massingham had said.

'I'm Maggott.' A friendly middle-aged Saint led me into a room under the battlements like an ancient wine cellar, but with racks of heavily bound tomes in place of bottles. 'Cecil Maggott, archivist.' He pointed to a spotty young man. 'And this is my assistant, Hansel Williams. He's the fast bowler of the Sandy Beach team, is Hansel. Yes. Now, what would you like to see?'

'Anything from Napoleon's time, please.'

'Hear that, Hansel? Napoleon.'

'Who?'

'Napoleon Bonaparte, Hansel. Now then.'

There was a long table and soon a good number of books were on it, smelling dusty and old.

'See this, perhaps,' recommended Hansel. He opened St James's Church Burials Registry for 1821:

May 9th Napoleon Bonaparte, late Emperor of France, he died on the 5th Instant at the old House at Longwood, and was interred on Mr Richard Torbett's Estate.

The Emperor's name lay between 'Edmond Hawes, Inhabitant' and 'Maria Mills, wife of the late Major Mills, St Helena Artillery'.

John Massingham had mentioned Sir Hudson Lowe, the Governor appointed to St Helena, with a heavily augmented garrison, specifically to keep an eye on the great exile, who, after all, had already escaped from Elba to perpetrate his own second downfall at Waterloo. Lowe was a man whom Napoleon and his entourage swiftly came to hate. I read the careful instructions to Lowe, signed in London by Lord Bathurst of the War Department in July 1815, concerning the treatment of the prisoner, who is referred to merely as 'the General':

He's to be allowed his plate, furniture, books and wine, but his money, diamonds, and negotiable bills are to be given up, and it is to be explained to the General that it is not the intention of the British Government to confiscate his property, but to prevent their being converted by him into an instrument of escape. . . . The General must always be attended by an officer. . . . The General must be given to understand that in the event of his attempting to escape, he will be afterwards subject to close custody.

Any letters, written or received, were to be censored. Ships of every description were to be prevented from touching at the island with the exception of those belonging to HM Service or the East India Company.

Hansel Williams brought me tome after tome. Angry old letters came to life again. General Count de Montholon, of Napoleon's suite, wrote to Lowe: 'It is hate that has determined the choice of this place, just as it has determined the instructions given to the commanding officer here . . . to call the Emperor Napoleon "general," wishing to oblige us to recognize that he never reigned in France.' To this, Sir George Cockburn, the British admiral who had transported Napoleon to St Helena on his flagship *Northumberland*, gave a reply that must have flown in through the front door at Longwood like a cannonball: 'Sir, You oblige me officially to explain to you that I have no cognizance of an Emperor being actually upon this island, or of any person possessing such Dignity, having come hither with me in the *Northumberland*. . . .'

I reported to John Massingham on the archives. 'Frankly,' he said, 'the way I look at it, Bonaparte was a war criminal. He introduced a new form of warfare to Europe – total war. His picture was on the wall here. It seemed to have no place among the British royal family so I took it down. I've been attacked by the Napoleon lobby for doing so, of course. You must meet Gilbert Martineau, who's in charge of Longwood; honorary consul and curator. Longwood's a bit of France, you know. We gave it to them in 1858. I have to admit Martineau's very hospitable. He pondered for a moment. 'Martineau. . . . Frankly, we don't really speak much. I forget the reason. Oh, yes, I know why. The trouble between him and me started when I put a lot of children's swings – playground swings – on the green at Longwood. He regards the whole place as a French shrine and protested really quite vigorously. He said, "The French would never stick such things just outside a war cemetery."'

He considered the matter again. 'Yes, Martineau. He really is a most extraordinary chap. It only goes to show how bizarre legends grow up in a small place like this, but he is supposed to have had his old mother shipped back to France in a barrel of brandy. She died quite recently.'

'A barrel of. . . .'

'Oh, yes. Brandy. To have poured a lot of good brandy into a barrel with her. As a preservative. Well, you see what I mean. . . .'

I drove to the hamlet of Longwood through green lanes and hedges of spiky flax. It was very seldom that I met another car, but when I did and we squeezed past each other, or when I came upon a man driving donkeys laden with grapes, the Saints always waved or called a greeting. I had a beer in the little pub on the green and then went round it to the huddle of trees on the far side. Gilbert Martineau was waiting at the gate of the garden of Longwood House with an abstracted air.

'What can I do for you?' he asked in breezy tones. I had expected a portly, moustached mixture of Hercule Poirot and Jean Gabin. What I saw was an elegant, good-looking man, tall, slim and well dressed in a pale blue seersucker suit with a dark blue knitted tie (he had bought it at Harrods, he told me later): a dandy, in fact.

'You invited me to lunch,' I said. 'I'm writing. . . .'

He interrupted. 'I'm writing, too. Oh, yes, indeed. In fact I've written fifteen books and three more are in progress. I'm working on Byron and preparing something else on Berlioz.' He waved an elegantly deprecating hand, 'And Tchaikovsky as well. Apart from that I have written plays and film scripts. And I've just won a prize. So?'

I was glad that he had to stop to draw breath. 'So. You invited me to lunch.'

'Of course, of course. Come in.' He led the way through a well-tended garden into a wing of an attractive single-storey house painted a pleasing, delicate shade of pink. This was Longwood – or rather the part of it Martineau lived in. It was beautifully furnished with things he had brought from France. On occasional tables stood framed portraits of de Gaulle, Churchill and Serge Lifar, the ballet dancer.

'Do sit down,' Martineau said. 'By the way, if you think my English is very good, it's because I was with the Royal Navy in the war.'

A servant appeared carrying a bottle and two glasses on a tray.

'Champagne?' He popped a cork, pouring into a fine glass. '*Salut!*'

I liked Martineau. He was not only a good host, as John Massingham had acknowledged, but also an intelligent and indefatigable talker – a facet of his nature no doubt encouraged by isolation. Not that he regretted Longwood's isolation. He said he adored Longwood and hoped to stay for ever – with periodic visits to France, of course. Actually, he had his eye on a flat in Monaco.

He showed me his books. Many of them were about Napoleon or his entourage on St Helena. Martineau talked affectionately of them, rather as though he knew them all personally. He had written a bestseller about Madame Mère, Napoleon's formidable and long-suffering mother. 'I call her the Corsican Niobe,' he said. 'Am I lonely, you will ask? Let me only quote Napoleon. He said of St Helena, "Here, one must socialize with a budgerigar if that's all the company one has." I have people out to stay. I have books. The ship brings pilgrims to the shrine.'

'What Napoleon said about the budgerigar was not very complimentary to the people exiled here with him – Montholon and the rest.'

Martineau laughed. 'No, not very. People say Napoleon had an affair with Madame de Montholon. But life here was all too cluttered. Too crowded for that sort of thing. An affair? No, not that. People say so, but I doubt it.'

Martineau's exile was self-imposed and a good deal more comfortable than Napoleon's. His cook was every bit as good as Napoleon's Cipriani, and his equivalent of Napoleon's Mameluke servant Ali was an old Saint called George Benjamin who, after lunch, showed me round while Martineau wrote a letter or two for me to post in Europe.

Longwood House is a pleasant building, surrounded by trim lawns and carefully sculptured hedges. Some of the paths had been sunk into the turf to enable Napoleon to stroll about below the level of prying eyes. By a door in a second wing we entered the part of the house kept as a museum, and still more or less as Napoleon knew it.

We came first into the billiard room, which had also served as antechamber for those who had applied for audiences with the Emperor. 'See that billiard table, sir,' said Mr Benjamin. 'Made by Thurston & Co. No slate. All wood.' I crossed the teak floor and looked at the pictures on the walls. There was a print of Napoleon saying farewell to his troops at Fontainebleau, portraits of him by David, Gérard and Delaroche. The room was full of busts.

'Cold, isn't it?' Mr Benjamin said. I looked at a Steuben print of the Emperor and his baby son, the King of Rome.

' I've got swollen legs,' Mr Benjamin remarked.

'I'm in no hurry,' I said. 'Please take your time.'

The salon where Napoleon received his guests was next to the billiard room. Here the Grand Marshal, Bertrand, had announced visitors as if they were all still in the Tuileries, while Napoleon stood by the mantelpiece, leaning against it.

I, too, leaned on the mantelpiece, with old Benjamin beside me blowing dust off the back of an elegant dark wood chair with gold-leaf mouldings. The great battle pictures, or prints of them, were here. David's *Bonaparte, Commander in Chief of the Army in Italy*, and Delaroche's *Bonaparte Crossing the Alps*. 'I have to wear a couple of sweaters all the time,' Mr Benjamin was saying. 'I've had a heart attack.'

We moved from room to room – eleven of them, none of them large and all with low ceilings. In a cramped room I came across the camp bed Napoleon had used at Austerlitz, tested it and found it hard. In size it was like a child's cot, unsprung, with a mattress that might have been stuffed with straw. I bent over the Emperor's death mask, noticing that it seemed unnaturally small, diminished perhaps by the process of moulding. The closed eyes were deeply sunk into their sockets, the cheekbones harshly prominent, the nose under its fine long sweep of hairless brow as thin and sharp as a quill. In this room he had murmured his last words: '. . . at the head of the army' – and had then lain on view in the uniform of the Guard and the cloak he had worn at Marengo.

I had expected to find Gilbert Martineau as rabidly pro-Napoleon as John Massingham was clearly anti, but he didn't seem to be much of a chauvinist. When I mentioned the story, promulgated by some Napoleon worshippers, that the British had had Napoleon poisoned with arsenic, Martineau laughed the idea away without hesitation.

'Ha! That was a story thought up by a weightlifter in Canada in cahoots with a dentist in Sweden. Well, that's what I say. The obstacles to a methodical investigation of the Emperor's medical dossier are innumerable. The doctors at his deathbed were notably mediocre. The journals of Bertrand and of the valet Marchand – well, neither was a doctor. You see, the autopsy showed a perforation in Napoleon's stomach. Madame de Montholon found she could put her little finger into the hole. Symptoms were – exhaustion, loss of appetite, fever, vomiting of blood. The experts hesitated between a peptic ulcer and cancer.' Martineau certainly knew the details. 'As for the arsenic, that came from the arsenic powder they used then to preserve people's locks of hair. That's all. Napoleon had an internal haemorrhage. His heart rate was below fifty all his life. Very unusual. He had always vomited when he flew into his furious rages and he ate all his meals in seven minutes. He'd have the whole meal set out, and he'd pick a bit of ice cream here, a bit of mutton there. Actually eating very little and drinking not much at all. He was a very sober man; like a camel.'

A sharp wind whisked through the hibiscus bushes beyond the window. 'Cold,' said Martineau. 'But it's not always like this. Sometimes the Emperor used to sit out of doors, reading Racine – *Andromache* was a favourite – to his entourage. He read badly and Madame de Montholon would fall asleep. . . . Napoleon was only fifty-one years old when he died, you know.'

When I commented that the camp bed seemed hardly big enough for a boy scout, he said, 'Well, Napoleon was about five foot six or seven.'

Martineau even had a compassionate word for Sir Hudson Lowe. 'You know what happened to him?' he asked me.

'I've no idea.'

'Well, after St Helena he was offered the governorship of Ceylon, but by the time he got there someone else had the job. He died in poverty in Chelsea. Without a *sou*. And that was his reward for doing what he was told to do.'

Before I left Longwood, Martineau talked of his new book – *Byron: Pilgrim of Eternity*. 'Good title?' He had a ouija board at Longwood and sometimes Byron spoke to him.

'Byron talks to you? What on earth does he say?'

'Oh, terrible things. Things like, "You are a very clever bastard. Why do you take the piss out of me?" That sort of thing.' Martineau's English *was* very good.

262

'Byron says that to you?'

'Oh, yes. And worse. What a fellow! What a diabolical fellow! Do you know what he said once? He said, "Shakespeare's *Midsummer Night's Dream* is a real fuck-up." What a devil! But what a fabulous letter writer.'

I set off with Hansel Williams and his friend Stedson Stroud to tour the rest of the little island. St Helena is perfectly preserved, like a piece of old English countryside before the intrusion of pylons, airports, motorways or factory chimneys. Tiny Georgian farmhouses spring into view from behind folds in the hills and in terraced valleys full of spreading trees. Napoleon had chosen one such fold to be buried in; it was quite hard to find. We walked down a short, wide path springy with grass to the original tomb – a slab of concrete enclosed by railings and clumps of amaryllis and hibiscus and tall dark cypresses that stood to attention like grenadiers. Mynah birds chatted round a spring nearby and bees hummed round the stiff bayonet-like leaves of flax.

Of course, the grave is empty now. Nineteen years after his death, the Emperor was exhumed and taken to Les Invalides in Paris.

The Haunted Pass

The flying bullet down the pass
That whispers shrill, 'All Flesh is Grass' . . .
    Rudyard Kipling, 'Frontier Arithmetic'

16 NOVEMBER 1977

'Of course, I think the women lost us India,' said the charming, elderly Indian Army lady from Bude in Cornwall. The dust of a Peshawar street behind the cantonments speckled the dawn air; a knot of inquisitive Pathans with curious pale eyes and flat woollen caps stood gazing at us. It was chilly so near to the Khyber Pass.

On the steps of the simple hotel, thirty or forty elderly British ex-Indian Army officers and their wives were gathering for a group photograph before taking the bus for a trip along the North-West Frontier to Swat.

'Come along now, girls and boys,' boomed retired Brigadier John

Woodroofe, the leader of this annual voyage into the imperial past, clapping his hands. 'Please gather on the steps, chaps. We're going to have our picture taken.'

Mrs Rodgers from Bude went on, 'I'm not sure I should be saying this, but the husbands got on so well with the Indians, and then the wives came out and put up those barriers.' She added nervously, 'I don't suppose Brigadier Chadwick agrees, though, for a moment.' A small, spry old man with a white moustache and a soft hat had pottered up to us. Brigadier Chadwick is ninety-two and he first came to India in 1909 as a Mountain Gunner.

'Wives?' he said loudly. 'Quite right. Oh, definitely, I should say so.'

A lot of changes, Brigadier?

'Oh, many changes, many. All for the better. Take the marvellous way the Pakistani officers allow their ladies into the mess. Very attractive, too. All for the better.'

Our small group expanded slightly. 'The old *burrah memsahibs* were terribly spoilt and overbearing,' continued Mrs Rodgers. 'They played bridge all the time, but I managed to avoid that.'

A Major Blessington said to her, 'You came out and joined the Fishing Fleet in '36, Betty, I think?'

Fishing Fleet? I said.

'Yes, that's what we called the pool of unmarried daughters out here,' said Major Blessington. 'But you know Peshawar wasn't just a pleasant station. A lot of unsung heroes went up to the Frontier – it was a little like Ulster, I suppose. Nobody knew much about it at home. The casualty figures weren't put about much.'

Someone added, 'There was a charming gent in the hills called the Fakir of Ipi, who kept on bumping our people off.'

'Come on then. Hurry up, all,' trumpeted Brigadier Woodroofe. 'Now where's Brigadier Chadwick?'

'Answering a call of nature, I think.'

'A trunk call,' said a jolly woman in a hat, looking at her watch.

Presently the photograph was taken. Jostling and laughing, the party clambered stiffly into the buses, and drove off, waving, in a swirl of dust, towards the distant snow-lined ridges of Chitral.

Just before you reach the Khyber Pass, you come to a checkpoint next to a stone arch, impressive but newish, with 'Khyber Gate' on it in

Arabic script. There is a small market and a bare, baked mud fort. Nearby a slab of stone has been erected with a few lines of Kipling's poem 'Frontier Arithmetic' on it:

A scrimmage in a border station,
A canter down a dark defile,
Two thousand pounds of education
Drops to a ten-rupee Jezail.

Reading it, I remembered that Sherlock Holmes's friend Dr John Watson suffered for years from twinges in his leg after stopping a Jezail bullet in Afghanistan. But the arithmetic has changed with the years. Two thousand pounds of private education wouldn't get you far, I suppose, these days. I discovered, by asking various squatting turbaned figures strapped round with cartridge belts and daggers, that a Jezail bullet costs, in 1977, no more than fifteen rupees (£1).

The commander of the Khyber Gate post ordered a young Afridi border guard with his rifle into the back seat of our car, and soon the road bent sharply upward into a pass between twin ridges of rock.

The pass is certainly forbidding – those Jezail bullets spring urgently back to mind as you look at it – and narrower than one had expected. It begins *very* narrow; the road snakes more and more steeply and the ravine drops away deeper and deeper as it penetrates into the jumble of mountains on the Afghanistan border. A goods train keeps pace with the road, plunging in and out of tunnels every few hundred yards, finally seeming to be overwhelmed by the mass of rock and disappearing for a mile or two – to shoot out, just as you have given it up, hooting, from a hidden cavern. The trains have small, snorting steam engines at both ends.

Our young Afridi guard, sitting in the back seat with his rifle between his knees, moved in and out of long silences like the train and its tunnels. He had eyes the colour of Portuguese oysters and a flat expression. His name, he said, was Jan Afzal.

His grandfather must have fought the British.

'Oh, yes,' he said, 'often.' Our interpreter, a Pathan poet in Government service in Peshawar, translated.

What did his grandfather have to say about the British?

'Good people in peacetime.' A pause. Then, without a smile: 'In wartime, we didn't like them so much.' Jan Afzal seemed quite a diplomat.

Small forts like stone boxes with gun slits perched on dozens of crag tops through the pass. Approaching a high-perched one, Jan Afzal stirred slightly and said, 'That's the Haunted Picket.'

Why haunted?

'Our people say that years ago some British soldiers went into that picket and never came out. Now no one will go into it.'

Would *he* go into it now?

'No, no, no!' he said, and laughed for the first and last time. Seven British graves from the Third Afghan War of 1919 lay on the roadside nearby, but the haunting did not come from there, it seemed.

The historian Herodotus, some 2400 years ago, called Afridis like Jan Afzal the *Apartae*. Like most tribesmen anywhere they set much store by the principles of hospitality and an eye for an eye. That second principle flashed unwelcomed through my mind later when my companion, Tony McGrath, levelled a long camera lens at some Pathan women in a mud-walled village. Instantly and out of nowhere, a cross-eyed and unshaven Pathan sprang up to the driver's open window, seized him violently by the ears and began to twist them. He was screaming something very hostile, to do with cameras and women.

Our guard, Jan Afzal, jammed in the back seat, seemed paralysed with shock or cramp. Our interpreter, however, threw a torrent of words across the driver's head with instant effect. To my surprise, the furious Pathan let go of his ears and, pointing down the road, yelled what must have been the uninhibited Pushtu for 'Scram!' Lucky, I thought, that he was about the only gunless man we had seen in the pass.

Weapons have been part of the Khyber scenery since the invention of the spear. The pass, after all, was the invasion route of every southbound conqueror. Alexander, Genghis Khan, Timur the Lame (Marlowe's Tamberlane), the amazing and witty Emperor Babur, who founded the great Mogul Empire in India, all tramped through it, heading for the Indus River beyond Peshawar. The British Army first arrived in Peshawar in 1849. The Second Sikh War gave them the pass. The Afridis seized it back in 1897, lost it again, and tried to regain it in 1919 – the year Jan Afzal's grandfather was sniping at us among those impossible crags.

The crags, by the way, are worth looking at. Their colour seems to be uniform. But when you pay attention to them, you see that the slabs of rock, the scree and scrub are variously rust-coloured or violet deepening into maroon; orange suddenly splashed onto black; green-black or purple-black lightening into a luminous silver-grey. Defiles disappear into deep, mysterious shadows. The pass floor is as tawny as a lion's pelt.

On the way up to Landi Kotal, the dusty market at the head of the pass, long mule trains, heavily loaded for Afghanistan, flamboyantly decorated trucks from Kabul, and old Chevrolet cars with as many as twenty-five men in them (including eight in the boot) struggle past the crests of British regiments carved on the rock walls – Dorsets, 1st Battalion the Cheshires, 'The Pompadours' (The Essex Regiment). At Landi Kotal itself there are shops of British cloth and Japanese sewing machines, and gun belts, and harness for horses or mules, and many other things. It used to be a big smuggling depot but Jan Afzal stirred himself to boast that his town, Bara, seven miles from Peshawar, is *the* place now – spare parts, cloth, radios, even chandeliers: a big industry.

We drove into the fortress in Landi Kotal that houses the Khyber Rifles. Inside a great gate, a guard was turned out in turbans with great sprouting of starched cloth. Orderlies with decorated cross belts and silver-tipped canes stamped about as though fresh from a drill course at the Guards Depot.

'So good of you to come.' A youngish officer with short black hair, an exquisitely neat moustache and a crown and a pip on his shoulder extended a hand. Could he be from Hollywood's Central Casting? No, he was, he said, Lieut-Colonel Gilani, the reigning Commandant of the Khyber Rifles, a real soldier who fought in the disastrous campaign that turned East Pakistan into Bangladesh in 1971, and who later survived two years in an Indian prisoner-of-war camp.

In his office he lay back in a swivel chair and said: 'I love it here. It's a gift from God being in a quiet, nice place like this.' Above him a board displayed the names of every commandant since the Rifles were formed in 1878. After 1919, the British names stopped.

'Very difficult, in the old days,' said the colonel, 'to defend those forts you saw. They were under constant harassment. The British found it was better to pay the tribes than fight them.' Indeed, the Frontier war was never 'won'.

A large officers' mess looked out on the panorama of mountains. The mess is obviously, in its way, a place of pilgrimage. A painting of the Shah hung slightly askew near the fireplace. Facing it was a portrait of Sir George Roos-Keppel, Political Agent, Khyber, and

Commandant of the Khyber Rifles, 1899–1908, stern in uniform and an immense fur coat. There were framed photographs of J.F.K. and Jackie.

Over tea and curry puffs officers joined us, some from neighbouring regiments – the South Waziristan Scouts, Dir Scouts, and the Kurram Militia from up round Gilgit on the road to Chinese Turkestan – Sandy Arbuthnot country, for those who read John Buchan. Outside, the colonel had marshalled the Khyber Rifles sword dancers and pipe band. The band banged and skirled away at 'Scotland the Brave', filling the surrounding hills and presumably the ears of elderly tribesmen crouched outside in the marketplace with incongruous but evocative echoes of the brave and grisly British past. Battle honours on the pipes read:

Black Mountain Expedition 1887
Siege of Landi Kotal 1891
Bazar Valley Campaigns 1908
Mohmands Operations 1914–17

Even Jan Afzal seemed impressed by the skirling. I looked across at him and he looked back impassively. But he raised his eyebrows twice Groucho Marx fashion; this, I assumed, meant he was beside himself.

'My men are all Pathan tribesmen,' said the colonel proudly. It did not seem the time and place, even though Colonel Gilani is from Rawalpindi and not a Pathan himself, to ask if the rude saying I had read the night before in my copy of *Kim* is still in common usage: 'Trust a Brahmin before a snake, a snake before a harlot, and a harlot before an Afghan.' Afghans are Pathans, so it seemed ungracious to inquire. Ungrateful, too, because it is not all that easy to get into the Khyber Rifles fort and take tea with Colonel Gilani. We left, indeed, gratefully.

It was not, in the past, the happy fate of every Briton to return from Landi Kotal in one piece. In the sombre beauty of Peshawar's old British cemetery I saw evidence of that. Beneath massive trees, where crows and mynah birds perch in a dusty canopy of leaves, you can read the gravestones, watched by a benevolent Pathan gardener. One impressive stone recalls how two British bank officials 'met their deaths by assassination in the Khyber Pass on April 20th, 1930'. There is the unusual grave of a man 'accidentally killed in the Soda Water Factory'. One of the earliest memorials is to

George Mitchell Richmond
Lieutenant, Late 54th Regt.
20th Punjab Infantry,
Aged 23 years,
who died on 27th October, 1863
of a wound received in Defence
of the Eagles' Nest Picket at
Umbeyla Pass

There are wives and babies, too: cholera did for many of them. It is hard not to be moved when you read 'Not gone from memory or from love . . .' on the old tombs of twenty- to twenty-one- year-old privates, gunners, fusiliers and drummer boys. You have to sweep leaves away and sometimes scrape moss off with your foot to read the inscriptions. And, by now, both the memory and the love have long ago expired.

Major Blessington is right: a lot of unsung heroes did go up here. Brigadier Woodroofe told me of one lady of his ex-Indian Army group who had 'two husbands shot from under her' hereabouts. There were more like her in the old days.

Things are different now, of course. We drove two former Frontier Force officers, Brigadier Bill Boulter and Colonel Janson (both Pushtu speakers) to the Khyber Gate. There, with a Pakistani ex-Commandant of the Khyber Rifles – an Afridi himself – they were soon in happy conversation with some rough-and-ready looking Pathans. A photograph! Good idea! Pathans and British officers huddled giggling together in a fraternal pose. Yet something was wrong. Why did the large blue-eyed elderly tribesman, who looked like an Irish actor, refuse to smile? Everyone else was grinning from ear to ear. He stared at the camera glumly, just as young Jan Afzal had done.

'Smile,' the Pakistani colonel pleaded. 'Please smile just once. Why be so stern and martial with friends?'

Under his turban, the man's craggy face slowly unbent; his mouth, as we waited intently, relaxed a fraction; and with a great diffidence he croaked: 'Stern, no. But I've no teeth!' And suddenly he opened a completely toothless mouth and bellowed and bellowed with laughter.

They all joined in – British and Pathans, standing in the dust of the Khyber road to Afghanistan, posing for a snapshot where, not so *very* long ago, those shrill bullets impartially whispered to one and all that all Flesh is Grass.

Journey on a Perfect Little Train

When I had the opportunity to take a trip by steam engine into the Himalayan foothills, I boarded at the first opportunity.

23 NOVEMBER 1977

At 8.40 p.m. sharp, the Kashmir Mail's whistle sounded its mournful invitation to everyone to get aboard damn quick or be left behind. The crowds thrust more urgently back and forth through the gloom and steam of Old Delhi's Number 6 Platform. Porters in red jackets with brass armbands, balancing suitcases, bedrolls and massive tin trunks on their heads, heaved them – 'Ugh! Ahh!' – through open windows. It seemed wise to skip aboard. I put my bag on the table of my sleeper and craned out of the window.

Under dim lamps a continuous hideous shouting prevailed. A man at a tea stall yelled 'Chai-ee!' at the top of his voice – a cup of tea for an English penny and a crisp chapati thrown in. Squawking, dark, birdlike men hawked small towers of books that teetered on their sleek heads. The train, I saw, was amazingly long. It bristled with heads and arms. About it, not unpleasantly, hung strong smells of frying food, urine, spices, steam and hot metal.

The Kashmir Mail is one of the best night trains I know. Presently it floated out of Delhi station and slid smoothly northwards towards the snows and hills. I ordered fresh, iced water from a steward and poured Black Knight Indian whisky into it. True, you need to bring your own bedroll in the ordinary, first-class sleepers, but the air-conditioned ones are luxurious, twice as large as the British Rail equivalent – also much cheaper and yet making a profit.

After roaring away the night, the Kashmir Mail makes an early morning stop at a small town called Pathankot. We left it there in a clear chilly dawn. And as it hooted and chuffed away we walked to a tiny branch line that would take us under the western edge of the Himalayas. The Pathankot assistant station master (chief bookings clerk) – a large, grey-haired man with impassive good manners – led us to a little metallic thing as different from the mighty, hissing Kashmir Mail as a miniature poodle from a Great Dane. It stood meekly at an insignificant side platform. Narrow-gauge, very short, drawn by what seemed like a toy engine, the low, dwarfish carriages resembled something out of E. Nesbit's *Railway Children* – in fact, this toy-like train seemed, during the next two days, to become more and more Nesbit-like.

A low carriage had four doors in it marked with a big I – and outside one door stood a knot of people. One of them threw open our compartment, an entirely self-contained, corridorless little room with doors each side and windows that let down if you tugged, a private lavatory through another door, a long upholstered couch, a folding table, and two ceiling fans with brassy attachments. At the door, we shook hands with our reception committee: Mr Krishna Gosain, the driver; Mr W.C. Mehta, the plump guard, with a blue uniform and Indian Railways cap, a whistle and a rolled green flag; a few others; all beaming.

'We have one minute to the go,' said Mr Mehta, round-faced and cheerful. 'Of course, sir, we will be stopping frequently, so we are meeting you for tea many times today.'

Good, we said, just what we want.

'You have official letter here from Delhi,' said Mr Gosain, the driver. He displayed a mouth utterly devoid of teeth except for two upper tusks that hung down at each corner of his mouth like tobacco-stained stalactites. 'So,' he pursed his lips for emphasis, 'I am able to welcome you to the *footplate* of my engine any time *you* may be willing.'

Doors were slammed. We ducked into our compartment. An unknown well-wisher thrust in a bagful of apples. Mr Mehta's whistle shrilled. The little toy engine hooted and very gently began to draw its toy carriages after it into the countryside. And what a countryside!

For seven hours on the way to the small north Punjabi town of Palampur we wiggled across ancient bridges and one very new one on a steep gradient towards the great snowy ridge. After three hours, that ridge began to tower into the middle distance like a foam-crested tidal wave. In the trough below, our little train fussed through an amazingly English-looking landscape, through groves of English-looking trees and English-looking grasses and ferns. Oranges and pale blue flowers brushed our carriage door and small moths flew in and out of it. There were frequent stops. Mr Gosain, the driver, yanked on the steam brake and we clattered lightly into a minute station, with a minute platform and a minute old-fashioned waiting-room and ticket office combined. At each stop, as railwaymen used to do in Britain (do they still?), Mr Gosain handed the token pouch on its football-size ring to a station porter. Mr Mehta and his assistant threw open the guard's van doors and porters languidly off-loaded bundles, sacks, bicycles and other cargo.

Nothing was hurried, thank God, on this perfect little train. The passengers were as varied as Mother India: young men in loose and highly coloured clothes, olive-eyed women partly veiled, turbaned portly Sikhs, dark-skinned soldiers, one or two holy men with long tangled hair and beards, yellow robes, one of them carrying a trident and a vivid peacock's tail like a large fan. They made for the tea cart that every station has.

Usually Mr Mehta had reached the tea before us, had ordered – and paid – for us, and then gone back to his luggage sorting. Looking round to rebuke him for his generosity, you could see him in a knot of porters near the guard's van, grinning back and miming, encouragingly, a man drinking a cup of tea. We grew to love Mr Mehta. The tea came in cups, was strong and heavily milked and sugared – first-class Railway Tea, in fact. Sometimes there were *grams* (lentils) on leaf saucers, and scented cakes. As the day went on, the heat increased considerably and people called '*Pani*' into the blue, and were answered by men who brought cool water in copper vessels.

At Jawalamukhi Road station a notice said: 'No roof riding is permitted due to fixed structure ahead' – anyone on the roof would have been swept off and deposited into the thick, deep grass over which the butterflies danced at the trackside. But we had no one on the roof. The passengers were content to open the carriage doors and stand laughing on the running board outside the stately moving train, or hang out of the windows waving to people in the fields, or bullock cart drivers at small level crossings, or at each other as we negotiated one of the many sweeping bends.

'Please join me on the footplate,' said Mr Gosain at one station. 'Interesting curves ahead, sir, you would like to see them.'

So I clambered up into the little engine cabin. Mr Gosain carefully put on his glasses, turned the driving lever to 'High' and we slowly gathered speed. There was a red mark – probably for danger – on the speed gauge where it said 30 kilometres per hour. The needle sailed past the red mark. The little engine shook and rattled and headed at what seemed like enormous speed towards a viaduct over an abyss.

Mr Gosain, ecstatically baring his twin tusks, shouted: 'How do you like my driving? I am the speed champion!' We were approaching 45 kilometres an hour – not, you may say, something to break any records, but on this track it seemed enough for Mr Gosain, had he so wished, to have retracted the undercarriage, pulled back on the lever, and lifted gently off the ground. But, of course, all was well. Mr Gosain's elderly co-driver, a small silent man in a corner of the cabin, motioned deferentially to the speed gauge. Mr Gosain casually flicked on the brake lever, and we racketed across the viaduct safely and in fine style.

Soon the landscape began to look lumpy, as if a green and brown blanket had been draped over sacks of outsize potatoes. We hooted past tea bushes and wheat and clumps of giant bamboo. We looked down at river beds where the water ran like grey-green silk over bone-white stones.

'All dam-water here, sir,' Mr Mehta informed us.

A Sikh, who had walked along the running board from another carriage, popped in through our open door saying, 'Good morning.' Soon he said, 'Do you see that temple there? It has been given facelift – you know facelift?'

The whole world up here might have been given some divine facelift. The beauty of it was almost too much to be absorbed, even trundling through it, as we were, at only slightly more than walking pace. We moved past houses with slate roofs, as if we were actually moving down the village street. There were a great many woolly trees and mango groves, cranes, small patches of water. Hour after hour, the backdrop of white-topped mountains loomed closer and higher. It finally blocked the horizon. And presently the 9.25 up train to Jogindernager chuffed into Palumpur station.

Mr Gosain and Mr Mehta were going on to Jogindernagar. But Mr Mehta would be returning on the down train which we were catching to Pathankot next morning. So we said goodbye to Mr Gosain. 'I will be driving the goods train down early tomorrow morning,' he said sorrowfully. 'But you will hear my whistle. I will definitely whistle several times, starting with two whistles – like *so*.' He pressed a brass knob and the engine let out two whoops that made several passengers rush in panic to their carriages. 'We shall be listening for you,' we said, shaking his hand.

I strongly recommend the railway resthouse at Palumpur. Like the railway line, it was built in 1928. It has cool, high-ceilinged rooms and fans on long stalks, and dark, solid wood chairs for lounging in. It is made of pink brick and its large, neat garden stares straight at the Himalayas. You think you could reach out and touch them.

In the evening the mountains have a bluish, hazy look; the snow is very white. On the lower slopes little lights appear from the doorways of peasant cottages. Flocks of green parrots and hoopoes fly between the trees. After dark, jackals begin to yowl.

At dinnertime, a skinny, birdlike elderly man, with white hair dyed streakily henna-red, hopped up with fish and bread and strong tea and Indian beer, and in the morning omelettes and more strong tea. He was the *chowkidar* (watchman-housekeeper) and we came to love him. The only other resident, who introduced himself as Mr Molhotra, the local assistant railway engineer, told us: 'This *chowkidar* is so good because he was once "bearer" to the Maharajah of Kapurthala State.'

'That is indeed quite right, sir,' said Hoshiar Singh, the *chowkidar*, perkily cocking his head to one side like a friendly mynah bird. 'I have been keeping this Snow View Rest House clean, sir, for nine years. I hope everything is to your liking, sir.'

Before we left next morning, he hopped stiffly up to us, beamed and flourished a small blue flower, a goodbye present. 'Come soon again, sir, if you please,' he said, with a little bow.

We had already heard Mr Gosain passing in the morning down goods. His two whistle blasts sounded from the first bend of the track; then a wild series of whistles and hoots rent the champagne mountain air, as if a flock of strange birds had escaped shrieking from a local aviary. I could imagine Mr Gosain's gleeful mouth with its twin tusk-stalactites, and the speed needle mounting unheeded towards 40 kilometres an hour. When, later, we embarked again on *our* train, the Sikh stationmaster of Palampur grinned under his robin's egg blue turban, and said that he had no news – despite Mr Gosain's dramatic passing – of a crash on the line that morning. (And, indeed, I think there has been only one serious accident since 1928.)

On the return journey the train was overwhelmed with passengers. The goods van was opened, and sweating families pushed up into it; women and youths stormed into the carriages through the windows like pirates boarding a prize. Scores of men hung onto the outside. Our Mr Mehta, the guard, hustled and bustled, his whistle peeping like a thing possessed. 'Phew,' he said to me at last, when everyone was – somehow – aboard. 'Come into the guard's place, sir.' In Mr Mehta's cabin I noticed a wire-fronted crate with 'Dog Box' written on it ('So hot. No one has dog aboard today, sir,' he said). I asked him why he seemed to have a green flag but not a red one. At once he produced a red flag from under some newspapers. 'What a question, sir,' he cried, giggling. 'How I am facing the danger without a red flag!'

He was obsessed with our welfare. 'Look, this halt is called Kopar Lahar. The best tea on the line is here, sir. Please get down and have some tea, sir.' Of course, we did so. Later he said, 'Food is ordered, sir, at the next stop. We telephoned down the line from three stops back' – and a serving boy hurried up at the next station with a large metal tray cluttered with curried meat, onions, peppers, stew, potatoes and flat bread, for which he was delighted to receive the equivalent of twenty-two English pence.

How can one do justice to the delight of being with these friendly, infinitely obliging people? At the night stop Mr Mehta had broadcast our presence on the train, so with us in the guard's van were three officials of this tiny line; they had come just for the fun and a chat with someone new. One introduced himself as Mr C.R. Sarkar, a Bengali, the permanent way inspector; another was Dr K.C. Bhasti – I saw from an imposing card he gave me that he was an MBBS (I am ashamed not to be sure what that is) and assistant medical officer up the line. Nobody seemed to mind when Mr Molhotra, the engineer, stopped the train for Tony McGrath to take photographs of it. 'We shall, I am promising you, reach Pathankot on the exact minute,' said Mr Mehta reassuringly. And so we did.

On the way, the smell of hot grass and flowers embraced us. Small dark butterflies flew in and out. Mr Mehta's commentary seldom ceased: 'Snakes, oh yes, a lot we are having. Dangerous some of them, and some not. Most are of gold colour.' At one point Mr Sarkar pointed to a copse and murmured darkly, 'Panthers are in those long trees.'

At last, in Pathankot Junction, the idyll had to end. Soldiers in crumpled khaki – Sikh Horse, Jats, Singallers, Mahrattas – carrying kitbags disembarked, yawning and stretching. Passengers clambered from the goods van. Dust rose from the platform into the pale yellow rays of the setting sun. Mr Mehta and his friends said their sad, warm goodbyes. Mr Mehta seemed quite moved. He took off his uniform cap with a formal gesture. 'Have my card, sir,' he said, handing me one. 'Have you a card, sir? Next time you could drink some nice beer in my small house here, sir.'

I shook his hand again and again. 'Mr Mehta,' I said. 'Tony and I shall never forget you or Mr Gosain or the Snow View Rest House or a single hoot or whistle on the Jogindernagar line.' And I meant it.

The Last Explorer: Wilfred Thesiger

9 SEPTEMBER 1979

You would hardly expect to find Wilfred Thesiger, pushing seventy, last from the Victorian mould of great explorers, close to fisticuffs up a side street in SW3. But you'd be wrong.

Imagine a tall, lean, tanned figure, not unlike Sherlock Holmes, dressed in an old-fashioned suit and waistcoat with a gold watch chain and carrying an elderly umbrella, progressing down Paradise Walk last June with the long, flat-footed strides so well remembered by the countless tribesmen from Kashgar to Arabia's Empty Quarter who have struggled to keep up with him. At the bottom of the narrow street a number of motorists had been blocked in by a bull-necked man of about thirty-six at the wheel of a large car. Amid the cursing and hooting, Thesiger asked the angry man, with the quiet courtesy of a bygone age, if he could help him to reverse the six feet necessary to let the others pass.

The reply was explosive. 'Je-e-e-sus Chri-i-st! How I *hate* the upper classes!' the man yelled, and when Thesiger repeated his offer ('The car was far grander than anything I or my friends could afford in a thousand years,' he told me), the man fumbled with his door. 'Right — I'm going to break your f—— neck!' It was, said Thesiger later, a lovely prospect. He put a long, hard hand on the door handle. 'I'll help you get out,' he said mildly. 'But I should warn you that you will get hurt.' Deep, pale eyes under shaggy eyebrows stared as blankly and steadily at the angry man in the car as they had gazed over a rifle's sights at lion in the Sudan and wild boar in Iraq. Crashing his gears, the angry man drove apoplectically away. And Thesiger was soon round the corner in his small sitting room lined with African and Arabian first editions and hung with Arab daggers, plaintively sighing over a cup of Earl Grey to his devoted housekeeper, Miss Emtage: 'The bloody man funked it!'

That's one side of Thesiger. A few days later he showed another. He and I were waiting in his flat for a taxi to take us to Heathrow. Wilfred had invited me to join him on a safari to Lake Rudolf and the wild Samburu country of northern Kenya, where he has spent much of almost every year since 1960. He had also insisted with surprising passion that we should leave the flat three hours before our flight time. 'Don't want to miss that plane,' he said, evidently terrified that it would sneak off without us. Thesiger would bravely face a lion in his tent; airline schedules give him the vapours.

Wilfred Thesiger was born in Addis Ababa in 1910; so he is not a true Victorian, he only looks and acts like one. To me he has always had a timeless quality, and today I see more or less the same man I saw first in Basra in 1952 when, on his advice, I abandoned a job in a shipping office for the Marsh Arabs of Mesopotamia.

Now Wilfred still has few grey hairs and looks ten years younger than his sixty-nine years. His hard brown face still looks like a splinter of hard knotty wood; his oddly long nose still has curious kinks in it, the mementoes of four years as undefeated light heavyweight champion of Oxford University. He looks like a print out of old books of fantastic exploration – out of a tome by Mungo Park of the Niger, Charles Doughty or Richard Burton of Arabia, Younghusband of Tibet. If he had been born in 1836 – the year he would have chosen – he would have been a respected colleague of all these men.

The tally of his travels is so impressive that it is hardly surprising that he sniffs at some more publicity-minded people. ('Any fairly adventurous British Embassy Secretary might go where *she's* gone,' is a typical sally.) He has a prima donna's sharp tongue.

It all began at the age of nineteen, with a walk across the wild and hostile Danikil country of Abyssinia. (The British Ambassador said, 'Don't let the Danikil castrate you. That would rather spoil the effect of the show.') Then came a stint in the wild Sudan as an assistant District Commissioner. In World War II, Thesiger was with Orde Wingate in Ethiopia, where he won a DSO for capturing 10,000 Italian soldiers with a force of 300 tribesmen. Later, he spent weeks behind the German lines in the Western Desert with David Stirling's Strategic Air Service.

After the war, Thesiger stunned the old gentlemen of the prestigious Royal Geographical Society with two crossings of the great waterless sands of Saudi Arabia's Empty Quarter ('Several people warned me that my pint of water a day wouldn't be enough in that heat').

Then came travels in Kurdistan and Iran on horses and mules, through the Iraqi marshes by canoe, on foot in Nuristan and the Karakoram, the Ethiopian Blue Nile gorges ('Oh, the strain of crossing them with failing mules!'), up the Chitral River and to Hunza on foot with yaks ('Maddening animals'). After the war, too, came the CBE and the sort of prizes Buchan's intrepid Sandy Arbuthnot would have coveted – the Founder's Medal of the Royal Geographical Society, the

Lawrence of Arabia Medal of the Royal Central Asian Society, the
Livingstone Medal of the Royal Scottish Geographical Society, the
Burton Memorial Medal of the Royal Asiatic Society. Add to all that
two books, *Arabian Sands* and *The Marsh Arabs*, a Fellowship of the
Royal Society of Literature, and a marvellous book of photographs.
Not bad for a man who jokes that he's never done a stroke of work in
his life.

At Nairobi airport we are welcomed ecstatically by Wilfred's
entourage of four young Samburus. Soon we are driving Land Rovers
north towards the Samburu tribal lands, Mount Kenya in cloud on our
right; the Aberdare ridge on our left. Lush green hills; coffee, maize,
bananas. After a few hours, the landscape fades into rolling bush
country. The Land Rovers bounce and trail plumes of dust. I see
antelope and a giraffe. A tall tribesman holding a spear shyly waves
under an acacia tree. We are in Thesiger's home-from-home.

En route I begin to learn the characters of Thesiger's Africans: Kendawa, nineteen, a plumpish, easy-going Samburu from a buffalo-infested clearing near Maralal, the hill township we are aiming for; Chugana, shy, dreamy; a short, barrel-bellied sixteen-year-old, who cooks and clowns in equal measure, nicknamed variously Bonzo, Charlie (after Chaplin), and the Hobbit; and Lawi, the most remarkable of this quartet.

Lawi is one of those precious human beings who seem endowed with an extra ration of warmth, sense and goodness. He is twenty, six feet tall, quick-witted, humorous, amazingly good-natured. He is a first-class driver-mechanic; a natural rock climber; he can sew and cook; he is a good shot, and a good boxer in the classical style (taught by Thesiger). 'In fact,' said Thesiger, teasing him, 'there's very little you are *not* – in your own estimation, Lawi.'

'Now then, *mzee juu*, don't be unkind like dees.'

Mzee juu means 'top elder', a term of particular respect (Kenyatta was *Mzee* to Kenyans). Thesiger was addressed as *mzee juu* by nearly every tribesman we met in northern Kenya.

Lawi winked at me: 'The Samburu also call *mzee juu* the *Sangalai*.'

'The Old Bull Elephant That Walks by Himself,' translated Thesiger, pleased.

Maralal is the heart of Samburuland. We drive into a short, dusty avenue of jacaranda, pepper and eucalyptus trees, backed by small stores with corrugated iron roofs. We buy petrol under a signboard that says, 'Bhola and Sons, Land Rover Service', and Mr Bhola, a pleasant Kenya Asian of Punjabi origin, gives us tea and biscuits. They are welcome extras since Thesiger has decreed only one meal a day (in the evening) with mugs of tea for breakfast and lunch, teasing me by saying, 'I hope you have the stamina.' The remark reminds me of what Thesiger said to Eric Newby and Hugh Carless when, years ago, he found them 9000 feet up near the Hindu Kush about to inflate their air beds: 'God, you must be a couple of pansies.'

Wilfred is not quite as tough as of old. Now, he sometimes wears dark glasses, and I notice he is casting covetous glances at my new sleeping bag. When he and I were with the Marsh Arabs we slept on bare reed matting and stoically wrestled with hordes of fleas.

In Maralal, I have my first glimpse of an astonishing spectacle: tall, half-naked Samburu warriors, their heads and shoulders daubed with ochre, their ochred hair meticulously worked into peaks and ringlets, wandering about or leaning in attitudes of kingly disdain against store entrances, long legs crossed under a brief crimson cloth, as exotic as unicorns.

Soon we bump into the bush to the small house Thesiger bought for Lawi last year — cedar-beam walls backed with hardened mud and cow dung, a sloping corrugated iron roof, three rooms, a narrow veranda. 'Thank God, we're home,' says Thesiger. Soon he wanders off to nearby thatched huts to see Lawi's neighbours. I hear cries of 'Jambo! Jambo!' (How are you!) and the sound of cow bells on the smooth green hillsides round the house. Lawi shows me his 'garden': a hedge of cactus; morning glories round a water tank; bougainvillea and jacaranda; beyond that a thicket of maize and the ravaged remains of a potato patch — 'The porcupine ate them all up!' said Lawi sadly.

Later, at night, I heard long, bloodcurdling cries and the strange bark of zebra: 'Kwa-ha! Kwa-ha!' Peering out, I see Lawi and the Hobbit with my big Cogswell and Harrison torch, driving about sixty eland and zebra away from Lawi's valuable maize.

During the day, painted Samburu warriors frequently stride into the compound to chat, eat pocho (maize meal) and pose for photographs. 'They'd charge a tourist a couple of quid a picture,' says Thesiger. 'Lucky you're with me.' Many warriors speak English, having been to mission schools, passed their 'O' levels and happily reverted to their traditions.

'We say, if a man neglects the old customs, he's a slave,' Lawi explains. The young warriors, leaning on their spears, smile through the paint and gravely agree.

People are far more important to Thesiger than places. Watching Kendawa and Chugana gambolling on Lawi's veranda, he says: 'I'm much happier in Kenya now that Africans rule it. It does away with all that Bwana nonsense. Now I can say what I like to Lawi, Kendawa and the rest, and they say exactly what they like to me. It's like the relationship you and I had with the Marsh Arabs.'

He much admires the dedicated District Commissioners of the British Empire who lived cheek by jowl, speaking the language, with the Africans or Indians they administered. (His new book is dedicated to the late Guy Moore, his DC in the Sudan.) Memsahibs and British clubs, he believes, destroyed the Raj by planting an unbridgeable gulf between the races.

Ask Thesiger, 'Why travel?' and he replies, 'First, the challenge, the danger — then, the people. I love the people. I'd risk my life to save a black man or a brown one. I'm not so sure I'd do that for a white.'

Later: 'The thrill of the desert, yes. But the desert was meaningless except as a setting for the Bedu. If there'd been no Bedu, I wouldn't have been near the place. It would have been a meaningless penance.'

After two days at Lawi's, we head for Lake Rudolf (Thesiger typically refuses to call it by its new name, Lake Turkana). The bush is alive with zebra, giraffe, Grant's gazelle, Thomson's gazelle (Tommies), impala and ostrich. The camp we make every evening is basic. People who cry, 'Bring whisky-and-soda for the *memsahib*!', women who wear jodhpurs and drink too much and are handy in bed with white hunters and own houses on Fifth Avenue – that's Hemingway, not Thesiger. Hemingway's world is a world of ice boxes, chairs and tables, collapsible washbasins and canvas cooling bags. A world where the African bearers are sent to camp 200 yards downwind. Not Thesiger's world.

In Thesiger's world, under huge spreading trees between rocky hills, the Hobbit puts water for tea on the fire. We unpack: a sack of maize meal; a battered Blue Band butter carton containing Oxo cubes, packet soups, onions, potatoes, mugs, spoons (no forks or knives), tea, sugar; one paraffin lamp; metal cooking pots and a frying pan; plastic bowls; cheap torches with broken bulbs; pangas and a spade; blankets; loo paper; Thesiger's towel and sponge bag.

The sight of a toothbrush lying on top of an old Ribena box sparks off a Thesiger reminiscence: 'I think Orde Wingate was one of the greatest men I knew. Eccentric. In the Abyssinian campaign, he once gave all his officers our battle orders lying in his tent stark naked and smoothing his pubic hair with someone else's toothbrush.'

'How do you know it was someone else's?'

'I don't suppose he ever had one of his own.'

We hear goat bells, and tiny herd boys emerge cautiously from the bush. 'Give those *totos* a bowl of maize meal,' Thesiger orders. We buy a goat from them for dinner, and while Lawi is skinning it I remember Wilfred in those Marsh Arab days. In my mind's eye, I see a tall figure squelching briskly through mud and reed stubble. Huge wild boar lurk ahead. At his side, calm and alert, young Amara (the Lawi of that place and time) carries Wilfred's rifle, a Rigby ·275. Thesiger is wearing a tweed jacket, is barefoot, has tucked up his Arab ankle-length nightshirt, exposing hugely muscled calves and baggy knee-length white drawers. He looks like a cross between the ultimate Great White Hunter and Widow Twankey.

Next, I see him as my guest in 1977 aboard a sixty-five-year-old ketch, on a six-month voyage to discover Joseph Conrad's eastern world. Floppy hat, dark glasses. Thesiger was an improbable figure jammed into the straitjacket of a twenty-foot sailing boat. But he wanted to see Borneo. He is a voracious reader, and his favourite books are *Lord Jim* and *Kim*. So he was happy when I took him to see the place where Almayer and Lord Jim died. It made up for cramp and mild seasickness.

In London, he likes the comfort of the Travellers' Club. He shuns the bar and usually eats in the cheap quick-lunch room. He is very careful with money. In Samburu, he reclines on the sleeping bag he used in the Karakoram; wears an old floppy hat he bought secondhand in Nairobi twenty years ago; slips on the ancient sandals he'd had 'run up' by a native in a hut on the Kenya–Ethiopia border when his shoes disintegrated on a 400-mile walk from Addis Ababa.

'Where was the most dangerous time,' I asked. 'With the SAS in the Western Desert? With Wingate?'

Thesiger considered. 'My first crossing of the Empty Quarter was physically the hardest. There were moments when I felt the camels wouldn't make it – and if the camels wouldn't, we wouldn't. In the great sands, when you got to the tip of a 700-foot dune and saw another 700-footer in front of you, and another beyond that, you felt a little. . . .'

'Despair?'

'Well, disquiet. My second crossing was dangerous, too – a tribe or two were out to get me.'

We lay looking at the African stars. Faint animal noises came from the bushes. 'Five years ago,' said Thesiger, 'I'd sit here after dark and see the shapes of elephants going noiselessly by, like galleons. No twig snaps, not a branch cracks. One moment they're there, the next moment you hear a few watery gargling sounds, then silence, and you know they've gone.' Sadly: 'I've seen three hundred elephant here. Lucky to see *one* now. So much poaching for the tusks by Samburu tribesmen or Somali *shiftas* [bandits]. Now Kenya's admirable President Moi is trying to stop it. Forest fires have done for a lot of Kenya's forest. No one gives a damn. There's no replanting. In any case, you can't remake indigenous forests.'

'We're living in a dying world.'

'Undoubtedly. That's the theme of my book.'

Lawi came up and Thesiger said casually, 'They say there's a man-eater around here.'

'I hear that too, *mzee juu*.'

'Don't worry. Lions have walked about in camps of mine. It's leopards that would take sleeping dogs off people's beds.'

Lawi said: 'I'd seize a lion by de whiskers if it came to me.'

'I'd like to see that, Lawi. Actually its jaws would take you just below the eyes and under the chin. You couldn't even scream. I doubt if we'd wake up. Sweet dreams.'

On the move next morning, we pass eland – huge beasts five feet at the shoulder; vultures unspeakably evil on the ground and oddly beautiful in flight; gerenuk – Waller's gazelle – long-necked, wide-eared, like (as a game expert has accurately stated) those blown-glass animals people put on their mantelpieces. We see fresh signs of elephant: Homeric droppings. And soon an elephant blocks our path and seems to be considering a charge six feet from Thesiger's Land Rover.

'Look at it waggling its ears at us,' Chugana says. 'It's trying to leesten to what dee hell we are saying.'

I notice the odd fact that an agitated group of male baboons are sexually assaulting the elephant as it stands gazing at us. The elephant seems not to notice them. It is more or less eyeball to eyeball with Thesiger. Lawi cautiously reverses, and soon the elephant turns away and we can pass. The baboons go with it, chattering – presumably comparing notes.

'A buffalo would have charged,' Thesiger said. 'It can turn on a sixpence, quicker than a polo pony. To be caught in the open by a buffalo would be like running down the track in front of an express train.'

Hundreds of zebra, impala, eland and various gazelles suddenly explode into the landscape, a galloping cataract swirling past. We stand in the bush and stare, and when they've gone Thesiger, visibly moved, turns and says, 'That was two thousand head of game. That was the old Africa, before the poachers. You are privileged.'

On the shores of Lake Rudolf pelican, flamingo, ibis and geese wade in the shallows. Some Molo fishermen with nets push palm-trunk rafts into the water. Samburu boys of about sixteen squat around us wearing black ostrich plumes and black goatskin cloaks, carrying small bows and arrows. They chatter away in Swahili, Samburu and excellent English. 'They're waiting for me to doctor them,' Thesiger says. 'Their own people circumcised them recently – you tell that from the black plumes – and made a terrible hash of it. It's by far the most important event in a man's life here – only after circumcision can you become a warrior and eventually a *mzee*, an elder.'

We talk of big game shooting, which these days is illegal in Kenya. 'In five years in the Sudan before the war I shot seventy lions,' Thesiger's tone was matter-of-fact, not boastful. 'Tracking them for hours on foot or on horseback. When you dismounted they'd come straight at you from only twenty yards. I was criticized for shooting so many. But then lion were all over the place, like vermin. Now I have no desire whatsoever to shoot anything.'

Big game hunting was big business in Kenya: 'Before they banned it here safari operators used spotter planes to direct hunters to herds of buffalo. Like a military operation. Idiotic . . . I remember once a white hunter, a nice man called Shaw, came to my camp near here – I had only camels and a few Turkana tribesmen. Would I come over to dinner at the camp of his American client? One American; eight bearers; several tents; a truck or two of baggage; two Land Rovers. Cocktails before the meal. Smoked salmon; steak. Wines. An excellent dinner. Nice old American, too. About seventy. Had a lifelong dream to shoot a buffalo before he died. So he did – or perhaps Shaw really shot it for him. Pretty pointless. Suppose he got something out of it, though.'

Thesiger has strong views on Americans: 'I don't much like those Persian *ayatollahs*. But they are right to be disgusted with the false values the Americans have smothered everyone with – the cars, TV, drugs, drink, shrieking transistors, the vulgarity foisted on proud peoples.'

We see two lionesses lounging at the roadside. They are very beautiful and very languid. I remember that Thesiger, at the time of the worldwide success of the books about the Adamsons' famous lion, Elsa, was engaged in a long and acrimonious debate in the letters pages of the *East African Standard*. He bitterly attacked the Adamsons' much-publicized release of domesticated lion into the bush. 'These animals,' he said, 'have no fear of man and they are incompetent killers. When they cannot kill, these animals will turn on the easiest prey available – man. . . . To return a tame lion to the wilds is to turn loose a potential man-eater.' Such a view resounded round Kenya and the Elsa-loving world like a shot in a closed room. The furore increased when George Adamson's cook, Stanley, was killed by Boy, one of Elsa's grown-up cubs. Thesiger fired off a second letter. The Elsa- and Boy-lovers fired emotionally back.

Thesiger says now that he cannot stand the foolishness of people who believe that because they see lions being fondled and having their ears tickled, the animals are really just big, harmless, cuddly cats. 'Though I've nothing against pets,' he says. 'Serval cats and genets make marvellous pets. Even cheetahs. So why all this nonsense over lion, which can kill your house guests and eat your servants? Sheer lunacy.'

We camped one night at a river. Warthogs ran through bushes full of vervet monkeys. Partridge cautiously drank in the mud near a dead giraffe. Crocodiles lazed watchfully in the water. Painted warriors — like Spartans before Thermopylae — stalked smiling into the camp, calling: 'How are you, *mzee juu*?' They put off their crimson cloths and, in a leisurely ritual, bathed and painted each other. When darkness fell, elephants advanced inquisitively down the bank towards us. Thesiger said: 'If they come in the night, don't clap or shout or they'll flatten the tent and you in it.' The elephants faded into the shadows. My big torch lit up crocodile eyes in the river like cat's eyes on the main road. 'Nobody wash in the river after dark,' ordered Thesiger.

We drank Twining's Earl Grey at the fire. 'America has nothing like this,' said Thesiger. 'As for you, Lawi, I suppose some people would call you Kipling's bloody 'eathen, wouldn't they?'

Lawi laughed. '*Mzee juu*, you know I'm a Protestant.'

'Well, I'm an atheist, so I'm the bloody 'eathen.' Thesiger turned to me. 'I simply cannot believe in an afterlife, can you? All those saints eternally casting down their golden crowns into the glassy sea — I ask you! Lawi, don't forget — when I die, I want my corpse laid out in the bush for the hyenas. I mean that.'

'Anything you weesh, *mzee juu*,' said Lawi, fondly.

285

From Tweedside to the Karakoram

This article was written in the week that saw the centenary of John Buchan's birth.

24 AUGUST 1975

About the time of the Suez crisis of 1956 a magazine article appeared whose author – only half seriously – bemoaned the great, lost days of British espionage. 'Even now,' he said, 'in the depth of some Eastern bazaar and confronted with a hideously maimed beggar, I cannot resist murmuring as I drop my piastre into his filthy claw, "Jolly good show, Carruthers. Keep it up."' A John Buchan reader knows that that beggar was not called Carruthers at all. He was Sandy Arbuthnot: Old Sandy who had passed, among other things, as a *guru* – you know, the one who lived at the foot of the Shansi Pass as you go over to Kaikand – and later as a star of that dervish troupe on the Bosphorus.

John Buchan told us such unforgettable things years ago, and that is why we remember Buchan himself, born a hundred years ago. He was the eldest son of a poor minister of the John Knox Free Church in Perth. He died in 1940 as Lord Tweedsmuir, Governor-General of Canada, aged sixty-four. So his career was spectacular and might have been more so (he had once dreamed of a cabinet post) if he had not been handicapped by weak health. But today it's through Sandy – and Hannay, and Leithen, and Archie Clanroyden (the Bertie Wooster of his books) – that one remembers Buchan.

In the beginning, his talent and dogged hard work led swiftly from the manse to Glasgow University and an Oxford scholarship. He took a First in Greats at Oxford, became President of the Union (where not everyone understood his broad Scots accent), and won the Newdigate Prize for poetry. He was also accepted (despite the accent and his lack of cash) into a brilliant upper-class undergraduate 'club' – names like Asquith and Herbert were prominent in it – whose members nearly all left Oxford not only with first class degrees but Blues for boxing, rowing or rugby football as well. They were the stuff of which Sandy Arbuthnot and his chums were later created. After a short time at the Bar and writing for the *Spectator*, Buchan was recruited by Lord Milner, High Commissioner for South Africa, into his 'kindergarten' – an elite group of young men hand-picked to rebuild the republics of Transvaal and the Orange Free State after the Boer War.

Buchan fell for Africa at once. He wrote home: 'It is splendid swinging along in the cool veld air.' He had found the Africa of a boy's dreams. The weight of the White Man's Burden settled on his shoulders as cosily as an old tweed jacket. *Prester John*, the first grand Buchan 'thriller', was the upshot. It echoes Stevenson and Rider Haggard, but it has for hero a simple Scots storekeeper, alone with his knowledge of rock-climbing, tremulously heading off a great African rising against the Whites.

Buchan's two 'stars' soon followed: Richard Hannay in *The Thirty-nine Steps* (1915), and Sandy Arbuthnot joining him in *Greenmantle* (1916). Hannay started well by finding a man called Scudder skewered to death in his Portland Place flat, but he ended up as Major-General Sir Richard Hannay, KCB, DSO, Légion d'Honneur. Like Buchan, he had begun life as a lowly Scot, then spent thirty-one years 'making his pile' in Bulawayo as a mining engineer before *The Thirty-nine Steps* led him to life at the top in London. He and Sandy between them had most of the characteristics that make up the word 'Buchan-esque'. Hannay was no good at office work, but spoke twelve languages. Both knew all about firearms (though what, I wonder, was a Lee-Speed carbine?). For Hannay, plunges in icy burns were good, hot baths ('liverish') and beards ('needless hair') bad.

Sandy was an Old Etonian, slender, almost girlish. He once thought of standing for Labour, but the idea seemed too boring. He was a 'master of disguise': when not a *guru*, he turned up as a Communist Clydeside boilermaker, a Turkish gypsy dancer, even (perhaps most daring of all) a London drama critic. In *The Three Hostages* he appeared in a turban as Kharama, a 'foul thing out of the east', and poor Hannay, unsuspecting, went for him 'like a wild beast'. ('Don't be an old ass, Dick,' said Sandy lightly, tossing the turban in Hannay's face.)

Leithen, another prototypical hero, hunted, fished, climbed, joined the Guards as a 'private at the start of the War and finished up a GSOI' – then went on to be Attorney-General. Still another hero always wore his Brigade tie in the Balkans. Several were good milers – even Archie Clanroyden's wife was 'famous for her wind'.

Sandy had been an intelligence officer with General Maude 'and then something in Simla'. Friends of his had been 'spoken of for India' (i.e. for Viceroy). But both Hannay and Arbuthnot were too harum-scarum for serious appointments like that.

Buchan's characters are wonderfully unassuming. Hannay is

frequently self-doubting – not a bit like James Bond. David Crawfurd in *Prester John* admits to being terrified most of the time. (Buchan himself feared the moment in *Alice* when she plunges into the rabbit hole. And sometimes a deserted Scottish valley would suddenly seem too 'silent and aware', and he would rush out of it in panic.)

Hannay and Co. sit perfectly in their frames. Plots move fast through threats of monstrous risings or invasion. ('Some mischief is afoot in those hills,' someone blurts out. And you know it's more than a spot of ivory smuggling.) The key to a horrendous conspiracy often lies buried in a cypher: 'Seek. . . . Where beside the sacred tree spins the seer who cannot see,' for example. That proved a tough one to crack. At the eleventh hour, Hannay inadvertently snaps his pipe-stem against the mantelpiece and the sound triggers a memory of the villainous Medina. Someone springs up, yelling: 'I've got it!'

Of course, Buchan's snobbery is tiresome. One just has to face the fact that he felt proudly at home in the elitist world of club and country house he had arrived at through his own efforts. To be fair, he could write lovingly of 'common' people like Dickson McCunn, the Glasgow grocer-hero of *Huntingtower*, and the little gang of slum boys, the Gorbals Die-Hards. He was not a bellicose imperialist of the Churchill stamp. He opposed military intervention in Soviet Russia in 1919. He liked Americans and was one of the earlier pre-World War II supporters of the Atlantic Alliance. He was pro-Commonwealth rather than pro-Empire and understood people like Pandit Nehru and Gandhi. In his early books, he certainly writes insultingly about Jews (one is 'the whitest Jew since the Apostle Paul'), often bracketing them with Bolsheviks and anarchists, whom he naturally detested. In this he reflects the common attitudes of the time; no excuse, I admit. Later, he became an outspoken pro-Zionist, and a friend and admirer of Chaim Weizmann. His name is inscribed in the Golden Book of the Jewish National Fund of Israel, beside Lloyd George, Balfour and Smuts.

Hannay and his friends are not nearly as ruthlessly, unthinkingly violent and vengeful as Bulldog Drummond, James Bond and Co. Buchan produced awesome villains worthy of his awesome heroes. The Rev. John Laputa, the black African villain, is noble enough to emerge a kind of hero, and David Crawfurd is left at the end respectfully contemplating Laputa's statue. The murderous German mastermind in *The Thirty-nine Steps* who looked like Mr Pickwick and could 'hood his eyes like a hawk' was, Hannay said, 'more than a spy; in his foul way he was a patriot'; and so Hannay respected him.

The traitor Dominick Medina in *The Three Hostages* was an MP, a poet, had the brains and charm of the devil and was the best shot in England 'after His Majesty'. Hannay risked his own life to save him. Buchan's heroes usually treated their enemies leniently whatever their colour or creed or – fitting the Buchan code of chivalry – they took them on fair and square in single combat, preferably with sporting rifles in mountainous country.

It is here in that sort of terrain, I think, that John Buchan really comes into his own. Snobbery, anti-semitism, any and all flaws are forgotten when Hannay and the rest take to the hills in wind 'enough to take the wings off a sea-gull'. Buchan himself had poached salmon and walked the headwaters of the Tweed. He had swum in freezing lochs, slept rough round fires of heather and bog oak, followed spoors of men and animals, and ridden the high veld. What sticks in the mind is the chase in *The Thirty-nine Steps*, the distant figures of Hannay's pursuers on the bare moorland. Or the deadly stalking match between Hannay and Medina in *The Three Hostages* which ends with Hannay trying to lower the villain over a Scottish cliff to safety (' "Medina" – my voice must have been like a wild animal's scream – "I'm going to try to let you down a bit. ..." The answer out of the darkness was a sob. ... Next second the strands had parted'). In what T.E. Lawrence called Buchan's 'clean-limbed, speedy, breathless' books, landscape, animals and birds, minutely observed, actually affect character and action. One man recovers his courage watching a wild goose evading a falcon; another is saved from capture because he knows that pink-foot geese, when alarmed, move *nearer* the enemy.

I remember years ago, before I slipped into journalism, sitting among Marsh Arab tribesmen in a reed hut in a remote part of Iraq, trying to decide if I should throw up a future in shipping and travel in Arabia indefinitely. Skeins of geese and wildfowl crossed the sky; the Marshmen, eager to set out on a wild boar hunt, clutched their rifles; the canoes stood ready. In a moment, thank God, I had left the shipping office for five uncertain years with the Bedu. It was a Buchan-like opportunity. In *Memory Hold the Door*, his autobiography, Buchan writes, 'I regard the shrinking of opportunity as one of the gravest facts of our age. The world must remain an oyster for youth to open. If not, youth will cease to be young, and that would be the end of everything.'

Pink Gin and Panama

This interview appeared the weekend before Graham Greene's novel, The Human Factor, *was published.*

12 MARCH 1978

A pageboy was waiting on the steps of the Ritz when I arrived. 'Mr Young for Mr Greene?' he asked. His room, 612, was none too easy to find, because they are improving the Ritz. On the sixth floor, workmen were whistling and hammering in gutted rooms. Graham Greene's nicely painted door seemed as incongruous as if it stood in a bomb site. He opened it cautiously, smiling and holding out his hand. 'I'm glad you could find me in all this.'

The expected pale, fleshy face was there, with blue protuberant eyes under unexpected brown eyebrows. I suppose I had anticipated baggy grey trousers and a rumpled Viyella shirt. But in flared trousers, a cheerful shirt of brown, black and white splodges, a light brown tie and a smart brown ribbed wool jacket with a zip, he was looking distinctly spruce and much less than seventy-three.

Knowing I had just arrived from New York, he said: 'Jet-lag. I've got a marvellous cure for that.' He popped a large orange pill into a tooth glass of water. 'You can get this in Paris. It's amazing how it picks you up. I can't bear Fernet Branca, can you?'

His pale blue, battered suitcase stood on a luggage rack. On the mantelpiece there was a quart bottle of Teacher's whisky, not quite full. An old copy of George A. Birmingham's *The Inviolable Sanctuary* lay on a table.

Was he glad to be in London?

'I find it rather depressing. It's so dirty now.'

Since 1966, he has divided his time and his collection of books, including many first editions, between a small flat in Paris and another in Antibes.

Did he ever go to America?

'Not if I can help it. But I *can* go. All the hassles over my visas came to an end when Kennedy came in.'

His new novel, *The Human Factor*, is published on Thursday. It concerns the British Secret Service, the South African Intelligence Organization BOSS, and Maurice Castle, the ageing MI6 desk officer, responsible for southern Africa, who is married to Sarah, a black

South African. Castle defects, reluctantly, to Russia. The story, of course, has undertones of the Philby case.

'No,' said Greene,' I didn't choose the name Maurice after Maurice Oldfield [the then head of MI6], though I did send him a copy. He should see that he is not at all like Castle – nor really is Philby.'

In the novel, Castle commutes from MI6 to Berkhamsted. He bicycles from the station there to his small semi-detached. Greene was born in Berkhamsted, where his father was headmaster of the school. 'I revisited it before writing my autobiography [A Sort of Life] and again before this book. I rather enjoy going back to Berkhamsted because I was happy there. The only sad thing is that the sinister old pub – the Crooked Billet – has been rebuilt in the most appalling modern style.'

On The Human Factor's title page is a quotation from Joseph Conrad's Victory: 'I only know that he who forms a tie is lost. The germ of corruption has entered his soul.' 'I reread Victory a year ago,' said Greene. 'I've always liked it – except for the ending. Conrad over-romanticized a bit there.'

Photographer Tony McGrath came in and began to take pictures. I told Greene that McGrath and I had been in the Khyber Pass together recently.

'Did you read G. A. Henty up there?' he asked.

'No, Kipling.'

'I've never liked Kipling's prose much. But I admire his poetry.' Greene began to recite: 'Cities and Thrones and Powers...,' emphasizing the lines 'Out of the spent and unconsidered earth/The Cities rise again.' 'I think "spent earth" is so good,' he said, 'don't you?' He broke off to say: 'I've booked a table in the Ritz's Marie Antoinette Room.'

I pointed out that in the book Hargreaves, the head of MI6, and his assistant, Dr Percival, lunched at the Travellers' Club – so why didn't we?

'A nice idea,' said Greene – and he rang the restaurant to cancel his booking. Then he said: 'Before we go – G.K. Chesterton was another underestimated poet. Put "The Ballad of the White Horse" against "The Waste Land". If I had to lose one of them, I'm not sure that ... well, anyhow, let's just say I reread "The Ballad" more often.' Still talking, he tugged on a large, glossy fur coat, very 'trendy', from Simpson's of Piccadilly. 'Forster? I liked A Passage to India, but I'm afraid that's all. I once met him. He was carrying one of those curved

Victorian bags and I said, "What a nice bag," and he said, "It was given to me by an aunt in Portsmouth." That seemed to me to be Forster.'

Greene sprang to the window as a hubbub drifted up from the street. 'A demo!' We looked down on Iranian demonstrators, sinisterly masked and chanting anti-Shah slogans outside the Iran Air office.

We bustled downstairs and across the lobby. Greene strode with casual eagerness across Piccadilly and through the line of shouting Iranians like a revolutionary general inspecting his troops. 'This must be the right thing to do, don't you think?' he said, obviously enjoying the situation. Later, when we were near the bottom of St James's Street, he stopped to point. 'That's my old flat over Overton's. Colonel Daintry of MI6 lives there in my book.' Round the corner into Pall Mall: 'See that tiny passage? Kim Philby and I used to drink a lot at a nice little pub up there in the war and fire-watching days.'

'Let's have one there now.'

In the pub's crowded bar, Greene had a large pink gin. He told me with relish about how, at the recent meeting on the Panama Canal Treaty in Washington (which he attended as a guest of his friend, the Panamanian President, Torrijos), an official of the Paraguayan dictator, Stroessner, had refused to shake his hand. Evidently he had read *Travels with My Aunt*.

Farther up Pall Mall, the Travellers' was sombre and almost empty: Saturday. 'I rather like the emptiness,' said Greene. 'In the book, Hargreaves and Dr Percival lunched in their clubs on a Saturday for peace and quiet.'

In a nearly empty smoking room I ordered more pink gin for us both. 'There's the possibility of a film of the new book,' he said. 'Otto Preminger is interested. I'd like Trevor Howard as Maurice Castle. But I don't enjoy cinema writing. I can't work for a year after a film. One feels exhausted. Not that book writing is fun; I only manage two hundred words a day now. But it's a boil that has to be drained.'

On the Victorian staircase we passed an elderly member and Greene murmured happily, 'Could that be the ghost of H.G. Wells?' Only half a dozen members were lunching. Under the chandeliers the empty tables stretched away like tombstones. We were met by a forbidding head waiter, who, looking past us, said: 'I'm afraid the gentleman should be wearing a jacket, sir.'

'Oh, dear,' I said. 'But on a Saturday. . . .'

'What's that?' said Greene, amiably pressing forward. But we were given a table. 'No jacket!' said Greene. 'What's *this*, then?' And he pulled merrily at his smart brown cardigan with the zip.

A waiter in dark glasses brusquely thrust two menus under our noses.

'I say,' said Greene, who now seemed alert for anything, 'there was a hint of menace in *that* gesture, don't you think? Still, we *are* late. . . .'

The dining room emptied, the waiters vanished. Greene and I were left drinking the last of the wine. A bespectacled man in a cash booth, far away by the door, peered at us from time to time. One half expected Harry Lime to pop in. 'Melodrama,' said Greene. 'I have a great liking for melodrama, and from *A Gun for Sale* I thought I'd drain it off into books I called "entertainments", though there is melodrama in some of the other books, too.'

Downstairs again, over Calvados ('brandy doesn't agree with me'), we turned to Panama. What had taken him there? 'Partly Drake and Portobello Bay.' He broke into jovial song: '"Drake is in his hammock. . . ."' A solitary member looked up startled from his paper and cleared his throat. 'Good bad poetry, don't you think?' said Greene. 'I'd love to go back to Panama if there's trouble if that treaty's not signed. Torrijos would fight and even the Pentagon have said they'd need a hundred thousand men to defend the Canal. But the Canal would be inoperative. It's easy to sabotage. And I doubt if the Americans would put up with a war against a small nation like Panama. Torrijos is a fighter. Not a man to be flown to exile in Miami. He told me he liked Carter, luckily.'

I wondered if Torrijos might be someone he'd like to put into a novel.

'I find it impossible to write about real people. One doesn't know enough about them, even about friends. Characters have to come out of the subconscious.'

I reminded him about the terrible American journalist in *The Quiet American*.

'Ah, yes,' Greene replied. 'He *was* drawn from life, as a matter of fact. What a dreadful man. Although I felt sorry for him towards the end and made him rather more human.'

Walking back to the Ritz, he said: 'Do you know Yevtushenko? He came to see me in Antibes. I wondered why. He is so charming and yet so name-dropping. An official dissident allowed to travel. One has a certain unease. Anyway he came and was slightly critical of the KGB. I said, joking, "Be careful. I've a friend in the KGB." He was astonished and said "Philby?" "Yes," I replied. He said, "What, that traitor?" "But he's a Communist," I said. And Yevtushenko said, "Do you *believe* that?" ' Greene laughed.

Back in his room, Greene asked: 'Who was the man who wrote *The Last Days of Hitler*? Yes, Hugh Trevor-Roper. He took much exception to my comparison of Kim with those Catholics who accepted Torquemada in the hope of better things to come. Communism is a Christian heresy. I have hopes. We do hear, don't we, of more dissidents coming out of Russia? I have hopes of Carter, too. Fingers crossed.' He smiled, and in a moment we found ourselves on the subject of death.

'Death? At seventy-three, I don't suppose a day goes by when it doesn't cross my mind. One hesitates to start a new book. . . . It's not death that worries me, it's the process. I hope it'll come quickly, say in an air crash. The thought of being wounded in Vietnam – kneecapped, for example – scared me. Under bombardment, I thought, "Why am I here?" But when I was on a dive-bombing raid, I was concentrating too much on not being sick down the pilot's neck. Of course, death used to attract me as a young man. But that's when it was a choice. When it's an approaching certainty, it's much less attractive. After-life?' – another smile – 'I'm a Catholic agnostic. But living too long worries me. My family tends to. An uncle of mine fell out of a tree at ninety-one – and lived.'

He put a long, strong finger on the Teacher's bottle. I nodded and he poured out two large ones. 'I drink more perhaps when I'm happy, like today, than when I'm bored. Boredom? I'm sure everybody has it. I *just* don't know how bank clerks or factory workers cope. *We* can *escape.* And you asked me if I thought of my books as comforting tokens of my immortality. But what twentieth-century books will survive thirty or forty years more? Even Shakespeare has no comfort – he doesn't *know* he's being read. How long will *anyone* be read? How long will this sort of life go on at all?'

I sipped the whisky and said, 'Sounds grim.'

Greene pointed that strong, admonishing finger and fixed me with his popping blue eyes. 'No,' he said gaily. 'Realistic.'

Drinks at White's with the Colonel

Was David Stirling, founder of the SAS, to be the saviour of Britain?

25 AUGUST 1974

At first sight, Colonel David Stirling, sitting on a black leather sofa in White's, his club in St James's Street, London, doesn't look like someone who might imagine himself running Britain's power stations, sewers and such like if a general strike hits us. A few members around on a Friday evening flitted about in baggy tweeds, collecting canvas grips, cashing last-minute cheques to cover August Bank holiday weekend in the country. None of them greeted him and Stirling, a very tall, clean-shaven man with white hair and – for fifty-eight – a youngish face, watched them pass with a sort of mild curiosity, as if they were total strangers who had blundered into the wrong club by mistake. A waiter brought him a small glass of Campari and gin.

'Have you read that book – you know – by the Russian with the unpronounceable name?' he said, fitting a beautifully tight, nine-inch cigar into a dark wood holder. (Of course he meant Solzhenitsyn.) 'I've read about half. It's absolutely terrifying what he says can happen if no one stands up and speaks up. . . .'

His suit was single-breasted and dark, his tie salt-and-pepper, his shoes those black Italian-style slippers with a brass chain across the uppers. He might, I suppose, be expected to wear something tight, aggressive and double-breasted, or Bulldog Drummond plus-fours. Nor does Stirling bark or boom. His voice is quietly good-mannered, and though words come tumbling out, they sound spontaneously jumbled and unrehearsed.

'I am utterly without ambition, too old for that. But I do believe that the human spirit and human society need disciplines. Yep, I do think this time Britain is heading for real disaster. The Communists are out of the woodwork after all these years and they have declared themselves.' He becomes quite vehement when he denies that he would approve a right-wing military take-over. 'Anyone who calls me Fascist I will take for a ride in court,' he said.

'Really?'

'Well, no, not really. But it's an outrageous thing to say about me.'

Amazing to say, Stirling seems to see himself as left of centre, and General Walter Walker, the founder of the vigilante force Unison, as right of centre and undesirably military, even someone to be mistrusted. Stirling gave me the impression, in fact, that he fears Walker is the sort of man who gives right-wingery a bad name.

'One difference: I am a prohibited immigrant into Rhodesia. Walker is not.'

Stirling also thinks military ranks (such as his own) are a political disadvantage. It would be better for a civilian to take over command of his 'GB 75' *and* Unison. He does not seem to care – or see – that in such an amalgamation his group would be obliged to accept some very objectionable people.

Even so, when Mr Roy Mason, the Defence Secretary, let fly at Stirling last week for being 'blimpish', he showed himself to be either wildly ill-informed or a staggeringly bad judge of aristocratic character. Blimpish, after all, implies doddering, obese, reactionary bluster rooted in stupidity. David Stirling is not that sort at all. He seems much more a kind of post-imperial John Buchan character, full of cunning, a patronizing mistrust for the workers and a sense of mission. He probably feels that by training people to keep the sewers and power stations running he's helping to save the Crown. Although from time to time he does seem to be a bit dotty, he is certainly not a silly old buffer.

When you ask about him, those who have known him well immediately start using adjectives like 'high-minded' and 'sly'. Perhaps his ardent Catholicism is a key to his motives. His upper-class background and education are obviously another. He was at Ampleforth. His younger brother, Peter, who is married to a pukka Persian, has a gravel business in Tehran. Big brother Bill looks after Keir, the very grand family house in Scotland, which needs money to keep it up, so he has dabbled in contracting and oil drilling abroad.

World War II was Stirling's high spot. In 1941, when he was twenty-six, he and Peter invented the Special Air Service (SAS), an almost freelance affair officered mainly by the likes of Randolph Churchill and Fitzroy Maclean, which confused the enemy by popping up behind the lines and attacking him from peculiar angles. He initiated, before he was captured, a new form of warfare in which the master idea was to go so far behind the lines that the Germans weren't watching, walk casually onto airfields with bombs and stick them in, and then retreat *deeper* behind the lines.

Someone who was in the war with him said: 'He was always a freelance, hardly in the Army at all. He was incredibly brave. He was a charmer, too, and a very, very good officer.' He saved his men's lives on occasions through cunning and quick wits, shouting angrily in instant German invented on the spot if they ran into Italians, and Chico Marx-type Italian if they met Germans.

'I once saw Fitzroy giving some Germans a magnificent dressing down in mock Italian,' Stirling said.

Evelyn Waugh was another colleague-in-arms. 'I remember him sitting here on that very fender – see it? – swinging his legs and glaring at people. He said he wanted to antagonize a few people so as not to have to waste too much time being polite to too many chaps. He was never rude to me. As a soldier, his moral and physical courage were amazing. He was determined to be always up at the sharp end of things.'

In 1943, David Stirling was taken prisoner in Tunisia. He soon escaped from the Germans, but was retaken by the Italians. He made himself such a pest, however, that he was quickly – to his delight – transferred to the Eton of prisoner-of-war camps, Colditz. He spent the rest of the war there. 'No swankers,' he said modestly, 'but they really thought me *pericoloso*.' (Stirling's talk of himself is littered with 'No swankers . . .' or 'It seems so like swanking, but . . .').

Strangely enough, General 'Bob' Laycock, his commanding officer, once said Stirling almost seemed a bit lazy. There *is* a smooth, soft, lazy look about him. For instance, in the war, Laycock said, he would wander off on some hair-raising adventure as if bound for a day's deer-stalking on a Scottish hill. But his nerve was never in doubt.

On the other hand, his political judgement seems shaky, to say the least. One old chum says, quite fondly, that in politics David Stirling's ideas are quite unreal. A fellow-member of White's, the smartest of all the smart St James's clubs, says that Stirling has a sense of humour, and it's always 'rather fun' to meet him there in the crowded, poky bar among the blue pin-stripes, the carnation buttonholes, the odour of Mr Trumper's hair tonic. But even he, liking him, thinks of him as someone who believes you get around any kind of obstacle with courage and a bit of luck.

The strange case of his involvement in the Capricorn Africa Society, which he founded in the fifties, illuminates some major weaknesses and strengths in a man who, whatever his judgement, is intellectually serious if indelibly romantic. It also perhaps throws light on the sort of methods Stirling prefers. Capricorn was an attempt to maintain the white presence in East and Central Africa by forging, in the teeth of the upsurge of militant black nationalism, an alliance of the whites and the right kind of blacks. The attempt was doomed from the start – but thought of failure did not deter Stirling. Indeed, Stirling himself and the sort of whites he attracted believed they could form a common front with equally superior figures among the leaders of the Africans.

The main idea was to persuade Africans in Kenya, Tanganyika, the two Rhodesias and Nyasaland (as they were then called) 'to reject the barren doctrine of racial nationalism ... and acquire a common patriotism.' Stirling's black supporters mostly belonged to multi-racial circles anyway and were therefore 'Uncle Toms' to the black nationalists. As for the whites, at a conference Stirling convened on the shores of Lake Nyasa in June 1956 one observer had the impression 'of having got inside the Officers' Club for a party to which the more presentable wives had been invited'. Generally speaking his whites were apt to be ex-something on a lofty scale, like ex-Governor or ex-Brigadier, and young Kenya ladies from the White Highlands. Stirling effectively controlled every moment of that conference so impatiently and with such fervour that some present felt they were at one of those Moral Rearmament house parties. (He had a discreet walk-out with MRA at about this time, but neither would join the other.) Nevertheless, and inevitably, the tide of African nationalism came in, and Capricorn sank quietly into the sand.

Last week, eleven years later, puffing on his cigar in White's, Stirling said: 'Well, Capricorn was Utopian, almost Walter Mitty. I've talked to Julius Nyerere and Kenneth Kaunda about it and they always said that the Africans had to go through the process of proving themselves on their own. We were a total failure.'

After Capricorn came an interlude when Stirling helped the Yemeni royalists 'fight the Russians who were experimenting with new types of poison gas on Yemeni civilians'. And then came Watchguard, a commercial organization providing Third World heads of state with bodyguards and intelligence agents. Kenyatta of Kenya, Kaunda of Zambia and several Gulf rulers employed Stirling's people.

In 1970, Stirling became involved in a madcap scheme to raid the main jail in Tripoli and release several score of Libyan political prisoners from the clutches of Colonel Gaddafi. It is characteristic of Stirling that he dropped out when the Foreign Office asked him to come off it.

Now Stirling is director of several conventional companies, including Television International Enterprises Ltd, which has dark-panelled offices at 22 South Audley Street, where you find three nice secretaries with an electric kettle, a yapping Yorkshire terrier and a switchboard jammed with calls (since *Peace News* last week revealed the existence of GB 75 – 'rumbled it', in David Stirling's parlance).

'A pity we were rumbled – prematurely,' he said. 'Our recruiting will stretch right the way across the classes. But so far it's only just begun – so you see our membership gives a wrong impression.'

He added that, as a Scotsman, he finds it difficult to understand class. 'Class is something generated in England,' he said.

When he gets up to go, he stares thoughtfully at you as if trying to read by your expression if he should tell you something more.

I remembered part of a speech that someone made at the Capricorn conference in a bankrupt hotel on the shores of Lake Nyasa in 1956: 'Responsibility should be left to those people of all races who are qualified for it.' That Buchanism seems to summarize David Stirling's creed. Stirling swears he would act only at the request of, and in support of, the elected Government of the day.

Maybe so. But while everyone agrees that David Stirling is likeable, amusing and will listen, they also agree he is virtually unstoppable when he's decided where his duty lies. So he is, you might say, quite a formidable bloke.

Saved from the Wreckers

4 FEBRUARY 1979

I wish to make a claim: that the oldest-feeling, most soul-subduing and cosily creepy part of England-on-Sea is almost hidden between Britain's battered kneecap and its battered shin. I mean between Devon's Hartland Point and Cornwall's Fire Point Beacon above Boscastle. This is the Wreckers' Coast: a place of buzzards and seals and effigies of knights in dim, half-lost churches, where seas pound into cliff-bound bays that have swallowed seamen from a hundred wrecked schooners, and in wartime, perhaps, harboured German U-boats.

Once, poor children in these parts prayed, 'God save Father and Mother and zend a ship ta shore vore morning.' And on cold, rainy days there has always seemed to me to be an aura here of doomed ships and silent watchers on terrible cliffs – an aura that survives the asphalted roads and the romance-killing caravan sites. Yet, with the summer sun, it all looks quite different. Everything smiles – on picnickers, surfers, flower gatherers and adventurous walkers with bird and butterfly books in their haversacks next to the sandwiches and the hip flask.

Under the sun, these cliffs give almost theatrically splendid views. South of Bude between Compass Point and Widemouth Bay's Black Rock (actually, locals say, a Cornish giant eternally plaiting ropes of sand), my grandmother, years ago, would jerkily brake the Austin two-seater and exclaim: 'What a lot of sea!' And raised on R.L. Stevenson, Captain Marryat, Crosbie Garstin (*The Owl's House*), and R.M. Ballantyne, I was almost convinced that one clear day I would see on the horizon the Indies . . . tall ships . . . Hispaniola. 'Fifteen men on a dead man's chest.' Even today, that conviction returns to sidle up to me, like Blind Pew to Billy Bones. Further south the cliffs are as high as 720 feet. The sea moves restlessly at their feet; larks and hawks move restlessly above. The biggest gulls I've ever seen strut there with eyes as cold as the sea below.

The coastline is a chain of tall headlands with names like Cow and Calf, Sharpnose Point, Wrangle Point, Longbeak, Dizzard. Their angry shapes and the prevailing west winds have done for dozens of ships, provoking the sailors' saying,

From Trevose Head to Hartland Light
Is a watery grave by day or night.

At the Falcon Inn, in the old part of Bude, Desmond Gregory, the licensee and a pillar of the hard-working Bude lifeboat team, lets off his signal rockets among the drinkers outside the pub if a boat is in trouble off the harbour. Spectacular wreck photographs adorn his bar. And I myself have a fine photograph at home of the Austrian barque *Capricorno*, her sails in tatters, her skipper drunk, being pounded to pieces by enormous seas below Compass Point in December 1900. Only two men were saved. In the picture a solitary seaman stands on the doomed deck, like Steerforth in *David Copperfield*.

By contrast, the nub of the region, Bude Haven, lies behind its long nineteenth-century breakwater, placid and homely. Sun and wind haven't changed Bude much over the years. It is peacefully remote, with its nearest railway station at Exeter.

Its two wide sandy beaches are its glory, perhaps the finest in England. Under a summer sun there can be few happier places for children than Bude, what with the cliffs and those beaches. It is a treat to run down to them, as I once did from my grandmother's Victorian house in Ocean View Road where surfboards and buckets and spades cluttered the hall, when the wind was just right for the surf. On a good day the surf comes in six lines of foam, head-high and not too far out (or you have a long wade). We used to fling ourselves prone just before each wave broke, with or without a surfboard. These days young men in rubber suits balance standing up, as in Hawaii.

The nannies who used to help dig sandcastles are no more. But the dogs still dig their way to Australia through the sand. The kids with kites still shriek when mother capsizes in a shrimp pool ('Oo, Ma, you're showing all you've got!'). And the long black lines of rock still run out into the booming surf, knobbly with mussels and limpets, like arthritic fingers.

Behind the beaches, there are villas called 'Saratoga' and 'Camelot' with cedars and red-hot poker plants in their gardens and bees and lavender. Downs View skirts the golf links, where in the war American GIs littered the bunkers with French letters. The GIs, raucous and randy, enraged retired Indian Army officers who crouched like tigers in nearby villas with rooms full of bamboo furniture, Benares trays, Alma-Tadema prints and metal statues of dying Pathan tribesmen. Landladies put up 'B and B with EM (evening meal)' signs on those villas now and make a tidy living in the summer.

Bude's only cinema, the art-deco Picture House, still dominates the links. It was opened in 1936 by Ambrose and his Orchestra with 'Soft Lights and Sweet Music'. I just remember being banned from it by my parents because they thought *King Solomon's Mines* would give me nightmares.

Let us be frank: Bude is not Brighton. Sir John Betjeman (gallantly) has said it is the 'least rowdy resort'. Yet it has a very comfortable and genuinely friendly old pub – the Falcon Hotel – run by the Brendon family since the 1800s. Boats still sail into the nearby lock used for 125 years until 1936 by Bude's famous ketch *Ceres*. There is a self-possessed little smack called *Fruitful*. It's only recently that the old whiskered sea captains have been, as they say here, 'called to rest'.

Bude is ennobled by its beaches and its hinterland. Inland, the sheer *age* of the region envelops you. You can ramble for hours across headlands that run back forming broad, high land on which scattered farms seem settled hull-down in wriggling lanes to escape the winter gales which have forced trees here to grow almost parallel to the earth. In long, deep, dark valleys you come upon small, ancient churches in small, ancient graveyards smelling of flowers and grass. Huge trees loom over them. Many of these churches are oddly far from any village. Royal coats-of-arms hang in some (in the Civil War this was Royalist country). Under stone canopies armoured effigies turn up stone toes (one inscription: 'Edwarde Arundell read and ruled well – 1624') and fine wooden pews are fighting erosion by age or insects. If a cloud covers the sun, you may feel uneasy. On solid gravestones the same names return and return, century after century: Muttons, Sleemans, Okes and Prusts. Frequent Christian names are Eli, Caleb, Joshua, Reuben. And I found one woman called, surprisingly, Salome. Launcells, Poundstock, St Juliot's (where Thomas Hardy, helping to restore it, found his wife Emma Gifford, the vicar's step-daughter) are three very satisfactory churches-under-the-hill.

An equally pleasing church on a cliff is at Morwenstowe, high over the sea, where the opium-eating Parson ('Passon') Hawker buried drowned sailors from 1834 to 1875 and wrote outrageous poetry. A practical joker, Hawker clambered onto a rock one night to impersonate a mermaid. 'Dressin' up in sea weed and not much else,' a local inhabitant noted, 'and combing his hair and zingin', till all the town went down to see 'un; they thought 'twas a merry maid [mermaid] sure enough.' Then he frightened the daylights out of them by standing to sing 'God Save the King'. Near his church, there are seals in the ocean and a good old pub called the Bush selling real ale and Cornish pasties.

All the same, Stoke is *the* church of the region. Near Hartland Light, off which Lundy Island squats fatly, Stoke's square tower and four pinnacles soar above the nearly empty landscape. Driving to it through lanes only wide enough for one car, trees meeting overhead and grass brushing the window, is like following Alice's White Rabbit down the rabbit hole. But once there, the grandeur of Stoke's tower imposes itself. A cheerful old gravestone reads: 'For evr'y man who lives there is one debt to Nature due./I've paid my debt/And so must you.' And a plaque on the church wall says that John Lane, founder of the Bodley Head, and Sir Allen Lane, his son, are buried here. What, as J.B. Priestley thought when he saw the plaque, could be more incongruous, among these remote fields and lanes, than echoes of Beardsley and the *Yellow Book*, Beerbohm, Le Gallienne's 'Quest of the Golden Girl'? Or 'I have been true to thee, Cynara, in my fashion'?

But the sun-and-gale-hammered character of this Far West of England is strong enough to absorb incongruities. Even – I hope – the incongruity of the jumbo motor coaches which these days, increasingly, trumpet their way down to the Wreckers' Coast.

Unadulterated Spirit of Brighton

30 AUGUST 1981

The other day, looking for a bit of Bank Holiday spirit, I went to Brighton for the first time, and found it was like going abroad. I still haven't decided why. Perhaps I was partly affected by the Royal Pavilion's Oriental domes; partly by the Sassoon family's Persian tent mausoleum in Kemp Town, which is now the 'Bombay Music Bar'.

But I started out in a very English frame of mind, with *Hangover Square*, Patrick Hamilton's good, drab English novel of the Brighton and Earls Court of 1939, open on my knee, waiting to see if the train, as he describes it, really would hesitate as if on the brink of a dangerous zone before 'lolloping methodically' into Brighton station.

There was no sense of danger. Only a totally unexpected aura, between station and hotel, of Caribbean carnival. A happy flood of black families seemed to have taken possession of the town. They overflowed into souvenir shops, cafés, buses, cars, and lapped round me in the Babylonian lobby of the grand Metropole Hotel. What could it all mean?

In the lift, jolly West Indian-born ladies from Manchester or Swindon, wearing startling hats, cried 'Good morning'; black men and boys, dressed to kill, were genially concerned to know how I was with Jesus. Later, hundreds of them quick-timed it gaily along the Front behind a band, singing 'Onward Christian Soldiers'. 'Victory!' they shouted, and 'Jesus!' Brixton was rioting, but the Church of God of Prophecy was enjoying a joyful twenty-eighth Annual Convention in Brighton.

A few days later, figures in fish-scale costumes were huddling on the windswept Front clutching rubber tridents and inflatable whales. Evidently a 'Save the Whale' get-together was in the offing.

Brighton is obsessed with conferences. It's whales one week, the

TUC or the Tories the next. From September to June, in the howling gales of winter, delegates of some sort regularly toddle away from the rhetoric-ridden Brighton Centre for their reviving double Chivas Regals in the twentieth-century Victorian grandeur of the Old Ship (built 1670), the Grand (1864), the Royal Albion (1826) or the modernized Metropole. Brighton is no longer a 'bucket-and-spade town'. The family holiday trade ('two weeks by the sea') began to slip fifteen years ago and has never stopped slipping. Package tours have done for them. So hotel owners have changed Brighton's face, building halls like Zeppelin hangars to house massive conferences and exhibitions of everything from soap to machinery. Where the Metropole's Winter Gardens once were, they could almost stage the Aldershot Tattoo.

I have to admit that the Metropole's very name had aroused the frivolous in me. I felt perhaps I should have arrived in squeaky, black-and-white co-respondent shoes. In the thirties, Brighton was the Mecca for aspiring divorcees manufacturing evidence of adultery, and the Metropole was just the place for a carefully surveilled 'dirty weekend' with a girl 'friend' supplied by an agency. I peered about its lobby for lurking detectives – 'cheerful middle-aged men', according to Evelyn Waugh, 'in soft hats and heavy raincoats', with names like Blenkinsop. A.P. Herbert, in his deliciously comic novel *Holy Deadlock*, unveiled the farce behind the 'adultery' game. You didn't actually *do* anything; you merely had to be *seen in bed* with someone who was not your wife. A.P. Herbert's John Adam and his 'friend', Miss Myrtle, were typical. They went to Brighton and slept fully clothed in separate hotel bedrooms (probably at the Metropole). In the morning, Miss Myrtle, businesslike, pushed the bell for the maid and slipped into Adam's bed. 'I'm sorry to trouble you, Mr Adam, but this is where we have to be matey. Allow me.' Her tiny arms round his neck, waiting for the maid, she added, 'Take your spectacles off, I would. It looks funny.' The elderly maid, as A.P.H. wrote, had left her bed at six and walked a mile on a cold Brighton morning. A hippopotamus in the bed could scarcely have excited her. Nevertheless, well tipped, she came up trumps with her evidence before the Probate, Divorce and Admiralty Division of the High Court of Justice.

I wondered about that maid when the manager of today's Metropole showed me a recent letter from a lady who got a job there in 1925, aged fourteen. Her terms had been: 12/6d a week, including bed and board, plus two candles, ½ lb sugar, 2 oz tea and half a day off weekly. One thing was good, she wrote: 'You could walk around safely winter evenings. Not like now.'

It's a pity that the tarted-up entrance to the Metropole makes it look like a fairly high-class Leicester Square Steak House, because Brighton's hotels can still speak of a high-flying past of unusual aesthetic and social interest. The Royal Crescent is very pretty. The Grand is the handsomest: its Fitzherbert Room housed a conference of international scent-makers when I was there. Entrance apart, the Metropole retains much of the red-faced, expensive façade designed for it in 1890 by Alfred Waterhouse, architect of the South Kensington Natural History Museum. It caused a stir in its youth. Lillie Langtry liked it. Later C.B. Cochran, the impresario, called it 'very flash'. Others thought it quite hideous. An exotic highlight was the Russian and Turkish 'vapour rooms' – gone, alas, with the Winter Gardens and Miss Myrtle. The manager showed me two poignant mementoes. The first was a dinner menu for 28 August 1914 – 'Plat de Jour: Boiled Leg of Mutton, Turnips and Caper Sauce 2/6', with an orchestra to provide a selection from the new musical smash, *The Girl from Utah*, and a *pièce de genre*, *Danse Caprice* by Monti. Only four months later, war fever had enveloped the hotel's diners. The Christmas programme began with 'Land of Hope and Glory', continued with the 'Heroes of the Empire' waltz, and 'Your King and Country Needs You', led onto a gusty climax – Mrs Webster Millar giving out with 'The Boys of the Old Brigade'.

What an impression of imperial solidity Brighton must have given then! An impression the Chinese Ambassador's secretary sought to convey in a letter home about 'Pu-lai-tun on the coast of Ying south of Lun-tun'. 'It is strength and security which breeds good order, and by the possession of a Pul-lai-tun a country's might may well be judged.' Today mods and rockers still occasionally mill about and make the headlines: often the police meet them at the station, remove their bootlaces and put them quietly back on the train. Brighton, contrary to rumour, is not a violent place.

I walked along the Front in a stiff breeze, viewing an unbroken swell of dull waves and a line of beached pleasure boats. The West Pier is a sad sight; empty, grimy, it waits for a rich admirer like an ageing beauty at a ball. (*Two* 'Save-the-pier' societies are failing to raise money: surely a minor national disgrace.) The Front is still very fine. Who can fault Brunswick Square; its rich vanilla pillaring and billowing façades, its delicate balconies? But you can see the uncared for parts too – the parts that make some people wonder if conservation concerns Brighton Council quite enough. (Take a look at the urban mange near the Mermaid Hotel, for example.) Modern 'improvements' have menaced older, better buildings. The little, clean, white-faced King's Hotel and the dignified creamy Apollo are unacceptably overshadowed by the bunker-like face of the new Bedford.

Towards West Street, the wind pushed paper refuse against the legs of young skateboard riders and the Edwardian shelters with their strings of coloured lights like ping-pong balls. In one such shelter on a December night years ago, Graham Greene heard a voice from the darkness saying, 'I'm Old Moore. I live alone in a basement. I bake my own bread,' adding humbly, 'the *Almanac*, you know. I write the *Almanac*.' Now the shelters sometimes house Brighton's drunks. 'Brighton Crawling with Alcoholics, says AA', a newspaper headline read the day I arrived, and I did notice a remarkable number of Skid Row types about the town. In a pub I saw a bearded man slip money into an old derelict's claw and heard him mutter, 'Here, take this. Just don't let me catch you round the Steyne nights. Never. I'd really hate you to be in trouble, y'know. Be wise, Charlie.' Sinister words.

Down the street, teenagers find the phone booths useful for stand-up sex. And then the Odeon cinema's handy, close to the monstrous Kingswest Entertainment Centre, where the Church of God convention was singing 'Bring them in, Bring them in, Bring them in from the fields of sin'. Kingswest has no windows on the Front at all – it's a long, off-white, cracked, blind streak of Festival of Britain ugliness stuck slap in the face of Brighton. No one in authority seems to know why it was permitted, but at the time, so people said, Sir Hugh Casson somehow convinced Brighton Council that it would look very nice.

Better to turn your back on Kingswest and look at the sea, however grey. The sea, after all, is why people came here in the first place, and is a good reason for coming here now. Brighton was an unknown fishing port called Brighthelmstone until the mid-eighteenth century. Then a best-selling book by Dr Richard Russell of Lewes made it (and himself) famous – a dip in the briny (and a mouthful of it) would work wonders for young and old, he told the fashionable world. Soon the sea teemed with bodies in waterlogged garments. Bathing machines were invented – about twice the size of a sentry box; for hire: Gents 6d, Ladies 9d, attracting crowds of young men with spy-glasses. Mansions were built round the Steyne – pronounced 'steen', a flat, level place near Dr Russell's house (now the Royal Albion Hotel). The exodus from

London across the South Downs had begun. Mrs Hester Thrale took a house in West Street and enticed Dr Johnson to take a dip (he disliked the sea and Brighton intensely): Gibbon rested there after Volume 3 of *Decline and Fall*, avoiding the water, until the winter fogs drove him off.

Of course, the real miracle of Brighton's second birth was the work of the Prince Regent. He first came to rouse the spirit of the place on 7 September 1783. A ring of bells announced him, and a royal salute from the guns at the battery, one of which went off accidentally and killed the gunner, whose 'body was blown off the battery to some distance on the beach'. Never mind; soon, Brighton was alive with 'morning rides, champagne, dissipation, noise and nonsense'. *Le tout* London hurried down. In 1787 Henry Holland, who later designed Carlton House, began his sketches for the translation of a respectable farmhouse into the Royal Pavilion.

Regency Brighton flourished between 1788 and 1823. In 1784 'Prinny' had met Mrs Fitzherbert, a twice-widowed, much respected young lady with golden locks. The two of them provided the nub of the highlife there for some twenty years; a curious, sad, doomed relationship that involved a secret marriage, before the Prince Regent showed her the other side of his nature and, subsequently, the door. Good, gentle Mrs Fitzherbert outlived early happiness and later sorrow (and the Prince Regent), dying in 1837, aged eighty. In 1811 Lady Hamilton appeared, fat, broke, friendless, pensionless and homeless (despite Lord Nelson's dying plea) to earn a few shillings performing her '100 Classical Poses' – at one moment a plump Medea brandishing a dagger, at the next a portly Niobe defying heaven's fury. She died soon after, bankrupt, in Calais.

One reason for Brighton's popularity was its easy access to London. Forty-two stagecoaches ran daily, taking five and a half hours in ten stages and a mere minute and a half at each stage to change the four horses. Off on the Grand Tour, you could stay the night at the Old Ship and catch the steam packet to France.

John Nash finished the Pavilion – at last – in 1824. Some people hated it, calling it 'a pot-bellied palace' and 'a *congerie* of bulbous excrescences'. To Hazlitt, it resembled a lot of stone pumpkins and pepperboxes; Sydney Smith said the dome of St Paul's must have come down to Brighton and pupped. The Prince Regent fled to it from hostile mobs that scared him in London. Later, William IV used it too. Queen Victoria, who couldn't bear it, ordered the Brighton Council to relieve her of it for £50,000. Wounded Indian soldiers were nursed in it in World War I, lying under the bogus minarets and mock-Mogul domes in God-knows-what confusion of dreams. The present curator, John Morley, told me that £2 million are needed to clean and replace the stone. Replica minarets of fibreglass have not been a success, and something else must be tried. Much of the interior of this glorious Xanadu-in-Sussex has already been meticulously revived, and appreciative tourists crowd into its golden salons across the lawns between the Museum and the Theatre Royal.

It was nice to see the Pavilion pulling them in. But it's the ugly things that make Big Money for the council: things like the conference centre – and the Marina. The Marina is a concrete colossus. Conservationists bitterly opposed the idea of it; it would interfere with the fine sweep of white cliffs to Beachy Head, they said, and so it does. It has the delicacy of design of something built to shelter the D-Day armada from heavy bombing. But some people are proud to have the 'largest pleasure craft facility this side of Leningrad', and Mr Reg Morgan, Brighton's Town Clerk, claims it is 'the most significant development since the Royal Pavilion'. Anyway there it is by the nudist beach (quite an innovation, too, by the way, where Japanese families gather to snap England in the raw).

The spirits of Prinny and Queen Victoria are all around you. But the 1930s, too, are very close – the raunchy seaside picture postcard thirties; of C.B. Fry and Ranji; of Noël Coward, Douglas Byng and Ivor Novello; of Patrick Hamilton's beery schizoid murderer, George Harvey Bone, and Graham Greene's vicious boy, Pinkie.

Greene has written that his setting of *Brighton Rock* may in part belong to an imaginary geographical region. Much less than he thinks, I venture to say. The slums of Nelson Place are gone, it's true. And Mutton's restaurant. The racecourse gangs have long ago retired into well-heeled respectability. But one night I found Sherry's bar. 'Sherry's Music, Entertainments, Novelties – a Night Out in Another Galaxy.' An Asian in dark glasses stood guard behind a glass entrance where Pinkie the Boy had paid three bob to watch the rumba-ing partners with their bright metallic hair and little black handbags. Now teenagers formed long queues to pay £3. A twopenny ice from an Everest tricycle had been the whole extent of Pinkie's girl Ida's knowledge of luxury. Now, around Sherry's huge, dark, animated though still delightfully Edwardian dance floor, fivers and tenners kept a dozen barmen busy until early morning, while spinning spheres drenched them in showers of light. Shining rods of coloured laser stabbed down on the dancers through the smoke, and a Tannoy boomed: 'Let's say hullo to Tracey who's twenty-four today!'

Next day, in sunshine, the half-familiar vignettes multiplied. Towards the Palace Pier, black boys (not the Church of God) roller-skated past kebab shops, steak houses, fish and chip takeaways and places selling sailor hats and postcards of Charles and Di. Waiting for the miniature railway at Black Rock, a fat woman kicked off her shoes and groaned to her husband, 'I'm fooked!'

'There's always something new at the Palace Pier,' said a sign on the gate, and a punk leaned against a girl with green hair and flicked his tongue in and out of her pursed mouth as if finishing off an ice cream cornet. Hearing screams from the Ghost Train, one swarthy man said to another in Arabic, 'I'm too scared.' Of course, there were electronic games now – but 'What the Butler Saw' machines survive as well. So do the jellied eels and mussels. And, of course, Brighton rock. I remember Pinkie's Ida, with her 'plump, good-natured ageing face', comparing Brighton rock to human nature: 'Bite it all the way down,' she said, 'you'll still read Brighton. That's human nature.'

Outside again, posters advertised a new play by Simon Gray, but it might have been something with Cicely Courtneidge and Tom Walls, or Max Miller, who died here in 1963. At the Norfolk, where Greene saw a blonde with Garbo cheeks pausing to powder her nose, red neon blared 'American Bar' and someone inside played the piano. The rather sinister man I spotted back in the Metropole drinking whisky could easily have been Greene's Cubitt having a 'Scotch and splash' among the gilt chairs at the 'Pompadour Boudoir' of the 'Cosmopoli-tan Hotel'.

During my week in Brighton, Britain's riots filled the front pages. Headlines in the thirties had the Depression and Munich – and two Brighton Trunk Murders: first, a torso and two legs in a suitcase at King's Cross (unsolved; head never found); second, a complete woman in a trunk in Kemp Street (Tony Mancini, a waiter, found not guilty). Perhaps a trip to Brighton seems like going abroad simply because the past, as L.P. Hartley wrote, is another country, and Brighton's various pasts cling to it as its sugary rock sticks to one's mouth and fingers.

I was sorry to leave, and my last call was to the town's unofficial patron spirit. In the church of St John the Baptist in Kemp Town, the oldest part of Brighton, gentle, much loved Maria Fitzherbert kneels, immortalized in marble relief. Her three gold wedding rings are clearly revealed. Facing the altar, you can find her on the right-hand wall, over a bright red fire extinguisher. I look forward to seeing her again.

Duel in a Damp Shangri-la

A report from Baguio City, outside Manila, 5000-foot-high scene of the 'million dollar wing-ding' world chess championship between the Russian Grandmasters Karpov and Korchnoi.

30 JULY 1978

At five o'clock sharp, Korchnoi and Karpov enter from the wings, right and left. You almost expect them to prance downstage and, grinning, swing into a soft-shoe shuffle to an invisible orchestra. But no. Their approach to the floodlit table with the black and white pieces set out all ready under the huge 'Silence' notice is sedate. Korchnoi taller, slightly bowed, balding, like a friendly bear. Young Karpov, a wisp of a man, brown hair falling boyishly over one eyebrow, slightly flat-footed. They pay no attention to the audience, a carefully measured forty-one feet away, or to each other. They shake hands (touch hands, really) with a blind, abstracted air. It is not dislike, Korchnoi told me. It is simply that, to each of them, the other simply might not be there in that concentrated moment when they are enduring an exactly timed three minutes of photographs.

The audience whispers. The cameramen are banished. The frail man in the light blue suit (Karpov) tests his white chair, rests his elbows on the table, locks his hands over his mouth like a squirrel munching an acorn, bends his flared trouser legs under him and crosses one brown shoe over the other, pale eyes fixed on the board.

Korchnoi, in his special $15,000 green chair, unhurriedly leans forward, adjusting between finger and thumb dark glasses which have mirror surfaces to block Karpov's unnerving stare.

Silence. Then eight minutes of moves – almost a flurry. It subsides, and Korchnoi gets up and strolls away, hands in coat pockets, to an armchair on the edge of the stage. There he sits down, crosses his legs, and calmly watches Filipinos struggling to mark up the moves on two huge boards on each side of the stage.

Through binoculars, I see Karpov's smooth cheeks twitching slightly, his lips very slightly pursing and unpursing, as he ponders Korchnoi's move. He ponders it for twenty minutes. He may ponder it for twenty more. People leave for a drink.

There's no hurry. This tournament is bound to go on for three months, maybe much longer. Chess, we all know, is slow, like elephants making love. But here the slowness suddenly astounds you. Every other evening, perhaps until Christmas, these two men will enter this half-empty 1000-seat hall, and play chess from 5 p.m. to 10 p.m., until one of them has won six games.

Baguio (the 'A' is long as in Yorkshire: 'Ee bah goom') is a five-hour drive from Manila, almost 5000 feet above the sea in northern Luzon. I drove up jungle canyons full of waterfalls with taxi driver Rommy (Boy) Perez at the wheel of his 'Easy Rider' taxi. It is Baguio's rainy season. It will rain every day until October. Sometimes the little town is blanketed in dense fog. The small, friendly, Malay-like Baguio people say 'Have a nice day' in American accents. They carry umbrellas. Middle-aged men, with the features of bronzed Somerset Maughams, sip San Miguel beer ('Cerveza Negra -- Packs Vigor') in bars, wearing sweaters like Welsh miners in November.

Viktor Korchnoi is at the Pines Hotel. It has a vaguely Bavarian look and a blazing wood fire in the hall. He can be seen any day genially chatting in the cafeteria. Anatoly Karpov and his henchmen, including two Soviet Grandmasters, a taciturn manager (ex-KGB) called Viktor Baturinsky, an interpreter and a cook, live in a tower of the very modern, neo-Babylonian Terraces Plaza Hotel, isolated from the world like the Prisoner of Zenda. Everyone feels very isolated here. In an ocean of pine trees, Baguio is like a very damp Shangri-la near (say) Midhurst.

Politics got into the act early. Korchnoi sat back at the opening ceremony under President Marcos's eye and hooted with glee when the Philippines Army band played the 'Internationale' instead of the Soviet national anthem. It more than made up for the Soviet refusal to let him use the flag of his recently adopted country, Switzerland.

Then came the great yoghurt controversy. Karpov liked having yoghurt -- usually violet-coloured -- delivered to him during play. One of Korchnoi's seconds, British Grandmaster Raymond Keene, wrote a letter to Grandmaster Lothar Schmid, the West German arbiter of the match: 'It is clear that a cunningly arranged distribution of edible items to one player . . . could convey a tiny code message. A yoghurt could mean "we instruct you to offer a draw". A dish of marinated quails' eggs could mean. . . .'

Surely a joke of sorts? But careful arbiter Schmid, a young fifty, neutral as a pat of butter, said to me, 'Well, you know, there could be a code in a split banana. But no one suspected Fischer's sour fish in 1972.'

Mrs Petra Leeuwerick, Viktor Korchnoi's constant and voluble companion, is his formidable political tricks master as well. The sinister Baturinsky is Karpov's. Originally Austrian (now Dutch), Petra was seized by the Russians in the Soviet zone of Vienna after the war and given twenty years as a spy in the infamous Vorkuta labour camp. No wonder she loathes Baturinsky. She served nine years there, leading occasional revolts. She is beautiful, forty-nine, and very tough. She met Korchnoi three months after his defection in 1976. 'Our meeting was Kismet,' she says. 'The Soviets want to kill him in a mental way.'

'You say they are using microwaves?'

'Who knows? From the Soviets I expect many things – all bad! Baturinsky? He was a military prosecutor in the Stalin era. Just like the man who gave me twenty years!'

Further talk of Kismet from Michael Stean, another British Grandmaster and a Korchnoi second, a slightly built, quietly affable man, who overlapped at Trinity, Cambridge, in 1971 with the heavy-weight, ebullient Raymond Keene. Keene had met Korchnoi in Havana in 1972 and again in Geneva after his defection. Korchnoi likes having supporters around – unlike Bobby Fischer, the genius who distrusts everyone – so he recruited Keene, and Keene recruited his friend Stean.

For Stean 'it was an act of fate'. It has, he says, improved his chess enormously. After every game Keene and Stean go into a huddle with Korchnoi, trying to analyse Karpov's state of mind from his moves.

I ask Stean about chess. 'Chess,' he says, 'is a talent for pattern recognition. Compare it with music or maths. Or code breaking. Memory? Fischer's chess memory is fantastic.'

Another chess champion here told me, 'I can memorize pages of poems and so on.'

I asked how long, then, would it take him to memorize, say, 'Pippa Passes' or a Shakespeare sonnet? Half an hour?

'About that.'

'This?'

I held up the Pines cafeteria menu: *potage*, kare-kare (braised ox knuckles with eggplants, banana blossoms and beans), coffee or tea — seven lines of print.

'No, no,' he said quickly. 'You see, I'm not interested in that.'

Stean said, 'I can't remember verse. I even forget my key in my room.' He can remember telephone numbers, though.

Most people, Keene says, are at their chess peak at about thirty — his own age, as it happens. Korchnoi, forty-seven last Sunday, is, statistically speaking, over the hill. 'But Viktor is an exception to all the rules.'

Under the Baguio convention hall, when the play is on, the players' seconds, security men and journalists wander about between a restaurant, a telex room and two bars. Tangle-haired Grandmasters fling pieces about chess boards in a haze of smoke, trying to work out what the two Titans on the stage overhead are up to.

We watch in sweaty heat despite air conditioning. A German Grandmaster is booming: 'How to liberate Karpov's position, which is passive?' It sounds a tricky question.

'Viktor,' Stean is explaining to journalists over pineapple juice, 'has always played Open Defence to the Ruy Lopez. Karpov has played the Queen's Gambit Declined and one Nimzo-Indian.

An American gasps: 'Wild!'

As the five hours drag on, I tell myself to remember never to ask *anyone*: 'Who's winning?' The reply would be almost as devastating as a flamethrower.

At one point, I am slammed amicably into a chair by the excitable Filipino organizer of this million-dollar wing-ding, Florencio Campomanes, and simultaneously bear-hugged by joyful Soviet cosmonaut Vitaly Sevastyanov, a two-time Hero of the Soviet Union, two red ribbons with stars on his lapel, and a full tumbler of neat vodka in his powerful hand.

'Name? Young? Ha, you always young man.' We drink several tumblers and he tells about flying through space in Soyuz and Salyut. 'Come home,' he bawls, handing me his address. 'Star-Town, Moscow.'

Baturinsky looks in at me, narrowing eyes behind thick glasses. When I say goodbye to the heroic cosmonaut, my notes are sodden with vodka, my cheek scratched by medals.

In the Pines cafeteria Yasha Murei, a young Russian in Korchnoi's party who recently left Russia for Israel, says to Campomanes, 'Bed noos forr you.'

'Bad news?'

'You hef fetal kees.'

'My kiss is fatal, ha!'

'No, no. Baturinsky he kees you lest night. Fetal. Maybe you die.'

Next night, a choral concert on the chess stage by the Philippines Opera chorus, vigorously conducted by Tessie Agana-Santos, a handsome lady in ankle-length white. We hear an aria from a Filipino opera called *El Filibusterismo*. Korchnoi cocks a quizzical eye. Karpov is absent in his tower. Baturinsky wears a small smile.

I decide to beard Baturinsky. A deep voice answers the telephone from room 424. 'J'ai une meeting at onze heures,' he says. The R's roll like balls in a skittle alley. 'Mais possible for you at quatre heures, four hours?'

At four o'clock, over coffee, we meet. Baturinsky is short, vastly tubby, baldish, wears specs. He looks to me like an old Hollywood comedy actor of the 1950s called 'Cuddles' Zakal. Through a smooth, blond Russian interpreter in a blue blazer he says: 'This yoghurt business – rid-ee-culous! And they say we held Korchnoi back to advance our pet Karpov. Quite untrue. . . .' Baturinsky blows out thick smoke from a fat cigar.

'*Does* Karpov – so thin – need special food?'

'Some. But that's in the confidence of our cook.'

'Can I see the cook?'

Baturinsky smiles, puffing smoke. 'No. Sorry. He's not around.' He adds: 'You know, the Korchnoi people say I have no humour. But those who know me say I am a humorous man. My age? Well, I was born in 1914, but that is not the reason the Great War began.' He beams.

'I like that,' I say.

But the Korchnoi people claim his team is in touch with Moscow to receive tactical advice.

'Yes,' Baturinsky surprisingly replies.

Smoke envelops me from both sides.

'Through the cook. 007! Later, we may bring up space rockets.'

I say I'd like to see Karpov.

'I'll do my best.'

We shake hands. I say: 'And the cook?' He turns to the interpreter, puzzled: 'Engliski humour?' And he waddles away, trailing smoke.

I saw Anatoly Karpov (Tolya to his team) in the lobby at ten paces. People say he weighs only fifty kilos. He certainly looks frail. He has a romantic look. In fact he likes reading Lermontov, the Russian romantic. He has few friends. No girls. He is cautious, defensive at chess. (Korchnoi is the romantic, dare-devil counter-attacker.) Soviet Grandmaster Mikhail Tal says, 'He's a minor genius trying to become a major genius.'

'He's so cool,' Michael Stean told me. 'I played with him once in Spain in a disco, and the air-conditioning failed. Everyone sat there streaming. Karpov wasn't even sweating.'

Lucky for Karpov, because chess is, physically, immensely taxing. Players can lose two or three pounds in a game. Hence Korchnoi's jogging, and Karpov's tennis at the US Army rest camp here. Keeping up championship stamina plays havoc with daily routine. After matches Korchnoi stays up late analysing them with Stean and Keene. In the morning, he gets up at eleven o'clock. Before a match he sleeps for one hour.

His breakfast is porridge, laced with whisky or honey. Between games, he gulps Iranian caviare ('good for the brain'). He is volatile, brave ('I fear only the dentist'), and although he is a naturally heavy drinker and smoker, he gives up smoking and most drinking for the two- to three-month match. He likes Tolstoy, Solzhenitsyn, Sherlock Holmes, people and cats.

I talked to him in the cafeteria about bribery in the chess world. Ray Keene had told me of a bribe offer from a Romanian in Reykjavik in 1972.

'Let me explain you,' Korchnoi said, relaxed in an open-necked shirt. 'In Soviet Union bribes are not always in money – but something more precious. Travel, for instance. Only sportsmen can travel. I know one who threw a point to Karpov, he's with him now! I know a Yugoslav player who gave a point to a Soviet Grandmaster for $400. And a Romanian Grandmaster who lost to a Brazilian for $1000.'

Later, I heard harsh words, too, for the Soviet-dominated World Chess Federation (FIDE). I had imagined it to be as upright an institution as, say, the Athenaeum. But no.

'About as full of politics as the UN,' according to more than one international chess master.

Bribes or no bribes – and a top master winning a major tournament will get only about what a first-round loser at Wimbledon gets – 'jet-set chess' is a game for the utterly dedicated. Chess is as mind-boggling as studying the universe. There are, I am told, 10^{70} atoms in the universe. The number of possible chess games is reckoned to be 10^{120}. There is no end to chess. Stean compares it to an ever-expanding balloon. 'The surface – our knowledge – gets bigger all the time. I think of Humpty Dumpty in Lewis Carroll's *Alice Through the Looking Glass* – 'I can explain all the poems that ever were invented – and a good many that haven't been invented yet.' But Michael Stean hasn't read *Alice*, as I discover when I thrust the mock chess problem at the beginning of it under his nose, momentarily flummoxing him. There are twelve Grandmasters here, carrying on like a clutch of prima donnas in a teashop. Between games, one can hear these Einsteins of chess playing without boards over cream cakes at the Pines. And the noise of genius at play is considerable.

'Listen, what about this: P–QB4, N–KB3, P–Q4? Hey, I ordered milk.'

'Vot is he showink you?'

'Just a minute. *Moment!* P–K3, N–QB3, B–N5, how's that?'

'Kindly speak Spanish so I can understand.'

'Wait, *ja*? P–K3, P–B4 . . . that seems to work.'

'Vy you not trying N–K2?'

'Oh, what's the Russian for "forget it"?'

The names echo out cheerfully: 'Yuri . . . Yasha . . . Dragan . . . Max . . . Eugene . . . Miguel . . . Bob . . .'

Viktor Korchnoi has written a book, *Chess Is My Life*. It *is* his life. He has been a Grandmaster for twenty-four years. He defected in 1976 for chess reasons, not political ones. ('His chess in the USSR was being throttled for the sake of bringing on Karpov,' says Stean.) But now he has become, unwittingly, a (non-active) political dissident, although he has had no contact with people like Solzhenitsyn. His wife and son, Igor, blocked in the Soviet Union, are the cause. The other day, Viktor Korchnoi wrote a letter to Brezhnev. 'My family submitted a request to emigrate from the Soviet Union. . . . This request was refused. . . . Their situation is now catastrophic. They have been robbed of their means of existence. . . . I invoke your mercy, Mr Chairman.' He took this letter to the Soviet Embassy in Manila. It was returned to him unread. Yet his son is due for military call-up: five years more in the Soviet Union.

I asked Grandmasters Tal (USSR), Najdorf (Argentina), Schmid (Germany), Keene (UK) and Byrne (US) how they saw the play so far.

They agreed: level very high and controlled – a hint of pressure from Korchnoi.

'Three months more?' I asked Byrne.

'I'm afraid so.'

In the Pines cafeteria someone says: 'Viktor, the weather here is bad until October. So, thirty games of bad weather. Then seventy games of sun, no?'

Petra Leeuwerick says: 'Viktor *likes* bad weather.'

Korchnoi, in a Sussex University T-shirt, roared with laughter: 'Yes, yes.'

'What patience you must have,' I said.

Petra grinned darkly: 'If you go to the Soviet Union for ten years, you'll learn patience, too.'

Soon the clouds came down. A typhoon was approaching this hill-top Sussex-in-the-Philippines.

Getting 'Laid Back' in Hollywood

A cool look at new trends among the movie moguls.

18 FEBRUARY 1979

It's funny that the rulers of Hollywood, once so contemptuous of writers when they had many good ones, are now scrabbling around to find someone – anyone – who can put one idea, leave alone one word, behind another. If you have a single good idea to help an imagination-starved Hollywood mogul, go West. With a little luck and push you might soon find yourself, like film star Martha Dodd in Scott Fitzgerald's story, 'up to your ass in daisies'.

I returned to California the other day and made some notes on a scene that one might expect to have changed dramatically during the past ten years.

Beverly Hills. The warmth, the tropical greenness, still alert one for parakeets, cicadas, even tom-toms. The approach to one of the most satisfactory hotels in the world has hardly changed. The same noble avenue of gleaming palms leads you to the same tricky crossing of

Sunset Boulevard. Up the same short curving driveway, through shrubs and tailored grass, to where the blond young giant in shirt-sleeves takes your keys and parks your rented convertible among the Rolls and Lincoln Continentals. The pink pillars of the Beverly Hills Hotel still announce '*Bien venidos amigos*'.

At the poolside, among the oiled bodies, Curt Jurgens strolls, white suit, white shoes, white hair, with a lady friend tanned the colour of a Mars Bar. The musak plays 'Close Encounters' and 'Flying Down to Rio', and a loudspeaker summons an invisible John Travolta to the telephone. The smog has gone. 'You can see forever today,' a waiter says chirpily, dispensing towels. 'As far as Catalina Island.'

I was last in Beverly Hills in 1968: a time of all sorts of anxiety. The film colony seemed doomed. I remember Jules Stein, the dapper multi-millionaire boss of Universal Studios among his own English furniture and pictures in the mansion high above Beverly Hills: 'TV will be the death of the movies.' Sam Goldwyn, the doyen of studio heads, made his famous joke, 'Who wants to go out to see a bad movie when they can stay at home and see a bad one free on TV?'

December 1978: ten years later, in Universal's Madison Avenue panelled offices in New York, the same Jules Stein, eighty and still dapper, happily admitted that films are again big business. Universal had, in fact, just put out *The Wiz*, a black version of *The Wizard of Oz* that cost a record $35 million. In the current jargon, movie making is a 'go-project'; movie makers are 'laid back' (i.e. relaxed) again.

So, in the event, the film sun never did set on Hollywood. Still, many would say that those ten years have shaken Hollywood like a terrier shaking an exotic species of rat. Newspapers chitter excitedly about radical change in the control and pattern of movie making. In New York, someone handed me an article from Rupert Murdoch's magazine *New West*. A headline said: 'Hollywood's New Power Elite: The Baby Moguls'. The writer had discovered a zippy new generation of studio executives, directors and producers – 'young, well-educated, many from radical backgrounds' – who shared the common cultural experience of growing up in the 1960s. They had been, apparently, rebels of the New Left in that anti-war decade.

To get a fix on this film revolution I first bearded a friendly guru: Ken Tynan. Tynan has been engaged on a series of long, 'insightful' *New Yorker* magazine profiles of show business giants like Johnnie Carson, Ralph Richardson and the comedian Mel Brooks. A short twisting drive – left off Sunset Boulevard, up Foothills Drive, a hairpin climb into thick smog, brought me to the door of a sprawling bungalow poised on one of the many wooded spurs inhabited by film people. Tynan met me clutching a cool bottle of the delicate pink Californian 'champagne' called Chandon Blanc de Noirs, and murmuring cheerfully: 'You see me here as the Writer as Hermit.'

I asked him if radicals were making a better Hollywood.

'Well, we're back to the days of wine and grosses. But you really don't have to be a radical 1960s' anti-war marcher to make a quality, socially aware movie. Remember *Grapes of Wrath*? John Ford, the director, was right-wing, but just got on with it. Hollywood studios in 1979 no longer have pools of 200 marvellous stars to choose from, or the old minor gangsters and comics like Edward Everett Horton and Eric Blore.'

Tynan's wife Kathy comes in, hair wet from the small pool.

'Let's think of a memorable Hollywood movie in the last year,' Ken says.

Kathy says, '*Chinatown*?'

'Four years ago.'

'*Godfather*?'

'Five years old.'

We rack our brains some more.

'An Ingmar Bergman film . . . ?'

'That's Swedish, not Hollywood.'

We give up. No really memorable films? It doesn't say much for the baby moguls.

Presently, I walk past a guard ('What is your wish, friend?') into the Universal Studios tower that soars like a shining black mackintosh above the San Fernando Valley. I want to ask Lew Wasserman, the successor to Jules Stein and, at sixty-five, a still-active *old* movie tsar, about the baby moguls. He is tall, slim, has longish grey hair, thick specs and the warm smile of a genial college president. He says, 'What *baby* moguls? Irving Thalberg [Universal's 'boy wonder' of the 1930s] was head of production at twenty-one. Jules Stein took me in when I was twenty-three. But yes, movie makers *should* be younger. *Movie goers* are young. Ned Tanen's the man to see.'

Ned Tanen, forty-eight, with his open, tireless look, as much resembles an ogre mogul like Louis B. Mayer, with his tight mouth, as Rin Tin Tin, the Wonder Dog, resembles Godzilla. But he is no less forthright. 'There's nothing new in the movie game. It's about making money like any other business. I can't think of anything we want to make less than *radical* movies. Social significance almost killed off French and Italian films.'

I remembered another of old Sam Goldwyn's precepts: 'If you want to send a message, hire Western Union!'

Tanen, thank heaven, seems equally unlike the hideously brash young executives in other American industries who delight in their 'upward mobility', the ones with hard eyes and slick, brass-buttoned blazers and blow-dried hair. The ones who use phrases like 'Hitting the old Boozola, ha, ha?' The ones obsessed with 'Numero Uno'.

A new jargon, however, is common to all today's American executives. 'Laid back', of course, means 'cool': 'the bottom line' means 'the final outcome' (of a deal); people no longer confer, they 'take a meeting'. If you are a nice, normal 'super-achiever' you take meetings as often as you take your status-packed Glenlivet-on-the-rocks: regularly and with brio. The rat who tells you you're strictly 'off the wall' means you're a nut-case. It's wise to 'make nice' and show that you really have 'white sugar in your veins' – i.e. are sensitive. If not, you may find yourself 'going down the tubes'. In super-achiever land even saying goodbye is an esoteric ritual. Try it. Raise an outward-turned palm to breast height; twitch up one corner of your mouth about the width of a fingernail; bend your eyebrows into a half-pained, half-quizzical posture – and let drop one word, as cool and expressionless as a sea pebble: 'Enjoy!' That's enough. Now turn on your two-inch heel and saunter away.

1968 was a time when stars gave parties to show their own movies in their own homes. They liked the flattering comments of their guests ('For Chrissake, Kirk, how in hell did you drag that goddam horse up that mountainside with the boulders falling...?'). Racketeering killed such innocent fun. 'The studios decreed there was too much copying of films. They were showing up in the Far and Middle East or some place,' was the explanation given to me by Irving Paul 'Swifty' Lazar, probably America's most successful literary agent. Lazar, diminutive, perky as a budgerigar in his South Beverly Drive office, favours a yellow baseball cap, a pink shirt and green trousers. Bald and seventyish, he looks, someone has said, like a very expensive beach toy. Lazar's handling of Richard Nixon, Irwin Shaw, Lauren Bacall and many others has bequeathed him a house that, in the words of Scott Fitzgerald, 'looks built for great emotional moments' and from which you can look down like God from the pool to the Pacific Ocean.

When I ask him about 'radical' movies in 1979, Lazar snaps,

'Radical? No, that's bullshit. They're rather conservative. A real bore is all those remakes. I believe Tanen wants to redo *Gone with the Wind*. That's in terrible taste. More than that, it's peculiar.' As for the baby moguls – 'well, they've got a hell of a lot of energy. College educations. Better manners, maybe. That's all.'

Unexpectedly, the 'hot' young man who could be the film world's 'Swifty' Lazar of AD 2000 agrees with that. Agent Michael Black – a thirty-year-old 'workaholic' – pooh-poohs reports of an austere new life. 'Pur-lees! My friends *do* have BMWs and Porsches. I have friends in *grand* houses. Of course, a few may have a bug up their ass about austerity.' Black has a sun-fed, sleek intensity. He represents George Segal, Fred Astaire, Tony Perkins, Michael York. One imagines he represents them twenty-six unsleeping hours out of twenty-four. Was *he* out protesting in the 1960s? A grin: 'Well, if there was a peace demo and the sun was out. . . . But look, Ned Tanen – no baby, right? – Tanen is as hip to what's going on in the country as anyone.'

But there is one aspect of Hollywood in 1979 that is different: the appalling, unprecedented scarcity of good writers. In the 'bad' old days famous writers – Faulkner, Huxley, Robert Benchley, Scott Fitzgerald – sat around like highly paid, although much despised, battery hens. Scott Fitzgerald had to plead with a contemptuous producer, 'I'm a good writer – really I am.' Irving Thalberg kept several writers working, unknown to one another, on the same screenplay. Recalling that time, Ken Tynan says: 'You had no liberty to write, but you got four films in a year, and although three were crap, one was probably a film to remember. Now it takes two years even to cast a Hollywood film.'

It's odd that a paucity of good movies and a dearth of new writers coincides with superlative acting ability. English director Tony Richardson says, 'This is a great age of American actors.' He rattled off a list of today's most 'bankable' stars: 'Women – Barbra Streisand, Liza Minnelli, Diane Keaton, Jane Fonda. Men – Redford, Travolta, Pacino, Hoffman, Beatty – probably Clint Eastwood – oh, yes, Burt Reynolds, Jack Nicholson – Brando when he's not directing himself, Woody Allen, Newman, de Niro. Then think of George C. Scott. The discipline, the range!'

I returned at last to the dark, shimmering tower at Universal City. There, on a high floor over the straggling wooded Universal lot and the Sheraton Hotel, I found a genuine baby mogul, Thom Mount, twenty-nine, the only baby mogul, everyone said, with *real* power. Baggy jeans, Pancho Villa moustache, dark check open shirt, warm smile, in that *New West* article Mount had been quoted: 'One of the major problems here is that people who run studios have absolutely no social responsibility.' Strong words. True or false? Universal had, after all, *allowed* Mount to make 'socially aware' *Blue Collar*, and in spite of critical acclaim it had flopped.

So crusading does go on – spasmodically. Obviously *plus ça change* . . . Obviously, too, the Tanens and Mounts are not the sort of illiterate mocked by Evelyn Waugh, who paid secretaries – 'pseudonannies' – to feed them classical novels, the Book of the Month, anything, and, like spoiled children shouted at intervals, 'Bags I. Daddy buy that.'

The young moguls are tied, of course, by what Thom Mount calls 'the straitjacket of this business – that if you don't make money you had better leave it'. As 'old' mogul David O. Selznick said, 'If you are primarily concerned with something called personal artistic integrity, you should get yourself a paintbrush or a typewriter.'

On the other hand, public taste is more sophisticated, techniques have moved on startlingly, censorship is minimal. Today, no one can say 'the only thing producers produce is relatives' – nepotism ('the son-in-law also rises') is out.

So we come back to the question that baffled the Tynans and myself that smoggy morning – 'Why have so few recent movies stormed and occupied the mind for ever?' – like the *Gone with the Wind* of Clark Gable and Vivien Leigh? Why should people ever be obliged even to contemplate a remake of *Gone with the Wind*?

Leaving Thom Mount, I descend, as darkness falls, to the Universal Tower's lobby. An elderly doorman calls for a taxi for me. People stream out past a determined-looking bronze bust of Jules Stein. Soon the whole building is empty except for me in the vast, towering lobby and the grizzled doorman at his desk. As I pace about, waiting, the doorman puts down his newspaper. To my surprise he begins to address me like a character in Chekhov: 'What's life but waiting? You're born to die, know what I mean? I retired five years ago from my business. What happened? I retire; my wife dies. Is it fair? I don't know the size of my own underwear. I can't boil an egg. What's a man to do? Start again at sixty-five? So I take this Mickey Mouse job to keep from boredom. From sitting at home, see, measuring my underwear.'

'That's pretty deep,' I say.

The taxi passes the Goldwyn Studios where ten years ago I arrived an hour late for lunch with the bald, eighty-four-year-old mogul. I recall Sam Goldwyn's strange, piping, friendly voice saying: 'You haven't asked me what my second favourite movie was.'

'What was it, Mr Goldwyn?'

'I'm glad you asked that question. It was *Withering Heights*. We had a great actor in it – Oliver somebody. . . .'

Next day, on the way to the airport, I leave the pink pillars of the Beverly Hills Hotel with their farewell inscription, '*Vaya con Dios*'. Presently, the tropical shrubs, the avenues of silver-stemmed palms give way to the tangled horror of the freeways.

It seems good that the Never-Never Land of Hollywood–Beverly Hills survives more or less intact. It has made history. It is – as Samuel Goldwyn once said, introducing Jackie Coogan's mother – 'The goose that laid the golden egg.'

The Million-dollar Suburb

It costs between $1 million and $2 million for a three-bedroomed villa in Beverly Hills. And, they say, you don't meet your neighbours unless there's an accident in the street.

BEVERLY HILLS, 1981

'No smog today. Who can say Beverly Hills isn't beautiful?' I stood near the pool on the small terrace of the house of the screen-writer George Axelrod, high on Coldwater Canyon. It was Christmas, but the sun gave us a good 88 degrees. The ridge of Mulholland Drive wriggled through a line of cypresses behind something like the bridge of a liner. 'Charlton Heston's house,' George said. 'For sale, I think.' A silver jet plane rose in the clear sunlight over the San Fernando Valley and then swung back over Studio City and Univeral Studios. 'At night you hear nothing but coyotes and raccoons up here.'

Later, I drove with George down the canyons to the southern edge of Beverly Hills, the city within the City (strictly, the County) of Los Angeles. Bungalows of the kind you might find in, say, Sunningdale, with tangled gardens and small garages, hugged steep, serpentine roads. Further down, a scraggy piece of bare ground and a ridge of tropical trees which hid part of a palace. 'Harold Lloyd's old place,' George said. 'I think an Arab's bought it.' A yellow awning on a spur: 'John Barrymore's hideaway. And there's where John Gilbert had a torrid affair with Garbo.'

'The man with the squeaky voice?'

'Right. The revisionist historians say that's not true.'

'A highly flammable place this,' George said as we came to exotic trees and flowering shrubs, expensive wrought iron, white villas. George reeled off the residents' names: 'Peggy Lee there. Danny Kaye. Jack Lemmon. Fred Astaire.' Rolls-Royces poked their noses out of circular driveways (Mr Lemmon was driving a sporty, low-slung 1950s' MG).

Across Sunset Boulevard the land levels out. Down Beverly Drive you pass between neat lawns and two sorts of palm tree. Beyond Santa Monica Boulevard you enter the chic shopping area: Bally, Cartier, Gucci, Tiffany, St Laurent – Rive Gauche. Then comes the drabness of Cienega and Olympic Boulevards; the tropical trimness of Beverly Hills melts into the mean sprawl of Los Angeles. We had driven through Beverly Hills from top to bottom; from bare hilltops to asphalt jungle. Or – to put it into the language of the studios – from yesterday into today.

To take yesterday first. The last Red Indians to raid Beverly Hills were shot dead in 1852 and lie buried under a walnut tree in Benedict Canyon not far from the present site of the Beverly Hills Women's Club. Recorded history of the 'golden ghetto' seems to start in 1769 with the purchase of the region by Spanish colonists and missionaries from Mexico, who paid the local Indians beads and tobacco worth even less than the $24 in beads the Algonquin Indians were paid for Manhattan. Soon, Maria Rita Valdez established a 4500-acre ranch at the Rodeo de las Aquas, the Gathering of the Waters, where the winter streams came together at the bottom of what are now Coldwater and Benedict Canyons. The arrival of the United States Cavalry in 1848 secured California for the Union. American ranchers replaced Spanish ones and hopefully planted wheat, lima beans and barley across the plain. A railroad pushed west to Santa Monica. Then oil prospectors came and with them the man who might well be called the maker of the Golden West – Burton E. Green, the boss of the Rodeo Land and Water Company – who put $670,000 into Maria Rita's old ranch and began to turn it into his dream city.

Burton Green's daughter still lives in Bel Air, an ultra-plush district bordering Beverly Hills, and I found her a lively source of information about her father. Petite, humorous, she sat in an elaborate Italianate villa, with red curtains and mounds of red cushions, wearing a red calf-length dress, stroking a fluffy St Bernard.

'My father,' she said, 'wanted wide streets, like Paris, with trees and curved streets. He brought out a French architect who had designed part of Washington DC. A beautiful city, that's what he wanted. It was a wilderness, then, just bean fields. We children used to ride horses down a dusty bridle path where Sunset Boulevard is now.'

Between marble pillars, over her shoulder, I could see a gleam of the Pacific Ocean. 'It was kind of lonely here in the early days', she said. 'Only the Mexican kids in the fields to play with.' I asked Dolly Green where the name Beverly Hills came from. 'Well, my father was rather modest in some ways. They said, "Call the new city Burton City or something." But he said no. And one day, driving through Massachusetts, he came by chance to a town called Beverly and said, "That's a beautiful name."'

I drove from Dolly Green's to the Beverly Hills Hotel, built in 1912 when the population of Beverly Hills was about 500. Bright sunshine beat down on the avenue of palms her father had planted. By 1919 the film industry that was to make Burton Green's city the most luxurious dormitory town in the world was well established. And then a turning point occurred: Gladys Mary Smith of Toronto (better known as Mary Pickford) and Douglas Fairbanks built their mansion, Pickfair, and put in Beverly Hills's first swimming pool. It was as if someone had pulled a switch. From the new studios a mile or two down the Sunset bridle path came Gloria Swanson, Chaplin, Will Rogers, actors, producers, writers, studio technicians. Someone wrote a popular song: 'I'm on my way – here's my beret – I'm on my way to Holl-ee-wood!'

By 1924 the population was up to 5000. Between then and 1930 it was to grow 2486 per cent. Old photographs show avenues curving up to only a few isolated villas near the newly built Beverly Hills Hotel; beyond the villas the canyons are still green, dry and empty. The plain was all terraced agricultural land, avocado and citrus plantations; and the tentative lines of Burton Green's baby palms. Its innocent look didn't last long. As Scott Fitzgerald said, Beverly Hills soon became 'a very fancy lot of pastry'. Like the discarded star Martha Dodd in his novel *The Last Tycoon* (I have fondly quoted her before), many young hard-working people could say, 'I had a beautiful place . . . 30 acres, with a miniature golf course and a pool and a gorgeous view. All spring I was up to my ass in daisies.'

Even so, Beverly Hills remained a rather village-like city up to a decade after World War II. 'It smelled of orange and eucalyptus, not smog,' says Ivan Moffat, an English screen-writer who went there in 1945. 'There was ease and affluence, because the movies were at their most buoyant up till 1949, before television.' The feeling of living in a corporation town was enhanced by its isolation. In those days the eleven hours or more it took to fly to New York made you think twice before travelling. You commuted to work like any other worker. In *The Last Tycoon* someone says, 'My father was in the picture business as another man might be in cotton and steel.'

Hard work, of course, did not exclude parties. Dolly Green again: 'Nobody sat down to dinner under fifty people. Cole used to sing his songs at the piano. Of course, sometimes people overdid things. Dear Marion Davis had a drink problem. One night, she was a little woozy, you know, so I offered her a glass of water. "Hey," she snapped, "I'm thirsty, not dirty." Oh, we had Clark Gable, Jack Warner and Louis B. Mayer, Irene Dunne and Loretta Young . . . Garbo, of course. It was unreal and showy, but great fun.'

What is it like today? Who lives in Beverly Hills in 1981? In the 'Spanish baroque' City Hall erected in 1931, young Mayor Edward Brown told me that 31,200 people slept in the 5.7 square miles of Beverly Hills; another 120,000 came in to work there in the daytime. In recent years many Iranians had moved in.

Ken Peters of the Unified School District told me: 'Farsi [the Iranian language] has become an important concern. Some of the Iranian kids can't speak English at all. Substantial numbers of Hebrew-speaking Israelis have moved in, too, but few Arabs.'

There are many more businessmen and professional men living in Beverly Hills than formerly. In a scathing put-down of the 'home of the stars', a Los Angeles writer recently wrote that the film stars are moving out, 'happy to leave the tinsel to affluent doctors, shrinks, dentists, lawyers, promoters'. But there seem to be a good many stars left, and many others are only a stone's throw away in neighbouring bits of 'Hollywood', in Bel Air, Brentwood, Malibu or Santa Monica.

Ed Kreins, the bulky, affable City Manager, lists the little city's proud possessions: one police station, three fire stations, two recreation centres, a senior citizen's centre, a public library, six parks, three playgrounds, 28,000 trees. Kreins and Police Chief Lee Tracy admit that the crime rate goes up, but less than it does in the rest of Los Angeles. They say that relations between the public and the 235-strong police force are 'outstanding'. Policemen here, said Kreins, will be the highest paid in LA County. I was assured that the emergency response time – the time it takes for a patrol car to respond to your home's alarm signal – averages three to four minutes. 'Sixty-eight per cent of our robberies,' he said, 'are cleared up against only 18 per cent nationwide.' Clearly the inhabitants of Beverly Hills have an elite police department.

There is an endlessly repeated story – I have heard it many times stated as fact – that no one is allowed to *walk* in Beverly Hills. The police are liable, the story goes, to pick you up for loitering with intent. But the police deny this. You can walk, they say, but, of course, if you *look* suspicious you may be checked up on. I had two major occasions to walk suspiciously, and I wasn't stopped either time. On Christmas Eve I walked from the Beverly Hills Hotel for drinks with the actor James Stewart, his wife Gloria and a daughter, Kelly, who studies gorilla behaviour at Cambridge University. It was nearly sundown. I strolled along Sunset Boulevard for quite a way. In the Stewarts' street, unfenced lawns run like green baize from houses built shoulder to shoulder as in any English suburb. A cat chased a squirrel across a lawn and up a cedar tree. A Mexican gardener picked up a lawn sprinkler and disappeared with it into a garage. Otherwise I was alone, turning up the crazy paving to the Stewarts' warm, homely, brick house, where a Stewart tartan ribbon hung on the door for Christmas. The second time, invited one night to a party at director Vincent Minnelli's I walked up a dark driveway to a tall, lighted window and a massive door. A bell clanged deep in the house. A Korean opened the door a crack and peered at me over the chain.

'Mr Vincent Minnelli's house?' I asked. The Korean slammed the door in my face.

Wrong house. Unsavaged by guard dogs, I beat it round the corner and found another doorway. A tall man with the heavy shoulders and trim hips of a night-club bouncer was silhouetted menacingly against the light. I tensed myself for another slam or a shove in the chest, but a deep friendly voice said, 'This is Vincent's house. Come along in.' He put out a hand, 'I'm Cesar Romero. Happy Christmas.' I was glad to disprove a famous myth. You *can* walk, even at night, in Beverly Hills.

'It's our concern to preserve the unique, garden-like character of Beverly Hills,' Mayor Brown said. So apartment blocks are restricted to three storeys. In the business section, between Santa Monica Boulevard and Wilshire, there is one outstanding eyesore – a black glass monstrosity (a bank), but the Mayor says such things cannot be repeated. Beverly Hills will remain an oasis in the high-rise sprawl of LA.

An expensive oasis. If you want to live there you'll need about $1 million for a house the size of a three-bedroomed villa in, say, Woking or Chepstow. Two years ago I saw on my TV set in the Beverly Hills Hotel the face of a young man called Marty Trugman, self-styled 'real estate superstar'. I found him, looking like Warren Beatty, in his Santa Monica Boulevard office, gold chains round his neck and a claret-coloured shirt open at the neck. Musak swirled lightly round his mock antique mirror and antique books, as he went through his prospectus with me.

'The Feeling of Bangkok or Kuala Lumpur' (I read). 'Lush foliage and glass-panelled entrance . . . three bedrooms, projection room. . . . Every room has a fireplace. From every room you walk into a garden. Pool . . . sauna . . . jacuzzi . . . electric gates. $12,500 a month.'

A jacuzzi?

'A teeny little pool; like a bathtub of wood, very hot water and whirlpool.' How many people fit into one?

'Anything from two to twenty, I guess.'

I read on: 'A Must-see! Minutes from the Beverly Hills Hotel . . . Two-storey Spanish hacienda . . . cathedral ceilings . . . quality of a by-gone era. $1,150,000.' A tennis court would add $100,000 to $500,000.

This year, Marty Trugman talked of the influx of Iranians and rising prices. 'No way anything under $1 million,' he said. 'I have a house on the market for $6,760,000. A lot of Canadian money is coming in here. Also British, since Mrs Thatcher said you could send out as much as you wanted.'

I asked to see the $6,760,000 house and he delegated a girl as beautiful as one of Charlie's Angels to drive me there. As the open 1980 convertible floated through the residential area between Santa Monica and Sunset Boulevards, the exotic, hybrid homes stared back at us like rare creatures in a rich eccentric's zoo: here a wing of Hampton Court coupled with the Taj Mahal; there, the hunting lodge of Mayerling mated with a miniature Versailles. Trugman's girl laughed when I pointed at something Tudorish and said, 'Anne Hathaway's garage?'

The iron gates to the $6,760,000 house opened when the girl spoke a password into a voice box. We inspected an acre of property and 9000 square feet of house: five bedrooms (each one had a 'panic-button' alarm), eleven baths, sauna, a 'champion-sized' tennis court; a sand-pebbled pool with waterfall; a ballet room, a barber's shop and four different security systems. Underneath everything else – a 'period' nuclear bomb shelter, with panelling and a Hollywood-medieval wrought-iron chandelier hanging from the ceiling. Period: early Errol Flynn, I guessed. I opened a cupboard and found tins – no, *canisters* – of dehydrated stew and vegetables.

Marty Trugman's angel said, 'Julie Andrews lives next door; that raises the value.' And added, winningly, 'You could have this place for $4 million – cash.'

There are plenty of people eager to run Beverly Hills down. Film director William Friedkin (*The French Connection, Cruising*) is quoted as saying, 'You make a lot of money, you buy a house in Beverly Hills, and the only guys you ever see are your butler and your cook and the guy who drives you to the studio. You never touch a dog in the street or talk to a guy in a bar or on a subway or know what the hell he wants, and that's why a lot of guys don't know who their audiences are.'

James Stewart and his daughter confirmed this, saying that they hardly ever met their immediate neighbours 'unless there's a traffic accident in our street' – but, by the way, I don't think they particularly want to. These days, in any case, Hollywood people are constantly breaking the old isolation by jetting to New York, Hawaii, Europe and Asia. Criticism of the vulgarity and tastelessness of many rich people is reasonable comment, no doubt.

It is not difficult to resent the boastful braying of the 'upwardly mobile' executives who pack the Polo Lounge of the Beverly Hills Hotel every noon and evening, their skin wrinkled from jacuzzi over-exposure, blow-dried hair, designer clothes. But in comparison to businessmen, movie stars are decorous.

When I first saw Beverly Hills in 1963, the downtown area was much more relaxed. Today's common hazards, kidnappings and muggings, were hardly considered; you bumped into Groucho Marx, Jack Lemmon, Kirk Douglas and other resident stars in the streets and drugstores. Helen Chaplin, in charge of publicity in the other grand hotel of Beverly Hills, the Beverly Wilshire, agrees with this: 'I used to sit in a store and I'd see Barbara Stanwyck, Gracie Allen, Gary Cooper buying little things, candy and such. All that's gone. Now they go shopping in Santa Monica. They'd be too bothered by autograph hunters here.'

Nowadays rich, jostling tourists come from miles around to stock their wardrobes from Gucci or Ted Lapidus. More than a little bit of 'soul' has vanished in the last decade. More basically, Beverly Hills is no 'gourmet's ghetto'. About the expensive catering services the stars hire to feed their guests, Gore Vidal groans, 'You only have to see the old familiar catering woman's face for the twentieth time to positively smell that old, familiar and sickening guinea hen and wild rice, or whatever oriental thing it is they dish up.' And Sir Ralph Richardson's remark to Kenneth Tynan about wine in America gains added force in Beverly Hills – 'It's been my experience that most of the wine served is cat's urine disguised in French labels.' I have to report that much of the Californian wine is no better.

Some traditional Hollywood restaurants remain. A famous film stars' Beverly Hills restaurant, the Brown Derby still stands ('a languid restaurant,' Scott Fitzgerald said, 'patronized for its food by clients who always look as if they'd like to lie down,' and where, incidentally, Jack Benny confided to me that the two comics he was most influenced by were Britain's Will Hay and Sid Field). It has a salad famous since the days of Burton Green. The best hamburgers I've ever had came my way in the Beverly Wilshire. And Chasen's, another old and good restaurant, still displays a portrait of W.C. Fields dressed as Queen Victoria. (Of its excellent orange-yellow chilli con carne the humorous writer Harry Kurnitz once observed to director Billy Wilder, 'I like to eat it, but I certainly wouldn't like to step in it').

Beverly Hills is a sort of costly Fantasyland. By now years of sensation, scandal and myth have solidified like a Disney mask round the face of the city that Burton Green built. You can view it as you might an old-time movie queen – a Theda Bara or a Garbo: with affection and awe, or as a tasteless, tarted-up unreality. But it is comfortable. It serves a purpose: it houses rich people who commute.

I asked Dolly Green what went through her mind when she drove down Sunset under the palms where once she had cantered along a dusty bridlepath. 'Oh,' she laughed, 'I think of my father, and how the city looks – how beautiful. Just as he wanted it.'

Tuticorin, the Spirit of the Seas

I first sailed into the south Indian port of Tuticorin in 1980 aboard one of the great commercial sailing vessels still built there. Enchanted by the place, I vowed to return.

9 SEPTEMBER 1983

In the gloom of his Dickensian office, the Tamil shipping manager handed me a cable: '42 saled 22/6,' it said. I thanked him and stepped out into Beach Road. The heat of south India struck me as if someone had opened a furnace door.

'So Hentry here tomorrow,' said Raju, Hentry's brother-in-law: short, black, wagging his head Tamil-fashion. 'If the wind will be orderly.'

In the bay, strong westerly gusts lashed up water the colour of milk chocolate. It looked disorderly enough to blow any Indian three-masted sailing vessel the 150 miles east back to Sri Lanka. Alongside the wharves of Tuticorin's Old Port, the great black masts of the sister ships of No. 42 (alias the *Jacklyne*, whose departure from Colombo with Hentry aboard the cable had signalled to her owner) rose like fleshless fingers testing the weather.

Santa Cruz, Silver Cloud, Our Lady of Good Health, Philip Machado, Little Flower and many more, they lay at rest, lazily rubbing fenders, sails lowered and stowed. Their crews were busy chipping paint or caulking decks. In the sun, their crosses and amulets glinted on damp, black chests.

I saw the ships with relief. In the three years I had been away, they might have been done away with. But in India, thank God, things don't rudely disappear as they do in the West. In fact, Tuticorin hadn't changed at all since the day I had arrived there in one of the sailing vessels called *tonis* for which the port had been famous since before the Spaniards built the Armada. It is a small place, about the size of (say) Lyme Regis, or smaller. There are wharves for the ships and a battered main street, Beach Road, and behind that a shallow network of shabbily dignified houses in narrow lanes. For the rest, it is a noisy clutter of Hindu temples, Catholic churches, schools, houses, and a hundred pungent stores selling most things from incense and mangoes to saris and axle grease. The alleys furthest from the sea fray out unobtrusively into a flat and dusty plain. After that, the hills and forests of south India prevail.

Pliny talked of Tuticorin; Marco Polo called it 'noble'. For centuries, it was famous as a pearl- and conch-fishing centre as well as a port. In Raj times, the British expanded it into quite an important railhead, a link with Ceylon across the water.

I came here by chance. I was ship-hopping from Athens to Canton for a book, *Slow Boats to China*, and in Colombo harbour I saw a couple of these amazing sailing boats. One of them sailed me to Tuticorin (I was heading towards India), and at once I was enchanted with this place of courteous seafarers and their humble dwellings like Peggotty's in *David Copperfield*; by its atmosphere of another age. I spent a few days here and vowed to return.

Three years ago I had been lucky to be allowed to sail at all. *Tonis* have no accommodation for passengers; in sun and storm the crew sleeps on deck. Built exclusively by and for Tuticorin shipowners, the *tonis* have no engines either. My *toni* had weighed a mere 250 tons (they go up to 450 tons), but her mainmast was a soaring black tree supporting a yard curved like a scimitar that seemed to scrape the sky at one end and the sea at the other. She had only two masts, but with booms out she flew along under thirteen pieces of sail. And then she was beautiful.

In those days, Hentry had been one of her crew of eleven, earning about £30 for a ten-day round voyage to Colombo. A hard and irregular living; if the weather is very bad indeed, or cargoes are slow, there is no work. He had started sailing at the age of thirteen, like our two boy cooks, small Victorian chimney sweeps who in high seas produced curried fish, rice and coffee from a dark hole in the deck near the stern where two men wrestled with a 10-foot steering boom.

Leaving Colombo we had been becalmed, and some of the crew had had to dive into the harbour, carrying rope to the decks of moored ships from which they hauled the *toni* through the water inches at a time. Hentry was one of these divers. Short, slim and muscular, he paused only to place between his teeth the chain round his neck which carried the portrait of Vailaikanni, Our Lady of Good Health. The seamen of Tuticorin are devout Catholics.

In the Indian Ocean, the crew had swung about the rigging like miniature Tarzans and more and more sails filled in the wind. At sunset, every man repaired to the stern and squatted behind the captain, a solemn, youngish man moustached like a corsair, while he led them through a litany – twenty minutes of hymns and responses – as the great masts groaned, the deck rolled and dipped, and the sails thundered under the varying pressures of the wind:

'I fly unto thee, thou Virgin of Virgins, my mother.'

The cavern of the hold gave you an idea of what Drake's or Anson's men had been through. It was hot, damp and smelly. God was down there, too. Where the timbers arched together in the bows, a light flickered. Candles shone on the pale, waxen faces of a crowned Virgin, Jesus and St Anthony. The crew believed something terrible would happen if the candles went out.

Arriving at Tuticorin, I had walked to a doss house in the bazaar. But the crew took me over like a trophy of their voyage. Hentry and his brother, Romans, led me to their little dilapidated house, showed me churches like marzipan cakes, proudly dragged me before the 'kings' of Tuticorin, the shipowners and merchants whose venerable offices opened on to the potholes of Beach Road near the port. And here I had met the Great Man – the Chevalier Machado, papal knight, *toni*-owner, salt exporter, guardian of the Church.

Tuticorin brings two things to my mind: love, and Captain Cook. Cook, because, although I have never been there, I have a notion that his first workplace, Whitby in Yorkshire, home of the famous sailing colliers, was once very similar to this little place in India – in spirit, of course, not in climate. In Whitby, too, ships were built and sailed by a population linked by life and death to the sea. As for love, that word, like graffiti, is written everywhere – 'God is Love' – in churches, houses, offices. And the people believe in it. When I tried to pay for my voyage, the shipowner had smiled and said, 'Mr Young, I don't want your money, I want your love. Love is better than money. It is a pleasure to have you on my ship.'

This time, in 1983, I arrived by train, sixteen hours from Madras. Warned by my letter, Raju, his wife and Romans met me at Tuticorin station, chirruping happily in Tamil and English. It was too hot now for the doss house, so we bounced in an old taxi to a crumbling hotel instead. Here, a friendly room 'boy', fortyish with a waterfall moustache and thick glasses, warned me of the four or five electricity failures a day, and insisted I take his old copy of *Woman's Home Journal* with a cover picture of Lady Di and a story about Ava Gardner's love affair with Frank Sinatra ('It never ended'). He brought me palm juice, too, in an 'Old Monk' rum bottle (it tasted like chestnuts liquefied in sugar), warning me not to take tea after it. 'Juice and tea are all mangling up in the stomach, and this is leading swiftly to dysentery.'

I visited first a friend who speaks the best English in Tuticorin. Winston Corera is about thirty-two, married to the Chevalier Machado's daughter, and has a shipping agency in Beach Road near his father-in-law's office. To get there my taxi, honking like a demented goose, zigzagged skilfully between half-naked Tamils, stray donkeys, bicycles, rickshaws and – biggest obstacle of all – huge creaking carts drawn by ivory-coloured oxen with soft, long-lashed eyes and graceful horns that curved up like praying arms. A smell, not unpleasant, of cow dung, sandalwood, sweat, spices and petrol rose around us. Big Tamil eyes peered and fine white teeth flashed through the windows. A foreigner is a novelty in Tuticorin.

Beach Road has a nineteenth-century air about it; it has seen better days. Its cobbles have given way to potholed asphalt, and sand blown from the bay, and numerous straying goats. At one end is the Collector's office, where through arched windows you see the clerks thoughtfully picking their noses over pyramids of yellowing files; then the Sancta Fatima school; the prim Victorian façade of a bank; a ships' chandler; the Raj Café (vegetarian); and the three-storeyed edifice in which the Chevalier Machado receives the world. Beyond Beach Road, the region's valuable salt pans stretch away like paddy fields under snow.

I climbed the wooden stair to Winston Corera's office and found myself half blinded by pungent smoke. Was the place ablaze? No, it was a dense cloud of incense that almost obscured the 'Lloyd's Agency' plaque, the motto 'God is Love', and a noticeboard announcing, 'MV *Ava Minti* from Calcutta to Old Port. Discharge of Railway Coal, 4500 metric tons.' Evidently people liked it simply for its pleasant smell.

A roomful of clerks peered at me through the incense, and Winston's cheerful dark face showed over a pair of brass-hinged swing doors, like tavern doors in a Wild West saloon. 'Welcome! Come in!' He pulled up one of those beautifully made dark wood chairs India still produces. 'Three years, is it? Well, well!' A boy brought fresh lime juice, water and salt – not sugar – the most refreshing drink of the East.

Corera is a typically Portuguese Tuticorin name. The most common is Fernando, then come Machado, Gomez, Perez, Vaiz. The family name of my friends Nazarene and Daisy, and their sons Hentry, Romans and Johnson, and their daughter Rani (married to Raju), is Rodrigo. All these names date from the time of the conversion just before St Francis Xavier – who is buried in Goa – came here in 1544.

Winston (named after Churchill) had told me that there is little to know of the social life of Tuticorin. Merchants, he said, work until eleven at night; some then gamble till dawn. Art-deco cinemas showed mostly Tamil films, but occasionally an ageing American one (*Papillon* was on now).

Alcohol is sold in seedy back-alley toddy shops; you buy beer at the grocer's. But the shipping community, intensely Catholic, shuns toddy shops. Hentry and Raju cannot afford beer. They are content with the cinemas and the various and frequent festivals, often religious, that fill the dusty lanes with flower-decked floats and gaudy statues and transform them into thrilling whirls of light and colour and a joyous hubbub into which they rush ecstatically, shouldering garlanded plinths bearing the Virgin Mary or St Anthony and the heavy replicas of sailing ships paraded on days hallowed by seafarers.

On such exhilarating days the Bishop of Tuticorin and the Chevalier Machado are driven around standing side by side in a jeep – the Chevalier beaming, dignified, in full knightly fig, high-collared, laced and brass-buttoned, plume-hatted, with his sword drawn as befits the Pope's guardian of the Church of Tuticorin. On these days, the soul of Tuticorin is exposed.

I found the Chevalier, stout and genial as ever, in his dim, high-ceilinged sanctum behind another pair of swing doors. He sat under pictures of Nehru and Gandhi and a head of Christ. His own head is large and fleshy, his lips thick, his hair black, and he is in his sixties. He reminded me of a darker version of Charles Laughton. He remembered my unusual arrival by sea. As the port's biggest shipowner, he was happy to assure me that the *tonis* were not a dying breed.

'Let me tell you what-is-what,' he boomed, beaming under thick, black, mobile eyebrows. 'They try to put engines into *tonis* – but they don't work at all well. Boats' timbers are too *heavy*. Engines are too *weak*. You get awful *vibrations*. Planks *give*: caulking *goes*. Water leaks in. No good!'

Couldn't steamers do the job quicker?

'Aaah! Why not? You want the what-is-what?' His eyebrows rose and fell rhythmically like caterpillars on springs. He meant, you want the real truth? 'Steamers are too *expensive*. Suppose they go to

Colombo — they have to wait for cargo: so *expensive*. Fuel: expensive. Stevedoring: expensive — but a sailing crew offload their own vessel, so if the boat is delayed — never mind; it doesn't cost much.'

A power cut plunged us into near darkness and the fans stopped. I felt sweat trickling down my face. Invisible now, the Chevalier rumbled calmly on. 'Sail could survive twenty years more. If there's cargo. *To* Sri Lanka: onions, garlic, coriander, dry chillis, dry fish — very important item! — and the *tendu* leaf that the poor people wrap their *beedis*, their tiny, khaki cigarettes, in. *From* Sri Lanka: black *grams*, buffalo skins, graphite. Salt? No, our very fine salt goes to Bangladesh, Singapore, Malaysia, that way.'

The lights come back on again. 'Will you visit our Church of Our Lady of Snows again? Ah! God bless you,' he said, when I said yes, 'I am praying for you.'

Hentry, arriving from Colombo on *toni* No. 42, brought an ugly reminder of the hazards of life. Two big sailing lighters, he said, had just gone down in heavy seas in the bay. Luckily, their crews had been rescued. But the sailing community, though fatalistic, was shocked at the news.

I went with him on board the largest *toni* in port, the *Arokya Mary*, or *Our Lady of Snows*, 335 tons (about 130 tons less than Cook's *Resolution*). There, memories of my voyage took me by the throat. Think of the size of her. Her gnarled deck is 129 feet long and 30 feet wide; her mainmast looms back as a fiend, 66 feet high, 7 feet in girth (a complete *pinnai* tree from Kerala). The scimitar-shaped spar that must hold a mainsail which thrashes about like a giant ray is 139 feet long. Up there, the crew look like flies on a curtain rail.

The Rodrigo family lives in an old cramped house behind a textile mill and the railway station. I have to stoop through the door. They've recently moved; the roof of their former house fell in on them. The new house is so clean they might have gone over it with toothbrushes. Sitting on a chair too small for me, I found a garland round my neck. Friends and relatives crowded in from the hot street; laughter and the burble of Tamil filled the room. Hentry called for a bottle opener. I smelt scent and soap. The swirling saris and gold-coloured ornaments of these poor people at this special occasion were reflected in the photographs of his wedding Raju thrust at me. On an unsent invitation, I read: 'You are requested to check in at: Sacred Heart

Cathidral Church 6 p.m. Mass, to Witness the departure of Batchlor-hood/Spinsterhood and arrival into wed-lock of Raju and Rani.'

Hentry's youngest brother, Johnson, introduced his friends, Nixon and John Kennedy. 'Yes, all are named after the presidents.' Kennedy, only sixteen, had written a novel in Tamil. Would I read it?

The men, I saw, had exchanged their sarongs for outrageously bell-bottomed trousers that flared out to hide their sandals, which they call 'elephants' feet' – long out of fashion in Britain. Their hair was carefully pomaded and whorled into shining quiffs like black ice cream, over faces made paler by a light powdering.

Hentry's mother and sisters covered a small table with green, yellow and pink cakes. Hentry poured Kingfisher beer. After the photographs, Raju showed me a massive tome in which he had inscribed his engineering notes at night school. The writing curled and looped like something in an illuminated holy book, which in its way I suppose this was to him.

His identity card shows his caste as 'Paravan'. All seafarers here are Paravans, yet no one knows the origin of the word. An old book I read said: 'The Moors had spread themselves over India. They were strengthened by the privateers of Calicut. Thus the Parruas (Paravans) were oppressed, until in a pearl fishery at Tuticoryn, they fell upon the Moors and killéd some thousands of them' (*pace* Bizet and his opera *The Pearl Fishers*, this coast was more famous for pearl- and conch-fishing even than Ceylon). Terrified of Arab vengeance, the Paravans begged the Portuguese for protection and the Portuguese, the strongest European power before the arrival of the Dutch and the British, promised it 'on condition that they should become Christians and this they generally agreed to do'. Presently, on cue, St Francis Xavier arrived.

All Catholic Tuticorin prays on Sunday. Most worshippers head for the Chevalier's lavish wedding cake of a church – Our Lady of Snows – from the steps of which you can see the masts of the *tonis*. The men in white sarongs shuffle in shyly, eyeing their bare feet and crossing themselves. Their wives and sisters follow, soft-eyed, beautiful, half veiled in saris as delicately tinted as butterflies' wings. A church full of Tamil madonnas.

After Mass, the captain of my *toni* and his wife put out a curry lunch in their small mud-floored yard where two goats bleated under a stunted papaya tree. Their children showed me the moral stricture inscribed in their schoolbook, 'Untouchability is a crime. Untouchability is a sin,' and read out an invocation they'd written which seemed to hint at their pre-Christian past: 'Praise unto You, Goddess Tamil, whose majestic youthfulness inspires awe and ecstasy.'

On my last day, Winston Corera drove me and the Rodrigo family to a famous oasis down the coast: a Paravan pilgrimage, as it turned out. Manapad, once prosperous, now an overgrown fishing village screened by palms, celebrated the fourth centenary of its church in 1981. It's a strange, much revered place with a seaside atmosphere of southern Europe. Its elaborate Portuguese-style mansions, porticoed and pillared, are incongruous, like grand opera sets on streets half swallowed by sand.

Scores of fishing boats tacked across the bay. Commanding a headland a mile off, the old church stands near a grotto which once sheltered St Francis Xavier, approachable along a trail of monuments representing the stations of the cross. Inside, in the gloom, a blood-streaked statue of Christ in a crown of thorns posed in a niche. Hentry, Romans and Raju made a beeline for it. With tears in their eyes, they rested their fingers on the gore-stained feet and then touched them to their own lips, forehead and eyes; and seemed comforted.

I took the train to Madras with Hentry, Romans and Raju, seen off by their families and friends. Nazarene presented me with one more garland, a gift of cakes, a purple towel, Oasis soap, a tube of Binaca fluorescent toothpaste ('for tender gums'), a tin of Britannia Assorted Biscuits, a sliced loaf of bread and jam for supper. Two grey business-men, with identical grey briefcases, shared our compartment and nibbled at the vegetarian dishes brought in by a steward. Hentry had refused it for all of us, and instead, under the businessmen's cold gaze, spread jam on pieces of Nazarene's bread and handed them round, then sat calmly or slept. Perhaps Raju was composing in his mind the letter that reached me a week later: 'Your stay is evergreen in our memory, and I have to write same in diary in golden letters. God has consoled us by your presence . . .'

Madras was a Paravans' holiday, though they considered the city was really a bit too big for them. I took them to the top of the new lighthouse (their first ride in a lift), to clothes shops, to the church in which the Apostle Thomas may be buried, where they bought cheap St Thomas amulets from the verger.

Then I took them to Chaplin's film *The Great Dictator*; they found it hilarious. But when we came out, they felt they should say goodbye for a while. Raju said, doubtfully, 'You want to visit friends – important people? If so, we shall wait for you somewhere.'

Important people? I looked at their good-natured faces; I thought of that world of poverty, work, thrift and devotion into which they are locked until the moment of their deaths. A real world to be faced up to, because no Paravan believes, as spoiled Westerners believe, that life owes him happiness.

'No,' I said to their anxious upturned faces. 'There's no point in that.' And, relieved, they wagged their heads back at me; silently, happily, agreeing: 'No point whatever.'

A week after my visit, Sinhalese mobs rose against the Tamil minority in Sri Lanka. Many Tamils were killed (quite a few burnt alive), more were made utterly destitute and are now refugees. Five *tonis* from Tuticorin were in Colombo harbour. It was feared that the ships and their Tamil crews were lost too, but eventually they sailed into Tuticorin. Soon, Hentry dictated a letter to me. His family's life is in ruins. 'Our boats are not allowed any more voyage to Colombo . . . I have no more income . . . I must go to Jeddah [Saudi Arabia] to save the family in these hard days. But for this I must pay recruiting agent rupees 10,000 [about £700]. Also I have debts in connection with the marriage of sister Rani.' He ended: 'We never fail to pray to Lord. . . .'

To Jeddah! £185 a month as a contracted labourer, where the swift retort to any complaint is, 'There are thousands more where you come from.' But – 'Unless I move to Jeddah,' Hentry says, 'I cannot support my family.' Others in Tuticorin share his plight.

Thus, the unrelenting family responsibilities of the poor inexorably combine with the forces of politics and racialism to torment the devout, thrifty and ceaselessly struggling peoples of Asia.

New York Revisited

De gustibus non est disputandum – Latin tag.

4 JANUARY 1987

'De gustibus ain't what dey used to be,' the American humorist S. J. Perelman was wont to moan. De gustibus seldom are, and returning to New York this year, twenty-four years after I first set foot there, I wasn't bowled over to find quite a few changes. Whether for better or worse is another matter.

Designated by Mr David Astor, Editor of the *Observer*, to be the newspaper's New York correspondent, I arrived there on the old *Queen Elizabeth* in a thick February blizzard. A dismal landfall if ever there was one. Staten Island and the Statue of Liberty were blotted from view by whirling snowflakes. A taxi driver somehow fumbled his way from the West Side pier to my hotel – the Bedford on East 40th Street – where for some time I sat in a pit of gloom staring out of the window at the desolation and feeling like Captain Oates in Scott's tent. When I finally ventured out to call on my only friend in the city my sense of location had quite gone. I have never since been able, mentally, to place Manhattan Island in correct relationship with New Jersey (west) and Long Island (east).

I took a fourth-floor apartment on Second Avenue a week or so after that unpromising arrival. It is still there: I gave it a friendly wave only the other day. My mind's eye can see its narrow stair, the rusty metal fire-escape two burglars found useful one night, the hole in the ceiling (has it been mended yet?) between the fireplace and the TV set on which I watched the Jack Paar talk show give way to a twitching newcomer called Johnnie Carson ('He'll never do,' I thought, and twenty-four years later Carson is still around and a multi-millionaire). The 'Gold Coin' Chinese restaurant that was below me is the Irish 'Green Derby' now, and smiling Fred Ferraro's grocery on the corner is a French restaurant. But, miraculously, that part of Second Avenue has escaped those money-vultures, the developers.

All the talk in Mayor Koch's New York is about money – or AIDS. In 1962 – the Kennedy Spring time – we had no AIDS and no money; the city was going broke. By 1974 it *was* broke, without money even to pay the city's cops, a third of whom were laid off (and no one has seen a cop walking a sidewalk since). Streets were suddenly dangerous, there was garbage all over, and you could have buried a bus in the largest pothole. Apart from the rats and roaches, who wanted to live in New York?

A speck in time before jungle reclaimed Fifth Avenue – and before I could summon the courage to buy an East Side apartment for a tenth of what it would cost now – things changed. The new wealth – from Europe, oil, real-estate operators – that is now transforming the city poses a different and equally disquieting danger: that soon no 'ordinary' people will be able to afford to live there. The cosy brick-and-brownstone Manhattan I knew is fast becoming a forest of sea-green, blue and black glass office blocks towering over plate-glassed boutiques which few but Texans, 'Eurotrash' jet-setters and Imelda Marcos would dare to enter. Sixth Avenue is already a mind-deadening corridor of glass – towers reflecting still more towers, blocking out the sun, magnifying traffic noise. Philip Johnson, the eighty-year-old blithe spirit of American architecture, has recently encumbered Third Avenue with an immense and seemingly pointless cylinder the colour of undercooked liver, although P. J. Clarke's red-brick saloon a block away (it's where Ray Milland filmed *The Lost Weekend* and still there because its owner, Danny Lavezzo, continues gallantly to defy the developers) retains more dignity in its one humble storey than elsewhere is contained in hundreds of feet. It's happening all over. Even elegant, limestone Fifth Avenue is threatened.

My friend Ved Mehta, a veteran *New Yorker* writer, is not alone in blaming Mayor Koch: 'He has sold the city to the real-estate operators.' One result: prices are up to Himalayan heights. I used to eat in Prexy's snack bars (remember? – they served 'the hamburger with the college education') for less than a dollar. 'Never more than $9 a meal in a restaurant then,' Ved recalls, 'and a glass of wine with it, too.' Now the bill for two is usually around $60. No wonder actors, dancers, painters can no longer afford to live in Lower Manhattan, SoHo, Chelsea or anywhere else. New York has become Yuppieville. Only yuppies can pay the rents.

In 1963 things were more lively. The Leonard Bernstein–Stephen Sondheim musical *West Side Story* was still highly topical. Youth gangs were an adolescent cult, particularly among blacks and Hispanics. So I wondered recently what had happened to the Young Assassins, the fighting gang that had 'adopted' me then. Were the kids still around – Robert ('Brutus') Feliciano, Luis ('Daddy') Rodriguez,

341

Micky ('Chino') Moreno, Luis ('Little Cuba') Rivera, Jerry ('Blue Eyes') Lee, and Carlos ('El Cid') Garcia? I spent some time with these jumpy, leather-jacketed youngsters twenty years ago, roaming the half-dozen poor, mean blocks around West 33rd Street, on corners and in Catholic social clubs, but even though I think eventually they trusted me they would never cross to my pad on Second Avenue. They were scared some rival gang would jump them if they left their 'turf'.

Those kids, once so quick with lethal switch-blades and zip-guns, would be middle-aged men by now, store-owners perhaps, or truckers, maybe even cops – if they hadn't ended up in Sing-Sing. In an effort to find them, I went first to New York City police headquarters. There I read my notebook of 1963 to Officer Fred Eldrick, who listened with growing fascination. '179 gangs, mostly black or Puerto Rican. Number of homicides in 1961: 11 – an increase of three over the previous year.' Interestingly enough, the notebooks recalled, only about 5 per cent of those so-called dangerous tearaways of the Sixties experimented with drugs – which in those days meant glue-sniffing, 'goof balls', aspirins in Coca-Cola, pot. A mere 2 per cent were hooked on 'horse' (heroin). 'Some addicts spend $30–40 a week,' the police briefing officer had sighed, shaking a bewildered head. 'You see how serious it's getting.' 'Ha!', Officer Eldrick snorted scornfully twenty years later.

At least the gangs had some good names, I reminded him: names like the Forty Thieves, the German Army, the Be-Bops, Suicide Mau Mau. And, in Harlem, the Ballerino Bopping Dragons and the Egyptian Warlords. 'All "rumbling" like crazy. Where are they now, do you think?'

'The gangs died in the late Sixties,' Officer Eldrick told me. 'You won't find 'em now.' He made it sound like a hundred years ago. 'A lot were drafted to Vietnam, and drugs are antisocial – don't make for membership of gangs. The youth's into "crack" (smokable cocaine) these days. Seventy-five per cent of all today's crimes are drug-related.' He laughed. Thirty to forty dollars a week on drugs, you said? That's more like the daily figure now. And the homicides – 11? Do you know the homicide figure for 1985? 1384.'

I had lived through an age of innocence. In 1962, when the Puerto Rican had crept in through my apartment window, waking me up, I had chased him out – and then opened the front door to find his mate there; and had had to get him out, too. (Fortunately, they were smaller than me.) I'd been lucky. Today they would have been on crack and used knives. 'An age of innocence, then,' I repeated. 'I guess so,' Officer Eldrick said. Of course I failed to find the Young Assassins on their former 'turf' – 'Hell's Kitchen', people had called it – and I found instead an old brownstone church and a Catholic priest. Father Mackay had seen all the changes. He pointed to builders working on a four-storey house opposite. 'See that building, Mr Young? That'll go for half a million dollars. Two or three poor families used to live in houses like that. Gentrification.'

Gentrification, one could say, means tarting up cheap housing for interior decorators, hat designers and poodle trimmers to live in expensively. Like tower-block building, gentrification is forcing simple people out of the city. The new Eldorado has little room for simple people. 'Small neighbourhood stores have been squeezed out by higher and higher rents,' Father Mackay said sadly. 'And what comes instead? Boutiques and ritzy restaurants.'

This had been a dangerous area in 1962. But with crack, this ubiquitous, easy-to-get drug, as common as tobacco, it's dangerous in a much more lethal way. 'Yes, we had a youth gang here in the old days,' said Father Mackay. 'The kids came to our church dances. They even kept order at them.' He spoke with something like nostalgia. 'The family ethos was strong then. And we'd go in to bat for 'em in the courts. Translating. Back then, you see, language was a problem for the Puerto Ricans. Now the Reagan administration has cut back on social services. There's unemployment, poverty. And, well, with crack around . . .'

The old youth gangs had beaten each other or cut each other up. A crack freak would kill anyone; and crack has nothing to do with family ties. It came to this then, that hard drugs and gentrification between them had driven 'Little Cuba', 'Blue Eyes', 'Chino', their wives and children clear out of the city. They had thought that in some measure they *were* the city. What slum were they in now? Yes, how innocent they – all of us – had been!

I remembered another thing. Back in 1962, at a fashionable church on Park Avenue, a dynamic priest called Father Hill had launched 'Operation Yorkville', a well-organized and fervent campaign against printed porn. Porn was, so to speak, in the air, and it was a time when the definition of 'dirt' was a highly charged topic. Legally, it was a muddled time. William Burroughs's *The Naked Lunch* was freely on sale, yet Henry Miller's *Tropic of Cancer* was facing indictment in Brooklyn. Soft-porn magazines had suddenly boomed on every bookstand. A couple of decades later, I wondered what had happened to Father Hill's campaign.

It had thrived at least in one sense. Its headquarters had moved, I found, from the old Park Avenue crypt to a building as big as a government department near Columbia University. Father Hill had recently died, and I was received instead by a well-dressed, humorous woman with the commanding presence of a Roman matron, on whose door a notice said, 'No one gets in to see the wizard, not no one, not no how,' and on whose waiting-room table lay a copy of *Screw* magazine. 'So you knew Father Hill. I'm afraid porn has exploded since the 1960s,' she said, indicating her suite of offices. 'So we had to expand, too.'

The 'explosion', she explained, had come with the advent in the 1970s of things like live sex shows, video and Dial-a-porn. 'These days any college kid can just pick up a phone, dial certain well-advertised numbers and hear – well, really *terrible* things. Violent, masochistic, sadistic things.' She pushed over her phone. 'Like to listen?' I shook my head demurely and asked her instead if she ever felt like King Canute.

'Well,' she said sadly, 'pornography today is no longer downtown; it's actually *downstairs* in every home. It's become a $9 billion-a-year racket. You see, you can make a hardcore film for $120,000, and porn movie-houses bring in $500 million a year.' A photograph on the wall showed the late Father Hill with President Reagan. 'President Reagan is right with us,' she said pointing to it. 'Lots of people are. And the laws are there, too. The trouble is that in New York City there's absolutely no law *enforcement*. None at all.'

Soon, a euphoric Vietnamese taxi driver swept me downtown at such speed someone might have told him the Vietcong had occupied Central Park. It made a nice change to see him – and the Chinese and Korean drivers – all part of the most recent wave of immigrants. Indian taxi drivers, too, are replacing those fibrous old gnomes with names like Czolczynsky or Pyszczuk who ended every utterance with an aggressively rhetorical 'Know what I mean?' Not all the old unpronounceable names have vanished, thank heavens. This year I was glad to note down one pretty good specimen: Faraschivoiu, Alexandru. It was pleasing to be told yet again what Winston Churchill said to Lady Astor by a bald-headed old character called Faraschivoiu.

What one really misses is good things to read. A minor tragedy of today's New York is that there is only one serious daily newspaper, the

New York Times, and a rather dull one at that. I miss the old *Tribune,* the very name of which reminds me of the long newspaper strike of the winter of 1962–3, when readers, deprived of the *Times* and the *Trib,* were thrown back on whatever unstopped publications they chanced to subscribe to. The great *New Yorker* reporter, the late A. J. Liebling, wrote that his own list was short, consisting principally of the *Wall Street Journal,* five days a week, and the airmail edition of the London *Observer.* 'The *Observer,*' he said, 'does me almost too well for foreign news, speculation and meaning-musing, and it also keeps me posted on British racing and intellectual knife-throwing.' What he really missed during the strike, he confessed, was ordinary run-of-the-mill newspaper news, 'mostly crime and shenanigans'.

These days Liebling would miss, as I certainly do, the wit and humour that was one of America's greatest contributions to the world. Humour seemed to disappear around 1979 with the death of Sid Perelman. Even at The *New Yorker,* that once unfailing source of wit, it has dried up. For a thrilling moment the other day I thought I had stumbled on a rare sample of humour in, of all places, the *Times* food section. With thumping heart, I read: 'Even a sliced tomato with basil can be absolutely symphonic when the ingredients in question have been picked earlier that day in a country garden and raced to town before the mist dries . . . Our corner of the dining-room [was suffused] with the aroma of autumn in a dew-moistened forest.' A whiff of Robert Benchley there, surely. But, alas, the wretched fellow was being *serious.*

The 'Humor' shelves of the major Manhattan bookstores carry nothing but the latest slim volume of Art Buchwald and a few booklets of cartoon strips. When I mentioned this to Joseph Mankiewicz, director of *All About Eve* and a delightful old wit himself, he could only shake his head sorrowfully and murmur, 'Yes, it's a lonely life.'

Humour is out, but jazz is back. In 1963 both were gloriously combined at the Strollers Theater Club on East 53rd Street, where jazz pianist Teddy Wilson and his trio backed Eleanor Bron, John Bird, John Fortune and Jeremy Geit, the British satirical group called The Establishment. Teddy, Oscar Peterson and Dudley Moore got together one afternoon in my Second Avenue flat with the hole in the ceiling and in the course of a liquorous conversation revealed, among other things, that their major influences, respectively, had been Fats Waller, Art Tatum and Erroll Garner, and that as children they had preferred violins and trumpets to pianos. Teddy died recently, Dudley twinkles in Hollywood, but in New York jazz and Oscar were well and truly alive this autumn.

It is a great loss that one can no longer wander up to Harlem of an evening: to the Red Rooster, for instance, or to Small's Paradise. But other old landmarks remain. P. J. Clarke's, that symbol of defiance among the satanic towers of Mammon, survives now on the yuppy trade (better that than nothing) – and, as far as I am concerned, on nostalgia. In its back room I still think I see former fellow-regulars like Budd Schulberg, Norman Mailer, Jake La Motta, Teddy Wilson, Zachary Scott and the rest – whether they are there or not. I still hear Artie Shaw talking of his forthcoming novel, to be called *I Love You, I Hate You, Drop Dead*. And I still wave (figuratively speaking) at a quiet, sweet, doom-faced phantom in the far corner of the bar with a broad-brimmed hat and a tiny dog on a leash: Davis Grubb, author of *The Night of The Hunter*, one of the finest horror stories of this century.

I am glad to see Elaine Kaufman, of Elaine's famous 89th Street rendezvous, undiminished by the years. I love the clams, scallops and oysters of Grand Central Station. And a perfect chilled Gibson is still to be found in the Oak Bar of the Plaza – a magnificent dowager of an hotel peering haughtily down on Central Park through a hundred lorgnettes, harbouring hawks in her topmost pinnacles and representing Old New York at its worst and best. These and many other things – the bohemian alleys of Lower Manhattan, for example; the pungent Kills of Staten Island, the icebound Hudson River, and the East River from Brooklyn up to Hell Gate and Execution Rock in Long Island Sound – I have explored them all and they will draw me back to New York. It is still the most vibrant port-city in the world.

As I say, I see now that when I arrived in that blizzard, an age of innocence was passing. I don't pine for 1962, even so. But I do leave New York dogged by a question: Can wealth, greed and drugs destroy a great metropolis that has managed so spectacularly to survive decay and destitution? I wish I knew the answer.

New York Harbour

In 1986 I went to New York once more to see what twenty-four years had done to my first recollections of it in the early Sixties. I took the opportunity to do a little exploration on the waterfront.

10 MAY 1987

The sea-gateway to America should be the grandest in the world – and by a long chalk it is. You could cram most of Europe's biggest harbours into the bays and sounds of New York and have room to spare.

Think of London; think of Hong Kong. One, a series of docks up a famous river; the other, a single bay-like anchorage. New York has *two* big bays, a smaller one and a backdoor stretch of water (Long Island Sound) that seems more like part of the open sea. No fewer than seven rivers flow into the harbour – the Hudson, the East River, the Hackensack, the Passaic, the Elizabeth, the Rahway and the Raritan. That is taking the ports of Newark and New York together because they are run as one by the states of New York and New Jersey.

New York harbour has as many vibrant moods as it has rivers. It is diffuse and confusing. Setting out to explore it, I orientated myself with an overall view of it from a helicopter. We rose into a clear autumn sky from a pad on the Battery at the tip of Manhattan Island, swung right over the Hudson and immediately looked down on recent relics of a dead past. That was the sad part. The once busy piers of Hoboken, New Jersey, run out into the water like the snapped-off stumps of dead teeth. Where Elia Kazan in the Fifties had shot *On the Waterfront*, the Oscar-winning film of dockland racketeering, I saw burned-out warehouses, beached hulks like the blackened skeletons of whales, mud and reclaimed land patchily sprouting bad, wiry grass. Downstream, by contrast, there was the prosperous present – the sprawling Newark container port, the largest in the world, accounting for most by far of New York's shipping. Containerization has killed the old world of piers and masts and funnels.

Things are no better for shipping further up the Hudson. The cliffs and shore of Weehaawken are dotted now with neat clapboard houses facing the towers of Manhattan, and their inhabitants draw back their curtains each day to gaze at one of the wonders of the world.

We whirred low over the George Washington Bridge, banked right over the Harlem River, a sleazy ditch that cuts Manhattan from the Bronx, and then south over a Columbia University team practising football. The low-rise slums of Harlem look like ruins of a bombed city.

At the head of East River we dipped over Hell Gate, Randall's Island, and North Brother Island, an old typhoid station. Wallabout Bay on the Brooklyn shore is haunted by the American Revolutionary patriots who died in British prison ships. Their bones – Walt Whitman called them *'the stepping stones to thee today and here, America'* – are still dredged up. Next Brooklyn Bridge, sleek Coast Guard cutters alongside Governor's Island and, at last, the Statue of Liberty. I walked from the heliport through the trees of Battery Park, dodging a sweetly chanting mob of little black children rushing to board the Staten Island Ferry.

Not long ago, New York harbour was known throughout the world for its corruption and violence largely thanks to the success of the Elia Kazan–Marlon Brando–Budd Schulberg movie *On the Waterfront*. A major character in it, played with a fine ferocity by Karl Malden, was the feisty waterfront priest Father Barry – an amalgam of two real anti-mob crusaders, the late Father John Corridan and Father Philip Carey who is still very much alive. In his church on West 16th Street the other day Father Carey told me, 'You know, things have changed completely. As you see, the Manhattan piers are obsolete. The passenger ships are mostly gone – destroyed by the big jets of course. We had 53,000 longshoremen in 1952 – now there's maybe 7000, mostly in Brooklyn where they're Italian, or in Newark where they're hardworking Portuguese immigrants.'

Father Carey is seventy years old, shortish and square in a black raincoat over a black clerical suit and dog-collar; he has a strong humorous face and a round, strong head of short white hair. He looks (and is) tough and completely fearless. His rooms are lined with filing cabinets of his careful records of the old, evil days: the days of loan-sharking; the days of the shape-up each morning on the piers – the system whereby corrupt hiring bosses allotted work exclusively to men prepared to 'kickback' some of their wages in bribes. Those who went to the cops fell mysteriously from high windows or simply disappeared.

Schulberg's screenplay used fighting phrases from Carey's sermons. 'If you don't think Christ is here on the waterfront, you got another guess coming. Some people think the Crucifixion only took place on Calvary. They better wise up. Every morning when the hiring boss blows his whistle, Jesus stands alongside you in the shape-up . . .'

'The breakthrough came,' Father Carey says, 'with the publicity; with my files; with Budd's screenplay. Legislation finally weeded out the criminals. Johnnie "Cockeye" Dunn, who'd murdered several men, died in the electric chair in Sing-Sing.'

Father Carey is not afraid to criticize his Church. 'Cardinal Spellman was no help in our waterfront battles. Forgive me for saying it – he was a man whose stupidity was only exceeded by his piety. And he was an exceedingly pious man!'

Carey and containerization were allies in a way. Now that the waterfront piers are obsolete, land on the Jersey shore where they once were is worth $500,000 an acre to developers planning offices, hotels and marinas. 'There'll be a mini-Manhattan here,' crows the Mayor of Jersey City. But no ships or longshoremen.

Seventy-year-old Frank Schubert sees New York Harbour from a different angle. The last surviving lighthouse keeper in the United States of America, for twenty-six years he has tended the Coney Island light on the ocean side of the Verrazano Narrows Bridge. You can't find a more exposed or commanding position than that.

The Coney Island light is a red one that flashes twelve times a minute and is visible to ships fourteen miles away. Its tower, built in 1897, is seventy-five feet high (it felt higher when I climbed it), and Mr Schubert lives next to it in a hundred-year-old house with walls eight feet thick.

'There's nothin' to it,' he said about his duties: cleaning, maintaining, painting. 'I have it rigged to go on a half-hour before sunset and to turn itself off again a half-hour after sunrise. Sometimes the big Miller moths fly up on hot nights and damage the mantle. I have to climb up and repair it.'

Coney Island is sadly run down these days, the oceanside funfair almost derelict in an area of a slum where policemen walk in *fours* at night. The lighthouse itself is fenced against vandals. His wife died in May, but Frank Schubert is not lonely: 'I get quite a few visitors.' In his snug old house with beautiful furniture he has crafted from driftwood, we listened to a distant honking. 'That's the foghorn on West Bank,' he said. 'Fog sensors activate that. People think I do and phone in to complain. But it's not me.'

The house seemed terribly vulnerable to Atlantic winter storms. 'Oh, the light sways a bit,' Schubert said, 'but actually winter's not too rugged.'

From the shore a breathtaking view: a tanker in the Narrows moving slowly up the Ambrose Channel to the Narrows bridge; the distant green sweep of Sandy Hook, New Jersey; the tiny Swinburne Island in mid-channel, a wartime crematorium. 'No one there now,' said Schubert. 'Just urns with ashes.'

One night eight or nine years ago there was a terrible accident. A container ship's steering broke and she ploughed into a tanker. 'I heard a terrific roar like a thousand blowtorches,' Schubert said. 'Nineteen men lost. A blazing inferno, it was. The shore was ablaze and the rocks. My nice white lighthouse turned completely black.'

Now the sun glinted on the innocent face of Lower Bay.

'I never get sick of the view,' Frank said. 'It's beautiful with the snow. And even during a hurricane, it can be teeming with rain, just bucketing down, and the shore'll be lined with people, just watchin'. Just watchin' the beauty of it.'

'A car went into the water just here last night,' Kevin, the police diver, said. 'It's about 60 feet deep. A coupla passers-by pulled a guy and his girl out the water, but before the police arrived they jumped into a cab and vanished. Now we have to make sure there's no one else in that car.'

We stood on the deck of a small police launch marked 'Police Scuba Team' while two officers in wet suits dived in the dark, oily water of the East River, trailing bubbles. Overhead a train rumbled across the iron girders of the Manhattan Bridge towards Brooklyn Heights.

'Difficult to see in this water,' Kevin said. 'Usually you see about an arm's length.' He stopped to pat Charlie Dog, the launch's mascot, a lively black animal barking at the divers in the water. 'We found two floaters [bodies] yesterday. We average about 140 of those a year. Suicides? George Washington Bridge is more popular with jumpers than the Brooklyn these days. Two hundred and thirteen feet high – it's guaranteed to kill you. Often we fish 'em out naked; that long fall rips their clothes clean off.'

The divers surfaced making the thumbs-up sign. 'Found it?' Kevin hollered. 'A 1986 Caddy in good condition? Okay, see what's in the trunk. I'll call Salvage.'

While we waited, Kevin went on: 'There's lots of wrecks down in the harbour. The destroyer *Turner*, for example. A whole lot of big eels. Bodies with cement boots on. Lots of guns.'

When a salvage truck with a crane arrived, the divers attached wires to the car and the salvage crew began to wind it up. The pale-blue Cadillac Sedan de Ville appeared inch by inch. In that filthy water it looked very beautiful and oddly poignant. 'Expensive car wash,' Kevin grunted. Watched by a small crowd, the crane dumped the car with a crash on the stone wharf. Black water and silt poured out of it. No body, though. A pair of pantie hose was draped over the front seat and Kevin pointed to it, laughing.

'Jeez . . . the son of a bitch was gettin' laid. Car parked. Cold night. Engine runnin' to keep the heater goin' and the stereo. Plenty sex. He or she must have knocked the gear into "drive", and the car leaped into sixty feet of East River. Stolen car or illicit affair, that's why they ran.'

In the glove compartment a driving licence with a Spanish name and an address. A routine police investigation was beginning. I strolled downriver past the Fulton Fish Market for a bowl of clam chowder at Sloppy Louie's seafood restaurant, thinking of all those skeletons under the water with cement boots on.

Frank Duffy of the Moran Tug Company sent me out on one of his tugs, the *Judy Moran*, to bring in the QE2. I went aboard the tiny vessel at Pier 90 in the Hudson and had a mug of tea and an egg sandwich with her Master, Geoff Nelson. Then he roared up the *Judy Moran*'s engines and edged her through the dark into the river. It was well before dawn.

In the wheelhouse Captain Jimmy Ferguson, the pilot, grey-haired in a cloth cap and a smart grey ulster, asked, 'Any baseball news?' and tuned the radio to a radio commentary about the New York Mets gearing up to win the World Series. The spangled skyline of Manhattan glittered in the Hudson like silver foil.

'The last of the ebb-tide, Jimmy,' Geoff Nelson said, inspecting the water. 'Yeah,' Ferguson agreed, 'looks like the water's coming down pretty good.'

Soon, a pale tinge lightened the sky beyond the battery. 'I recall when this river was like 8th Avenue with traffic,' Captain Ferguson said. 'It's sad. These docks are almost human: if you don't use 'em they just die. In twenty years' time, there'll be all apartment blocks here.' As the light grew a small dark wedge crowned with a tiny tiara of small lights became visible ahead of us. Geoff Nelson cried, 'That's her, there!'

Stationary, from the darkened wheelhouse, we watched the *QE2* slowly approaching, trailing a smudge of smoke. As Captain Ferguson said to Nelson, 'Want to tell the *QE2* to take a line on the starboard bow eventually?' By the time a second tug joined us he was attacking the cost of living. 'When I bring my wife in to a theatre and dinner, it's $200 . . . Oh, yes, the city's changed. I remember we were tied up once off 123rd Street and I went into a bar and I was the only white man there. No problem. But *now* . . .'

The *QE2* slid up, huge, streamlined, a whale to a minnow. Strangely impersonal, too. No passengers looked down – perhaps they were all asleep. '*QE2*,' Geoff said in the radio handset, 'we have your pilot on the starboard side.' In a moment, a door opened low down in the monster's side, a short ladder was lowered and Captain Ferguson nimbly scaled it, disappearing inside. Engines roaring, we closed with the black overhang of the liner's stern and deckhands secured a towline. Nelson spun the wide metal wheel. Using a good deal of our 3000 hp, we pushed the *QE2* at right angles to the river, the second tug nuzzling her bows to check the rate of swing.

It was quite light now, the water a whiteish-yellow. Very slowly we moved towards the pier.

Geoff Nelson radioed to Ferguson a hundred miles away on the liner's bridge, 'She's still drifting. I'm going to push her stern a bit more.'

Ferguson's voice: 'Should be slack water. One bell, Geoff' – half ahead. I could see our twin, the *Elizabeth Moran*, worrying away bravely like a monstrous terrier chivying a bull, her screw thrashing the water, her Stars and Stripes straight out in the dawn breeze. The skyscrapers watching us were grey now, only the Empire State a sheer, clean-soaring needle. A sleepy passenger or two blinked down at us from the boat deck. We must have looked like a bath toy.

'*Judy*, easy.' Nelson eased back the throttles, and the black cliff above us, with infinite slowness, approached her berth. Geoff Nelson said, 'There's a fine line between a fine job and a disaster. At this minute you could say we've the *QE2* at our mercy.' If we let the *QE2* go she might plough half-way down 50th Street before she lost momentum. What a sight that would be.'

Ferguson's orders continued: 'Easy, Geoff,' or 'Come back, *Judy*,' and once, 'A little stronger back there, Geoff . . . ' Seagulls appeared and bright sun shone on the windows of Manhattan. The *QE2* edged into her berth and Geoff reached up – the *Judy Moran* whistled once, twice, three times. 'I don't like to use our horn with passengers sleeping up there.' Now the job was done. The *QE2* would sail back to England to be converted from steam to diesel.

I heard Jimmy Ferguson's voice from the bridge, saying, 'Hi, Cap. Thanks . . . How ya doin'?' I shook hands with Geoff Nelson and jumped down from the *Judy*'s fender to the pier. The sun was up. Another fine day on the harbour had begun.

Thomas Hardy in North Cornwall

I had revisited Bude and the Wreckers' Coast of North Cornwall where I spent a good deal of my boyhood. Now at last I went to find that hidden valley where fate brought young Thomas Hardy face to face with his first wife, Emma Gifford.

18 JANUARY 1987

Woman much missed, how you call to me, call to me,
Saying that now you are not as you were
When you had changed from the one who was all to me,
But as at first, when our day was fair . . .

These days I find it impossible on certain north Cornish cliffs near Bude not to think of Thomas Hardy and his wife Emma in her 'air-blue' gown. I spent much of my youth there, but as a boy I hadn't read Hardy's poetry, so as far as I was concerned those soul-subduing heights 'with the wind oozing thin through the thorn from northward' were mine alone. Now Hardy and Emma will haunt them for ever.

The region is old enough for ghosts, God knows – to me it feels older than any other part of Britain. Remoter, too. When my grandmother still lived in her tall house at the top of Ocean View Road with its single round attic window looking down on the Atlantic Ocean like a sailor's spyglass, the trains took a very long day to reach Bude (with a change at Exeter) from Waterloo. Now that Exeter is Bude's nearest station, you must drive across Devon or take a bus and will be lucky to get there by opening-time.

Nothing much has changed thereabouts. You still squeeze down high-banked, wriggling lanes barely wide enough for a single car; branches meet over your head and grass brushes your windows. On the broad headlands that shoulder their way in from the 700-foot cliffs towards Bodmin Moor and Dartmoor, winter gales have bent the trees almost parallel to the earth. And Edwardian Bude, with its two beautiful beaches, is as reticent as ever behind its superb, whale-backed, nineteenth-century breakwater, and much the same as I remember it as a boy. The lines of surf roll in six-deep; at high tide the Atlantic breakers batter the rocks with the sound of great guns; and children with buckets and spades still dig their way through the sand to Australia. It's a pity the Art Deco picture house has been demolished for a supermarket, but in the Brendon Arms by the old Bede Haven canal, genial Desmond Gregory still dispenses beer under spectacular photographs of some of the hundred or more shipwrecks this Wrecker's Coast lays claim to.

Even today it is not easy to find St Juliot's, where Hardy, the young architectural designer, arriving from Dorset on 7 March 1870 to restore the ancient, tumbledown church, first set eyes on Emma Lavinia Gifford, the vicar's sister-in-law. The journey took twelve hours from Bockhampton, near Dorchester. 'Rose at half-past three . . . raw wind . . . Good heavens, here's an undertaking!' he noted. Train from Dorchester; change at Yeovil Junction; change again at Exeter; then to Launceston. Even after that there were several hours and fifteen miles more to St Juliot's in a four-wheeler, up and down switchback hills through those impossible lanes to Boscastle. At last, in the dark, the hidden rectory. At the time he was too tired to do more than note, 'Received by young lady in brown', adding later, 'a full-bosomed creature with a high colour, bright blue eyes and masses of blond hair'. Emma Gifford, then twenty-nine years old, was six months older than Hardy. She noticed the architect's Dorset accent, his beard and, with surprise, the manuscript of a poem sticking out of the pocket of his shabby greatcoat.

It was a *coup de foudre*. Hardy was later to describe that first meeting in the rectory's darkened porch as 'magic' and 'unreal', and talked and wrote obsessively about it to the end of his long life. In 'A Dream Or No', one of many passionately lyrical poems written later, he asked,

Why go to Saint-Juliot? What's Juliot to me?

— answering that because he met Emma there 'much of my life claims
that spot as its key'. This conviction, enhanced by intense remorse for
the unfeeling way he treated her during the later years of their thirty-
eight-year marriage, brought Hardy as an old man to St Juliot's again
and again, the last visit in 1920, half a century after the first. By then
Hardy was seventy-eight and Emma had been dead eight years.

It is not surprising that to Hardy Lyonnesse — the poetic name for
Cornwall — was 'a region of dream and mystery. The ghostly birds, the
pall-like sea . . . an atmosphere like the twilight of a night vision'.
Luckily, the rector, Caddell Holder, was in bed with gout and his wife
with him, and Hardy and Emma could sit late in the rectory garden,
reading *inter alia* Tennyson's 'Break, break, break', a poem inspired by
those 'rocky crags' barely more than a stone's throw down the valley.
When they were not walking and sketching, Hardy rebuilt the
crumbling church. And on his return to Bockhampton he celebrated
that 'unreal' week with the lines

When I came back from Lyonnesse
With magic in my eyes,
All marked with mute surmise
My radiance rare and fathomless,
When I came back from Lyonnesse
With magic in my eyes!

As I have implied, you can miss St Juliot quite easily; it is not marked
on any maps. Hardy was lucky to have had a local driver. I overshot
the turning the other day, although I have been there often. The thing is
to turn off the Stratton to Redruth road when the signpost says
Boscastle, and then look out for Lesnewth. On the edge of a deep
valley, the Valency, St Juliot's square tower rises above the hedge
pointing four pinnacles skywards like arthritic fingers. The old rectory
where Emma greeted Hardy is nearly hidden in a wooded lane close by
— a fair-sized, pleasant building with a good view, through french
windows, down the valley. A retired wing commander lives there with
his wife and, in these vicarless days, a parson from Boscastle takes
services in the churches of St Juliot's, Lesnewth and St Gennys.

Remark the strange fact that St Juliot's (originally St Julitta's) has no
village. It is one of several ancient Cornish churches with small ancient
graveyards you discover with some difficulty shrouded by huge trees
and little else: Poundstock, Launcells, Morwenstow are examples.

They can be creepy if a cloud suddenly covers the sun. I am particularly fond of Poundstock. The ghost walks (or gibbers) there of William Penfound, clerk, murdered in 1358 by a gang of delinquent noblemen who also 'wounded certain of his kinsmen, desecrating the vestments and sacred vessels with splashes of their blood, in contempt of the Creator, in defiance of the Church, and to the disturbance of the peace of the realm'. The murderers had good Cornish names – de St Gennys, Hunta, Penwaryn, Polshaghwe – and were dealt with by the Black Prince (also Duke of Cornwall). Other good local names on gravestones are Dinner, Sangwin, Jewell, Jose, Honey, Prout, Jollow. And I like the gentle reminder on a sixteenth-century Poundstock tomb: 'We All Do Fade As A Leaf.'

It is just possible – a nice thought – that Thomas Hardy met the famously eccentric cleric of Morwenstow, Parson ('Passon') Hawker, who took opium, buried countless drowned sailors between 1834 and 1876 and, according to A. L. Rowse, was one of the best of the lesser Victorian poets. Scorning Victorian restorers like Hardy, Hawker restored his own church, opened his services to animals and collected charms against such things as snake bite and sleepy foot:

> Foot, foot, foot is fast asleep:
> Thumb, thumb, thumb, in spittle we steep,
> Crosses three we make for to ease us,
> Two for the thieves and one for Christ Jesus

He wrote the ballad 'And shall Trelawney die?' and noted down horrendous pen-pictures of the coast Hardy so lyrically loved. 'The Channel is full of wreck – Cargo – and among it corpses – 13 came ashore at Bude, some lashed to the raft – these are buried all in one pit in Bude Churchyard. This I do not call Christian burial.' Rotting bodies were washed into coves from Hartland to Boscastle, and sometimes Hawker had to drench his men with gin before they'd do any burying at all. The constant wrecks became too much for him. 'I hear in every gust of the gale,' he moaned, 'a dying sailor's cry.'

This day-to-day Cornish world of wrecks, lifeboats and drowned bodies hardly disturbed the two lovers of St Juliot's. Emma found 'an edge-of-the-world atmosphere' on this wild coast, and 'the great sweeping lighthouse eyes of Hartland Point and Trevose Head' seemed to her alarmingly like legendary Cornish giants. Undaunted, nevertheless, with Hardy beside her on foot, she careered recklessly about the cliff edge at Beeny on her pretty mare Fanny; they sketched each other; and they peered down the abyss at the seal-caves far below:

> O the opal and the sapphire of that wandering
> > western sea,
> And the woman riding high above with bright
> > hair flapping free –
> The woman whom I loved so, and who loyally loved me.

I spotted both seals and seal-caves last summer. Walking on Beeny Cliff with a writer friend, Rennie Bere, formerly Chief Game Warden of Uganda and a first-class naturalist born in Bude some seventy years ago, I watched the breakers battering Tennyson's crags and through Rennie's glasses saw three young, woolly grey seals lying impassively on a rock. Others swam in deeper water. A peregrine flew over – 'Peregrines are on the mend,' Rennie said – and huge gulls with arrogant eyes stalked the clifftop. The view to Lundy Island was breathtaking. Beeny is always bracing. No wonder that to Hardy it was always summer until that perpetual wintertime when

> The woman now is – elsewhere – whom the ambling
> > pony bore,
> And nor knows nor cares for Beeny, and will laugh
> > there nevermore.

One of the oddest of Hardy's poems has to do with an expedition he made with Emma to Reperry Cross, near Lanivet on the St Austell Road. It describes, Hardy insisted, 'a strange incident, which ... really happened'. Emma leaned back, exhausted, resting her arms, 'like one nailed', along the arms of a roadside Celtic cross. Hardy was suddenly horrified, crying 'Don't!' and in the poem Emma tells him, 'Something strange came into my head, / I wish I had not rested so!' Hardy, recovered, assures her there is nothing in it, and

> ' – O I know there is not,' said she ...
> Yet I wonder ... If no one is bodily crucified now,
> In spirit one may be!'

> And we dragged on and on, while we seemed to see
> In the running of Time's far glass
> Her crucified, as she had wondered if she might be
> Some day. – Alas, alas!

– as indeed in spirit she *was* crucified by her husband during the long years at Max Gate, their Dorset home. The symbol of that marital Calvary, the 'Christ-cross stone' (it's about three and a half feet high and half buried by grass), is some way up on the right after the overpass just off the A30 south of Bodmin.

That morbid incident once experienced, it's a relief to get back to something less self-flagellatory. A stroll up the beautiful Valency Valley below St Juliot's will blow the blues away. Its connections with Hardy and Emma are all happy ones. One day they strolled together down the valley to Boscastle and, 'by a sparkling little brook', made a picnic of fruit and wine, and Hardy lost a glass in a waterfall –

I held the vessel to rinse in the fall,
Where it slipped, and sank, and was past recall.
. . . There the glass still is.

The glass became an instant symbol of undying love. It may still be there, but I failed to find it. Never mind; the isolated Valley is still a happy place of soft water meadows, a clear brook with a stony bed, waterfalls and copses where cattle ruminate in the summer shade. The National Trust has added a discreet footpath and a well-made gate or two, on one of which someone had painted ungrateful messages: 'F--- the National Trust' and 'Gus, Audrey, Alex are 2-faced bastards'. What, I wondered, would Hardy have made of that?

Rennie said, 'Hardy and Emma jumped from stone to stone coming down this stream. I wish I could. But I wrenched my leg some years ago trying to keep up with a family of gorillas in the Ruwenzori. Got it caught in a giant fern root.' But there was no hurry, no gorillas, and the fern roots here were little ones. We, too, picnicked – without losing a glass – and climbed slowly on up to the church.

The Valency Valley is long, deep and silent. Restored by Hardy, St Juliot's church stands equally silent, isolated in its trees. We puffed up towards it from the stream. Buzzards circled a hamlet high up on our right and a solitary farm building hid the old rectory's gate behind which we could hear the wing commander revving his car. The gate in the churchyard wall is guarded by a Celtic cross and the shifting shadows of trees can make it so startlingly alive that you jump. We found the church empty and watchful. Within it is the lectern at which one Sunday Hardy read the lesson (Jeremiah, Chapter 36, and rather dull); a visitor's book with a sinister entry – 'Earth, Air, Fire and Water. The Devil I do love'; and Hardy's memorial plaque to the wife he so neglected in life and so passionately and remorsefully loved in death.

'She opened the door of the West to me,' he wrote in one of the best-known of the poems that celebrate her.

Its wistful last stanza matches perfectly the gentle melancholy of a summer's afternoon in St Juliot's churchyard.

> She opens the door of the Past to me,
> Its magic lights,
> Its heavenly heights,
> When forward little is to see!

Home Thoughts from Abroad

15 JANUARY 1984

Nostalgia has a lot to answer for. Why, for instance, would anyone in his right mind choose to return to England in midwinter, after two years in the sunny seaports of Asia and the South Seas? After all, I was brought up in the British Isles, and I know what to expect.

For a start, my plane may never land at Heathrow – fog could close it as tight as an oyster. I am prepared for that vigil at the baggage chute; black ice on the M4; and street after street blocked by a motor show, a demo or frozen slush. I am girded up for what Dickens, a passionate lover of English life, called 'the monotony of London's seventh day, when everything is bolted and barred that could possibly furnish relief'.

These are only some of the black thoughts that being abroad induces. So why on earth am I coming back? I am in a Singapore garden at the coolest season. Sunlit lawns are fresh with rain; squirrels run up and down bamboo thickets; tiny kingfishers dart like brilliant arrows among yellow cassias and scarlet flame trees. For dinner I shall eat a perfect Malay curry off a banana leaf. So why move? The answer is simple: after two years away, I miss Britain and I can't wait until summer. I have gone down with a bad attack of nostalgia.

Nostalgia. Webster's Dictionary says it comes from the Greek – *nostos* (to return) and *algia* (a painful condition), and that it means, 'severe melancholia caused by protracted absence from home', or 'wistful or excessively sentimental yearning for a return to some real or romanticized setting in the past'. The second definition is the relevant one for me.

There is no doubt that most people long abroad should run a mile from a sentimental yearning to return to settings in the past. Old settings have a nasty habit of deteriorating as soon as your back is turned. And unassuaged nostalgia will not be mocked. It will strike back, painfully. Two object lessons stand out. Robert Louis Stevenson cannily decided to bury his nostalgia in books and wrote several novels about his chilly native Scotland without moving an inch outside Samoa. Once in exile, he wisely never risked a return to the land of David Balfour. Yet the stories of Somerset Maugham set in Malaya are full of victims of unassuaged nostalgia. They are usually planters and their wives who, after years in the back of beyond, dreaming of the Britain they knew, eagerly sail 'home' on leave and find a desperate disillusionment. When you came down to it, they soon decided, the life people led in England was *deadly*.

My view is that their imaginations had trapped them too exclusively in a tarted-up past to remake a livable present. The trick is to combine, in the mind's eye, Past with Present, as cartoon film makers superimpose foregrounds onto backgrounds to make pictures with the perspective that creates atmosphere and character. It's the layered spirit of a place we should search for. Perhaps this is obvious. I can only relate a personal case in point.

My boyhood holidays were spent in North Cornwall and in South Wales. Not in the pretty-pretty part of Wales – Pembroke, Cardigan – but in the curious half-green, half-grit area of Gwent, where the coal-pitted valleys run down like curling fingers to meet a rolling, wooded landscape that looked far closer in spirit to King Arthur than to the National Coal Board. One odd thing about this corner of Gwent is that, although it can seem almost as remote as wild, weird North Cornwall, it is accessible two-and-a-half hours from London down the M4 which carries you over the Severn Bridge (if it is not closed for repairs). Perhaps because it is so obvious, people miss it – in the same sort of way that the gigantic man in Chesterton's *The Man Who Was Thursday* was so *exceptionally* gigantic that he was easily overlooked.

For me, this is Nostalgia Country. All eastern Gwent from Monmouth to Caerleon, from Abergavenny to Chepstow, to me is part of the once and future Camelot. There are other claimants to Arthur's Kingdom – Tintagel, Camelford, Glastonbury: they cut no ice. You only have to look at the slumberous half-ruined castles in the woolly, folded hills of Gwent to know that somewhere here the Round Table is safely mothballed in a dungeon waiting to be excavated by the University of Wales. (I don't know in which water Excalibur is to be found, but you can bet your bottom dollar that it's only a stone's throw – well, a sword's throw – away.)

Actually, the precise few square miles I grew up in are not wholly Arthurian. They are pastoral-industrial, which makes them less bland and more exciting. On the pastoral side, there was my grandfather's old creaking house, a walled garden with perpetually buzzing bees, crumbling farm buildings and two great carthorses, Bonnie and Violet, with horse brasses clinking on their forelocks. Naturally, nostalgia says it was *Go-between* country; always sunny. And the hay smelled new-mown all year round in the Nine-Acre field (where I read W.H. Davies's 'Songs of Joy' and Walter de la Mare) and fox cubs played all day long in the shade of the 200-year-old trees in Park Wood among conkers like newly varnished knobs of wood. Watson, the gamekeeper, wore a moleskin waistcoat. When the shooting parties came for the pheasants, the child's eye saw the drops of blood on the ferns as jewels, and the shiny spent cartridges, scarlet and brass, were playthings of beauty. There were ground mists of bluebells under the trees; and by a stream kingcups reflected butter when you held them under your chin. Nostalgia cannot dream convincingly of what was never there, so it does not remember fish in the Rhymney River, which brought almost to the door a reminder of unemployment farther north. Its water flowed oily and black with coal-dust from the mining valleys, past Machen Plas, the old fortified house where Sir Henry Morgan, the pirate, was born, and on down to the Bristol Channel. No fish lived in that pollution. If you fell in, you came out black as soot. It was like falling into an inkwell. Associating the Styx with the Rhymney, I believed that Achilles, dipped in it by his mother, must have been the only black Greek hero, except for that heel.

Nostalgia goes in for detail. Rabbits ran into the headlights of the Morris Cowley. A crooked little house stood by the railway bridge, and in it a funny old hunch-backed woman called Miss Thomas lived alone, sometimes leaning over the garden gate, waving, like a benign witch from a de la Mare poem. On quiet nights, the wind brought the barking of foxes and the sad whistle calls of the goods train striving up the gradient from Newport to Merthyr Tydfil.

Oddly enough, even the grim, industrial side had its quota of romance – perhaps because I was lucky enough not to have to live and work (or, more likely, be out of work) in those satanic, un-green valleys of the thirties. I only made visits by bicycle to the drab terraced streets of cloth-capped men and Bethesda chapels between hills topped by black pyramids of coal slag.

Is it sheer, haywire nostalgia-run-wild that says there was an odd charm even there? I don't think so. Joseph Conrad wrote of the London docks that they possessed an ugliness so picturesque as to become a delight to the eye. The same thing could be said of Newport, where we shopped, a city which even its own mayor would not, I imagine, claim to be a Venice-on-Usk. An inexplicable allure hung about the grimly ornate Victorian streets, the sooty shell of the castle standing like a decaying tooth by the bridge that leads over the River Usk to the rugby ground, and the National Provincial Bank with its barley sugar pillars. I even have fond memories of the Commercial Street trams that clanked past the Westgate Hotel (where the Chartists had paid a bloody price for riot), past the Lavender Tea Rooms (jam tarts and Welsh cakes), towards the old Lyceum picture-house, where I first saw Ronald Colman in *The Prisoner of Zenda* and Michael Redgrave in *Kipps*.

In general – I see it now from this oriental garden – the region was a sort of Pook's Hill. Apart from King Arthur, it had been a Cambrian junction of historical comings-and-goings. On the wide, marshy strip by the sea between Newport and Cardiff (a chip off the Norfolk Broads), among the willows, the snipe and the bittern, stand two or three of Britain's oldest churches, in hamlets with ancient names like Wentloog. An Anglo-Saxon barrow sits on the top of Twm Balwm mountain, like a pimple on a bald man's head, visible from four counties. Roman legions made Caerleon a major headquarters. English kings built castles. Someone built Tintern Abbey for Wordsworth to write some Lines about. George Borrow found a bit of wild Wales here: in his time the Welsh language was spoken up to the Wye.

World War II brings more poignant daydreams from abroad. The mines and steelworks in the hills made a favourite target for bombers. I remember carol singing with our five Eltham evacuees from the London Blitz, tramping across snowy fields, while the searchlights like restless white fingers groped for German planes over the Avonmouth or Cardiff docks. It was dramatic. Once, we had to shelter from shrapnel falling from anti-aircraft shell bursts, shivering under a blasted oak from which, recently, a man had sprung out at middle-aged Myfanwy Spooner, a pillar of the Women's Institute, as she bicycled home in the blackout from a whist drive. A German landmine fell near Rogerstone steelworks over the hill and killed one of these carol-singing evacuees who had just been rehoused there. It took me a long time to recover from that.

What are things like in those parts now? I have been careful to go back at odd times in recent years. The old house and the farm belong to another family, but they are friends and I visit them. The Forestry Commission did for all the 200-year-old beeches and oaks, just after the war, chasing fast bucks from the bleak clumps of conifers they planted in their place. But there is still a wood there; and the Nine-Acre field; badgers and foxes galore; and more bullfinches than ever.

The spirit of the place struggles on. Miss Thomas, the benign witch, and her house are long gone. And myxomatosis has cleared the rabbits from the drive. But in many ways things have improved. The Rhymney River reflects the rejuvenated shape of things in the valleys – its waters are clear at last; you can catch trout there now, and there are herons. Anti-pollution campaigns have done it. The valleys themselves have achieved a real charm. The slag heaps are levelled off for football fields and car parks. The terraces have been pulled down or improved, shining with bold-coloured paint. Oddest of all, industrial archaeology already thrives. Councils take preservation seriously. Scholars stare at the old brick and steel railway viaduct as if they see the aqueducts of Rome. The old Merthyr ironworks are an archaeologist's delight; the old Dowlais works stables are preserved, too, and the house of Guest, the ironmaster, where Charlotte Guest collected the Welsh legends into the *Mabinogion*, and which is, I believe, a museum. Richard Llewellyn, the author, died recently, but his valley is truly green again.

I had forgotten the pubs. The old Maenllwyd Arms still looks down to the Bristol Channel; under Fox Wood, the Rhiwderin Inn's walls are still decorated with Newport's rugby teams, and dear Kathleen Baker, who helped with our washing when I was a small boy, still opens her door nearby, smiling, 'There's love-lee, Gav,' with a fag drooping from the side of her mouth like a Frenchman.

Another sign of the times: the railway station next door has been sold as a house. The line is closed, so the sad train whistles we heard at night are silent. Now the ticket office is a parlour, and there are red-hot pokers in the signal box. Motorways have spread and widened alarmingly, but so far they skirt, not desecrate, the region. So old Gwent is still Arthurian enough. 'Those pastoral farms' of Wordsworth's are still 'green to the very door', and if at farmers' summer gatherings you find one or two Japanese from the Sony factory at Bedwas – even they will speak with a Welsh accent ('There's rovree!').

All this I see and see again in the many doldrum periods of travel. Past and Present melded together quite happily. The present wouldn't be the same without that past, so perhaps nostalgia isn't such a bad thing after all. Of course, these comforting recollections still leave me with London to face this January. But, bolstered by the recollections, I can face it. I know the East will still be there when I want it. And in any case, at Heathrow, in spite of all its shortcomings, an irresistible psychological process of adaptation begins. I can see it already.

The plane is down; the passport checked; the bags have appeared. In the taxi, in a rush of the immediate present, the Eastern vision – of a sunny garden, of brown bodies in sarongs, the white sands of Samoa or blue sails on the Java Sea – shivers like a ghost scenting the dawn. Inside the flat, familiar books, mail, an invitation. The telephone rings – yes, I'll be in Gwent next week – and now my Eastern vision is dead. Long live Nostalgia.

FOR THE BEST IN PAPERBACKS, LOOK FOR THE

In every corner of the world, on every subject under the sun, Penguin represents quality and variety – the very best in publishing today.

For complete information about books available from Penguin – including Pelicans, Puffins, Peregrines and Penguin Classics – and how to order them, write to us at the appropriate address below. Please note that for copyright reasons the selection of books varies from country to country.

In the United Kingdom: For a complete list of books available from Penguin in the U.K., please write to *Dept E.P., Penguin Books Ltd, Harmondsworth, Middlesex, UB7 0DA*

In the United States: For a complete list of books available from Penguin in the U.S., please write to *Dept BA, Penguin, 299 Murray Hill Parkway, East Rutherford, New Jersey 07073*

In Canada: For a complete list of books available from Penguin in Canada, please write to *Penguin Books Canada Ltd, 2801 John Street, Markham, Ontario L3R 1B4*

In Australia: For a complete list of books available from Penguin in Australia, please write to the *Marketing Department, Penguin Books Australia Ltd, P.O. Box 257, Ringwood, Victoria 3134*

In New Zealand: For a complete list of books available from Penguin in New Zealand, please write to the *Marketing Department, Penguin Books (NZ) Ltd, Private Bag, Takapuna, Auckland 9*

In India: For a complete list of books available from Penguin, please write to *Penguin Overseas Ltd, 706 Eros Apartments, 56 Nehru Place, New Delhi, 110019*

In Holland: For a complete list of books available from Penguin in Holland, please write to *Penguin Books Nederland B.V., Postbus 195, NL-1380AD Weesp, Netherlands*

In Germany: For a complete list of books available from Penguin, please write to *Penguin Books Ltd, Friedrichstrasse 10 – 12, D–6000 Frankfurt Main 1, Federal Republic of Germany*

In Spain: For a complete list of books available from Penguin in Spain, please write to *Longman Penguin España, Calle San Nicolas 15, E–28013 Madrid, Spain*

A SELECTION OF FICTION AND NON-FICTION

A Confederacy of Dunces   John Kennedy Toole

In this Pulitzer-Prize-winning novel, in the bulky figure of Ignatius J. Reilly, an immortal comic character is born. 'I succumbed, stunned and seduced . . . it is a masterwork of comedy' – *The New York Times*

The Labyrinth of Solitude   Octavio Paz

Nine remarkable essays by Mexico's finest living poet: 'A profound and original book . . . with Lowry's *Under the Volcano* and Eisenstein's *Que Viva Mexico!*, *The Labyrinth of Solitude* completes the trinity of master-works about the spirit of modern Mexico' – *Sunday Times*

Falconer   John Cheever

Ezekiel Farragut, fratricide with a heroin habit, comes to Falconer Correctional Facility. His freedom is enclosed, his view curtailed by iron bars. But he is a man, none the less, and the vice, misery and degradation of prison change a man . . .

The Memory of War and Children in Exile: (Poems 1968–83)   James Fenton

'James Fenton is a poet I find myself again and again wanting to praise' – *Listener*. 'His assemblages bring with them tragedy, comedy, love of the world's variety, and the sadness of its moral blight' – *Observer*

The Bloody Chamber   Angela Carter

In tales that glitter and haunt – strange nuggets from a writer whose wayward pen spills forth stylish, erotic, nightmarish jewels of prose – the old fairy stories live and breathe again, subtly altered, subtly changed.

Cannibalism and the Common Law   A. W. Brian Simpson

In 1884 Tod Dudley and Edwin Stephens were sentenced to death for killing their shipmate in order to eat him. A. W. Brian Simpson unfolds the story of this macabre case in 'a marvellous rangy, atmospheric, complicated book . . . an irresistible blend of sensation and scholarship' – Jonathan Raban in the *Sunday Times*

FOR THE BEST IN PAPERBACKS, LOOK FOR THE

A SELECTION OF FICTION AND NON-FICTION

Bedbugs   Clive Sinclair

'Wildly erotic and weirdly plotted, the subconscious erupting violently into everyday life . . . It is not for the squeamish or the lazy. His stories work you hard; tease and torment and shock you' – *Financial Times*

The Awakening of George Darroch   Robin Jenkins

An eloquent and powerful story of personal and political upheaval, the one inextricably linked with the other, written by one of Scotland's finest novelists.

In Custody   Anita Desai

Deven, a lecturer in a small town in Northern India, is resigned to a life of mediocrity and empty dreams. When asked to interview the greatest poet of Delhi, Deven discovers a new kind of dignity, both for himself and his dreams.

Collected Poems   Geoffrey Hill

'Among our finest poets, Geoffrey Hill is at present the most European – in his Latinity, in his dramatization of the Christian condition, in his political intensity . . . The commanding note is unmistakable' – George Steiner in the *Sunday Times*

Parallel Lives   Phyllis Rose

In this study of five famous Victorian marriages, including that of John Ruskin and Effie Gray, Phyllis Rose probes our inherited myths and assumptions to make us look again at what we expect from our marriages.

Lamb   Bernard MacLaverty

In the Borstal run by Brother Benedict, boys are taught a little of God and a lot of fear. Michael Lamb, one of the brothers, runs away and takes a small boy with him. As the outside world closes in around them, Michael is forced to an uncompromising solution.

THE PENGUIN TRAVEL LIBRARY – A SELECTION